Freedom in White and Black

Kara Walker, *no world* from *An Unpeopled Land in Uncharted Waters*, 2010. Etching with aquatint, sugar-lift, spit-bite and dry-point. Plate: 23⅞″ × 35⅝″ ; sheet: 30¼″ × 40¾″

FREEDOM
in White and Black

A Lost Story of the Illegal Slave Trade and Its Global Legacy

Emma Christopher

The University of Wisconsin Press

The University of Wisconsin Press
728 State Street, Suite 443
Madison, Wisconsin 53706
uwpress.wisc.edu

Gray's Inn House, 127 Clerkenwell Road
London EC1R 5DB, United Kingdom
eurospanbookstore.com

Printed in the United States of America

This book may be available in a digital edition.

Library of Congress Cataloging-in-Publication Data
Names: Christopher, Emma, 1971– author.
Title: Freedom in white and black: a lost story of the illegal slave trade
and its global legacy / Emma Christopher.
Description: Madison, Wisconsin: The University of Wisconsin Press, [2018]
| Includes bibliographical references and index.
Identifiers: LCCN 2017044805 | ISBN 9780299316204 (cloth: alk. paper)
Subjects: LCSH: Slave trade—Africa—History. | Slave traders—
Africa—Biography. | Slaves—Africa—Biography.
Classification: LCC HT1321 .C47 2018 | DDC 306.3/620922—dc23
LC record available at https://lccn.loc.gov/2017044805

ISBN 978-0-299-31624-2 (pbk.: alk. paper)

supported by a grant unslaved

Figure Foundation

For
Sergio,
with love

Contents

List of Characters

Tom Ball: Ball's origins and African name are unclear; he was possibly Temne. Ball was a factory slave belonging to Bostock who gave important testimony at Bostock and McQueen's trial. He was subsequently drafted into the West India Regiment and shipped to the Caribbean as a soldier, before returning to settle in Sierra Leone.

Robert Bostock: A Briton, Bostock was the son of a Liverpool slave trader of the same name. Bostock followed in his father's footsteps and co-owned slave trading factories at Gallinas and the St. Paul River in West Africa. He was subsequently arrested in 1813, convicted of illegal slave dealing, and transported to Australia for a term of fourteen years. He later had his conviction overturned and became a free settler in Tasmania.

Antonio Escoto (alias Anthony Scott): Escoto was a slave trader in Cuba who had links with Charles Mason and the *Fénix/Phoenix*. He later appealed to the British to compensate him for his losses through legal channels, but he was also believed to be behind the murder of Captain John Roach, committed by sailors aboard another vessel owned by Escoto.

W. A. B. (William Augustine Bernard) Johnson: A German, Johnson was a missionary and preacher at Regent, Sierra Leone, who lived alongside many of those who arrived from Bostock and Mason's factory. Together they founded what was acclaimed as a model village and built St. Charles Church, cited as the third oldest stone church in Africa.

Charles Mason: An American slave trader, Mason co-owned the slave trading factories at Gallinas and the St. Paul River with Bostock. Away in Charleston or Havana at the time of Bostock and McQueen's arrest, Mason continued slave trading but was later captured by another British patrol and taken to Freetown. As an American he could not be tried by the British court, but he drowned when his ship sank on the way back across the Atlantic.

John McQueen: Originally from Glasgow, Scotland, McQueen had been apprenticed to a slave factory in Africa as a child and later worked as Bostock's assistant at the St. Paul River. He was captured, tried, and convicted with Bostock and also went to Australia, where he again worked for Bostock in Sydney.

David Noah: A Bassa man whose original name is unknown. Noah was only a child at the time of his enslavement and the events surrounding his rescue. He grew to adulthood in Regent, Sierra Leone, and along with Tamba became an important member of the Church Missionary Society, later trying to fight the slave trade in his homeland.

Jack Phoenix (originally Za): "Za" (as written by the clerk) was likely Sahr or Saa, and so a firstborn Kissi or Kono child. He was the first captive embarked aboard the slave ship *Fénix/Phoenix* just prior to Bostock's arrest. Rescued during the events that followed, he became part of the crew of the *Phoenix* and took the name Jack Phoenix. He was recaptured during the revenge murder of Captain John Roach and was believed to have been sold in Cuba.

John Reffell (originally Yarra): Yarra's African origins are unclear, but at the time of his liberation he was a factory slave owned by John McQueen. He was the only man who testified at both Bostock and McQueen's original trial and at Bostock's appeal. In freedom he went to live in Hogbrook/ Regent and adopted the name John Reffell, after the superintendent of Liberated Africans, Joseph Reffell.

John Roach: A British mariner, Roach was captain of the brig *Kitty* with a letter of marque to capture enemy vessels and was trading with Bostock and McQueen. In 1813 Roach argued with Bostock and reported the latter's illegal slave dealing in Freetown, leading to the British naval attack on Bostock and Mason's St. Paul factory. Roach was later murdered, apparently in revenge for these actions.

Lawrence Summers (and other Anglicized aliases; originally Sessay): A Mende, Sessay/Summers was a child at the time of his rescue from Bostock's factory and was subsequently taken aboard HMS *Thais* as a "boy, third class." He gave an account at Bostock's appeal, revealing his capture and walk to the coast years before.

William Tamba (originally Tamba): A Kissi man, Tamba was involved in the slave trade at the Banana Islands, probably as a high-ranking slave of the Clevelands or Caulkers, and was then owned by Bostock. After his rescue at the time of Bostock's arrest he was one of the founders of the celebrated village of Hogbrook/Regent in Sierra Leone, fought against the slave trade, and helped settle the free American colony of Liberia. He worked closely with the Church Missionary Society for many years.

Robert Thorpe: Thorpe was a British judge who fought against illegal slave traders while occupying the bench in Freetown. Later, having being denied the chance to return to Sierra Leone, he fought for slave traders' rights and assisted Robert Bostock in appealing his conviction.

Freedom in White and Black

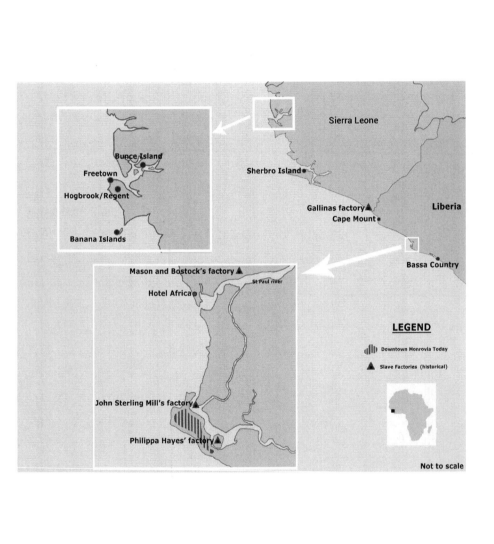

Sierra Leone

Bunce Island

Freetown

Hogbrook/Regent

Banana Islands

Sherbro Island

Gallinas factory

Cape Mount

Liberia

Bassa Country

Mason and Bostock's factory

St Paul river

Hotel Africa

John Sterling Mill's factory

Philippa Hayes' factory

LEGEND

Downtown Monrovia Today

Slave Factories (historical)

Not to scale

Prologue

On the banks of the St. Paul Rver, near Monrovia, Liberia.

It was at the ruins of Hotel Africa that I met a former slave. He was lean and unshaven with eyes that clouded dully across the whites. His name was Reuben.

"Have you come to buy it?" he asked.

"We need white man, American, to invest," clarified another Liberian dressed in a tattered T-shirt, who told me he was the caretaker of the wrecked building.

There was hardly anything left to buy. The skeleton was substantial enough to stake claim to its former grandeur, but it had been disemboweled. The outer walls and roof had completely gone, leaving a ghoulish honeycomb of steel girders holding up the floors. The wiring, pipes, and doors had vanished. Furniture, carpets, fixtures, and fittings were nothing but memories, although their imagined lavishness bloomed all the more as the old stories were retold. In their place, trees pushed up through the foundations with tropical enthusiasm. Nothing else had survived the crushing civil wars that tore the nation apart, first from 1989 to 1996, and then again from 1999 to 2003. Even the beach was being destroyed, ecological demolition from what locals described as the sea being angry.

It is all the more poignant because Hotel Africa was originally built for a summit of the Organization of African Unity (OAU) in 1979 and intended as a celebration of the continent. It was meant to symbolize that Africans would somehow somersault happily out of poverty and into a shining future. The centerpiece was the swimming pool, quarried in the top-heavy, lop-sided shape of Africa and surrounded by fifty-one luxury beach villas, one for each head of state. New roads and bridges were built, and cruise ships anchored just offshore.[1]

I asked the men to show me the famous pool, and we walked around the ruins. It had fallen into such disrepair that the shape was hard to figure out, the continent disfigured. Derelict in the middle was a bar where elegant bathers could once float up for another olive in their martini, now adrift somewhere near South Sudan. Nothing at all remained of the lavish villas.

"All finished," declared Reuben.

Rumors say that the OAU money was misspent or misappropriated. The entire OAU party cost the Liberian nation US $101 million, the hotel itself US $36 million, money that even then, in far happier financial times than today, it could scarcely afford. Now, decades on and with the hotel utterly destroyed, the country has still not paid off the debt. It is a ghost on the political landscape as arguments rage over where all the money went.[2]

The caretaker, some decades older than Reuben, remembered how it happened. He recalled the "Congos" (that is, Americo-Liberian people) coming to party at the OAU summit. But 1979 turned out to be the final year that this old elite ruled, and the next year there was the first coup in the nation's history. Years of instability and worsening corruption followed. Then there were two devastating civil wars. Hotel Africa survived the first part of the chaos and even hosted peace talks in 1998, but things were going downhill rapidly. Once the Nigerian peacekeeping soldiers left, the butchery began. By 2001 only one floor was operating, and that, in the words of a visiting *Observer* journalist, was the "centre of gravity," where warlord Charles Taylor ran his "new trade in misery." The hotel's owner, a close ally of Taylor, fled two years later, leaving looters to ransack the building.[3]

The caretaker asked about my interest in this story. There was nothing to do but dash their hopes, to confess that I am neither a potential investor nor a hotelier, but a historian. And so the conversation made its strange turn, Reuben looking at the packed earth, telling me that he had once been a slave.

"They caught me," he said simply.

"I was just a boy, and I came into the hands of bad men."

"They . . . I was a slave . . . I . . . no . . . everything is struggle for we [i.e., us]."

We stood in silence looking at the oil tankers moored on the horizon, unlovely in the afternoon haze. I did not know what to say. Words that were heartfelt as I considered them would doubtless sound banal, trite.

It was unbearably poignant because what had taken me to Hotel Africa was slavery and slave trading. Two hundred years ago, somewhere close to the ruins of Hotel Africa, an American, Charles Mason, and a Briton, Robert Bostock, together ran an illegal slave-trading business.[4]

It was a tiny fragment of the vast transatlantic slave trade. But, unusually, it is possible to trace a handful of the people—a few of the captives, factory slaves, the owners and their assistant—who were there at one particular moment in time. Some of those they held captive and enslaved can be followed from seizure to liberation and beyond.

Nor can this slaving business be entirely divorced from the far wider Liberian story. One of their former slaves went on to fight the slave trade, becoming part of the reason that the nation of Liberia was founded nearby as a settlement for the first of the Americo-Liberians, the people whose descendants would one day party at Hotel Africa. The threads that led from Mason and Bostock's business to Reuben's wartime enslavement are knotted and twisted, even sometimes threatening to unravel in places where different paths may have been taken, but nevertheless they are there. That the ruins of an illegal slave trading business lie beneath a destroyed model of Africa is painfully tragic symbolism you do not have to be a historian to interpret.

This is the story of that tiny illicit slave trading business, some of its people, and their very different lives.

Introduction

Early June 1813.

He knew that their vessels ate bodies. He knew because whenever one skulked into view he was bidden to help feed it. Half a moon before had been the most recent time. Then a boy, a firstborn son, had been the first sold. The child's hungry limbs had been pushed into the dugout that had conveyed him, mute with terror, to where the ship's wooden walls soared out from the water groaning and swaying. It had swallowed the boy whole.

But something had gone wrong. The white men had brokered a deal for hundreds of souls, but only nine-year-old Za had been handed over when a fight had broken out, and the ship sailed away. The rest of the designated cargo remained behind, and the pens were overflowing. Arms, legs, and torsos crowded together.

Tom Ball knew enough of their words to understand the fury and despair. He could read the cicatrices cut into their sweat-streaked backs. Many of them would have expected to go, dreading that those who stepped from the continent's edge were lost. Now, the vessel gone, he listened as they tried to push down shoots of hope for fear that it would betray them.

If the ship returned, they were destined for the auction block's sharp sting, chasms of broken lives lurking beneath, then slavery that neither they, nor their children, nor their children's children, would elude easily. The tethers around their limbs and necks would not leave them, not really. Tom Ball knew this because he too was enslaved. His owner, the slave merchant, had bought him a decade before. Just a child then, he had been told that his name was Tom Ball. Still, sometimes he used another name, the one that wove him into the fabric of life.[1]

A mere hundred paces across the rust-red earth separated his sleeping place from the holding pens, but these footsteps somehow encompassed the vast ocean. He was more fortunate than those being sold onward, but it was not much on which to build. He shared the compound with the bellows, bleats, and stinking dung of a hundred cows, a thousand sheep, and five hundred goats.[2]

They were so close to the ocean that its zephyrs cut benevolently into the burn of the late dry season. Sea air occasionally breezed in, providing fleeting reprieve from the stink of crowded, diseased, unwashed bodies and the open pits as toilets. It carried away mercifully the mosquitoes and the scavenger flies hovering over wounds. Yet the ocean's deep drubbing blows onto the sand, the gentle spent ebb, were drowned out by the keening. Its echoes would reverberate long after they had all escaped from this place.

He had no idea how soon that would be. Only a few days later he would be called upon to confess the courage and dignity he had been concealing for a decade beneath a costume of loyalty and submission. He would be asked to tell his story, and he would speak his truths far more poetically than the white man's cold words would convey. A ship was a beast, he intimated—*she*, in the usual feminine form for vessels, rather than *it*—and each one "filled her Belly with slaves." Slave traders might not literally feast on human beings, but Ball knew that somehow, in their own way, they greedily consumed African souls.

Tamba rarely had any easiness in his manner. Immovable and snappish, his powerful frame foretold the rigidness within. But his rigor, combined with a luminous intellect, made him a natural leader with a talent for the heroic. In the years to come the stories would be recounted far beyond Africa: of a man caught in quicksand, already up to his gullet when Tamba's arms wrenched him up, free and clear. A more adept boatman than many of the pilots along the coast, Tamba used his might to haul a canoe out of swells and whitecaps when those aboard feared that they would drown.[3]

He had been ensnared when young and, like Tom Ball, had somehow escaped the Middle Passage. A decade in the slave trade had honed his muscles and squared his edges. His owners valued him highly, and he called himself a servant instead of a slave. He rowed a dugout upriver to trade with headmen. He had lived at the Plantain Islands, exchanging men for rum, women for guns, boys for tobacco, or girls for cloth. He spoke some English and six African languages besides: his native Kissi, plus Sherbro, Mende, Vai, Kono, and some Gola.[4]

There were tiers of captivity, suffering, and pain in the slave factory,[5] and Tamba was well above Ball in the hierarchy. But all the factory slaves who

guarded and fed the human trade goods lived in no-man's-land, caught between survival and treachery. Tamba never revealed how deep ran the wounds
of this work. He gave only clues as to how being a proud Kissi man clashed
with the white man's ways. But its repercussions would haunt him long after
their liberation.

The pens both Tom and Tamba were guarding were too flimsy to imprison. In
the vast bamboo cages, those at the sides were defenseless against the ruinous
rains and the febrile sun. Here captivity was personal. At a nearby barracoon[6]
an observer viewed wares tethered individually to stakes, "their foot in the
stocks, a log with a hole in the center for the foot, and a peg drove in crosswise
to confine it." Around the whole compound were high mud walls, a further
deterrent to escape.[7]

The cages held captives from the patchwork of peoples that lived in the
river's hinterland. Mende, Gbande, Kissi, Loma, and Kono, smaller numbers
of Gola, Manding, and Sherbro. Kpelle, Vai, Dei, Temne, Bassa, and Belle
people sometimes arrived. Most were strangers and could not understand the
tongues of captives from distant lands, but others had their arm linked through
that of a family member or someone from their people. A small group were
from neighboring Gbande villages subjected to a violent raid. Two Sherbro
women called each other sister. There was a set of twins, twenty-six-year-old
Kono men who had taken every step of life together.[8]

Long journeys had led to this hell. For Sessay, eleven, it was two years since
he had been "stolen" from his family. "[D]riven down the Country," he had
been passed hand to hand, dealer to trader, "before they came to the sea."
When later he became familiar with the Bible, he would remember that the
duration of his walking had been forty days and forty nights. Those who could
not keep up were left to die like animals.[9]

The elders were a focus, a source of wisdom, as they had been in their
homelands. Boi, a Mende man, was forty years old; Fangha, a Kono, a similar
age. They and the younger men who were formidable warriors, like twenty-
three-year-old Canaba, who at 5 foot 10½ inches (1.79 meters) was a giant
among them, struggled surely with fury and mortification at finding themselves
in this most demeaning situation. They could do little to protect the others.[10]

There were no elders in the female pen. When buyers brought women
who had delivered many children, they were turned away. The four oldest
women the merchants had acquired recently were still in their twenties, the rest

teenagers and girls. The indignities they suffered are beyond knowing, violations that must have left torments, fears, and endless doubts. Safui held tight her three-month-old daughter Bessy, born on her walk to the ocean or into the distress of this gruesome place.

Three-fifths of all the captives were just children, eight, nine, and ten years old. This was the age of Za, already aboard the slave vessel, and many of those still in the pens like Eya, Famai, and Sarae.[11] They had only a hazy personal understanding of the monstrous trade that had netted them. As well as the loneliness, hunger, and exhaustion, they had specific distresses wondering about their parents and siblings. All ravenous, the children's hunger devoured whole days in raw anguish.[12]

Only the Muslims stretched their chains to kneel in prayer, but all came from societies that knew evil spirits. The Mende, Sessay's people, told of the Njaoli who would kidnap anybody foolish enough to go onto the big water. They warned people never to reveal fear to the Ndogbɔjusui, who looked just like a white man. Two Loma children knew that people with fairer hair were reincarnated water spirits and could not be trusted.[13]

So many died of hunger, disease, and exhaustion that each compound had its own graveyard. But they had only lost one in recent days to the water. Za had been pushed into a canoe and rowed out through the mangrove creeks until he passed into the river's mouth. They had expected him to be the first of many, but it had not turned out that way. Za had gone without them.

Briton Robert Bostock stalked by in long trousers and a fluttering shirt, king of the realm. He was of average height with pale blond hair, and his education and affluence gave him an aura of authority. Bostock jointly owned the business with his American partner, Charles Mason, but Mason was away, arranging trade in Charleston and Havana. So Bostock ran the business alone, aided by their assistant, John McQueen. A Scot, McQueen was younger and taller with blue eyes. His temper lay far shallower beneath the surface than that of his stolid boss.

Both Bostock and McQueen had years of slaving experience, both having been habituated to the trade's gory realities while children. Bostock's father, now long dead, had been a slave trader. McQueen had grown up on the African coast, apprenticed to his slave trader uncle at the age of eleven.

Finally, after years of toil, surrounded by Africans and their violent diseases instead of safe at home in Britain, it was all paying off. Bostock had a "very large" house within the compound. Their warehouses were vast emporia, and Bostock boasted that he had five hundred "stacks of gold dust," five thousand "pieces of Gold Coin," ten thousand "pieces of Silver Coin," five hundred gold bars, a thousand silver rings, a thousand amulets, and fifty thousand beads. The value of it all was around $10–15,000.[14] John McQueen was also building his own fortune and had purchased Yarra a year earlier, a factory slave of his own, who labored alongside Ball and Tamba.[15]

The problem was that their trade was illegal. Britain and America had both introduced laws five years earlier prohibiting the transatlantic slave trade. In Britain it had become anathema, considered a most un-British, treasonous business. Bostock and McQueen did not yet know it, but time was quickly running out. Only a few days later when it was all over, John McQueen would look back on his decade of trading in human beings and say, defiantly, "I liked it very much."[16]

Bostock and Mason's compound was on the banks of what Europeans know as the St. Paul River, a name bestowed by Portuguese sailors centuries earlier when they happened to first see it on the feast day of St. Paul. If any of Bostock and Mason's business remained today, it would be in Liberia, a country that did not yet exist in 1813. Founded by black Americans as a colony of freedom and named for the Roman word *liber*, Liberia would take its first tottering footsteps almost eight years later on a tiny island just south of Bostock and Mason's factory. In 1813 an ally of theirs had his slave barracoon on that small island, and within days of Ball loading Za aboard a slave ship hundreds of their captives would be hidden there. Its reincarnation as a place of freedom was in part an act of redemption by Tamba, one of the African men they owned and whom we have already briefly met.

Bostock, Mason, and McQueen could not possibly foresee this new country of liberty, but they knew that calamity was skulking offshore. They were on the frontlines of a battle over slavery and freedom, so close to their abolitionist enemies that they were virtually spies behind enemy lines. Just up the coast, a scant two days' sail away, was the free British colony of Sierra Leone, founded twenty-eight years earlier. It had begun as a place of freedom for Africans, a way to exhibit what Africa could be without the slave trade. Since 1808 and the outlawing of the slave trade, it had become the base of the British Navy's anti-slavery patrol and home to a growing community of "recaptured" Africans freed from the slave ships seized for illegal trading. Ships traded food and household goods in Freetown, the capital, then crossed the invisible divide and sold them at Bostock and Mason's factory.

Other dangers were also afoot. Privateers—who partook in a type of piracy supported by the state in wartime—were a constant hazard to shipping as both the War of 1812 and the Napoleonic Wars were ongoing. The *Fénix*—the slave vessel that loaded aboard the young boy named Za—had been unlucky to be caught up in both conflicts. A French vessel had plundered it as it cruised down the African coast. It then sailed away from Bostock and Mason's factory without its full human cargo because of a threat from a British privateer ostensibly involved in the War of 1812.[17]

Despite all this, seen across the reaches of history, it was an ordinary enough day at Bostock and Mason's slaving factory. At the end of the dry season, light rains sometimes came in the night, but there had not yet been crescendos of thunder crashing across the sky. The compound was a bedlam of tortured captives overtaken by sickness and hunger, children screaming, dogs barking, roosters crowing, cows lowing, women puffing as they chimed giant pestles into waist-high mortars and pounded clothes with lye. Free African Kru seamen used their extraordinary maritime skills to work the river, moving merchandise back and forth. Goods were loaded and checked. Food stuffs had to be prepared for the coming rains when so many of the stores would otherwise be ruined. Out on the river canoes paddled by, one carrying two Dei traders with five tusks of ivory they hoped to sell.[18]

Another canoe lapped up onto the small beach with two traders from Cape Mount bringing a male and a female captive. Bostock or McQueen had to assess their profit potential in the manner of the coast:

> As each negro was brought before him [a slave dealer] examined the subject, without regard to sex, from head to foot. A careful manipulation of the chief muscles, armpits and groins was made, to assure soundness. The mouth, too, was inspected, as if a tooth was missing it was noted as a defect liable to deduction. Eyes, voice, lungs, fingers and toes, were not forgotten.

They had to be alert for trickery, of the sick made to look healthy with "bloating drugs," their skins glistening with lemon juice. They had to weigh up whether they should add two more to their swollen barracoon or turn them away.[19]

Tom Ball carried foodstuffs to the pens, grains of life among the death, walking back and forth with precious drinking water. Yarra and Ball were guarding, ever watchful for signs that the despair had reached the cusp where men and women could take no more and would try to find a way to death's soft fall.

Yet, of course, it was not an ordinary day that we are regarding. If this had been an average day at an African slave factory we would not know about these particular ivory sellers or the final two captives arriving. The names Bostock, Mason, and McQueen might be clear in the records—though merchants sometimes hid their identities in the illegal period of trading—but it is very unlikely that those same documents would reveal the stories of Tamba, Ball, and Yarra. They would not contain these men's own words. There would be no names for those chained in the barracoon. The identities of the men, women, and children who we know as only Sessay and Za are tentative at best,[20] but they are uncommon wealth in the history of the transatlantic slave trade.

To slave traders, captives were notes of credit as much as people, so names, family ties, and ethnic identities simply did not matter. More than this, it was an important part of the dehumanization process that captives were not known by their names. Across the hinterland from Bostock and Mason's barracoons, names told of family ties and ethnic origin. They interleaved each person into the rich tapestry of their people's story. Along with cicatrices, they were a type of passport that revealed personhood and consequently warded off the absurdity of being an item of trade. So, as the captured headed step by chained step across the continent and out onto the saltwater, names were stripped away. The identities of those taken from Africa in chains are overwhelmingly lost to history.[21]

This remains an open wound to the hundreds of millions of people who today trace their ancestry to them. The loss of these identities means that so much that was appropriated has still not been restored, though DNA analysis is making inroads. Their extraordinarily rich heritage of beliefs, languages, cultural norms, songs, dances, folklore, crafts, jokes, festivals, expressions, and ways of being was splintered. Henry Louis Gates has written, "Almost all African Americans wonder where their ancestors came from in Africa. What languages did they speak? What was their music? Their religion? Their culture?" The answers, as Gates puts it, are "long lost in the abyss of slavery."[22]

The loss of these names and identities matters greatly—or at least should matter—to the wider world too, to those not of African origin. These victims, largely nameless and faceless in the voluminous records the slave trade has left about profit and loss, changed the world. The numbers alone are horrific: around eight million by the time of Bostock and Mason's (comparatively tiny) slaving operation. Twelve or thirteen million before the trade ended. It was enough stolen labor to change everything, to make the people and places that

had access to their muscle power wealthy and for that money to flow into industry, insurance, and banking.[23]

For Africa it was a devastating loss. Twelve or thirteen million families,
entire ethnic and family groups, whole swathes of the land, were eviscerated.
Whether this was the first major step on the way to the poverty and conflict
suffered by the continent today is still a matter of dispute. But while the answers
are complex, scholars are completing studies that prove the links. Places that
lost many of their people are still among the poorest today. They struggle more
with issues of trust and good governance.[24]

A significant percentage of captives, the exact amount still in debate but
around 7.5–20 percent, died or were murdered as they crossed the saltwater.
Some leapt overboard because the voyage was unendurable, and death would
carry them home. But those stolen, captured, kidnapped, traded, and tricked
were a tide. Enough lived to be whipped onto the auction block to number
four-fifths of all immigrants to the Americas up to 1807, the year the trade was
made illegal. As Edward Baptist has written, "the whole history of the United
States" can be found "behind a line of people in chains." Pushing north into
Canada and all the way south to Brazil and into Argentina, they were the back-
bone of the economies and cultures of the Americas. Today, more people of
African origin live in Brazil than in any other country of the world except
Nigeria.[25]

The lack of known identities for almost all of the victims is arguably part of
the reason that white society has found it possible to look away, to sidestep even
apology. Uncomfortable truths are so much more easily shrouded when victims
lack names and faces, when millions of stories of a stolen child, kidnapped
parents, a forced march in chains, a rape, a brutal whipping, pitiless starvation,
how the skin smoked as the branding iron hit are all trussed together into one
impersonal mass of history. It is easier to pretend it is of the distant past, to dis-
avow its legacy today. It is simpler to tell of the great white liberators whose
names, images—even how they enjoyed their breakfast as schoolboys—are all
within easy reach.[26] The original violation of treating people as merchandise,
their identities deemed irrelevant, is now used to rebuff their descendants' claims
for recompense.

So it is vital, as many other historians have noted before me, to recount as
many of these stolen lives as possible. It is imperative to try and locate them not
just as the gross number of their total mass accumulated over centuries, or on the
profit and loss sheets that whittle their heartbreaks into economics—although
all of this is the crucial work on which biographies can be built—but as they
were. They were multifaceted, imperfect, irrepressible human beings.[27]

This story can be told, and most of these names appear in the archival records, only because in mid-1813 the end for Mason and Bostock's slaving enterprise was lurking just over the horizon. Within days the Royal Navy's antislavery patrol assailed them, and in desperation Bostock and/or McQueen set the barracoons aflame. Such palpable disregard for human life compounded rather than hid their crimes. Both men were arrested and taken to Sierra Leone, and in the resulting court case the detail of this story was first laid bare. In the makeshift dock in Freetown girls' school, with a jury made up principally of men of African origin, Bostock and McQueen revealed their backgrounds. They pleaded for mercy based on childhoods in the slave trade, cited previous slaving businesses where they had worked, and named some of their equally guilty colleagues. Desperate to save themselves, they provided the kind of information usually hidden after the slave trade became illegal in 1808. These details provide a portal to explore their illicit activities.

The charges against them revolved, of course, around the captives found in the burned barracoons. Without victims there could be no case: a slave trader found without captives walked away scot-free no matter the weight of other evidence against him. So, to build the case of *The King vs. Robert Bostock and John McQueen*, as well as to fulfill the British antislavery agenda, Africans found amid or near the razed slave factory were also taken to Freetown. There a clerk of the Liberated African department wrote their names. He sometimes misunderstood, misheard, and mangled, but this list was more information than Bostock and McQueen had ever gathered. In fact, it revealed far more than the British knew since these names were often identifiers that make it possible, even now centuries later, to try to trace the African captives, to attempt to uncover something of the people they were. Through their names the barracoon's noxious grasp is revealed to have ranged out beyond the hinterland of the St. Paul and far into the interior. It gives a very rare view, however incomplete, of those caught in one slave trading business at one moment in time.[28]

Two Africans gave statements for the prosecution's case. Summoning remarkable courage, for they could not possibly know whether the two white men might go free and enact revenge, Yarra and Tom Ball gave brief but startling accounts. Yarra named his previous master from the time before McQueen had purchased him. Ball, owned for much longer by Bostock, spoke of Charles Mason, of their other slaving factory north at Gallinas where he had previously been enslaved, and even named ships that he had helped load with tragic human "cargo." They are short narratives, but within the language and syntax of these two men's testimonies are evocations of each man's perspective, an extraordinarily rare peep into the lives of these most marginalized workers.

Luckily for Yarra and Ball, Bostock and McQueen were found guilty and sent into exile for fourteen years. But it was far from the end of the affair. Charles Mason carried on slave trading and was captured by the patrols in 1816. His arrival in Freetown terrified his former bondspeople. Bostock then managed to return to Britain from banishment, and he both pleaded his legal case and demanded compensation for his losses. Faced with this foe, the British sent word to Freetown asking his former slaves and captives to testify once again. It was at this point that Tamba first gave evidence while Yarra added to his original account. The appeal also led the British to track down Sessay, by then known in his new life aboard a Royal Navy vessel as Lawrence Summers. He gave the significant details of his capture and subsequent sale into Bostock and Mason's "slave yard," recalling also the terrifying day that his prison had gone up in smoke.

Having entered the voluminous paperwork of the British Empire, a handful of the rescued Africans remained within its crisp edges. Some, like Sessay/Summers, were listed on muster rolls and in logbooks. Then, a few years later, the Church Missionary Society (CMS) began to oversee the lives of those who remained in Sierra Leone, and two of those liberated from Bostock and Mason became highly literate. Tamba and David Noah, the latter of whom was a child, his name unclear, at the time of their rescue, both joined the CMS as "messengers of salvation in native districts." Unusually, they corresponded directly with the venerable society. These sources—letters and journals sent by the two men to London—are remarkable, the most direct insight into those saved in mid-1813 from the slave trade. Within them are glimpses of Tamba's traumas resulting from these events: his torment when Charles Mason appeared in Freetown and Tamba relived the burning of the factory, his determination to gather testimony against Bostock's appeal, and his anxiousness to keep together those with whom he had arrived in the colony. Tamba also revealed his battle to be treated as an equal by the CMS. Once or twice he hinted at his despair at the relentless racism he endured.

The letters go far beyond the personal. Both Tamba and Noah ventured heroically back to the places they had been enslaved, begging local chiefs to stop selling their countrymen. Tamba wrote of trying to reason with Siaka a few decades before, as King Siaka, he was involved in trading the men who would become known as the *Amistad* slaves. Noah planned a mission to Bassa to educate his people against the slave trade. Tamba even went back to the St. Paul River, confronting the slave traders whom he had known during his days at Bostock and Mason's. He was also seemingly instrumental in promoting that location to the agents of the American Colonization Society for the colony of Liberia. It is a story from which he has been whitewashed.

All of these sources, rich as they are, have blatant shortcomings. The captives and factory slaves enter the historical lens only because of the deeds of white men and are all but exhibits in their legal cases. An amanuensis inscribed the scanty words of Yarra and Tom Ball. Even the letters and journals of Tamba and Noah are part of a European-led narrative. To try to "writ[e] into the historical silence," I have read between the lines, appraised from clues told by Europeans and North Americans. I journeyed several times into the Liberian and Sierra Leonean upcountry regions to sit down with chiefs and elders of the places the names on the Liberated African list are known, following up on the suggestions provided by linguists. A few beautiful slivers of oral testimony are used. All of this is imperfect by nature, but it is all there is to set against the (also imperfect) written archive.[29]

It is a great loss to the story that the female captives, even Bostock's and McQueen's African wives, are missing. It is another testament to the inequalities of the times that we know almost nothing about these women. There is no comparison across the racial cleft, yet even Bostock's white wife is seen only through the words of others and the birth dates of her eleven children. McQueen's common-law white wife, of a less privileged social class, appears in the records most notably while being sentenced to the ducking stool for unladylike conduct and being "a scold." Tamba's wife appears only in a note expressing how he missed her while on one of his missionary journeys, Noah's wife at his sadness at her death. The women and girls rescued alongside them are almost entirely obscure, leaving no traces that allow even an attempt at reconstruction. The women were certainly there and changing history; we just do not see them.[30]

Despite these limitations, accounts of Africans caught up in the slave trade are very rare pearls. Tom Ball, Yarra, and Tamba gave some of the only factory slave testimonies that exist. Sessay and the unnamed Bassa child who grew up to be David Noah provided compelling testimonies of their paths into slavery. Sessay/Lawrence Summers; David Noah; Tom Ball, who may have also been called Banna; Tamba/William Tamba; and Yarra/John Reffell were two captives and three factory slaves among hundreds of thousands at the Windward Coast, but very few had the opportunity to leave their name, let alone have their own words recorded. Their declarations stand as acts of rebellion against those who sought to dehumanize them into merchandise. They speak their stories for the lost.[31]

This was not a gruesomely average slave trading tale of Middle Passage and auction block. Far from it: beyond the slave factory the usual trajectory of the transatlantic slave trade was, superficially at least, turned upside down. The captives and factory slaves were declared free; it was the British slave traders who were sent off aboard a ship in chains to labor on somebody else's account in a land far away.

Flipped over like this, stark truths about the era are revealed in new ways. By 1813 the transatlantic slave trade had so twisted the racial landscape that, regardless of their granted liberty, the Africans who escaped the Middle Passage were grossly disadvantaged in their later lives under British control. Stripped of the horrors of the Middle Passage and its violence, denuded of the chains and the cane fields, the specter of race still prevailed. By the time the British and Americans banned the transatlantic slave trade in 1807–8, the dominance they had marshaled through profit, power, and faux science was all but unassailable. Behind the bulwark of their self-proclaimed piety as antislavery champions racism festered and metastasized.[32]

On the other side of the coin, Bostock and McQueen's story reveals what privileges and esteem British nationality, middle-class status, and masculinity could bestow, whatever the gravity of a man's transgression. In New South Wales, the penal colony to which they were banished as sentence for their crimes (today part of Australia), both men became successful, wealthy, and respected astonishingly quickly. This was possible in part because of a mistake in the legal case against them, but there was a far bigger picture too. They were thought to be entirely different creatures—often quite literally—than hungry, near naked, deeply traumatized West Africans.

Some of this was tangible. Bostock and McQueen were given vast tracts of land by the colonial authorities in Australia, whereas those rescued had their greatly smaller plots—land they had already struggled to clear and plant— taken away. African men and women were not deemed to be deserving of such resources. Bostock's children in Australia got a degree of self-government decades before those of Tamba, Noah, and the others in Sierra Leone, who were supposed to be akin to children needing education. Britain spent enormously more money on its Australian colonies than it would on Sierra Leone.

This upturning of the slave trade therefore casts an intriguing, provocative sidelight onto the thorny question of slave trade legacies. Here, upturned, it is possible to see the specifics beneath the general picture. A few of the Africans can be traced from their approximate place of capture, through the barracoon and then down through the generations to their descendants today. The slave traders' descendants, with the exception of Mason's, are much easier still to find. Side by side the contrast between these families' situations remains stark, varying only really for Bostock's nonwhite descendants (about whom more later). So if, overturned, the transatlantic slave trade has left palpable inequality, what might this imply for those who made the Middle Passage? Atypical it may be, but this story provides a sliver of headland, a place from which to view the journeys that contributed to today's disparities as they sailed off along the sea lanes that lead to the present.

Part 1

Journeys
to the Slave Factory

1

Son of a Liverpool Slave Dealer

The slave trade was the scenery of his childhood, the fresco backdrop to the months and years as he grew. In other parts of Britain the abolitionist movement was making huge inroads in popular opinion, but Robert Bostock was raised in Liverpool, heartland of the centuries-old trade. Carrying Africans across the sea for sale had made their city wealthy, and its tentacles reached unashamedly onto the cobbled streets. Captains paraded through the town proudly trailing a black "servant" brought home from their travels. Liverpool had a Jamaica Street and the Goree Docks. Paradise Street housed the sailors' taverns and brothels. Shops openly displayed handcuffs, leg irons, thumbscrews, and the *speculum oris*: a device with which to wrench open the jaws of any who might try to starve himself or herself to death. Liverpool Exchange celebrated its trading successes by having opulent "Busts of Blackamores" carved for its frieze. Their money was even called *guineas*, a quarter ounce of gold in each.[1]

Perhaps we catch sight of Robert Bostock, a tow-haired boy, watching his father's ships being repaired at the old dock, amid the "gigantic docks of almost Titanic masonry" where sugar, rum, cotton, and coffee from around the globe were offloaded. Or perhaps we imagine him visiting his father's office on Union Street, bustling with seamen and only steps away from major slave traders like Henry Blundell and the Backhouses. A square red pennant was his father's personal signal, hoisted when a slaving vessel was safely back from the treacherous seas, leaving the family rejoicing.[2]

Slave trading was Robert's family business, shoes that he would one day step into just as other boys inherited a career as a carpenter or shopkeeper. His father, Captain Robert Bostock, had joined the Royal Navy as a boy and afterward had been drawn to Liverpool and the slave trade. It was hardly an unusual or controversial decision; even people without seafaring skills joined in the bonanza. By the mid-eighteenth century Liverpool was the center of Britain's slave trade, and it grabbed the imagination of "every order of people," with whirlwind rumors of vast fortunes made selling human beings at the markets of Barbados, Jamaica, or Virginia. It "dazzled their ideas" like a gold rush, so that "he who cannot send a bale, will send a bandbox."[3]

Robert's father, Captain Bostock, first commanded the tiny sloop *Little Ben*, setting sail in August 1769 for Cape Mount and then selling 79 captives across the seas at Dominica. There had been a second voyage in the *Little Ben*, then another in the bigger *Townside* with the *Little Ben* in tandem. By 1773, Captain Bostock was master of the *Burrowes*, yet a larger vessel. When his youngest son was born and named for him, Captain Bostock was at the helm of the *Bloom*, taking 239 captive hostages across the Atlantic for sale at St. John's, Antigua.[4]

The slave trade may have lured with vast potential profit, but the risks were legendary. Slave revolt, at worst a brutal death at the hands of a cargo of "savages," was the ultimate horror story luridly retold among Liverpool traders. Larger crews, more weapons, and carefully crafted instructions from the merchants were carried in hope of maintaining security. The muskets and chains gave the whiff of protection.

The African coast was also notoriously deadly for Europeans. Written half a century before and still in use, *The Guinea Man's Vade Mecum* described the "evil, malevolent, contagious, destructive fogs" that seemed to carry healthy men away within a few hours. Things only got worse when they weighed anchor for the transatlantic crossing. Imprisoned in the hold were bodies prostrate with alarming diseases to which they had no resistance. Slaving vessels were hothouses of malaria, yellow fever, hookworm, tapeworm, leprosy, syphilis, yaws, opthalmia, elephantitis, trypanosomiasis, and dysentery, all generating terror for Britons—especially middle-class Britons like Captain Bostock—who were more familiar with smallpox, influenza, and tuberculosis. Some slave ships employed a surgeon, but their skills were rather rudimentary even by the standards of the day.[5]

There were other common difficulties too, problems his boss, slave merchant Thomas Radcliffe, would have warned Captain Bostock about most sternly on his earliest voyages. There was little trust of African dealers, with language gaps, cultural misunderstandings, and overweening xenophobia charging negotiations. Stories of long-winded haggling, bluffing, trickery, and false promises were so rife that the word *palaver* had been adopted into English to describe it.

So when Captain Bostock and his crew anchored at the Banana Islands off the coast of Sierra Leone on one of his early voyages, conceivably aboard the

Little Ben, he could only have been immensely reassured to meet the local chief. His name was James Cleveland. It was an encounter that would not only profoundly change Captain Bostock's life but would have lasting repercussions for his family, especially his then yet-to-be-born youngest son and namesake. Captain Bostock likely anticipated some half-naked, wild African, but here was a man so "polished in his manners" that he appeared like one of their own. "With a White Man he is a White Man," as one Englishman put it, and what finer compliment could a late eighteenth-century Briton proffer? The son of an Englishman and Ndamba, a Kissi woman, James Cleveland had been educated in Liverpool. He knew how to "address an European with fair words," flattering his visitor by claiming that as the son of a white man he could not treat another white man, another father to him, grievously. He promised Bostock a good deal.[6]

In terms of how Captain Bostock saw Cleveland, it mattered that James Cleveland spoke English fluently, ate with a knife and fork, and slept in a European-style bed. It was not long past the days when ideas as to what constituted a person's race encompassed far more than skin color. Lineage, education, religion, culture, and even dress had all been signifiers as to a person's "race" in previous decades, and there was certainly not the attitude that anybody with one discernible drop of African blood was "black." This was deeply reinforced by the fact that Cleveland's whole family lived in a wholly different way than the Africans they bought and sold. James's half-sister Elizabeth, also educated in Liverpool, moved to South Carolina and "lived her life as a member of the white planter elite," yet never attempted to hide in any way her African heritage.[7]

Cleveland was ruthless. He had expanded his territory by marrying the sister of a neighboring rival, Charles Caulker, and then having him beheaded. In his vast dominion he coaxed people into debt by forwarding goods that they could not afford, then sending his personal militia, sometimes with deserters from slave ships acting as officers, to harry the debtors. Homes, livestock, and crops were laid waste, and anybody captured was made a slave. Those within Cleveland's reach gave up the age-old tradition of clearing the ground around their homes and left bushes and trees to grow in order to provide cover if they were forced to flee. Others simply abandoned their homes and built new ones at the ends of creeks so narrow that only a single canoe could enter.[8]

Captain Bostock was so impressed by Cleveland, so relieved at the ease and speed with which they had done business perhaps, that he continued to visit on subsequent voyages. There is no record of it, but it is not improbable that Captain Bostock had an African "wife" who was a member of the Cleveland family, as other slaver captains did. Over the course of the next sixteen years,

Bostock and Cleveland certainly became allies. Having a man like Cleveland to vouch for him was the best way that a European could do business in this part of Africa. Even the Reverend John Newton, later one of the most assiduous abolitionists, had an African patron while he was employed in the slave trade. It was a relationship that endured so that even forty years later, vehemently protesting the slave trade, Newton called his patron "my friend Harry."[9]

Captain Bostock was yet more attached to James Cleveland than Newton was to Harry Tucker, however. After a final slaving voyage aboard the *Jemmy* in 1787, Captain Bostock decided to retire from the sea and become a slaving merchant, leaving other, younger men to the dirtier, more dangerous side of the trade. It was a regular career progression, but Captain Bostock made an unusual decision. While the vast majority of Liverpool slaving merchants instructed their captains to buy from whosoever was selling, Captain Bostock sent his ships to trade solely with his old friend James Cleveland.

This was rather extraordinary as their relationship was a friendship as much as a business agreement, at least on Captain Bostock's part. Mercantile grievances he framed in terms of what he saw as their particular personal attachment. It was a strange way of doing business. What exactly Cleveland felt about all this is unclear, but young Robert Bostock and his siblings grew up very much aware of their father's great friend in Africa. Daughters Elizabeth, Maria, and Margaret (young Robert's older sisters) sat in the drawing room meticulously embroidering ruffled shirts with James Cleveland's name and then sent them off to him aboard their father's slave ships. Believing that Cleveland had named a son Robert after him, Captain Bostock sent a gift of a silver coral to the baby, and young Robert Bostock grew up thinking that he had a namesake out in Africa. The Bostock family fully expected Robert Cleveland to live with them in England during his education.[10]

So Robert Bostock was a boy sure of one thing: venturing to Cleveland's stronghold on the Banana Islands would be his destiny. It was probably an exciting proposition despite the risks of the "white man's grave." Both his older brothers were sent out to the Banana Islands, and if they were like most other young men of the era, they returned with tales of exquisite islands filled with sandy beaches, palm trees, and people who wore rather less clothing than was fashionable in England. Captain Bostock too could not forget his time with the Clevelands and, sitting in his office in Liverpool, daydreamed of being back on the islands; happy memories he likely passed on to his children. It must all have seemed most exotic to the young Robert Bostock. Even the name of their islands, *banana*, spoke of a fruit about which he had heard but had certainly never eaten.[11]

Yet as the years went on it all went fearfully wrong. This was perhaps unsurprising, since whether Bostock's friendship with Cleveland was truly reciprocated is far from certain. In Bostock's mind their closeness meant that Cleveland should give him special treatment, but it was not to be. In 1789, frustration building, Captain Bostock wrote to Cleveland: "I think [because of] the Friendship subsisting betwixt you & me that if you wou'd not give me the preference you wou'd certainly give me my turn." When Bostock's ship *Kite* was wrecked at the Banana Islands, misunderstandings and debts escalated. Captain Bostock became increasingly enraged over money that Cleveland owed. He began to write Cleveland very out of character and not very gentlemanly instructions, at one point ordering him not to "involve yourself again in so much Debt." "[N]o Man that means well" could possibly act in such a manner without regret, Captain Bostock wrote, a staggering change from his usual florid compliments for his friend. When even these petitions failed, Captain Bostock began ordering his ship captains to trade with other African merchants, in what amounted to a seismic shift in his business tactics and ethic. But by that point he was mired in debt, too.[12]

Whether from necessity or loyalty, he also continued to trade with Cleveland. In May 1790, during a time of crisis when Liverpool's sailors were on strike, Captain Bostock wrote to Cleveland complaining that he was so "much distressed for want of Money at present" that he could "scarce keep my Credit up." I have "so much Property in your Hands," he wrote, "I hope you will take it into consideration and release me from these difficulties as soon as possible." The worst of it was that he believed that Cleveland had the money to repay him but was declining to do so. Even the safe arrival of the Bostocks' youngest daughter Amelia failed to cheer him, and he lamented that he would rather have received the money owed. It was all going horribly wrong. By December 1790, Captain Bostock's account at Heywood's Bank in Castle Street, Liverpool, was overdrawn by £1399 8s 3d. His business was failing, but he still hoped it would be saved if Cleveland would repay him.[13]

Robert was only seven years old when these hopes were dashed. Captain Bostock's square red pennant was raised, but the cheer was cut short as his returning ship carried terrible news. James Cleveland had passed away. It signaled a bitter financial reverse for the Bostock family. "Riches or ruin on an enormous scale" had always been the Liverpool merchants' way of doing things, and Captain Bostock seemed close to ruin. At the time of his death Cleveland owed Bostock £1,237 3s,[14] an amount that Captain Bostock, rather understating matters, described as "a large Sum." Bostock wrote urgently to James's heir, nephew William Cleveland, enquiring desperately "how you Intend to settle his Affairs." But William Cleveland would not or could not answer in a way that satisfied Captain Bostock. Nevertheless, Bostock had a tombstone engraved for his old friend and sent it out to the Banana Islands to stand over his grave.[15]

In 1792, at his Bootle home three miles to the north of Liverpool, Captain Bostock became ill. He had been indisposed with gout for some time but now became so sick that he abruptly stopped writing the letterbooks and ledgers he had previously completed with meticulous care. The family tiptoed around him.

During his years first as a captain and then as a slaving merchant there had been sustained attacks on the slave trade, but Captain Bostock's sickness came at a time when the abolitionists seemed to be winning. Only twenty-odd years before, most Britons had believed that the Bible condoned slavery and that Africans were both lesser people and especially suited to hard labor. But a succession of Enlightenment thinkers, Quakers, and evangelical Anglicans had brought a remarkable change. Some former slave traders like John Newton had turned against the business, and Newton's *Thoughts on the Slave Trade* castigated his former profession, making Britons aware of the horrors and cruelties. Gustavus Vassa, later known as Olaudah Equiano, published his autobiography, allowing a peep into the African side of the story. Many in Liverpool held firm in support of the trade that had made them so wealthy, but in the rest of the country abolitionism became a very popular cause. An unprecedented one in six people signed a petition against the slave trade between 1787 and 1792.[16]

As Captain Bostock ailed, the abolitionists secured their first real parliamentary victory. In April 1792, a bill ensuring the gradual abolition of the slave trade passed the House of Commons and only failed to become law when blocked by the House of Lords. It turned out to be only the first of a series of shocks. In January 1793, Louis XVI went to the guillotine in Paris. Within weeks, to the bewilderment and dismay of many, Britain declared war against republican France. The abolitionist movement was temporarily silenced for fear of appearing unpatriotic, but that suddenly turned into a relatively benign problem. Now all maritime commerce would be quelled by the war.

The consequences were dire. A capital crisis gripped the country, with regional banks faltering. Wretched confusion was wreaked in Liverpool when one of the city's major banks failed, owing "upwards of two millions." Heywood's bank, where Captain Bostock held his account, was forced to borrow £40,000 from the Bank of England in late March and then a further £30,000 in May. Smaller merchants in the city were the hardest hit. For Captain Bostock, sick and desperately anxious, it was a miserable summer, particularly after the bankruptcy of Bristol slave trader James Rogers, who had also dealt extensively with James Cleveland. There were over 1,300 bankruptcies in Britain in 1793, more than two and a half times the usual number, but Rogers's was one of the most staggering.[17]

The toll on Captain Bostock was inestimable. A few months later he passed away at the age of fifty. Robert Bostock, then nine years old, could only walk behind his father's coffin in the funeral procession as it led up the hill to St. Anne's Church in Richmond Street. The words "Tho mortals weep a Christian dead" were selected for the tombstone.[18]

We cannot know if the young boy was aware of his father's debts at this age. As we catch a glimpse of the sad, small figure walking behind the coffin, perhaps he was simply proud of the legacy he was inheriting. Tales of his father's derring-do would be more familiar to him than the children's books that were just coming into fashion. Captain Bostock had chased off a French ship in 1778 despite taking three broadsides. On his final voyage, while selling slaves at Antigua, he had seen the king's younger brother, accompanied by a dashing young officer named Nelson. They were the kind of tales a young boy might relish, as yet unaware of a more far more complex world.[19]

Besides their personal loss, Captain Bostock's death delivered a devastating financial blow for his family. The demise of the breadwinner meant an acute drop in their living standards even after the debt-fuelled struggles of the previous years. Adding significantly to their troubles was the fact that Robert's father failed to leave a will, and it would be decades before his estate was finally administered. In the meantime Robert's mother, confined to widow's weeds, was forced to work, a situation considered most indecorous. Robert's eldest brother John, away at sea, was the only one of the children able to help the family financially, and his loss in a shipwreck not many years after Captain Bostock's death left the family devastated once more. Robert's elder sisters' suitors began shying away—wealthy debutants were credited with beauty, good character, and accomplishments that the indebted were not felt to possess—and only Maria ever married.[20]

Beyond the Bostock family's personal instability, the nine years between Captain Bostock's death and Robert's coming of age were a time of tumult in Britain. In 1794, the government was so fearful of wholesale rebellion that habeas corpus was suspended. "Tyger! Tyger! burning bright," wrote William Blake, continuing with lines that seemed to incite revolt: "On what wings dare he aspire? What the hand, dare seize the fire?" The war with France was going badly, and in 1795 Prussia and Spain both sued for peace. The Industrial Revolution, spurred by the cycles of slave trading, slave-grown crops, and their processing, had already created population growth, increasing urbanization and overcrowding, but when the added uncertainties of the war led to food shortages, riots erupted in 1795–96 and 1800–1801. In 1797, major seamen's strikes broke out at Spithead and the Nore, triggering fears that Britain would succumb to Jacobin-style revolution. The following year a widespread revolt against British rule erupted in Ireland, agitation that Britain attempted to crush with carnage and bloodshed. By 1800, Britain alone was left fighting France after Austria, the Ottoman Empire, and Russia were defeated. Throughout the British Isles, these were hard times.

When Robert turned eighteen it must have seemed evident what he must do. Seafaring and trading had always been his calling, following his father and older brothers. So, in 1802, Robert Bostock decided to sail for the Banana Islands. His father's money was still there—the will remained unresolved—and with it the possibility of vindicating his family. Going to Africa was a rite of passage for Bostock boys, and it was not difficult to find a berth. When Britain and France signed the Treaty of Amiens, the temporary truce brought an upsurge in maritime trade. Just that year, twelve slave ships were leaving Liverpool for Sierra Leone or the Windward Coast.[21]

There would have seemed few moral grounds to stop him joining the slave trade. As Robert departed for Africa, it appeared as if 1792, as his father had lain sick, had proved to be the height of the abolitionist campaign. The French and Haitian Revolutions had halted the abolitionists' crusade, and Liverpool had just elected another noted slave trader as mayor. Others even seemed to be rallying to the slave traders' side. The French Revolutionary government had abolished the trade, but Napoleon Bonaparte had introduced it once more. The following year South Carolina also reopened its ports to slave ships. Even if it should come to pass that the slave trade was outlawed, Robert Bostock could always do as his father had once instructed and "make hay while the sun shines."[22]

2

A Kissi Child Caught
in the Slave Trade

The boys laughed as they scared away the birds, running with arms flapping wildly when one dared to get too near. They made it fun, but it was a solemn duty, a task they had to complete to ensure a good harvest, to prove they were able to take on bigger jobs. Each evening on their way home they collected firewood, entwining the branches into a rough bundle, then straggled gleefully but sleepily back to the village. In the middle of the line we imagine Tamba, average height, quick-witted, and tenacious, a well-made child who would grow into a brawny adult.[1]

Nothing is known of Tamba's childhood, but the Kissi people to whom he belonged lived on the margins. To the north were savannah and hills, to the south thick forest. The Kissi were rice farmers and knew that land and rainfall were everything. The earth was the wife of the sky, and the sky shared its name with the supreme god because it was from there that rain fell, fertilizing the earth so that everyone could eat. Rice and rainfall marked out the seasons. Each November as the rain stopped, families joined together, rushing to bring in the harvest before the animals and birds stole the crop. As soon as it was safely stowed, the celebrations and thanks to the gods and ancestors began.[2]

Homes were circular, made of clay from the riverbed, a conical roof of carefully bound *tuhuwe* grass rising above. Tamba lived there with his mother, his brother Saa, and sisters Sia, Kumba, and Finda. There could be other brothers and sisters who had the same father but a different mother, and cousins and second cousins and friends and relatives who, either by blood or marriage or through the myriad other lines that spun out, embraced almost the whole community. Tamba's father would be the head of the immediate family, but uncles, aunts, great uncles, grandparents, older cousins, and big brothers were all respected, as of course were headmen and chiefs. Uninitiated boys like Tamba knew their place. Within that role was life.[3]

The Kissi lived at the far reaches of the river that the Europeans called St. Paul, but to the Kissi it was Diani or Nianda. Europeans believed that a mysterious mountain range called the Mountains of Kong began in Kissi territory, but they were wrong. The hills to the north of the Kissi were the highlands of the Futa Jallon. It was from there that terror came.[4]

In the time of Tamba's grandparents and great-grandparents, the Fula had founded a theocratic state in these highlands. They had launched jihad against nonbelievers like the Kissi, enslaving infidels. It had begun a time of tragedy. So many of the Kissi were sold to the coast that they were among the biggest victims of the slave trade in the region. The sale of all those stolen then earned the raiders more money to launch more raids. During Tamba's childhood, the elders would still remember brothers and sisters stolen away. They gathered the young to tell of the great tragedies that had befallen their village. Boys like Tamba grew up hearing warnings.[5]

Yet Kissi people took pride in their resilience. They were far from defeated. Life went on much as it always had, moving forward with new ideas and discoveries while honoring the wisdom of the past. Cotton cloth was woven into the dramatic designs so treasured by everyone, and kola nuts and sometimes salt, carried overland from the coast, were used as currencies. The elders taught the lore and wisdom of the past to their grandchildren and great-grandchildren, passing on knowledge of seasons and harvests. The rains fell each year, bringing a time of sickness and hunger, and in the dry season crops were harvested and life seemed bountiful. The gods and the ancestors were usually generous.[6]

Being quite a small ethnic group, the Kissi knew their immediate neighbors since they traded with them at market. Many Kissi could speak in part the languages of the Manding, Kono, Gbande, Gola, or Loma, at least enough to buy and sell and to hear news of lands further away. Apart from the Manding they were all small groups with their own languages and religions so that a map of the area by ethnic affiliation resembled an intricate patchwork.[7]

Other than the Manding and the Fula, the other contiguous groups—the Loma, Gola, Kono, and Gbande—were also trying to defend their own gods against the Muslim deity. At times these fellow nonbelievers were allies of the Kissi. At other times they were enemies. This had long been the way of things, but as the jihad destroyed communities and demand for slaves from the coast grew ever stronger, the balance of life shifted. During a particularly brutal time a "war hero" from a Gbande/Kissi conflict became the paramount chief, and those disloyal to him had their villages burned down, their people sold into slavery. Another warrior was notorious for his ruthlessness, and while he ruled, the slave trade with the Manding people flourished. Even the weekly market became such a dangerous place that husbands went with their wives to prevent them being captured. Things became so desperate, rumors so malicious, that stories spread that the Kissi were reduced to the "wretchedness and barbarism" of husbands selling unfaithful wives or parents selling their children.[8]

Whatever their languages, gods, and beliefs, common ideas ran through the region's peoples, extending out far beyond the Kissi and their nearest neighbors. Within each group, from the oldest to the youngest, each person was part of a pattern, their piece interlocking with all the others to make one element. They were individuals, of course, but all together they made life itself, something far greater than any one of them alone. Little personality, little of the very quiddity of a person, existed without family and wider community. People did not say that they *had* a brother or a child or a nephew, but that they *were* a brother or a parent or an uncle/aunt, since it was this that most defined them. The Kissi people's neighbors, the Gbande, made boys memorize their entire lineage by heart before they could be initiated into adulthood. The mark of a true man was to know his place among other men.[9]

Lineages encompassed the ancestors and the ones not yet born. Their people were their people and always would be, ties that transcended feeble earthly constraints. To the Kissi the dead were not really gone but sleeping, able to speak to the living through the wind and other natural phenomena that were revered as manifestations of Malika, the Supreme Being. For the Mende, a large and powerful people to the northwest of the Kissi, two or three generations of the dead, collectively called "grandfather," were ancestral spirits who dwelled among the living. Poised between worlds, they could intercede between the living and "the all-seeing, all-knowing father-protector" called Leve or Nwegɔ. The Gbande regularly delivered food to their dead who had "gone to gather herbs," and they were always consulted on major decisions. Newborn Gbande children were believed to be gifts from these ancestor spirits.[10]

Since belonging was vital, and identity beyond the bounds of kin group was hard to conceive, leaving the homeland permanently was unthinkable. It was so monstrous a fate that the Kissi would only forever banish one of their kin for witchcraft. Each society incorporated within itself disagreements over land, unhappy spouses, rebellious young men, or other fissures that ensued. Only in the most extreme circumstances would somebody be forced to leave.[11]

Banishment was by far the worst thing that could befall anybody. It was graver than poverty, sickness, or war. Even death was just another stage of the human journey. But to be alone without the kin and wider clan that made life livable was so alarming that it incited all manner of disasters including mental breakdown. "To be at the mercy of strangers in a strange land" was the epitome of human suffering.[12]

Since belonging was life, parents gave their children names that told of their place in the world and wove them into the family and through that into their wider clan and society. A name spoken out loud gave the listener information since everybody in the region knew the order of names in families. When Tamba spoke his simple two-syllable name, people across a vast area knew that he was his mother's second-born son and that his family were Kissi or perhaps Kono, a related people whose names overlapped with those of the Kissi. First-, second-, and third-born Kono and Kissi sons shared their names, although fourth-born sons did not. Other names were given to twins, children born directly after twins, or a child born after their previous sibling had died. It was through a name that a person became part of society. It was how they would take their place in the warp and weft of history.[13]

The Sherbro people, distant relatives who had been neighbors at some point in the past, also had these "umbilical names." So too did the Mano, whose land was to the south and east, near the Kpelle and Belle. A Mano mother called her sons Saye, Nyahn, and Paye in the order of their arrival, and her daughters Kou, Yah, and Yei, although she might also choose a different name that had come to her in a dream, derived from an elders' comment, or was in honor of a godparent or ancestor. A middle name was the child's "story name," telling of some event around the time of his or her birth.[14]

People from further away had names that spoke of the time or place in which they had been born, or relayed a message or a parable about their life or character. Some names told of a father's profession or a characteristic of their mother during her pregnancy. Most people did not have any equivalent of a surname or lineage title, and normally clan names were things to keep secret, not to be revealed to anybody outside of their home village. Different names were used in different situations for it was only while safely at home that all the facets of a person's being could be revealed without fear of misfortune.[15]

Whether Tamba was initiated before he was stolen away is unclear. He did not bear any Poro cicatrices, but that does not necessarily mean that he was uninitiated. He might well have been old enough to live through the Poro bush but still young enough to be called "boy" when he arrived at the coast.

So now we must imagine him slightly older than when he had been collecting firewood. Now the end of early boyhood has brought with it a most anticipated occasion, when a boy became a man through initiation into the men's society. It was a mark of great pride, knowing that childhood was to be cast off and his abilities and strengths would help sustain and defend his people. But even if no boy would ever admit it, that excitement was mixed with dread. He would be away from his mother, father, brothers, and sisters for months or even years while undergoing initiation. Only masked spirits would pass between the world of the initiates and the village delivering news of how the children were progressing. In the sacred bush he must learn all the skills and knowledge—laws, social norms, lineages, songs, dances, stories of the ancestors, specialized skills, fighting tactics—to see him through life.[16]

Adding to his hidden fears would be the older boys' teasing, terrifying tales of wild animals that would claw the boys' backs or spears run through initiates' bodies. Nobody could or would tell Tamba and his age mates what was really going to happen since to know the rituals prior to initiation risked death. So clandestine were the rites and rituals to non-initiates that they were termed "secret societies," even though there was nothing else secret about them. It was certainly no secret who was a member since everybody was. There was no other way to be a full human being. The societies stretched far back into history uniting the past and present, the "all-pervading spirit world" with the everyday realm of mortal men. There was a society for the men, and Tamba's sisters would go through parallel rituals to join a counterpart society that meant that they were no longer girls but women.[17]

The wild animals and the spears had to be faced, come what may. Although most of the stories of the initiation bush would prove to be myths, some parts of the process would be painful since preparing children for initiation also meant physically readying them for marriage and parenthood through circumcision. A boy who still had his foreskin was condemned as "a weakling, an inferior being." For girls, a clitoridectomy was considered to be having their last bit of maleness removed so that they were fully women and could therefore become pregnant and give birth.[18]

Boys and sometimes girls had cicatrices cut into their backs: the origin of those myths of wild animals' claw marks. Delicate, dainty scars were desired, and it was important to show no weakness as the knife sliced. Some groups cut scars to signify the order in which boys entered the initiation bush, or their (ritualized) escape from the wild animals or devils said to inhabit the sacred spaces. Some told of their homes: Mano boys had scars cut "around the neck" and down across the chest "where they branch[ed] into several double rows" swirling around and back up to the neck. Some Mende boys had "a main line running from the neck to the base of the spine, and from this roughly horizontal lines passing under the shoulder blades and along the waist." Any special skills learned in the Poro bush might lead to extra marks, such as "circles round the breasts," which was a mark of great honor.[19]

At the end of this lengthy period of study, practice, listening, and being tested, the initiation ceremony would be the biggest day of Tamba's life so far. Like all initiates he would take a new name, sometimes something told "from the tree-tops, from the sleeping amphibian, from the prowling animal, and from the very deeps of the earth." Other people's names were already decided, such as clans who had names for the order in which the boys and girls had entered initiation. Boys who learned a specialized skill or job adopted that as their name. Forever after it would confer status. Among other peoples it was very bad luck to later mention a boy's or girl's birth name, as it invoked the impure person they had been before initiation, but the Kissi retained the names that told of their birth order. Tamba remained Tamba, though perhaps he had an initiation name with his age mates, a more personal, secret name that would be their bond.[20]

Returned to the village, after the celebrations and congratulations, Tamba and his brother initiates would be considered suitably prepared for adulthood, and they would now be able to one day marry, own property, hold office, or participate in important discussions. Connections made in the initiation bush would be a haven through whatever life would later become.[21]

They would also form connections across their different ethnic groups for those who suffered the fate of being separated from their people. Since the societies in various forms existed across the region, they were the stitches holding together the patchwork of different ethnicities. Only the Muslim Manding and the coastal Kru stood apart, and their refusal to recognize the sacred spirits of the Poro and Sande societies was one of the reasons they were outsiders. For so many, membership of the Poro and Sande societies would be the power clung to when life fell apart.[22]

It is not possible to catch sight of Tamba as he was somehow caught up in the waves of enslavement and made his way to the coast. He was in the historical shadows, unseeable as the waves of violence ensnared him and carried him away. He never left any record of these events, only that they happened while he was young. It was perhaps during the journey that he suffered the punishments or injuries that led to the scars that he would carry for the rest of his life on his right knee and lower back.[23]

We can surmise that there was mental trauma, but that has left little direct record on the page. Since Kissi land was far from the coast, the walk must have stretched him to the limits of endurance and then beyond into realms where life ceded to mere existence. The stars in the cooler evening, the rare sips of water, these were in all probability his only comforts when tethered in a coffle, trying to synchronize each footfall with his fellow sufferers to minimize the injuries from the chains. He was part of a swell, thousands of others captured, sold, or pawned, all walking across Africa toward the sea. It was a procession of pain, despair, and fury.

He survived to reach the seacoast. There, instead of being sold to a ship to cross the Atlantic, he was kept to be a factory slave. Amid the hell and chaos that the trade in human beings visited across the land, exactly how this happened is unclear. Maybe it was James Cleveland, himself the son of a Kissi woman, who recognized Tamba as a relative of his mother Ndamba. Such chance meetings could change the fate of anybody, could save a child at the last moment from a slave ship's hold.[24]

Tamba, though a slave, was destined to stay in Africa.

3

The Banana Islands
to Gallinas

For most young British men the Banana Islands were an earthly paradise. The
sandy beaches enticed, and when the heat got to be too much, there was the
shade of a palm tree or a swim in the aquamarine waters of the bays. Robert
Bostock could taste tamarind, wild plum, guava, and yam and admire the birds
with plumage far more brilliant than anything he had previously seen. At night
the stars were charming.[1]

But Bostock discovered a major flaw in his plan to reclaim the money
owed to his late father. When Robert arrived at the Banana Islands in 1802, the
Clevelands, his family's debtors, were not there. Even the gravestone sent out
by his father for James Cleveland was gone. Instead he found himself in the
midst of a war between the Clevelands and their enemies, the Caulkers. After
James Cleveland's death the Caulkers had scented weakness and lost no time in
punishing past wrongs. Stephen Caulker, brother of the man whom James
Cleveland had once had beheaded, swiftly attacked. In early 1798, the Clevelands fled aboard a slave ship to Sherbro, and the Caulkers took control of the
Banana Islands. Inevitably, it was not the end of the affair. European slave
traders advanced William Cleveland, James's nephew, goods and arms to wage
war on the Caulkers, sure that conflict would increase the number of captives
brought to market. A shocked British man observed that the victims of the war
were not just men holding muskets, but women and children, captured and
sold.[2]

Robert Bostock was alone in Africa. But the possibility of slave trading was
open to him, particularly with the ongoing conflict, and perhaps this had been
his intention all along. He needed a patron, and Stephen Caulker was happy to
stand in that role. Caulker made a further offer: Bostock would marry one of
his daughters. It was a way to assure loyalty and an investment on both men's

part. Even had he so wanted, it was an offer Bostock could hardly refuse. To do so would cause the greatest offence.[3]

Marriages in England were solemn affairs of the church, one woman for a lifetime. This was nothing of the kind. Robert surely believed that he would later return home to find a suitable English wife, a demure girl who embroidered and played the pianoforte like his sisters. The celebration of this marriage required drumming, rum for everybody on the islands, and the sacrifice of animals. The earlier wedding of an Englishman to one of James Cleveland's daughters had been celebrated with a chorus of epithalamiums, the firing of one hundred cannon, and the slaughter of the only bull for miles around. "Gad so! I believe I am in love with her!" the groom had written back to England, praising his new wife's shape as "like the Venus of Medicis."[4]

Robert Bostock married a daughter of the powerful Caulker clan. He sat watching the drumming, made the required offerings of beads, cloth, and handkerchiefs. He watched as his young bride was brought toward him under the shade of an umbrella.[5]

Shortly afterward, on the island that his father had loved, he did his first deals as a slave trader. He began to learn the tactics, the way to deal, the local headmen, and whom to trust. The Caulkers were his in-laws, his patrons, and his financiers. For the next few months, the Banana Islands were his home.[6]

Tamba lived on the Plantain Islands, tiny dots of tropical beach three miles off the mainland and just south of the Banana Islands. The men engaged in fishing while the women grew crops, particularly the Egusi seeds for which the islands were renowned, but it was also a strategic post in the slave trade. A few decades earlier John Newton had been a slave trader there, and the mighty Caulker family had taken it as their headquarters around the 1780s, just a few years before James Cleveland beheaded Chief Charles Caulker. Under their ownership the slave trade flourished, and barracoons were constructed with metal shackles fastened into mud walls. By the early nineteenth century it was "one of the greatest slave markets on the coast."[7]

Like John Newton before him, Tamba lived on the largest of the islands, "low and sandy, about two miles in circumference and almost covered with palm-trees." The population tiny, everybody knew Tamba, and he knew them. The Sherbro and Bullom languages spoken at the islands were related to his own Kissi language, and Tamba quickly became fluent. And as traders came by to purchase Egusi and sell slaves and other commodities, he learned words of Mende and Vai and of the other languages that stretch down the coast. He also grew accustomed to the white men who came to call in their crowded, putrid slave ships and soon understood many of their words too.[8]

Tamba became a polyglot and knew that the richness of the African languages, with their many words for each permutation of domestic slave and trade slave and so many other levels of servitude, represented clearly his position relative to those chained in the barracoons. "Slave" could be *cɛ* in Kissi, *woko* in Bullom, *nduwe* in Mende, *wono* in Sherbro, but there were many more alternatives in all of these languages, words that could account for his own status. This was the truth he clung to: he was not being sold across the ocean. There was safety in belonging to such a powerful clan as the Caulkers. The white men who came to buy, with their words *slave*, *esclavo*, and *escravo*, did not have this richness of understanding. He learned the English word *servant*. It was the closest thing he had.[9]

Only three miles off shore, he grew to adulthood an expert canoe man. Climbing into a dugout and paddling it over to Shenge on the mainland, or taking one of the bigger craft to make the longer journey northwest to the Banana Islands or southward to Sherbro, was as familiar to him as walking the golden sands of the Plantains. He also knew that directly inland from the Banana Islands was the southernmost part of Sierra Leone, the British colony. As the slave trade was pronounced to be illegal by the British and Americans, the Caulkers looked to the south, away from these enemies to their business empire. And at some point, conceivably as part of his marriage deal, the Caulkers gave or sold Tamba to Robert Bostock.

Sailors knew it as the Windward Coast, rolling the first word off the tongue and eliding the two halves to make "Winerd." Sometimes they called it the Pepper Coast after the "grains of paradise" whose purple flowers lined the inland waterways. Until the turn of the eighteenth century, slave ships usually sailed right by, leaving crews to the more mundane business of working the ship all the way from Bunce Island in the Sierra Leone River to Fort Appollonia at the far west of the Gulf of Guinea. The surf was too rough; immense waves arriving from their transatlantic swirl meant the landing was not worth the risk.

In the early nineteenth century, however, as the illegalization of the transatlantic slave trade seemed to be in the cards, the Windward Coast beckoned with new prospects. Just beyond the pounding waves was a separate world. An

Atlantic sea bar stretched down much of the coast, and hidden behind it was a network of placid mangrove creeks. It made trading easy. Canoes bringing captives in ones, twos, fives, and tens could easily paddle down the mellow rivers and creeks to sell their human wares.[10]

Working for the Caulkers at the Banana Islands, Robert Bostock heard about this potential, and soon a new opportunity presented itself. He was offered the job of second-in-command to a slave trader named Lancelot Bellerby, who owned a factory at Gallinas on the Kerefe River. Bellerby, like Bostock, was from Liverpool, and it must have seemed like a good fit, so Robert Bostock and his new young wife set off on the short voyage.[11]

Bellerby's business was booming. Ships owned by the DeWolfs of Rhode Island—the most avid of North American slave traders whose head was soon to be the second richest man in the nation—patronized his factory. It was the DeWolf dynasty's heyday in the slave trade: they were taking advantage of what turned out to be a brief lull between earlier attempts to outlaw the trade and its eventual ban. Under the terms of the U.S. Constitution, the first date by which the trade could be outlawed was 1808, and moves were being made to make that a reality. The DeWolfs intended to profit as much as they could in the meantime.[12]

In just one seven-month period in 1804, the DeWolfs dispatched eighteen slaving expeditions to Africa. They were making a fortune, and James DeWolf soon began building his mansion, the Mount, just as his brother William built his own grand home, Hey Bonnie Hall. Daughters of the family rode around in carriages, wore fresh ribbons in their hair and silk stockings, had music and dancing lessons, and learned to play the harp.[13]

The Windward Coast was far from the only area that the DeWolfs favored for their slaving expeditions, but it was a place to which they kept sending their captains, sure that their usual dealers would provide them with human cargoes. In 1804, their small sloop *Nancy* visited Gallinas to purchase slaves. Their slaver *Hiram* visited in 1805 followed by the *Three Sisters*. DeWolf vessels *Jane* and *Charlotte* also called at Bellerby and Bostock's factory that year to trade for captives. Captain John Sabens of the *Charlotte* purchased some girls called "Tully, Peggy, Purrow and Naco" that he chose as "cabin girls." He hoped that later slave buyers in Havana would find them equally sexually desirable and pay up to "$350 a head" for them.[14]

It was not just for their wealth and the scale of the operations that the DeWolf family and their captains were unrivaled allies for Bellerby and Bostock. They were steady friends in uncertain times. In 1804, word reached Bellerby and Bostock that the Society for Effecting the Abolition of the Slave Trade had again been meeting in Great Britain. Having paused its earlier campaign when war with France erupted, it was now once again pushing its cause. Slave ships arriving from Liverpool, Bristol, and London bore the news that bills to prohibit slave trading were once more being introduced to Parliament. It did not bode well, but a quick tot of rum and a laughing exchange with those who knew all about the exploits of the DeWolf family could only help ameliorate any unease. Captain Jim DeWolf was a byword of defiance toward abolitionist rulings and any who sought to check the slave trade's wildest reaches. In his career as a slave ship captain he had managed to sidestep two separate accusations that he had murdered slaves. He had been unruffled even by an arrest warrant from George Washington, and he remained so well respected that he was elected to the Rhode Island House of Representatives. Later he would move on to the U.S. Senate.[15]

Such feats made for fine tales over a bottle of port or beer in the humid evenings of Gallinas. They could laugh at the impotent thundering of the abolitionists who saw their hard-won laws scorned. In the 1790s and 1800s, when Rhode Island began controlling the slave trade, the DeWolfs had flagrantly flouted the rules. Even when caught out they had turned it into the stuff of legend. In 1799, when the *Lucy* was captured illegally slaving and was about to be sold as a forfeit, they had sent out some of their blackguards, dressed as Indians, to kidnap the auctioneer. Then they repurchased the vessel for a pittance.[16]

In a legendary act of bluster, a few years earlier they had succeeded in having their small town designated a discrete customs district. James DeWolf's brother-in-law, a former slave ship captain who "personified contempt for the abolition law," had been installed as its collector. Their ships' men boasted out in Africa of how they stole out of Bristol claiming to be bound for Cuba with rum, acquired fake papers, and then sailed for slaves.[17]

By 1805, the lure of all of those stories and the wealth to be had in Bristol was overpowering. Lancelot Bellerby decided to try a new approach to the business. Taking passage aboard one of the DeWolf slave vessels, he sailed to Rhode Island and linked up directly with the DeWolf family.

Robert Bostock, just turned twenty-one years old, ruled his own slave trading business for the first time. Within the crumbling walls of the compound he was feudal lord.[18]

At their home near Glasgow, Scotland, John McQueen's parents had to decide how to give their son the best chance in life. Young John was ten or eleven years old, pale skinned and blue eyed with hair that would be dark by adulthood. He was tall for his age. Apprenticeships were widely considered to be the best choice for growing boys, a good investment for sons of the middling sort. Increasingly, as Glasgow's Atlantic trading links burgeoned, boys went into maritime industries, learning trades and living under the strict rules that generally keep them out of trouble. Being apprenticed to a father or grandfather was common if that possibility existed, but McQueen's father could not offer such a role. The McQueens had another option, however. John Lascelles, an uncle to young John (whether biological or titular is unclear), owned a slave factory out in West Africa.[19]

A decade before, the year Olaudah Equiano spoke in the city, thirteen thousand Glaswegians had signed a petition against the slave trade. But there was always considerable support among Glaswegians for its continuation, even among those who did not have a close personal connection with it. Glasgow's boom times were built on slave-produced crops, mainly tobacco and rum, and many were loath to see the profits of trade fade away. Plus, in the decade since the petition, the abolitionist cause had been off the agenda, and other concerns had come to the fore. Two years earlier riots had broken out over shortages of potatoes and oatmeal.

John's parents would have known of West Africa's reputation as deadly to white men, but there were few certainties along any path: smallpox carried away nearly one in five people in their city. Did they also perhaps fear that John would not grow up to be the most *civilized* of men in Africa, being so far away from *proper* society? We cannot know, not least since there is little evidence of the family's financial standing or social aspirations. Lascelles was wealthy and far away from Glasgow, where the population was growing apace. Perhaps, struggling themselves, they were relieved at having one less mouth to feed.

A decision was made. Conceivably they hoped that Lascelles, apparently without a European heir, would pass on the business to his nephew. The McQueens decided it was their boy's best chance in life. John, still a child, sailed for Africa.[20]

John McQueen was not the only British boy growing up in West Africa's slave factories. Other families made the same judgment. Robert Bostock's older brother had been scarcely older than McQueen when he had first traveled to James Cleveland's demesne at the Banana Islands. Malcolm Brodie, later a colleague, arrived in Africa "as a young boy" to work at John Frazer's factory. Men and women walked out of Frazer's in chains and shuffled ashore in Florida. Richard Drake starting slave trading on the Windward Coast in his midteens. He became expert at turning a profit from sick captives, using "drugging, cupping and blistering" to render the ailing saleable. American families also made this choice for their sons. George Cook, another future colleague of Bostock's, claimed that he left his home when he was about ten years old to go to the Îles de Los to work for infamous slave trader Benjamin Curtis.[21]

Boys like John would learn the simplest tasks first: filling in the bookkeeping entries and arranging payments for local dealers. He also had to learn how to spot sick slaves who had been made to look healthy to trick the inexperienced buyer; to check for "yellow eye, swollen tongue and feverish skin." He got to know the other white dealers like Lancelot Bellerby, next door, and soon Bellerby's new associate, Robert Bostock. Bellerby and Bostock were older than McQueen, but the resident European population in Gallinas was tiny, and they socialized together, sharing pointers about African dealers and slave ship captains who came to call. Ships' captains left overseas mail with one man for delivery to another. They shared scarce items and a consensus of superiority.[22]

As the years passed, McQueen went from a boy playing on the back streets of Glasgow to a youth who was proficient in the nuances of palavers with local chiefs. He knew how to haggle with slave ship captains the way his contemporaries knew how to plane wood. The cost of each and every item in bars was as familiar to him as produce was to a Glasgow shopkeeper. Each dry season was a parade of dealers and deals, ships and shipments. The current of human merchandise kept walking out of their factory and onto the vessels that would carry them away. Each rainy season was a time of "insufferable lassitude and despondency" when there was little to do but listen to the sound of the deluge battering the thatch.[23]

In 1805 trouble came to Gallinas. The king was dead, and local chiefs including Siaka and Faŋsona engaged in a power struggle. Lascelles lent Faŋsona "forty slaves and ten puncheons of rum" for his fight. Then in the midst of the protracted battle, Lancelot Bellerby returned as supercargo of a fleet of DeWolf vessels. Bellerby was anxious to brag to his old friends about his many successes in Rhode Island, where young belles knew him as "rich Mr Bellaby" and he had begun courting Miss Jane Smith. But this venture, caught up in the Gallinas conflict, was ill-starred. With many slave dealers absent as the battles raged, the factories were all but deserted, and filling the holds proved impossible. Bellerby was forced to sail away with far fewer slaves than planned, and James DeWolf would pursue him for lost profits through the courts of South Carolina and Havana.[24]

John McQueen had bigger problems. Faŋsona was on the losing side. Then, with fighting at the factory gates, his uncle, master, and protector died.

Only in his midteens, John McQueen was alone in Africa and blockaded by angry armies. He smuggled himself aboard the first available ship and sailed away at the last moment. With little reason to return now that his uncle was dead, he took a job at Sherbro Island.[25]

4

Making Deals with Siaka, Selling to the DeWolfs

By 1807, when a ship arrived carrying the startling news that the king and country had illegalized his business, Robert Bostock was back in Gallinas. With avarice trouncing pique, as fighting receded the chiefs allowed the white traders to slink back. Now Siaka, Faŋsona, and the rest heard about the new law but were mystified. The white men had no control over their lands. Who could tell them what to do in their own territory? More mysteriously, white men had always been devoted to buying captives, had caused the trade to double and treble and quadruple with their incessant hungering for more African bodies. By what strange logic were they now saying that it was wrong?[1]

Bostock left no hint about his decision to continue slave trading when others hung up their manacles and sailed home. Perhaps he believed his father to have been nothing like the murderous, monstrous slavers the abolitionists described. Feasibly he was swayed by arguments that captives would still be there, and possibly be slaughtered wholesale, if he and the other dealers did not buy them. Slave trading could be posited as a humanitarian option if the lens was tilted far enough in the right direction. Britain sent off its own criminals in ships to the far side of the world, having founded the prison colony New South Wales in 1788 specifically for this purpose. Maybe it was the right of Africans to do the same?[2]

The color of the rationalizations, no matter their hue, was gold. There were still voracious slave markets to be fed, especially in Cuba and Brazil. Greed has never yet been overcome through parliamentary decree. DeWolf vessels still heaved into view, their holds full to the brim. An increasing number of vessels based in Cuba vowed to openly disobey the laws of the phlegmatic northerners. Slave trading had always been a high-stakes business, and becoming outlaws merely added a new frisson of adventure. There was camaraderie among brigands.

New men arrived, such as American trader Charles Mason,[3] lured by the higher profits as risks increased. Mason worked closely with William Crundell, a white slave dealer who had sided with Siaka in the recent conflict and so was now on the winning side. Soon Gallinas was once again an attractive destination for slave ship captains.[4]

They were precariously close to the enemy nevertheless. Sierra Leone, a tiny colony originally called the Province of Freedom, was just up the coast. It had been founded in 1787 by a group of blacks from Britain, mostly refugees from the American War of Independence. Others who had liberated themselves by fleeing ended up in Nova Scotia at the end of the war, then sailed in 1792 for Africa. In 1800 Maroons had also arrived in the colony, deported by the British from Jamaica for revolt.[5]

The settlement had been a mosquito buzzing the slave trading leviathan since Bostock was a boy. From the start the idea behind the colony had been to defeat the slave trade. Thomas Clarkson, second only to Wilberforce in the British abolitionist campaign, had written in 1788 that "the Establishment of a Free Settlement on the Coast of Africa for honourable Trade would be the most effectual means of destroying the Slave Trade." Its principles of free African labor and the reality of black men sitting on juries and holding their own government had caused many a slave trader's wry joke. But with the slave trade made illegal, the colony became a hazard. On January 1, 1808, the Union Jack was hauled up the flagpole in the capital, Freetown, and the settlement of around two thousand people officially became a British colony. The British government dispatched two Royal Navy vessels to be stationed there to catch illegal slavers. A Vice-Admiralty Court was set up to adjudicate anybody so captured. African captives found aboard illegal slavers would find homes in the colony.[6]

There were some who tutted at the absurdity of it all. Britain was tied up in a European war that had been virtually ceaseless since 1792. The Royal Navy needed to deliver troops and supplies, protect borders, and collect money to pay for it all. The nation did not have enough ships or sailors to launch an attack on a business that was so entrenched. More than one old seadog believed that they should concentrate on repelling the French rather than aiming their cannons at the slave trade.[7]

But for men like Bostock and Mason it was galling and risible more than threatening. The risks of actually being caught were low because Gallinas had a feature that allowed them to dodge unwanted scrutiny. The long sea bars that stretched along the coast separated the slavers from any bigger vessels hoping to capture them. Merchants were already sending out smaller, livelier craft for just this reason. These compact vessels from Havana and Matanzas in Cuba and from São Luís do Maranhão on Brazil's Caribbean coast could get over the bars at high tide, gliding into the languid waters behind. There they were safe to go about their business since the navy's bigger vessels could not cross.[8]

Gone were the days when slave ships meandered down the coast purchasing captives in small lots. Now merchants had an entire shipload readied in advance so that captains and supercargoes could embark the captives in less than forty-eight hours and sneak away. A few years later, the governor of Sierra Leone would lament that "vessels coming to the Coast for Slaves are now so quick in their movements that I generally get information of their arrival & departure by the same conveyance."[9]

So Bostock and Mason's Gallinas factory developed a rhythmic spirit: gentle trading down the mellow creeks in the dry season, a long, dull hiatus as the deluge hit, and the lurches into action whenever slave ships came to call, transforming their simple factories into choreographed commotion. It was an auditorium of inhumanity and misery, an epic performance of greed and violence.

But then a strike sliced through their secluded creeks that involved an American DeWolf vessel. Although the Americans had banned the slave trade from 1808, the earliest date allowed by the Constitution, this move had been far less controversial than in Britain. So when James DeWolf's brig *Baltimore* had arrived back in Rhode Island with a cargo of slaves at the end of 1807 he had dispatched it to the Windward Coast once more. It weighed anchor in November 1807, only weeks before the ban would start. He was pushing to its limits the concept of a grace period in which to complete delayed voyages, in true DeWolf style. (Another DeWolf vessel, *Three Sisters*, left for Africa on December 21, 1807, a mere ten days before the ban.) Having traded through earlier sanctions, he evidently saw no reason not to carry on.[10]

It proved a miscalculation. In March 1808, the *Baltimore* was cruising off the Îles de Los with seventy-two captives aboard when the crew spotted a vessel flying the Union Jack. The British boarded and questioned them. Captain Slocum failed to argue convincingly that he was not breaking regulations as there were obviously slaves aboard. The *Baltimore* was carried into Sierra Leone, where the captives were liberated.

Hearsay, rumor, and anger hove heartily down the coast. In Bristol DeWolf raged, but it did not stop the patrols. In November one French and two Brazilian vessels fell to the patrol's cannons. Then came a lull. In late 1809, come the dry season, it began again. More than a hundred African captives were rescued from the *Cuba*. The *Two Cousins* was carried into Freetown and made a prize of war. The Netherlands' schooner *Africaan* was forfeited for the three captives found beneath decks.[11]

Alongside these captures, nevertheless, ran stories of lucky escapes, fights won, and new methods of decoy. The navy's patrols were a tiny dam attempting to hold back a tidal wave. The risks of being captured were small and potential profits ever greater. It became a sport, slavers trying to outdo each other by inventing new ways to beat the patrol. Among the mangrove-screened inlets of Gallinas country, small slave trading schooners played a game of tag with British cruisers. There were stories of a ship that blatantly relanded its captives and compelled them to sing and dance on the beach, taunting the British, who could only detain a vessel if slaves were aboard. British patrol captains were rumored to occasionally be willing to take bribes to sail away when a slave ship was due, a game known wryly as "Johnee Bull."[12]

As 1808 became 1809 and then 1810, Bostock and Mason must have been slyly thrilled. Business was booming. Captains still in the slaving business no longer called at older, established slaving ports. More discreet places swept into fashion, and the geography of the slave trade shifted. They and their neighbors were clear winners, as Gallinas was the perfect place for these new times. Their trade swelled to a size never seen when it all had been legal. The hum of promise became a roar.[13]

In 1809, Robert Bostock and Charles Mason went into business together. While most British traders had left, and those who remained fretted about the proximity of the British Navy's patrol boats, American merchants were less abashed, even after the *Baltimore* affair. The British, with their cool climate and pinched cheeks, had suddenly become moralistic, but America still had plantations and farms that demanded slave labor. In many port cities across the South it was an open secret that slave trading continued. Illegalization was near to being a joke. Countless were in cahoots, and customs agents were simply bribed to look away. Abolition appeared to be a northern-led hypocrisy, and many wanted no part of it.

At least a thousand or so Africans were still imported into the United States each year, sneaked in under cover of night or aboard slave ships claiming to be "in distress." Tens of thousands more were sold elsewhere having been transported aboard American ships, with American crews, or funded by American money. The African Institution of London estimated that American ships carried a quarter of those still being taken annually from Africa. President James

Madison admitted before Congress that many Americans were still trading. The official penalty if Charles Mason was caught would be $10,000 and five to ten years in jail (the death penalty had been discussed and outvoted but would later be introduced), but it was such a remote possibility it hardly mattered.[14]

There seemed little doubt that the slave traders were winning. In London the members of the African Institution, the organization set up by the original Sierra Leone Company when they handed over control of the colony to the British government, were increasingly disillusioned and despairing. In 1809 they had given grandiose celebratory speeches about the "entire cessation of the slave trade" and discussed the agricultural crops that would flourish in Africa's bright new dawn. Around this time Sierra Leone's Governor Ludlam had left notes for his successors as if the end of the slave trade was a fait accompli and they would henceforth govern over "streams of plenty" instead of "thirsty land." But by 1810 the abolitionists were aghast that the abolition laws were defied wildly and openly, and they grieved that their "expectation has not been realized." By 1811 they raged that the "coast swarms with slave ships," many simply disguised as Spanish or Portuguese to cover their true origins.[15]

In 1810, a commissioner of the African Institution and a confirmed abolitionist—a sentiment possibly derived from his seeing slaves during his earlier posting in the Caribbean—became governor of the British colony at Sierra Leone. Edward Henry Columbine, watercolor artist and hydrographical surveyor, arrived in Freetown with authority to arbitrate captured slave ships. He was determined that the campaign against the slave trade would enter a new phase. Bostock and Mason were at first unconcerned, but Columbine sprung into action and captured the slaver *Esperança*, finding the captives aboard shackled "in the most cruel manner" with three sets of manacles on their arms and legs. Soon after, the slave ship *Mariana* was taken. Its captain, "a most ill-looking dog," told Columbine defiantly that he would simply return to the coast better armed and ready to fight.[16]

Columbine then made the decision that he would not even attempt the real, if utterly impossible, task of patrolling the African coast entire. He would instead target slave ships cruising the "coast and rivers adjacent to Sierra Leone." Suddenly vessels calling at Mason and Bostock's enterprise were squarely in the frame. Columbine sent out the *Esperança*, now crewed by three Europeans and ten Sierra Leoneans, as an additional patrol vessel. It swiftly captured the *Zaragozano*, which had purchased at least some of the 129 captives aboard from Mason and Bostock. (The captives had also rebelled, jumped overboard, and been recaptured by Bostock's old acquaintance William Cleveland.) It was a warning of how the abolition movement was encroaching.[17]

Columbine, a true believer in the abolitionist cause, next sent out a messenger, John Kizell, to visit slave traders in the region and command them to relinquish the trade in human flesh. Kizell was a living example of the message, a man born close to Sherbro Island and shipped for sale in Charleston, South Carolina. After enduring several years of bondage he had fled during the American Revolutionary War and found his way to Sierra Leone. Now he conveyed an exhortation from Columbine to slave traders: "the slave trade cannot be carried on much longer, and therefore I earnestly hope and entreat that you will turn your views to the cultivation of your land." This would prevent people being trafficked and, Columbine argued, allow Africans to "rise above the poverty which renders you so dependent on Europe."[18]

Mason and Bostock must have heard about Kizell and his message from both the Clevelands and the Caulkers. Then Kizell landed in Gallinas, where he presented Columbine's letter to William Crundell, Mason's old ally, who "curse[d] and swore and rave[d]." Bostock managed to dodge Kizell's attentions, but Mason was less fortunate. Kizell added the name "Mason" to his list of the region's white slave dealers. The list was sent to Britain, where Mason's name was printed in the report of the African Committee as one of the enemies of their noble venture.[19]

None of this appears to have perturbed Charles Mason very much. Not long after Kizell's tour of the region and a few months after the capture of the *Zaragozano*, he and Bostock upped the stakes.

Imperceptibly at first, the landscape shifted as the monster of increased demand crept inland. At Gallinas and further south, previously cultivated land returned to a "dense and lofty forest of timber-trees, entangled with vines and brush-wood" as people fled from captors. North at Sherbro it was said that "thousands of miles are now without an inhabitant" because so many had run in terror.[20]

Disaster encroached upon village after village. Those with diverse qualities and talents, who carried their families' hopes, were condemned by trickery, doomed by false accusations, sold for debts, or pawned. No man left home without a weapon anymore. Stories of those taken spread like a contagion with people heralding the names of the lost, those whom they would endlessly mourn.[21]

It was a wife snatched from the fields, simply gone. A son who went to fight the enemy and never returned, and whose parents suffered every day, always wondering. The tragic day when slave raiders came to the village and so many were gone, and the urgency with which those left that day tried to tell their children about it. It was all of these burgeoned together into infinitude.

Most of all it was children: the "age of abolition" was really the "age of child enslavement." Easier to capture, less likely to rebel, able to fit into smaller spaces aboard ship and so cheaper to transport, children were the archetypical captives of the era. It made perfect business sense, because traders knew that they would fetch high prices in the Americas, yet they could generally be frightened into saying nothing should the antislavery patrols catch them. In increasing numbers the young and the very young made their way to the coast.[22]

Wars had long been waged purely to make slaves, and the jihad was an ongoing scourge, but now warfare increased as demand for captives skyrocketed, and the stakes of power escalated. A Gbande village in Foya was one of those raided, with the devastating loss of many of its people. The women might be wanted as domestic slaves, junior wives, but the men and boys and the rest of the women were forced to march to the sea. Within a decade, as many slaves would be shipped from Gallinas in a single year as had departed in the entire century to 1800.[23]

Clan identifications began to bend amid the search for survival. Small, weaker ethnic groups like the Banta were becoming so decimated by the onslaught of the Mende that later those who remained would assimilate themselves, for there was strength in numbers. The Loma people lost so many of their kin to slave raiders that they began changing their way of life, moving from small hamlets into bigger settlements for protection. They made pacts to defend each other, to be brothers in the face of the enemy.[24]

Some tried to adapt. The Vai, whose land Gallinas was within, became more serious slave traders. Others sought safety in multiethnic alliances like the Condo Federation, whose capital was at Bopolo, fifty miles inland from Cape Mount. Founded by Loma, Dei, and Gbande, soon Kpelle, Gola, Vai, and Manding also joined, hoping to save themselves by being part of a group strong enough to partially control the trade. The leader at Bopolo had worked for the British and could speak some English: a major track from Bopolo led directly to the coast and was a main route along which captives were trafficked.[25]

Many of those who marched desolately through Bopolo, taking the fork in the road leading to the coast, had already journeyed far from their homes. The distance from the birthplaces of some of those sold at Gallinas to the coast was around 450 kilometers or 280 miles. Others came from lands nearer to the coast, but these expanses too were unbearable. Together they comprised a human disaster.

We catch an unexpectedly clear view of Robert Bostock and Charles Mason in November 1810. They were sitting down with five powerful local chiefs, the entourages of these men, their own servants, and the heady aspiration of building a new slave factory. The chiefs controlled the land, and their consent was needed if Mason and Bostock were to construct their own barracoon. It was likely Charles Mason who inscribed their names on paper so thick that the texture was slightly uneven, using elaborate curlicue capitals as if to render the solemnity of the occasion onto the page. "Mr Scearca," "Dewarca Soba," "Fanga Suna," "St. Medeina," and "Mattier Rogers," he wrote.

"Mr Scearca," was Siaka, the man who had been William Crundell's ally in the Gallinas conflict. Soon he would become King Siaka, the African trader involved in the *Amistad* case. In 1810 he was an up-and-coming chief and slave dealer and within the decade owned his own town with about three hundred houses. He was said to eat off a silver plate. Mattier Rogers was "the oldest chief" and so commanded respect; he was one of the vast Rogers clan who had an English merchant ancestor. They controlled forty separate towns and villages, including the village of Dibia or Liyia, on the banks of the Moa River. "Fanga Sunga" was Mason's misspelling of Faŋsona, John Lascelles's old ally in the Gallinas conflict. His descendants up until the 1970s would treasure an "embroidered gown said to have been given by European slave dealers." "St. Medeina" could have been a reference to Amara, a local chief and slaver who would later call his capital Medina.[26]

With such august company to entertain, the gifts given in the palaver would have been substantial. Another Englishman trying to rent land found himself giving out iron bars not only to chiefs but also to entire retinues including servants, "key keepers," "singing men," and marabous.[27]

Bostock and Mason's business must have raised the vision of mighty proceeds for the chiefs. On November 13, a deal was struck. The five chiefs agreed to accept "fifty Bars of Tobacco, Cask Rum," and gunpowder for the renting of some land for the factory. Iron bars were the standard unit of currency on the coast, the measure of just about anything a slave trader and his customers might need. A single bar at this time bought about four pounds of pewter, three cauldrons, one pound of coffee, or eighteen Flemish knives. A piece of "guinea cloth" was six bars, as was a twenty-pound barrel of flour, but a firkin (about fifty-six pounds) of butter was ten bars. The thick, rigid paper on which the treaty was written cost around five bars for a ream, more than a gun, which was only four bars. Each healthy slave was worth 140–50 bars.[28]

They undertook a solemn oath. Mason and Bostock could "cut wood, thatch, and get water and mud and anything requisite to the Factory" and were given "every protection in the Country." Underneath, each of the five chiefs signed with a cross.[29]

There was something more on the contract, the twinkle in their eyes and the whisper of insolence and bravado engraved solemnly onto the paper. Mason wrote that he and Bostock were building this slave factory at "the point of" Bance Island, Gallinas. While it has usually been assumed that this was a reference to Bunce Island, in the Sierra Leone River, on closer reflection it can only have been a jibe at the abolitionist forces. It could not have been the old Bance Island since that was far from Gallinas and not under Siaka and Faŋsona's control. By November 1810 the slave trading fraternity had largely had to abandon Bunce Island anyway because it was too close to the naval patrols at Sierra Leone. As one man put it in that year, perhaps overoptimistically, "Bance is now of no more consequence than the dirt under my feet." The name was not so much a reference to the old Bunce Island but a warning from Mason and Bostock that they hoped to found a New Bance as infamous as the last.[30]

The digging and the forming of mud bricks and timber frames began. A new barracoon was raised on Gallinas's gentle shore.

5

A Cargo of Slaves
for Havana

By the end of 1810, the new factory was up and running. Slave dealers came to call with men, women, and children to sell and slave ships began to add the place to their itinerary. The dry season was their major trading time, and a hubbub of activity reigned.

But Bostock and Mason were ambitious and scented ever greater profits. Over the Christmas season of 1810, as the New Year appeared on the horizon, they plotted expansion. By the first of January 1811 it was resolved, and they gathered their old friends Lancelot Bellerby, now back from his adventures, and William Crundell, to witness the new agreement. Mason and Bostock, both "residing in the River Galinas [*sic*] Africa," agreed to "Establish a Factory at St Pauls [*sic*] Mount Serrada on the Coast of Africa." Bostock "shall stay in the Factory and sell barter ship and dispose of the property as he may think most advantageous to the risk and benefit of both parties." Charles Mason, however, was not staying at their Gallinas business. The contract stated, "it is agreed that Charles Mason shall go off with such property as may appear to be shipped on the account of the said parties and he shall make use of the property as may appear to arise from the same to the best of his Judgement." Both men laid down £1000 surety.[1]

The next ship to arrive at their Gallinas business, a possible vessel to carry away Mason and his and Bostock's property, was the brigantine *Dos Amigos*. When it heaved into view its captain, William Richmond, had a story to tell that likely made Mason and Bostock all the more determined. Richmond reported that he had taken all the necessary precautions, sailing to Cuba and putting a titular captain, Don Ramón Amadas, at the helm. His false papers suggesting Cuban ownership were in order. Yet sailing down the coast a few weeks earlier they had been boarded by Governor Columbine. Columbine was certain that the *Dos Amigos* was "fitted out for the slave trade." Amadas and

Richmond had secured the vessel's release, but principally because they did not have any captives aboard, rather than because their Spanish flag put them beyond Columbine's remit. Richmond returned boldly to slave trading.[2]

Richmond bought a cargo of Mende warriors, Kissi and Kono men caught in warfare, Gbande women and children taken in raids while their menfolk were away, Temne children who had wandered too far from home and been kidnapped, and Vai who had been tricked or pawned or sold for crimes that they may or may not have committed. They were 328 in number.

By this time Robert Bostock had purchased the factory slave he called Tom Ball and had made the new Gallinas factory into Tom's prison. Perhaps originally called Banna, and if so likely Temne—the one local language, along with its offshoot Banta, that Tamba could not speak—Ball had been enslaved since he was a boy. When the *Dos Amigos* arrived, he was set to work filling the ship's "belly." It was he whose strength paddled the men, women, and children who would make the crossing in the *Dos Amigos*'s hold as they left Africa for the final time.

Then the vessel sailed away, Charles Mason waving goodbye to his old colleagues and friends from the deck as it slipped over the bar and out to sea. His agreement with Bostock had not specifically mentioned Cuba, or how the island was being used to ensure a steady stream of illegal slaves into the United States, but that was where he was headed. It was where a stream of slave traders had moved since 1807 to hide from the British abolitionists who called them "the pirates of the Havannah." They sought refuge in Havana and Matanzas, where they could trade "with more eagerness and rapacity than ever." The island became such an important market that African merchants began to send their sons to study Spanish on the island, whereas they had once sent them to England or France. A "passenger service" began, shuttling merchants between the Windward Coast, Cuba, and Charleston, South Carolina.[3]

As the *Dos Amigos* weighed anchor in Havana harbor, the incentive behind this move was clear before Mason's eyes. Vast profits were conspicuous along the Malecón with its fine business emporiums and glamorously dressed ladies driven around in *volantes* by "a large negro" wearing galligaskins and a red jacket with gold lace trim. Havana was said to have "an air of solid age . . . that gives it a *grand* appearance." Its "wealth and luxury" were so impressive that visitors "gaze[d] at the peculiar brightness and glitter which distinguish tropical scenes." It was utterly different to the mud brick compound he had left behind in Gallinas.[4]

Amid the narrow streets, "large solid houses" contained warehouses on the ground floor with the merchant's counting house above. The "moneylending

Havana, Cuba, in 1839. From Frédéric Mialhe, *Isla de Cuba Pintoresca* (Havana: Lit. de la Rl. Sociedad Patriótica, 1839).

middlemen and speculators" had "cash in a strongbox and credit in the major cities of the world." Major slave merchants were among the richest of all, and lesser players dreamed of rivaling their success. The year before Mason's arrival, Governor Columbine of Sierra Leone lamented—all the while sounding quite jealous, given his own inadequate salary—that a slave bought for £18 or £20 near Sierra Leone would sell for many times that price in Havana. Columbine had heard of an American slave dealer who made £10,000 on a single voyage. It was rumored that George DeWolf, scion of the DeWolf family, bought his Cuban plantation Arca de Noé [Noah's Ark] from the profits of one illegal slaving voyage.[5]

This vociferous demand for slave labor was in part because the Haitian Revolution had fuelled an upsurge in the Cuban sugar industry, creating "a wild millionaire orgy" as production soared. The island was utterly changed in just a few decades. Cuba's story became sugar, and with grim predictability slaves followed. In the 280 or so years until 1790, around one hundred thousand Africans had been imported. Then in just the 30 years from 1790 to 1820, at least three times that many arrived in shackles. It was an irrevocable transformation, and the *Dos Amigos*'s captives were at the cusp of the tipping point.

Their appearance in 1811, and that of six thousand or so others that year, meant that Cuba was no longer a society where people of European origin were the majority. Primeval feelings of insecurity, danger, and being engulfed by the enemy fossilized and fed the very worst of human instinct.[6]

At the sea gate, an "olfactory catalog" of dried beef and fish greeted them all as Mason and the crew watched the captives led away to the barracoons. There the stench was yet more overwhelming, including sweat, putrid flesh, and death. Many were "reduced to skin and bones." They were "spread out on wooden planks," and dysentery carried some away. Yet it was violence, terror, and "the demolition of the spirit" that made it so unspeakable. Visiting Havana's barracoons, one doctor would be moved to comment, "there is nothing worse in the world than to be a slave."[7]

Richmond prepared to bring them to market. Cuban planters, fancying themselves experts on Africans in chains, had long lumped slaves together in various regional groups. These spoke more to the place from which they had departed Africa than any sense of their actual identity. Those who left from the Windward Coast, like those aboard the *Dos Amigos*, were termed Gangá, perhaps a contraction of "Gangara," a term outsiders used for the Mende, rapidly becoming the biggest ethnic group in the region.[8]

Newly imported Gangá fetched fine prices. While some Cuban planters favored Lucumí (Yoruba) bondsmen, usually captives arriving from Senegambia fetched the best prices. But Gangá came only just behind. The adult men aboard the *Dos Amigos* sold for as much as $400 each, the women and children slightly less.[9]

Preparing their merchandise for sale in Havana, Mason and Richmond were among friends. By 1807, Havana was already one of the two most popular markets for American slave ships. Now fellow Americans were possible purchasers for their wares as Cuba was in the process of becoming dominated by Americans. By 1823, at least fifty plantations in Matanzas province alone were owned by North Americans, and that decade the possibility of making the island part of the United States would be much discussed. By 1841, visiting American Joseph Gurney was told that 90 percent of the ships employed in Cuba's slave trade had been constructed in the United States and heavily funded by U.S. capital. In the 1850s, British writer Anthony Trollope would claim: "The Havana will soon become as much America as New Orleans."[10]

Cuba was a considerable part of how and why American attempts to abolish the slave trade were failing so badly. Slaving merchants operated proudly among its cobbled, majestic streets, not even feigning to shun the viciousness of their profession for the sake of appearances. It was not until 1817 that the

Spanish government agreed, with the help of a £400,000 inducement "loan" from Great Britain, to halt the slave trade to Cuba. That and later legislation had little to no effect, and it would be half a century before any significant inroads were made into the slave trade onto the island. In the meantime, there was very little at all to stop Americans continuing to trade slaves there.

Among those moving more of their operations to Havana in this era was the DeWolf family, and somewhere in the wake of the *Dos Amigos* lies their trail. They had long been the employers of the *Dos Amigos*'s captain, William Richmond, and they maintained contact with him for the rest of his life. Who exactly was behind the *Dos Amigos*'s voyage when it arrived in Havana in 1811 nobody was telling, but one or more members of the DeWolf family are strong contenders. The DeWolfs' agents, Hernández and Chaviteau, received the living, breathing shipment and arranged their sale.[11]

After the illegalization of the slave trade for Americans, and especially after the capture of the *Baltimore*, James DeWolf made a public display of turning his back on the slave trade. Whether it was show or reality remains to be decisively proven. But others in his family were equally clear in their intention to defy the ban. James's nephew and sometime rival George DeWolf bought three of James's former slave ships to keep trading. Well into the late 1810s he sent them to Africa for slaves. Later he retreated to his base in Cuba.[12]

There was more than one man who knew or suspected that the DeWolfs were up to their old games. Charles Mason sailed away from Africa with an old employee of theirs, and he would become a regular visitor in Rhode Island. He sailed between Charleston, South Carolina, and Rhode Island, as well as to Havana and Africa, arranging deals and victualing more ships for the journey across the ocean.[13]

With Mason gone, Robert Bostock needed somebody to assist him. Two months after the *Dos Amigos* sailed he hired John McQueen, returned from Sherbro.

Not long after, word reached them of new penalties if they were caught slave trading. Now, Britons risked fourteen years' transportation or up to five years' hard labor if they continued trading in slaves.[14]

Again, Bostock's response was to raise the stakes.

Part 2

Burned
to the Ground

6

A New Slave Factory
at the St. Paul River

Bostock and Mason's new factory was on the "beautiful border" of the St. Paul, slightly upriver from where it emerged into the sea at Cape Mesurado. It was an area of "prolific" soil garnering "oranges, lemons, cocoanuts, pine-apples, mangoes, plums, granadillas, sour and sweet sop, plantains, bananas, guyavas, tamarinds, ginger, sweet potatoes, yams, cassava and corn." Bostock and his new assistant, John McQueen, aided by Tom Ball and perhaps Tamba, whom they had brought with them from Gallinas, were too busy arranging the business of the guinea trade to pay much attention to the area's natural bounty.[1]

There unfortunately does not seem to be any evidence of the chief or chiefs with whom they dealt for the right to found this business, but Chief Bagna, whose compound was very close by, must have been involved. Whether Bostock and McQueen married into Bagna's clan is also not spelled out in the records that remain, but it was a common pathway in such negotiations. Once the chiefs had been dashed there were wells to be dug, mud to be hauled, and wood to be carved. Pens had to be built to ensure the greatest security and shackles attached to the floor and walls to hold individual captives securely. Coopers, clerks, carpenters, and cooks had to be employed and sufficient Kru sailors engaged to ensure that trade would progress smoothly.

The new factory was not far inland from the mouth of the St. Paul, close to where a branch of the river flowed south and joined up with the Mesurado River at the Cape. This tributary provided a quick, sheltered way to reach the Mesurado, far easier than venturing out to the ocean. It became an important trade route, especially since there were two prominent slave traders established on small islands just hidden in the mouth of the Mesurado. Captives, food-stuffs, merchandise, and news passed through the creek on dugouts.

Dazoe, the westernmost of the two islands, was the business empire of John Sterling Mill. The son of an English father and African mother, Mill had been educated in England and held similar status to the Caulkers and Clevelands. His mixed heritage was interpreted in differing and telling ways to those who met him: an American visitor would describe him "a yellow man," while to an African he purchased he was "a white man."[2]

Across a causeway from Dazoe, a stroll at low tide or a quick canoe trip when the ocean swept in, was Balli (sometimes Gomez) Island, the slaving domain run by Philippa Hayes. The daughter of an African mother and American father, Philippa had married an Englishman, William Hayes. He was the official owner of the property but in mid-1813 had returned to England, leaving Philippa and their daughter Hannah behind. Both Mill and Hayes became close trading partners of Bostock and his trusted friends.[3]

Bostock and Mason appear to have established the Cape Mesurado factory as a sub- or feeder factory, and in this they were ahead of the game. Rare at other parts of the African coast, at Sierra Leone and along the Windward Coast the practice of transshipping captives along the seaboard was becoming commonplace. With the slave trade illegal and the patrols heating up, the main imperative was to elude their attentions, and transporting slaves along the coast helped. Slaves could be transshipped quickly and quietly to whichever place the patrols were not present, ensuring a full shipment was available to slave ships that landed there.[4]

In the following decades other traders would follow Mason and Bostock's lead in having smaller feeder factories to supply a main base as well as to provide alternative places of slave purchase. Pedro Blanco, dealer of the *Amistad* slaves, later owned at least four smaller slave factories that supplied his headquarters at Gallinas. Like his forerunners Mason and Bostock, he established one of these at the St. Paul River. Another slave trader, Theophilus Canot, boasted that he ran a "nursery" or "junior factory" close to the St. Paul, as well as having other sub-factories that fed his main base at New Sestros. He declared that as a slaving entrepôt Cape Mesurado was second in importance only to Gallinas.[5]

It illustrated the way that the trade was changing. Bostock and McQueen were ordering and watching, shouting and flogging as their servants and slaves constructed their fiefdom-compounds of a different order to the slave trading meccas of earlier times, like Elmina, Cape Coast Castle, Gorée, or Bunce. Grand fortresses, impregnable but highly visible, had given way to smaller, more adaptable edifices. Built with bamboo fence poles, mud, and mangrove staves, using stonework only where it was most needed, they reflected local building methods. The contrast to the earlier castles was so great that at Rio Pongo, not far to the north of the Sierra Leone River, several slave factories appeared little more than assemblies of mud huts to westerners who visited.

"The lower part of it is built on the ground," an observed noted, with "one storey with a thatched roof over it and a parcel of mangrove sticks laid across and a great deal of mud to make it fire proof."[6]

Yet this was something of a European and American misperception since the slave factories were showpieces, grander and more imposing than anything else around them either then or now. American dealer George Cook, once a boy working for Benjamin Curtis, described his Bengara factory as "130 or 140 feet in front." It was constructed of "stones and bricks and mortar and mud . . . a great quantity of mud," with a storeroom underneath and a house up above. Separate buildings included a rice house and tobacco store, as well as the powder magazine, all gathered around "Piazzas." "Negroe [sic] houses all built of stone and cement standing on about two acres of land enclosed on all sides with a Wall of 10 feet high" provided accommodation for the Africans, both free and enslaved, that worked at the factory.[7]

Pedro Blanco, so powerful that he was said to have created a "theatre of a new order of society and a novel from of government," built his headquarters in the same way. Blanco had an empire spread across the islands at the mouth of the Kerefe River, a harem on one island and a grand home on another, all constructed in this local style. These building methods are why their compounds have left remains only accessible through archaeological excavation, although the walls and cannons of one of Blanco's Cape Mount sub-factories were apparently visible above ground into the 1920s.[8]

Whatever they spent on living quarters, showrooms, wharf, and walls—and it was considerable, reflecting their highly profitable business—their greatest wealth was not in infrastructure but in trading goods. The wealth amassed behind the earthen brick and mangrove walls was astonishing. Vast caches of merchandise were held in the traders' storerooms. George Cook claimed that in 1814 he kept fourteen tons of rice, one hundred tons of salt, thirty-two hogsheads of tobacco, seven and a half tons of "prime Ivory," five hundred different India cloths, four tons of beads of assorted varieties, ten tons of iron, two and a half puncheons of rum, fifty-four barrels of gunpowder and a huge assortment of weapons and firearms, canoes, cutters and launches to load and unload passing ships, all topped off with 250 men's hats and 125 umbrellas.[9]

Robert Bostock would later say that his stores at his new Cape Mesurado factory in the middle of 1813 held "100 pipes of Rum," hogsheads of tobacco, "2000 weight of Ivory," five hundred gold bars, five hundred sacks of gold dust, five thousand pieces of gold coin, "1000 pounds weight of Gold," ten thousand pieces of silver, one thousand silver rings, one thousand amulets and fifty thousand beads. The armory comprised five hundred barrels of gunpowder,

five hundred carronades and their carriages, five hundred muskets, fifty pairs of
pistols, five thousand knives, one hundred cutlasses and five hundred bayonets.
His fabric warehouse contained "3,000 pieces of Romals" and two thousand
bafts (both types of Indian fabric), "2,000 pieces of check," "300 pieces of Satin
Stripes," three thousand chintzes, five thousand pieces of linen, and "5,000
pieces of Manchester goods."

For traders looking for simpler wares, Bostock also had ten thousand
earthenware pots, five hundred brass kettles, five hundred brass pans, two
hundred iron pots and, for the more cultured purchaser, one thousand books
and thirty "sets of Musical instruments." For construction, he offered ten
thousand loads of timber and five thousand "iron fastenings," one hundred
glazed windows and their frames, two hundred doors, one hundred wooden
shutters, and one hundred chimneys. Should passing slave vessels need any
repairs, he also kept a small shipyard, including fifty sloops, fifty pinnaces, fifty
boats, fifty canoes, five hundred sails, fifty anchors, five thousand articles of
rigging, five thousand ropes, one hundred bowsprits, five thousand yards of
canvas, and tools for carpenters, blacksmiths, and coopers.[10]

Bostock built a home for himself on the banks of the St. Paul River, a house
described as "very large" by a visiting slave ship captain. Yarra, the factory
slave purchased by John McQueen not long after the establishment of the
Cape Mesurado compound, reported that it was built "in the country fashion
with a thick solid mud floor between the cellar and second story." Around it he
had a palisade constructed for protection.

It was something like that later owned by slave trader Theophilus Canot,
who wrote:

> My house, built of cane plastered with mud, consisted of two earthen-floored
> rooms and a broad veranda. The thatched roof was rather leaky, while my
> furniture comprised two arm-chests covered with mats, a deal table, a bamboo
> settee, a tin-pan with palm oil for a lamp, and a German looking-glass mounted
> in a paper frame. I augmented these comforts with the addition of a trunk, a
> mattress, hammock and a pair of blankets.

But Bostock had been in Africa much longer than Canot when he built his
home. Bostock's home was likely grander and better furnished.[11]

Too young to be initiated, not yet the person the years and teachings would
mold him into, Sessay had not learned to hide his hurt and pain behind a

shielding guise of enigma. "Stolen from his parents," his heartbreak was worn like armor, as if the raw breadth of his suffering would make it stop. Unmoved, his captors sold him onward. His young, slight neck was secured with a leather strap so that if he slowed he quickly choked. There were twenty in his human chain, and some of them were men, able to walk as fast as the sputtering whips insisted.[12]

He was walking from far inland, from the Mendelands to the north and east of Cape Mesurado. The Mende were powerful, advancing across whole swathes of country as they trounced the less numerous Kono, Kissi, and Gbande. They would boast for generations that Kono people had been sold to buy Mende women's headscarves. Yet for all the bravado the Mende were smarting, losing their own people in wars and slave raids just like all the rest. The antislavery patrol had only been liberating captives for a handful of years before there were so many Mende in Sierra Leone, where they were known as Cosso, that they had their own settlement. Within a few decades the majority of the captives aboard the *Amistad* would identify as Mende. In the 1810s there were many Mende boys, girls, women, and men filling the barracoons of the coast.

Taken from his parents so suddenly that he would always say he had been "stolen," unaware of what was really happening to him, Sessay was force-marched to join all the others in the barracoons. It was a journey of tens of thousands of footsteps, each spent trying to align with the man in front to ease the hurt, each one hoping that the boy behind did not fall back and throttle him. Food was sparse, water as rare as relief, moistening the mouth but never sating. Many stumbled, and the others would try to jostle him or her forward so that the guards would not notice. It was the only way to stop the indiscriminate slashes of the whip across their near-naked bodies.

The first time somebody fell and, judged utterly worthless by the guards, was left to die, it was a psychic shock. But then it became part of the rhythm of cruelty. The country was scattered with bleached bones. A British man stopped his trek for the night and wrote in his journal, "round this spot are lying more than one hundred skeletons." He and his party had already seen 107 human bodies that day, the desiccating bones of those who had not survived to reach the sea. He believed that the death rate for those in coffles was more than a third. On one of the major slave routes down to Gallinas, so many died at Cambawama that a mass grave soon existed where locals offered libations for the unknown who died passing through. Later generations would not cultivate the land there in deference to their loss.[13]

Each day of the journey to the coast was not more terrible purely because pains accrued: weals cutting across yesterday's welts, the chains and cuffs rasping on already abraded necks, ankles, and wrists, and the hunger and exhaustion rucking together to threaten collapse. Each new day was also further from home. Adults knew the tongues of those who lived around them and could converse with the people with whom they had traded foodstuffs at market, but beyond that it was bewildering. The further from home they trudged the less everything was recognized, and as the boundaries of their old lives faded on the horizon, so did chances of escape. Hopes of making it back so that this would all be a nightmare of the past wavered.

Sessay would afterward remember his death march as lasting forty days. By the time he told of this memory he had grown up aboard a British naval vessel where the Bible was read on Sundays and quoted when one of the seamen's bodies was pitched to the deep. He would likely have known by then that forty, in Christianity as in Judaism and Islam, could represent an unknowably long time. Forty days and nights, he probably understood, was the biblical duration of great trials and tribulations. It is this perhaps that he was expressing when he remembered his walk to the sea as lasting forty days: it had been unbearably long, a trial so far beyond endurance that it was only survived through other-worldly strength.[14]

A few days' sail up the coast, past Lake Piso, Bostock and Mason's Gallinas factory, Sherbro, the Banana Islands, and the British colony at Sierra Leone, the next big slave markets to the north were the Îles de Los and Rio Pongo. There a larger number of renegades still sold African captives, clustered in the Pongo's tributaries and on Crawford, Factory, and Tamara Islands in the Îles de Los.

It was from there that shocking news arrived at Cape Mesurado. The British antislavery patrol had arrested two slaving merchants, Charles Hickson and Samuel Samo. Hickson owned an operation at the Îles de Los. Samo was owner of the slaving factory Charleston in the Rio Pongo, "a slave factor of great note . . . a man eminent in wealth and influence." Both men had been taken to Freetown to stand trial for illegal slave trading.[15]

For Robert Bostock and all the other slave dealers watching, this was a dis-concerting change of tactic for the Royal Navy patrol. Before they had focused their attacks on slave ships, disregarding those ashore, so this foray onto land was an unwelcome surprise. It was all the more unfathomable because Samo was Dutch, not British. As in the case of the DeWolf ship *Baltimore*, the British Navy had taken upon themselves to ban anybody from slave trading regardless of their origin.

In Freetown, the fact that Samo could quite clearly make a very sound case that he was not British caused alarm. But Governor Maxwell and Chief Justice Robert Thorpe were not willing to let the case collapse on this matter, so Maxwell launched an audacious plan. He sent an agent to the Rio Pongo on the pretext that a British man there was in danger, and persuaded the chiefs to sign an agreement that Europeans who lived in their realm were under British law.

That done, Samo's trial began on April 7, 1812. The character testimonies alone revealed a gulf between British abolitionists and the slave traders, with his colleagues proclaiming his rectitude, as if that might save him. One described Samo as "a very quiet man, one of the best factors in the Rio Pongo" while another averred that "he knew nothing bad of him except his slave dealing; he never was one of the active bad hands in the Rio Pongo." It did not help: to the British he was a "bad hand" *because* he was slave trading; there were no longer any gradations of wrongdoing where this was concerned.[16]

Samo was proclaimed guilty. As scandalous to those watching on as the actual conviction was the fact that it was decided by a jury on which sat a majority of black men. The judge had to explain to them "both the law, and the principles on which it was founded," it was claimed, since "he was speaking to men whom, in all probability, were first taught by the act itself that slave trading was a crime." Bostock and McQueen, not far south at Cape Mesurado, can only have been dumbfounded.[17]

The only consolation was that a few days later Charles Hickson was acquitted of all charges against him and returned swiftly to slave trading. But it was not the end of the affair. Next, Freetown's court tried two men who worked for the British at Bunce Island, the former slave trading fortress by then refashioned as a military depot. Again these cases contained what seemed to many the absurd, not to mention contemptible, spectacle of Africans giving evidence against a British man. A freed captive even gave evidence, proclaiming that the defendant, Joseph Peters, was the man who had enslaved him. Peters was declared guilty and sentenced to seven years' transportation. His African assistant, William Tufft, received a sentence of three years' hard labor.[18]

Ultimately none of these sentences were enforced. Samo lingered in jail until July as authorities dallied over what to do. Christopher Fyfe has written that they were "unwilling to discharge unconditionally so notorious a slave-trader," so Maxwell again sent an agent to meet with the chiefs of the Rio Pongo, this time asking them to petition for Samo's release. The kings of the Susu and Manding nations wrote to Governor Maxwell, as did his the headman of the Îles de Los, letters of "pathos, sincerity, and submission," agreeing to abandon the slave trade "and do all in their power to bring it to a total termination, upon condition that Samo be discharged." It was a neat result for all:

British authorities could claim that Samo had been punished while averting a crisis over his sentence. Samo was pardoned on condition that he forever turn his back on the slave trade.

Peters too was offered a pardon if he agreed to leave Africa and never return. It was, perhaps predictably enough, only Tufft who did not get away scot-free. His sentence of three years' hard labor was commuted on condition of his enlisting in the army for life.[19]

The bells were tolling for the British slave traders counting their gold coins up and down the coast, but they were deafened by desire, by the lure of another cargo of merchandise on the horizon. When Charles Mason visited his old friend Bostock and their new concern in 1812, all seemed normal enough. Again it was Tom Ball who loaded the cargo aboard the slave ship of which Mason was supercargo. "Mason . . . came in a brig to Mesurado," Ball would remember, "and filled her Belly with Slaves whom he took away with him." The captives were added to those toiling in perpetuity on Cuban or American plantations.[20]

In June 1812, faraway events again colluded to change business for Mason and Bostock when their nations went to war. The origins of the War of 1812 are convoluted, but the transatlantic slave trade and its morality and legality were caught up in the whole affair. The United States was fighting for free trade and the rights of its sailors to be safe from being impressed by the British Navy. This affected the right of Britain's Navy to stop and search American vessels believed to be illegally trading in slaves. Before the war, President James Madison had "quietly" permitted the Royal Navy to search American vessels believed to be slave trading, as in the case of the *Baltimore*. After the war began this was impossible. It led to something the United States did not intend: the US flag began to be widely used to hide the illegal slave trade from Africa to Cuba.[21]

Bostock and McQueen may have felt themselves to be safely entrenched at Cape Mesurado, but they must have feared a downturn in trade. French privateers had been harassing shipping for several years, getting ever more daring as desperation set in. Now American ships would also be the enemy. Illicit slave vessels would have to dodge not just the antislavery patrol but enemy privateers of two powerful nations as well.[22]

And more cannon fire soon resounded down the coast. In March 1813, one of the Royal Navy's antislavery patrol ships, HMS *Thais*, captured the 160-ton *Rambler* as it cruised offshore from Mason and Bostock's factory at Cape

Mesurado. It was a formidable fighting vessel but lost its topmasts trying to escape and was captured and carried into Freetown as a prize. The *Rambler*'s captain and his crew were adamant that they were privateering and had no cargo, but its owners were James DeWolf and his brother Charles, and the *Rambler* had made at least three previous slaving voyages. It was condemned as an enemy privateer, but more than one observer suspected that it was still slaving. Those who were watching would always associate the loss of this vessel with the danger encroaching on Bostock's domain, though whether it was going there to buy captives is uncertain.[23]

Yet again peril inched toward them.

7

In the Barracoon

A father summoned his two small sons home from their chores and told them that they must to go the "Headman of their country" to run an errand. They walked away jostling each other, a skip in their step, not once glancing back. The boys' mother had died some years earlier, and they did not pause to speak to their friends because they could not imagine a need to say farewell, did not know of life without them.

They were Bassa boys of the Kwa-speaking peoples like the Kru who were spread down the Atlantic littoral. The Bassa and Kru had been among the first to trade with Europeans who had come to call centuries earlier, selling them melegueta pepper, or grains of paradise, and so had unwittingly named their part of the coast on European maps.[1]

The brothers waited at the headman's compound. Two weeks later, he gathered a small group of men and told them that they must go on a trading mission further up the coast. The brothers went with them on a three-day walk to the lands of their trading partners. Still they suspected nothing.

Then, one day, one boy awoke to find that his brother had vanished. Everybody he knew had gone. "I looked about me but saw none but strangers," he would remember later; "my country-people had all withdrawn." An overheard conversation revealed the truth. The headman had sold him, possibly after being pawned by his father. While sleeping, he had passed into the realms of merchandise.[2]

"I cried very much," he would later recall, "but alas! . . . there was no pity." Instead he was tricked, told that he would be in the "pen" for a single moon and would then be returning to his family. The month was long enough for him to begin to wonder if his father had betrayed him, had been complicit in what had happened. He thought back to the last time, searching his memory for clues in his father's face that he was saying farewell.

Slowly the boy realized that the promises of return were a deceit. They had merely been a ploy to calm him long enough to try to break his spirit. Far from releasing him, things got far worse. "Like a beast they began to treat me, though I was free-born." He could find "no pity, no mercy."

Soon they again made him start walking. This time he was marched for fourteen days. They reached the "sand beach" where a "white man" took him. He was turned into a crowded pen. He did not yet know it, but he was now the merchandise of John Sterling Mill.[3]

Sessay, the Mende boy whose journey to the coast lasted forty days, was in another barracoon just a few short miles away. What had happened to him in the intervening time since he had been "stolen from his parents" has been concertinaed into history. In the lowlights he would later tell, at the end of his journey he had yet another shock to endure. Terrifying white men purchased him along with six others. They were "turned into the Slave Yard where there were many Slaves in Irons."[4]

Sessay did not know the names of these two white men any more than the tricked Bassa boy knew his owner. Sessay did not know that they were Robert Bostock and John McQueen and he was on the banks of the St. Paul River at Cape Mesurado.

Still at last, Sessay and the Bassa boy whose name we do not know must have listened intently for familiar voices or words they recognized. Human nature dictated seeking connections, shared languages, somebody who knew of their people. For those who arrived alone in the barracoon this was key. An ally might help interpret this utterly bewildering situation. Somebody who knew his or her people could be a ray shining out from the sordid, despicably dehumanizing, shit-filled, stinking factory. A shared worldview might provide a fingertip hold on identity and sanity, asserting who they were and uncovering common words, gestures, and expressions through which they could transmit information without calling attention to themselves. Friendship spoke of humanity; it disdained the lie of being a commodity.

So many ethnicities and languages were represented among those held with them, sharing their pain, that finding such ties was no easy task. As well as those who arrived overland from upcountry, boats brought captives along the big water, vastly increasing the reach of the slavers' grasp. Their homelands were in a huge swathe of the hinterland. Some were from so far away that the words of others were jarring, vexing to the ear. The whispered questions, the cries of agony, starvation, and sheer despair, the rages and threats to destroy those who had brought them to this, came in so many languages, dialects, and accents. A plethora of deities, spirits, and ancestors were beseeched for wisdom, strength, and help.

Within this jumble must have festered preconceptions, old feuds, misunderstandings, and hatreds born of wars and past wrongs. There was a young boy named Paye, for example, the name Mano women gave to their third-born son, and we are left to wonder if others looked at this eight-year-old and remembered the pervasive rumor that the Mano were cannibals, eating dead slaves. Paye had been badly burned on the head somewhere in his short life, perhaps adding horrible authenticity to the fears of the other children.[5]

But they undoubtedly had bigger problems now. The old feuds would not have died away, but they bent to new realities. Their captors were shape-shifting enemies who were widely believed to be cannibals on a scale far beyond the Mano. Such beliefs were a mixture of "fantasy and fact, fused at the ankles and wrists in the surrealism of the transatlantic slave trade." Europeans were also known to be strangely adept sorcerers who could turn human bodies into an astonishing array of commodities. They could make people float over the big water. This was mysterious since ancestral spirits propelled canoes, but who could say what type of spirit moved the white men's huge vessels?[6]

Long-running arguments over land and resources perhaps diminished with such immediate dangers to meet. Different peoples had specific reports, wisdom given them by the elders and learned through their own particular experiences in the centuries of slave trading. The Kono believed that white people lived under the ocean, emerging in the daytime to live on islands. Among the Mende, Sessay's people, stories were told of Tingowei, "a beautiful siren-like woman with a soft, white skin" who appeared in the form of a long, golden chain, and of Njaoli who lived in deep waters and "own[ed] townsfull of treasure." Njaoli was beautiful but also deadly, sometimes kidnapping those who were foolish enough to venture onto the big water. Then there was Ndogbɔjusui, "a white man with a long white beard." He appeared to "lonely travellers, whom he tricked into following him. Those who encountered Ndogbɔjusui were warned to never reveal to him what was truly on their mind."[7]

To the Loma and Mano people chained in the barracoon, bad spirits and other forms of evil lived in the water where they had entire submarine societies. People with "reddish hair" were reincarnations of these evil spirits. To the

Loma, white men like Robert Bostock and John McQueen must have looked like wickedness incarnate.[8]

Those who languished in the barracoon for some time came to know slave trading's recurring features. From the interior came coffles of the newly damned, prisoners who were possible messengers. They might carry news of loved ones, homes and villages, everything that had defined the limits of the world before prison walls and shackles. In return for fragments from that other life might be offered as succor just hard-won knowledge: the cruelest guards, the best ways to get food, the fragments of an endurance that was beyond the human spirit but was all that could be clutched.

Some were certainly freedom fighters, solid in defiance, but for most their sentiments were surely more complex. Psychological damage was and is so inherently personal, and though shaped by the streams of culture, those shapes defy easy analysis. Physical pain mingled with fear and the jagged edges of despair. Indignation cut through shame, because to be a slave was considered profoundly shameful, and then circled back once more so that sometimes anger oozed with each realization of their captivity.[9]

Women were the minority, and they were younger. The oldest held at Bostock and Mason's Cape Mesurado barracoon in mid-1813 were Safui and Safua, both around twenty-eight years old. Safui, a Kono woman, had her baby Bessy with her in the barracoon. The sexual violence at the factory, in addition to all the other forms of degradation they were forced to endure, remains hidden. The complexion of their specific agonies they bore silently, not least because the world of those watching and writing down was a male world, and such issues were rarely addressed. But Bessy, at three months old, had come into the world in the squalid barracoon or just prior. We cannot know if she was born from love or brutality or something between.

For everyone the loss of family and friends was incalculable, but for the children like Sessay, Za, Eya, and so many others who outnumbered adults in Bostock's barracoon in June 1813 by three to two, their pain was all the more amplified by their dependence on those they had lost. Hunger and dehydration could damage a child more swiftly than an adult, and the ever-threatening diarrhea and dysentery easily proved fatal. For those who survived, the psychological effects never ended. Those too young to know where they had come from or to remember the songs and dances of their village did not even have the vestiges of their former lives to cling to, the things that acted as the major comfort to many adults stolen away across the Atlantic. Child slaves today often endure *dysphoria*: "a state of confusion, agitation, emptiness, and utter aloneness," not to mention isolation, distrust, self-blame, and self-harming. Mindsets and ideologies change over time; we do not have enough evidence to know if it was all of this, or all of this and more. Those between the ages of eight and twelve—old enough to know what was happening but not yet possessing the tools of endurance—were perhaps the "hardest hit" of all those who made the transatlantic crossing. There were more than ninety children of that age in Bostock and Mason's barracoon on the banks of the St. Paul River in mid-1813.[10]

For many of their captives, adult as well as child, the physical wounds of the long walk from their place of capture would not have yet healed as they languished in the slave pens. Ankles, pared of skin, chafed around new tethers. It is possible that some had been drugged on the way to facilitate their dehumanization, to numb them for the transition to faceless commodity, so that they just felt perplexingly listless. For countless captives sickness allowed only shards of sentience amid delirium. Very few escaped the hunger. That meant passing through the stage of dry mouth and intensified urination, and then enduring extreme craving for food as edema painfully swelled stomachs and joints. The starved then entered a domain of susceptibility to all manner of diseases and complaints until the body simply could not function and the brain shut down. While it was in the interests of Bostock and McQueen to keep their captives alive and healthy enough for sale, it was sometimes a close-run thing. The weight loss of captive Africans sold at this part was very nearly a death sentence.[11]

Dying was not just the usual tragedy of passing. Dying away from home was a calamity in itself, needing a special ceremony to bring home the deceased person's spirit to its rightful place alongside the other ancestors. So this, dying tied up in a white man's hellhole, what kind of death was this? How would family and friends know? To their people they would be among the vanished, those who had simply disappeared, fate unknown. This meant that they would never, as the Kissi believed, become the wind, speaking words of wisdom and support to the ones still living.[12]

Since most, or many, lacked family members, they began the process of making new families, rebuilding the blocks that made life livable. For those who were Mende, Kissi, Kono, and Gbande, there were enough of them in Mason and Bostock's barracoon to gang together and speak in their own tongues.

It was a tragedy, of course, that they were so many. For the Gbande, Kissi, and Kono, who had long been traded down through Vai country with salt, the new realities after 1807–8 had again seen them lose out. There were more of them in the barracoon because they had been newly decimated, newly destroyed. Yet the tragedy of their numbers held captive was also their strength. They could share information about the others with whom they were imprisoned, remembering stories that might help them to explain their fate and sow seeds of hope. Burdens could at least be shared so that when one despaired utterly the others could soothe their pain, knowing that the next day it might be they who needed succor.[13]

For those who were Gbande there was considerable likelihood of finding others whom they knew well, or being chained alongside somebody whom they had always known. The commonest name in Mason and Bostock's pen in mid-1813 was Bala, and although this was a name known among Manding, among Gbande people it was especially prevalent in a few small villages, particularly around Balahun, which can loosely be translated as "Bala place." Besides the Balas, there are other captives too such as Sangaree, Famai, and Paway, whose names suggest that they could well have been from the same small area. We can only surmise that this is who they were, but it is likely as the Manding people had no concentration of men and boys named Bala that might account for this group.[14]

The Gbande who could unite in this way were at an advantage over those who were Manding, whose position among the others was precarious. Their trading prowess, coupled with their participation in the jihad and conviction that non-Islamic people could legitimately be enslaved, had led to their partial alienation. Their refusal to acknowledge the Poro deities also left them outside the main connection between the other disparate groups. Their isolation, conversely, could be a uniting factor for others. The Kissi and the Gbande, who had often come into conflict over land, could agree about the wickedness of the Manding in capturing so many of their people. So too could the Loma who were held alongside them.[15]

So many Kissi and Kono people were held in the barracoon that each part of the family line was represented, mirroring the broken families in the interior severed of so many of their branches. Several of the boys were called Sahr or Saa, the name both Kono and Kissi women gave to their firstborn son. There were two more Tambas, or second sons, in addition to the factory slave with that name. There was one boy named Eya (Aiah), or third son, as well as another called Eya Gombo, a third son who had a second name dependent on his parents' marriage and whether a dowry had been paid for his mother. There was a child named Fallah, the name Kissi mothers gave to their fourth-born son. Twenty-seven-year-old Mairing was the next to the last son born in his Kono family. Two men, both twenty-six years old and the same height, having stood shoulder to shoulder through it all, were named Fangha, the Kono for male-male twins.[16]

There were other Kono in the barracoon too, people who almost certainly had a name that told of their place in the family but who were not commonly known by it. Since fathers usually had several sons named Saa, Tamba, Aiah, and so on—as many sons with those names as they had wives blessed with male children—children were given other names too to avoid confusion. These spoke of character traits, recalled things that happened around the time of their birth, or honored an ancestor. So the twelve-year-old boy whose name was later recorded as "Fingacuree" by the British—probably Fainbaquee—was a shy, timid child, given the name for "one who is fearful." His parents' dismay at losing their apprehensive child who needed reassurance and protection, and his own sheer terror in finding himself away from his family and in captivity, can only be imagined.[17]

Kissi people too had other names than their birth order names. A nine-year-old boy later gave his name as Cosang, probably a misspelling of the Kissi name meaning "go and spread news," and a sixteen-year-old girl was named Kayang, likely meaning "loser in a fight." Yembo, aged fourteen, had the name for a single woman, which may have reflected her mother's status rather than her own, and it might even have been this that had made her vulnerable to en-slavement. Bondoa or Bendoa, a ten-year-old boy, had a name "given to a handsome child, meaning something like 'polygamous'": a boy so attractive it was thought he would have many wives. Bondoa already bore the marks of the Poro society so this name was likely his Poro rather than a birth name. A twenty-nine-year-old man who pronounced his name "Baloo" bore an appella-tion that could perhaps (if this was an accurate recording) have been the Kissi term for "waterfall."[18]

Another of the bigger groups in the barracoon was made up of Sessay's people, the Mende. Many would later give names that told of Mende origins, despite the mangling into English: Boye and Boy (really Boi), Quay, Gom-boyarra, and Messay, among others. Nine-year-old Bessay or Pessay had a name that revealed she was born to Mende parents after her mother had previ-ously borne twins. A boy was called Torgboh, the Mende term for "tree tapper," which suggested that his father was one of the people who tapped sap for palm wine. Gaywo, a nine-year-old, had a name reflecting the Mende word *Nwegɔ* (god).[19]

For the adults, beyond ties found through their ethnic group and language, their membership in the Poro and Sande societies provided commonality that reached out to others with whom they shared their terrible circumstances. In the barracoon these loyalties were needed more than ever, providing inner strength when despair threatened and sparks of understanding with strangers whose languages were impenetrable. Those high up within their home societies were focal points in the barracoons, regularly sought out for advice and strength, to provide wisdom and understanding, and relied upon to remain defiant and dignified in the face of such intense provocation.[20]

The societies were common beams to walk on, for surely unity was needed in this world where men no longer looked like men and the rules of behavior had skewed so badly. The men and women of other peoples, neighbors, even enemies, could suddenly seem similar enough in the face of such unimaginable travesties. Brotherhood had been forged from far less. They provided understanding that might be clung to among so many displays of behavior that scarcely seemed within the realms of possibility. They were ties that cut across languages, dialects, and religious differences to forge bonds. They were laws and social norms that could be remembered as standards of stability amid the bedlam.

Societies had left visual as well as aural traits on their members, so that even when captives were tethered to poles, very scantily clothed, the cicatrices cut into the body at initiation were clearly visible to those who could read them. They were identifiers recognizable to most of the captives even if their captors were blind to the meanings.

So the younger, as yet uninitiated boys held alongside fourteen-year-old Balo doubtless respected the "round scar [on his] right breast" that told of a specialized skill he learned while undergoing his Poro education. He was young enough that it was recent, a marker of the life he had been expecting to lead, a visual travesty on one who was now made into merchandise. Whyero, two years older, had similar marks, advertising skills his white captors knew nothing about. More unusually, a twenty-two-year-old woman named Sungbo was "tattooed down [her] cheeks" and with a cruciform cicatrix on her forehead.[21]

So essential, so central to their understanding of the way things were and should have been, that many carried rituals over the seas. Across the Americas, captives continued the Poro and the Sande as best they could. Sea Island slaves in South Carolina and Georgia knew the rituals well. Some decades later the *Amistad* rebels would show their gymnastic and wrestling skills, learned in Poro School, on the town green in New Haven, Connecticut. Another young girl, kidnapped and taken to Cuba on the eve of her initiation into her local society, would keep alive the songs and dances she had learned to perform for her ceremony. Centuries later they carried her descendants home.[22]

8

The Slave Ship *Fénix* and Setting the Factory Alight

As May limped on in a humid daze, Bostock and McQueen were anxious for a slaving vessel to arrive. They needed to sell as many captives as possible before the heavy rains fell, when food was scarcer and diseases proliferated, creating a mass of sweating, shaking bodies. Profits were always much lower in the rainy season when fevers stole away their merchandise and fewer vessels called.

So it was an immense relief when the brig *Fénix* appeared just beyond the mouth of the St. Paul River on the twentieth, sliding over the shallows into the river. The *Fénix* had made a slaving voyage the year before, taking 204 captives to Cuba, so those aboard were familiar with the St. Paul's headmen and pilots.[1]

This time it had varied its path. Leaving Havana it had paused at Matanzas to wait out a storm and had then sailed for South Carolina. At Champney's Wharf in Charleston its supercargo had sold 101 hogsheads of molasses and then shipped gunpowder, rum, and other items best calculated for the trade in "muzzled Negroes." This detour risked a $20,000 fine plus forfeit of the vessel if they were caught, but there were plenty willing to collude. Charleston's roots were in the slave trade, and there were many who thought the abolitionist turn was a northern folly. The *Fénix*'s Captain José Cábez simply claimed that they were sailing for Teneriffe in the Canary Islands, and no further questions were asked.[2]

After that, however, their luck had turned. Cruising down the African coast to Cape Mesurado, they had been attacked by a French vessel. Captain Cábez later told how they had been plundered, and it had been all they could do to keep the vessel and enough merchandise to trade for slaves.

By the time they got to Bostock and Mason's factory they were as glad to see the friendly faces there as the two Britons were to see eager buyers. They had to be hasty nevertheless. After the obligatory gentlemanly greetings, some drinks proffered and letters and bills passed on, they got down to business. A local headman was willing to do business. Bostock and McQueen offered a small boy captive as a trading token. He was not yet grown but looked healthy and might fetch a good price.[3]

To those in the pens, the big vessel can only have goaded a new level of menace ahead with its cutwater. Its first sounds surely brought panic among the children, but the cooler men, the elders, the adult women are hard to imagine at this moment. We cannot know the many emotions and responses that each lurched through, still less appreciate how they created pools of panic, calm, shock, sorrow, and distress amid the mass of people. Some of them had been trapped at the factory for four moons: had they begun to see clefts of hope amid the mud walls, inklings that it might not be true, that the stories of being driven out onto the big water might be myths? Was there defiance, a resolution that they would show no fear in order to not give their captors, their tormentors, leverage over them? Or did the *Fénix*'s arrival see a wail of visceral horror rise up on the banks of the St. Paul? It was so terrible a thing to contemplate that the children surely gripped each other in terror, as if the touch of a familiar arm might be all that held them to life. Mute from hunger, shock, fevers, terror, and heartache, did any have the strength to cry?

The compound was open enough within its walls that they could see out from the pens across the terror unfolding. Small boats came up onto the beach next to the compound. Pale men with string for hair knotted down their backs walked through the factory passing the barracoons. Their skin was marked with red blotches and pitted all over. They walked in a rolling manner as if their legs were bowed instead of straight.

The factory slaves came among them. They chose just one boy, Za. He was dragged away, doubtless leaving those so recently chained next to him mute with shock at his loss and the slenderness of their own escape. They could watch until he was out of sight and then try to hear, to make sense of where they might be taking him so that they would know what their own fate might be. It was difficult to know if knowledge would help them or whether it was better to go forward numbly as the best way to bear it.

They likely knew enough to expect that more would follow, disappearing over the sand bar, out onto the most fearsome surf where the Njaoli might get them. These would probably be their last hours on the land, perhaps as living people. As the sun sunk over the big water they must have feared that it was all over. Perhaps a few of the women tried to raise a solemn lament, singing out their songs of sorrow.

Niceties over, Bostock agreed to 150 bars of trade goods per captive. John McQueen supervised the factory slaves as they aided the ship's crew and super-cargo, Manuel Ruiz, unloading the *Fénix* of its payment. "Nineteen hogs-heads rum and four bales handkerchiefs," tobacco, "checks," "blue Bafts," and "beeds" came ashore. The following morning, the captives would be loaded.[4]

But another vessel appeared slithering gingerly over the shallows and into the river. It was the brig *Kitty*. At its helm was John Roach, an old Liverpool slave trader who Bostock and McQueen knew well. Roach had first captained the slaver *Cecilia* in 1799, buying captives in the Congo River and delivering them to Kingston, Jamaica. He had worked for John Bolton, a major Liverpool slave dealer, and had captained his vessels *Christopher* and *John* carrying captives from Africa to Guiana, where Bolton was involved in cotton production. On another voyage aboard the *John* he had sold his human cargo at the slave mar-kets of Havana, the destination for the vast majority of those sold by Bostock and McQueen.[5]

Almost exactly five years earlier, however, in late May 1808, Roach had dropped anchor back in Liverpool aboard the slaver *May* and had professed himself a changed man, about to embark on a new career. Slave trading was in the past. Abolition a reality, he gained a letter of marque and become a privateer.

By 1813 he claimed to be a patriot capturing enemy ships. This allowed him to also infer his abolitionist credentials—a slave trader shown the error of his ways—by capturing slave ships. Yet his first venture into this had been curious at best. The *Amelia* had traded at Cabinda and sailed with 275 slaves aboard before an African American crewman had encouraged the captives to revolt. The mutineers kept some of the crew alive to help and likely tried to sail back from where they had come. Instead they sailed around the coast of Africa for four months until, dying from hunger and thirst, they landed at Cape Mount to beg for water. But those who ventured ashore to ask for help were ambushed and again held captive. Roach, somewhere nearby, heard that a pirate vessel was offshore. He retook the *Amelia* from the vastly weakened rebels and carried it, along with the remaining 88 men, women, and children, into Sierra Leone. It was not so much an act of abolitionism, as Roach claimed, but the recapturing of men and women who had already freed themselves.[6]

That had been Roach and the *Kitty*'s only venture into capturing slave ships until a few weeks before when they had assisted HMS *Thais* to capture the *San José Triunfo* as it was loading its human cargo at Elmina. What else Roach was doing other than privateering remains unclear, but he had a lucrative trade. There may have been nothing particularly illegal about this as Africa had far more to offer than captives, and he was both delivering goods to Freetown and exporting produce from there. But Roach and the *Kitty* were also trading frequently with all the slave traders up and down the coast. Roach clearly knew Bostock was slave trading even if the *Kitty* was not directly involved in buying and selling slaves.[7]

A few weeks earlier Roach had come to call on his old friends Bostock and McQueen and they had shaken hands on a deal. Roach had delivered some goods, and now he returned for payment. But there was a misunderstanding, and Bostock got into an argument about the amount of the debt. To Bostock it was nothing out of the ordinary, simply a businessman's quarrel that would soon be sorted out with a handshake. But Bostock badly misjudged the extent of Roach's loyalty to slave traders; misread the lengths that he would go to in protecting the illegal trade. As Roach had shown in the capture of the *San José Triunfo*, he was eager to capture slave ships if there was nothing to be gained financially by dealing illicitly with the merchants.

Furious at Bostock and McQueen, Roach made a wild threat. He bellowed across the compound that he would attack the *Fénix* and carry it to Sierra Leone. He argued defiantly that he could prove that it was an American vessel and therefore a legitimate prize of the War of 1812. It was flying Spanish colors, but in 1813, and aboard a slaving vessel, that hardly ruled out American ownership. American ships routinely faked Spanish-Cuban ownership to disguise their illegal activities, and the *Fénix* had, after all, sailed from Charleston.

Bostock could not believe it. Perhaps, like his father's long ago trust of James Cleveland, he put too much reliance on friendship. He did not believe that Roach would really attack the *Fénix*, apparently thinking it all an act of bluster to sting him for more money. But Roach was irate, and he ordered his men to ready their weapons. The *Kitty*'s crewmen sponged into the cannons' breeches, added the powder, wadded them in, and then rammed in the balls.

Aboard the *Fénix*, Captain José Cábez was flabbergasted. Assured by Bostock that Roach was an old ally, he could not have foreseen the ambush.

His men, already plundered by the French, were in a defiant mood. Cábez gave "orders to put the *Fénix* in a position to fight." His men too began to ready their weapons.[8]

The *Kitty* was slightly smaller than the *Fénix*, 116 tons to the slave vessel's 124, but more heavily armed. The *Fénix*, hoping simply to outrun the naval patrols, mounted only four guns. Both men thought their chances were fair. Then, judging himself within firing range, Roach ordered his men to take aim. As he yelled "Fire!" the clap of cannonballs roared across the water.

From ashore Bostock and McQueen heard the boom ring out. It was unbelievable. An ally was betraying them. Utterly incensed, Bostock watched from his ringside seat. Then one of the *Kitty*'s cannons hit its target.[9]

Za was held in a wooden dungeon, alone for what was very likely the first time in his life. It must have been almost too much to bear: the utter darkness, the rough walls, the endless rocking that turned his empty stomach. He can only have wondered at how nine short years of life had led to this, never conceiving that anything worse could happen since he had been taken from his parents, and yet more terrible things piled on top, and more kept being added, pushing him down.

When a huge boom rang out and the brig pitched wildly, he surely feared that death had found him.

A small party of the *Kitty*'s victorious men rowed over to the *Fénix* to formally take their prize. Aboard, they found that one of the rewards was a nine-year-old captive boy imprisoned in the hold. They took him back to the *Kitty*. Then they began ferrying the *Fénix*'s beaten sailors to shore, intent on leaving them prisoners in Bostock's compound.

Robert Bostock had other ideas and had already armed some of his factory slaves. As the sailors stepped ashore, Bostock and McQueen seized Roach while their factory slaves held the *Kitty*'s seamen. John McQueen threatened Roach "that they would be the death of him" if he did not let the *Fénix* go. The *Fénix*'s seamen took one of the *Kitty*'s boats and returned to their vessel. Later that night, taking advantage of scant security in Bostock and Mason's compound for Europeans, John Roach managed to bribe some of the Krumen to return him and his men to the *Kitty*.[10]

Back aboard his ship, Roach sat down and wrote a letter to John Sterling Mill, the slave dealer in the Mesurado River. Annotating his letter "Brig Kitty, Sunday morning 5 o'clock," he addressed it "My Dear Mills." Roach told Mill that he was determined to prove that "I am not so great a villain as he is," but that he was incensed by Bostock's "obstinacy." He was willing to negotiate with Bostock over the capture of the *Fénix* and asked John Sterling Mill to mediate. If Bostock offered enough money then he would "pledge my word of honor that I will not hurt the hair of any man's head for what has taken place." He would wait twenty-four hours for Bostock's offer, but after that he threatened to take John McQueen to Freetown and have him arrested for debt. John Roach's motives—pecuniary rather than principled, grimy rather than grand—were laid out in elaborate curlicue.[11]

As an afterthought, Roach asked Mill to pass on a message to Philippa Hayes next door. Roach asked Hayes to let him have some ivory and other items she had promised him. Then he mentioned that he had lost his glasses case and asked Hayes to search for it in her closet, a place he had clearly been spending more time than might be thought appropriate for somebody claiming that his privateering activities in West Africa were virtuous. Roach also asked Hayes to "send the children off in a boat." What he meant by this—what children Hayes had that were going aboard the *Kitty*—is very unclear and is, obviously, suspicious, although they could possibly have been Kru children or even free passengers.

Upon receiving the letter, Mill simply sent it over to Bostock's place with the short message attached:

Dear Sir
        This Letter you read I rec'd this morning and I have sent it for your perusal according to Captn. Roach's wish, hope you are well
        And remain

                                                        Your Humble Servant
                                                        J. S. Mill.

Bostock was far too livid to negotiate with a man who he believed had blatantly hoodwinked him. He remained indignant. The twenty-four-hour deadline passed.[12]

Roach ordered the *Kitty*'s seamen to set sail. As Bostock watched them sail away, he must have hoped it would be the end of the affair. It was not. Aboard the *Kitty*, Roach's crew turned mutinous; it is unclear whether over the attack on the *Fénix*, the children that Philippa Hayes was sending them, or even perhaps just a drunken brawl. Roach, already fuming, was beyond a calm response. On June 8, not long after he had ordered the brig steered back around Cape Mesurado, he saw a British naval ship nearby and hailed it to ask for help with his insubordinate crew.[13]

It was HMS *Thais*, leader of the antislavery squadron and vanquisher of the DeWolf vessel *Rambler*. Just three days earlier the substantial prize money from that capture had been paid to the *Thais*'s men, and they were jubilant. At the helm was Captain Edward Scobell, a man whose family appeared in *Burke's Peerage* and for whom the antislavery station was a test of faith. "In great waters," it would be effused on his tombstone, "he saw the wonders of the Lord." Zachary Macaulay, one of the most prominent abolitionists, was his prize agent in London. His mission was both "the annoyance of the enemy" and catching illegal slavers; he was at Cape Mesurado searching for a vessel named *Governor Wentworth*, rumored to be illegally slaving. Scobell already knew John Roach as the two had worked together to capture the slaver *San José Triunfo* just the previous month.[14]

Scobell sent a party to investigate what was happening aboard the *Kitty*. Four mutinous sailors were clamped into irons and launched over the side into the *Thais*'s boat. But the *Thais* gained more than the rebel seamen. By the end of this encounter Edward Scobell knew that an "extensive traffick in slaves" was being carried on nearby "by one or two Englishmen, and some Mulatto traders."[15]

Scobell was alarmed enough to sail straight to Freetown and lodge the *Kitty*'s rebellious sailors in jail. Then he begged a meeting with Governor Charles Maxwell to report what he had heard. Normally the Royal Navy's small antislave trade squadron did not attack slave factories ashore. The arrests of Samuel Samo and Charles Hickson had been anomalies, though not unsuccessful ones with Samo's conviction. But for them to ignore this information would be an admission of feebleness, even cowardice. Maxwell fired off letters to the Colonial Office and the Admiralty reporting the disturbing news.[16]

Soon the *Kitty* also arrived in Freetown to "complain officially and claim redress." Bostock and McQueen had stolen his goods, Roach alleged formally, and McQueen had made threats on his life. A couple of Krumen from Bostock's were with him to corroborate his story. Za was there too and was officially declared to be free, his name recorded as "Za alias Jack Phoenix." The Kitty's sailors had renamed the child. He had become a Jack Tar, originally found aboard the slaver *Fénix*.[17]

Governor Maxwell and Captain Scobell came to a decision. They could not ignore this, could not be seen to ignore a flagrant contravention of the law by two British men so close to their territory. Scobell would go to investigate and would arrest the two men if he found anything suspicious. Scobell's crew were in a poor state, with many afflicted by fevers, catarrh, rheumatism, "flux," gonorrhea, tuberculosis, and boils. The ship was "very leaky," the running rigging "in a bad state, spliced and tail'd and not haveing any Reeve anew [*sic*]." But they readied the *Thais* once again.[18]

Within days they weighed anchor, running again out of Freetown's spectacular harbor and hauling south to find out what was going on at Cape Mesurado. Sailing with them was the colonial schooner *Princess Charlotte*, a relatively small vessel that was struggling to fight the "much superior" slave vessels that came to call at the coast. By some reports there was also the sloop *Juan*, another Cuban slave ship that the *Thais* had captured a week earlier north of Sherbro Island.[19]

The next day, June 25, they were rounding Cape Mount, some of the men busy scrubbing clothes. They did not go unnoticed in the vigilant environment of one of the major slaving regions of Africa. The Caulker family heard the news. They immediately sent men in canoes to charge ahead and warn Bostock, still allied to them through his senior wife, who belonged to their family.[20]

The lapping of paddles cutting through the water alerted them first, then shouts. In the tranquil early morning light, before the heat set the country ablaze with reds and golds, canoes appeared. As they pulled up onto the beach, Bostock heard their shouted news, the alarmed tone that brooked no debate. The naval patrol was on its way.

Bostock and McQueen agreed that they would try to hide their captives. They might brazen it out if all the captives were hidden, like slave ship captains who were caught but could not be prosecuted because of insufficient evidence. It was how William Richmond had secured the release of the *Dos Amigos* and how countless other illicit slaver captains talked their way out of trouble.

They began barking orders. The factory slaves were instructed to get as many captives as possible into canoes and take them to John Sterling Mill, still an ally whatever the business with John Roach. They worked quickly, losing the chains and tethers that held so many, selecting the first group to go off, then whipping them into canoes. Yarra and Tom Ball rowed off in convoy, rapidly steering around the weft of the island, nipping through the small creek that separated the Mesurado and St. Paul's Rivers. Jostling the captives over the side, they beseeched Mill's help. The captives were put into his barracoons, hidden in plain sight. Tom and Yarra returned and repeated the exercise. For the rest of the day they went back and forth. By evening, news reached Bostock and Mason's compound that the enemy was offshore.

The naval vessel anchored for the night out beyond the sea bar while Scobell ordered the "jolly boat and the cutter jawl [*sic*]" prepared. That night brought "light airs with rain." The next morning they began before daybreak. The mate wrote in his log, "5:30 armed the cutter yawl and a jolly boat to be readied for action."[21]

At the factory Bostock and McQueen also rose long before dawn, planning and plotting to do just enough to escape arrest. Using twilight as cover they urgently hid more of their captives, making it look as if they were trading in some other commodity. It would be a preposterous claim, but the onus was on the naval men to prove their case, and that could only be done if Bostock and McQueen were actually found with captives.

Again Yarra and Ball worked the canoes, removing more captives to Mill's and perhaps Hayes's places. It was a precarious task. Speed was of the essence, but taking too many risked revolt and mass escape. Bostock's wives threw their most treasured possessions into a trunk. It was still half an hour until sunrise when four small boats appeared at the mouth of the St. Paul, crossing the "dark sand intermix'd with shell" where the shallows of only fifty-one feet had previously protected them. Not far into the river Lieutenant Watkins, in charge of the boats, "gained intelligence that many Slaves were then ready for embarkation."[22]

It was frantic; the captives were not yet all gone. Yarra and Tom worked the canoes, loading another group of captives aboard just as the *Thais*'s boats approached. At the last minute, Bostock gave the trunk with his possessions to Yarra, bidding him to take it. The two factory slaves desperately pushed off from the shore and paddled away. One of the boats gave chase. Tom and Yarra reached the shore, and many of the captives darted off, fearing for their lives as gunshots ricocheted around. Those who dallied, stunned by shock, hunger, and months tied at the ankles and wrists, felt the whip's snap across their naked limbs as they were impelled to find the momentum to run.

All was chaos, and a new type of terror. Knocked out of their fastened shackles, the captives wore only the tethers that allowed them to go who knew where. They were driven to the waterfront and crowded into canoes. Terror surely reigned, but there was mystery too because they headed away from the big water, in the direction some of them had been carried from their homes, up-river to where a branch of the St. Paul hugged the island. Through the creek they were paddled, furiously, the few miles until it emerged into the Mesurado River, where they were disembarked and once again chained. New men and new dangers were all around.

More were pushed from the pen that had been their jail and loaded into a canoe on the small sandy beach. At some point it must have become clear that a boat of white men was chasing them. Amid the white men's shouts of fury they careened up onto the bank. Rolling over the sides, they splashed into the water and made for shore. Suddenly some found themselves alone in the bush, unguarded. Astonished and terrified as shots rang out, courage coupled with desperate fear propelled them forward, their feet cutting into the soft mud. They ran and ran and ran until, exhausted, they could run no more.[23]

The *Thais*'s men watched the last canoe get away, its people fleeing, before turning back and approaching the factory. There were about forty men in their party, advancing with "English colours" held high.

Desperate now, Bostock called on Tamba and told him to unshackle the rest of those in the barracoon and march them to Chief Bagna's compound. Tamba got seventy-nine or eighty captives together. It was a desperate move risking mutiny and even being murdered in vengeance, but it was all they had left. Time was running out.

Robert Bostock and John McQueen were determined to fight. They had large supplies of arms, and if necessary they could go into their storeroom where five hundred carronades and their carriages, five hundred muskets and fifty pairs of pistols were stockpiled. Perched behind the wall of one of their stronger buildings, they opened fire on the marines as they stepped onto shore. Protected by the building and with the element of surprise, Bostock and McQueen saw one naval man go down, then another. Realizing that they were under "heavy fire" the marines fought back. Volleys shot across the compound.

Offshore, Scobell and the rest of his crew were surprised and alarmed as they heard "several Guns and Musquets fired." They had apparently perceived no danger. Samuel Samo and Charles Hickson had been arrested with little trouble, certainly not open resistance. The *Thais* "Shift'd the Schooner and Sloop Close in Shore" in case they were needed. But Scobell need not have worried; the Royal Navy's men were far from beaten. They were quickly over the threshold of the factory.

Bostock and McQueen made a last desperate move. Though they would deny it always, and the naval men admitted that they did not know definitively what happened, several of those there that day reported that Bostock and/or McQueen ordered the barracoon put to flame. They only had to touch the thatch before flames shot up its sides. With smoke billowing they fled, choking, running in a manner they would previously have considered far from dignified. Only a few moments later they heard a mighty explosion as the fire ignited their vast store of rum. The barrels of gunpowder in the storeroom also exploded, creating fireworks visible for miles around. It was a blasting spectacle in the morning air.[24]

Sessay was one of the last, still there after the canoes had carried many away and others had been linked into a coffle and marched out. He had seen "four small boats with white men in them" approach. Others were still there too. The navy's men would find the last few in the razed buildings, some "running from it." For some reason—a rather strange implication that was later crossed through in the records—"it [was] supposed" that those who did not flee "were drinking in the Cellar."[25]

9

Leaving,
Never to Return

Robert Bostock and John McQueen woke the following morning to a burned-out world. They were hiding at Chief Bagna's compound, uncertain what on earth to do next. Word reached them that the *Thais*'s crew was intent upon rounding up all the African captives they could find.

That first morning the gig shuttled backward and forward from the *Thais* to the *Princess Charlotte* and back to the shore, everybody surveying the scene of devastation. The next day, Monday, June 28, the first thirty-two Africans believed to be Bostock and McQueen's captives were rowed out and embarked onto the *Princess Charlotte*. The following day another sixteen were carried aboard the *Thais*. The day after that twenty-six more were embarked. At some point in these days Tom Ball, Bostock's slave since childhood, was taken aboard the *Thais*. Then Tamba and Yarra joined them.

The following day, the naval men visited Bagna's compound, and the chief handed over some of the captives who had shuffled over in Tamba's hastily constructed coffle. Sixty-seven men, women, and children were rowed out to HMS *Thais*. Chief Bagna seems to have been intent on a palaver, arguing that Bostock and McQueen must give themselves up. They evidently hoped that Bagna could protect them, perhaps making offers of the deal he might have if he continued to hide them. It seems likely that at least John McQueen, who would later try to bribe others, offered money, and Robert Bostock had a whole trunk of his most valuable possessions with him he could proffer. But Bagna decided that he could not afford to enrage the British Navy, as his own business depended on them not looking too closely at the ships with which he was trading.

Hearing that he was hiding many of Bostock's captives, the men of the *Thais* next called on John Sterling Mill. By the account of the captive Bassa boy held there, this time the navy's men were prepared for trouble and sent five boats, one more than on the original mission. Realizing that he too might be swept up in the trouble, Mill sent his headmen with groups of captives off to the mainland where they would be away from the eyes of the British.

Unguarded for a moment, the Bassa boy seized his chance. He and another boy slid away and once hidden by the dense bush sped frenziedly away. It was not long before they heard the sounds of pursuit. They were children, and those stalking them were grown men familiar with the terrain. Strong arms grabbed him and towed him pitilessly back to captivity.

Back at Dazoe, Mill was negotiating for his business, his livelihood. From what we know of other such occasions the navy's men likely made threats gloved in the words of friendship: Mill's and Hayes's businesses would be left alone if they surrendered those they were hiding for Bostock and McQueen. If not, the navy would come after them long into the future. Into 1814 the patrol was still attacking factories believed to be hiding captives for Samuel Samo. On the other hand, if Mill and Hayes were to hand over those they were hiding for Bostock and McQueen and make written promises that they would trade in human beings no more, the Royal Navy would look away.[1]

John Sterling Mill handed over captives equal to the number he was hiding for Bostock and McQueen. It did not matter who was who, whether those handed over were truly Bostock's or whether they were swapped for captives of roughly equal value. The Bassa boy, who had never been a slave of Bostock and McQueen, transformed in only a few weeks from "free-born" to an interchangeable item of merchandise, was rowed out the *Princess Charlotte*.[2]

On July 1 there was little more to be done. With even Mill and Hayes pressuring them to hand themselves over to end the assault, Bostock and McQueen knew the game was up. Presumably they said goodbye to wives and children hiding with them at the compound, though no evidence of this exists. It seems likely that Bagna would have offered safety to Bostock's Caulker wife and her children, since he would not have wanted to make such powerful enemies over such a small matter. Bostock and McQueen's wives from Bagna's family and those who were the kin of other Cape Mesurado chiefs also seem to have returned home taking their children with them. Although some of the children taken to Freetown aboard the *Thais* and *Princess Charlotte* were listed by the British as having a "yellowish complexion" or even a "yellowish tinge"—terminology that raises the specter, at least from the perspective of American racial terminology, that these were Bostock and McQueen's sons and daughters—this is relatively unlikely, at least in some cases. One of these children said to have a "yellowish complexion," for example, named Doray, also bore Poro cicatrices, which seems unlikely for a child of Bostock's.

Bagna handed over Robert Bostock and John McQueen, claiming that they had "been taken in the Woods by the Natives" rather than admitting that he had been hiding them. They were summarily placed into handcuffs and rowed out to the *Thais*. Housed above decks, some of their former captives held below, they could only hope that the whole affair would be sorted out in Freetown. The *Thais*'s men broached a cask of pork and beef, a reward for a difficult job done well.

That same day John Sterling Mill and Philippa Hayes agreed to sign a deposition:

> We the undersigned . . . voluntary make oath and confess that . . . we have dealt in and carried on a traffic for slaves buying in this country and bartering to be shipped by sea and conveyed in Irons to a state of Slavery various Negroes Natives of Africa the last purchased of whom our Slaves we did during the month of May last sell to the concern of Charles Mason and Robert Bostock the former we believe being an American now there and receiving the return of the cargoes into that Country and the latter being an Englishman living in this Neighbourhood and managing their extensive slave concern at the Factory of St. Pauls from whence and personally from the said Robert Bostock we have within the last month received payment for the said Slaves in Tobacco Rum etc.[3]

Beneath was information revealing the nature of the leverage the British had applied to gain this "Recantation and Abjuration." Mill was made to admit that his father had been an Englishman. Hayes confessed: "my property derives from an Englishman my Husband W Hayes being of that Country and now in it." In other words, they had been warned that their businesses were liable to attack since they could conceivably be considered to be British property and therefore under British legal jurisdiction. The only thing Mill and Hayes had been able to do to keep their business was to confess. "Made sensible of the inhumanity and unlawfulness of bartering the liberty and persons of our Fellow Creatures," they wrote treacherously, "we will never henceforward be conducive in anyway to the enslaving of African Negroes."[4]

The *Thais* and the *Princess Charlotte* remained out at sea for a few more days. Their seamen were not finished. Thirteen more of their captives arrived aboard the next day. A boat going to fetch them overturned at the mouth of the St. Paul River, and a naval man drowned. The following day another forty-three Africans were embarked.[5]

⬌

Armed men came for the captives hiding in John Sterling Mill's barracoon or at Chief Bagna's compound. They were rounded up and ordered to march to the shore. Small craft, much inferior to their own people's canoes, lay in wait. And so, after everything, after the wars and kidnaps and raids and pawning, beyond owners and dealers and gunfire and barracoons, this was leaving. Sitting in the bottom of the dugouts, their legs circling the person in front, arms crowding, they made the terrorizing journey out over the sandbar. They were forced to climb up onto the giant vessel, the white men angry when anybody hesitated or stumbled. It floated on top of the big water as if between the worlds of the spirits and the living. They knew that the ones who went out onto the big water did not return.

The motherless, tricked Bassa boy would remember that he had been "so afraid when I got into the vessel. I cried very much, especially when I think about my father, brother and sister." Adding to their fear were the strange ceremonies. One day the drowned sailor was wrapped into some sort of cloth and with incomprehensible words, thrown overboard. Four days later one of the white men was hauled up on ropes, his back exposed. A giant whip lashed into his flesh, backward and forward, slashing the air hither and thither to the count of thirty-six. While he was enslaved, Olaudah Equiano had watched a sailor flogged and wrote, "this made me fear these people the more, and I expected to be treated in the same manner."[6]

The British naval men who took them on this journey, herding them along and using gestures to instruct, were certain that they were rescuing them, that their actions were on the side of God, morality, and mercy. Whether the Bassa boy, Sessay and the others, even the adults, appreciated this is far from certain. It may well have seemed like yet another scene in the ongoing spectacle of violence.

Eventually, 233 men, women, and children, believed to be former captives from Bostock and Mason's slave factory, were aboard the *Thais* and the *Princess Charlotte*. It was perhaps half of those whom they had already sold to the *Fénix* at the time of the *Kitty*'s attack.[7]

They weighed anchor on July 4. Charles Mason, away in America, would not hear of his factory's destruction for some time and was busy celebrating his nation's freedom from British tyranny. But for Robert Bostock and John McQueen it was all over. They left behind the ruins of the slave factory they had constructed only eighteen months before.[8]

Part 3

Different Types of Liberty

10

Arriving
in Freetown

Sailing away from the burned-out ruins of their business, Robert Bostock and John McQueen were in an awkward predicament. Shut in the space that had been used to confine the mutinous sailors from the *Kitty* just a few weeks before, they were allowed to stroll around the decks for exercise. When they did so they were among the *Thais*'s marines and sailors upon whom they had fired a few days earlier. Propriety demanded that they make small talk with men whose colleagues they had killed and injured, and it was this, the records suggest, that concerned them. McQueen in particular sought out William Chambers, one of the men who had been in the *Thais*'s boats, and expressed his remorse for his wounded friends.[1]

That they were partisan enemies meeting across the deck—illegal slave traders and the frontline of the antislavery patrol—does not seem to have fully sunk in. It may have been that this gulf was simply too vast for them to grasp. The fact that anybody might truly, deep down, believe that slave trading was morally wrong may have seemed too improbable or too dangerous an idea to contemplate. Such philosophies belonged to another world, and they were only a few days out from being potentates of their own slaving domain. They could not yet appreciate the full rush of the abolitionist movement, the way that it had sunk deep into British minds.

The cases of Samuel Samo and Charles Hickson likely reinforced this idea. Hickson had been acquitted, and even Samo, found guilty, had afterward been pardoned. If the charges against them were the same as those against Samo and Hickson, they might reasonably expect to walk away. But Samo and Hickson had not resisted arrest and had certainly not killed the king's men. There was also a whiff of the craven in their actions. If it could be proven that Bostock and McQueen had set fire to their business, it would suggest ungentlemanly conduct. The tenets of middle-class, white, male Georgian behavior meant

97

head-held-high acceptance of fate, back ramrod straight in order to assume the required stature of preeminence.

They were acting out a charade of British civility that stood apart from the Africans they had been buying and selling. Even in these earliest days of their post–slave trading lives there was another agenda, appeals to a shared heritage as sons of Albion, and above and beyond that as worthy gentleman rather than ragamuffin sailors. They were white men of the proper sort and demanded a certain sort of treatment no matter the allegations against them. They both approached Captain Edward Scobell during the short voyage, "begging his intercession." They did not deny their guilt but spoke openly about their business, even noting for Scobell the exact number of captives they had held at the moment of attack. Both admitted that it was far more than those now aboard the *Thais* and *Princess Charlotte*.[2]

John McQueen apparently also believed that they might bribe their way to freedom. One day he was on deck when quartermaster Thomas Lovekine approached, asking how he thought they would fare. McQueen is alleged to have blustered: "if money would get them off they were sure of their liberty." It was a very ill-advised thing to say, a swaggering boast that utterly misjudged the reverence of many abolitionist devotees. Yet in other times and places he might just have been right.[3]

At best it can only have been utterly mystifying. Tethers may have still chaffed at wrists as the *Thais*'s men did not usually remove shackles until the captives had been formally declared free, days later. For men, women, and children captured in wars and raids, the arrival of the naval men was most likely just another of part of their long journeys into captivity. Whether they had any idea that their lives were diverging from the vast majority of those who left Africa in chains is not clear, but the evidence would imply that many did not. There are numerous reports that those "recaptured" had no idea what had happened, and some threw themselves overboard after their rescue, still preferring the rebellion of the deep. The days of the voyage were much less than an Atlantic crossing, but so few had ever returned that no such comparison was possible. It may even have seemed that these new events presented a worse fate than their original one, since slave dealers were known to deliberately mislead their captives to fear grisly deaths if they fell into the hands of the naval patrol.[4]

Their conditions on this voyage are not recorded. Probably they were given water to wash and food (salted pork? cheese?), but their situation can only have

Freetown, Sierra Leone, in 1850. From Thomas Poole Eyre, *Life, Scenery and Customs in Sierra Leone and the Gambia*, vol. 1 (London: Richard Bentley, 1850).

been grim. The seasickness and cramped conditions were terrible enough; what the voyage might mean in its entirety was horrifying. They were diseased and hungry, crowded aboard wooden vessels: the embodiment of all their fears. For the Kru, going to sea was a way to communicate with the ancestral spirits, but the others could only hope that their cries were still heard.[5]

Tamba, Tom Ball, and Yarra must have understood some of the words, but it was all so improbable. Who could be trusted? In these earliest days of their journey they could not know if it was safer to keep faith with Robert Bostock and John McQueen as they were still their masters. Ball and Tamba knew little else.

After two days the ship no longer moved across. Those above decks saw that they were pulling through the heads of a giant harbor, buildings soon rising on the banks. The uniformed men came again, shouting strange words and goading them up and over the sides into more small boats. They huddled together as they set foot ashore. One man who watched recaptives arriving wrote that they often thought they were in the slave markets of the Americas.[6]

Within a few years a set of steps, forever after known (curiously) as the Portuguese steps, was cut and hefted into place and a "King's Yard" erected, complete with pontificating dedication to British justice. But those arriving aboard HMS *Thais* and *Princess Charlotte* were early recaptives, and none of that yet existed. They walked ashore up a muddy bank with planks set down to gain traction. They were rounded up into what was described as a "cattle-pen" near the levee.[7]

Back on solid ground, they were pulled from their huddle one by one. They were measured. The strange men asked for their names. An African clerk wrote them as best he could. Some of the children were too shocked, too fearful, to speak. They were all allotted a number, a simple count of arriving Liberated Africans; in later times numbers would be inscribed onto a "small metal ticket" and tied around the neck.[8]

Tamba was the first to step forward. It was seemingly the first step toward the new role he would carve out for himself as their leader. The English guessed his age as thirty-three, around ten years older than his real age, and noted that he had several scars on his body from his life of enslavement in the slave trade. The others watched the strange dance as a stick was laid against him. Fears of being eaten likely menaced the children's minds as they watched. Tamba was recorded as being 5 feet 4 ½ inches tall and was given the number 4338. His well-known name gave the clerk no problem. Next a man whose name was recorded as "Kangaree" stepped forward. He was judged to be twenty-five years old and stood only 4 feet 8 inches tall. They noted that he was tattooed down his right arm. He was now number 4339.

The other men were jostled forward, one by one. Yarra, the property of John McQueen, became number 4405, the Poro cicatrices down his back noted. They guessed that he was twenty-nine years old, and he stood 5 feet 6 ½ inches tall. The name Tom Ball does not appear on this list; instead he gave an African name. It was perhaps a simple act of dignity. Calculating backward from what appears to have later happened to Ball, he possibly gave the name Banna, which would imply that he was perhaps Temne. If that was the case, then he had tattoos on his left wrist and a scar below his shoulder blade. A lifetime of enslavement had left him 5 feet 3 ¼ inches tall.

Though they could not know it, these checks and notes spoke of many things. There was the British desire to tally and a need for numbers to be sent back to London as matters of accounting. The numbers also would serve to illustrate how the campaign against the illegal slave trade was progressing. They intimated that Africans' complex naming systems were not understood and so thought best reduced to numbers. More portentously, they marked the recaptives' unwitting entry into the British Imperial world. They would not be enslaved, but their labor was nevertheless requisite.

A whole world of Poro membership, specialized skills, pride, and belonging was noted into the ledgers, though the clerks—certainly the European clerks—had little idea what they were noting. Their scarification was a type of passport (albeit the information was more nuanced), and it is our tragedy that so much that the ledgers contain is now ambiguous.

Boi—written *Boy* by the British—around forty years of age, had his proud marks of identity and status boxed into the cool, slightly puzzled description "very much purrahfied." They were turned around so that their scarification born on different parts could be noted: Canyarra had "purrah each side"; Sangolee wore his Poro marks on his back; Wojoe's were "on breast"; Fandee's on his cheeks. For the two Kono twins named Fangha, their scars were the things by which they could be separated. The second Fangha had "purrah" marks noted to be "curious."

Some found that their facial scarification was sketched into the white men's big book. A twenty-nine-year-old man whose name sounded to the clerk like the English word *Gray* had his cicatrices drawn into the ledger. The cross on his forehead bore circles on the end of each branch. Coseree, whose age was estimated to be twenty-one, had a single two-stroke cross, while another man named Fangha, older than the twins, bore a star.

After the adult men came the teenagers: Tambo and Bondoa, each with an extra finger, and Kong, who had the scars of smallpox, lines of newly acquired Poro cicatrices, and marks of medicinal healing.

Then it was the turn of the children. Sessay hung back, waiting for more to go ahead of him. When most of the other boys his age had already gone forward he was pulled to the front. He was just over 4 feet 5 inches tall, and it was noted that he had a "bump" on his left knee and a long face. He was now number 4516. A boy who did chores aboard the ship did not have his name written down, only the strange word *Prince* that the white man shouted when he wanted him. He was eight years old, and they looked closely at his face, writing that he had "a yellowish tinge" to his "complexion."

The women and girls were last. The first was Kayang, around sixteen years old and probably Kissi. One fourteen-year-old was recorded by the name Charlotte, after the *Princess Charlotte*. Perhaps she simply was too traumatized to speak, but the specter of the *Charlotte* seamen's lusting for her "round face" is also raised. The last of Bostock and Mason's captives to be counted was Dee, an eight-year-old girl with a round face who became number 4570.[9]

British authorities claimed that they had all been saved from being sold to a passing slave ship, but this was not entirely true. Tamba, Tom, and Yarra had been factory slaves, unlikely to be sold away. At least the one Bassa boy, and likely others, had belonged not to Bostock and Mason but to John Sterling Mill. And another man was astonished and angry that these white men were not acknowledging what they obviously knew. When his turn came to give his name he said, "Joshua Krooman." While Kru sailors regularly took wondrous names like Bottle of Beer, Frying Pan, Mashed Potato and Bubble and Squeak—there had even been letters written to London demanding that this levity in Kru naming be stopped—they seldom used Kruman as a surname. Joshua must have added it to say that he was most definitely not a captive, not in the same category as the others. His cicatrices told of his freedom. He bore the "black mark down forehead nose and inside eye" that Kru seamen adopted to prevent them being stolen away as slaves.[10]

Two of the children were also Kru. A seven-year-old girl gave her name as Bassa Kroo. It could be that the child simply gave the name of her region and her people as she knew them, proclaiming herself to be Kru from Grand Bassa. Another child, a nine-year-old boy named Saree, did not give "Kroo" as part of his name that day in the King's Yard but soon afterward declared himself to be Kru.[11]

Joshua Krooman was testimony to the fact that the campaign against the slave trade had become a money grab. There is little doubt that the naval men knew that Joshua was not a captive awaiting sale. They had worked alongside Krumen and recognized what their facial scarification meant. But they had captured him and brought him to Freetown nonetheless, conspiring to get the head money that he would accrue.

Stepping ashore in Freetown, Bostock and McQueen passed into the hands of George Clarke, the colony's jailer, one of the last of the original settlers who had founded the Province of Freedom twenty-six years earlier. Freetown had no jail. Two houses were being used, and Bostock and McQueen were lodged in one of those. They wore no shackles.[12]

The captives languished in the cattle pen. Large cauldrons of rice were cooked to keep them fed, but it was too little too late. "Emaciated, squalid, sickly looking and ill fed," the newly Liberated Africans were often "nothing more than living skeletons." An observer of another group of recaptives wrote:

The expression of the countenance indicated suffering, moral and physical, of the most profound and agonizing nature. . . . The belly is, as it were, tacked to the back, whilst the hip bones protrude, and give rise to foul sloughing and phagedenic ulcers. . . . The squalor and extreme wretchedness of the figure is heightened, in many cases, by the party-coloured evacuations with which the body is besmeared. The legs refuse to perform their functions, and with difficulty support the emaciated, tottering and debilitated body.[13]

It was hellish. Recaptives died in their first days in Freetown as diseases and hunger overtook them. Of Bostock and Mason's slaves, one of those lost in the early days was probably fourteen-year-old Bessy, for whom no later fate was recorded.

Yet, in that darkness there were shafts of light. They were not alone. The pen stood only yards from the center of Freetown, and many recaptives from the earliest days of the patrols lived on the fringes of the settlement. So visitors came to see them, recaptives descending en masse to search for family members and countrymen. The question would seethe through the town whenever new people arrived: "who is of my country?" For those brought in before, it was a way to try and reach the homes and families from which they had been stolen, to hear news of loved ones and remember their lives before. The starving, sick, and exhausted arrivals were the only communication route most had. It was also a way to offer support and hope for those arriving after them, to rebuild kinship and community according to their own understanding that food and shelter, like pain and suffering, were shared.[14]

For those in the pen who were found by a countryman or countrywoman, the relief can only have been overwhelming. An observer of such a reunion wrote, "The poor creatures being faint . . . and unconscious of what had befallen them, did not know whether they should laugh or cry when they beheld the countenances of those whom they had supposed long dead." The scene was "too affecting" to be described, and "no one could refrain from shedding tears."[15]

Kinsmen and kinswomen were safety, sanctuaries after journeys through the perdition of strange lands. Countrymen were a pathway to a future that was, at last, imaginable. They could be interlocutors explaining to the newly arrived the dimensions of their scarcely comprehensible fate, teaching them how to negotiate the place in which they now found themselves. Through these visitors they began to learn something of this strange place and catch sight of the future.

A recaptive Kissi man who had been in the colony long enough to take the name Mulberry arrived to meet the newcomers. Kayang, the sixteen-year-old who had stepped forward first of all the females, was one of his kinswomen. He held out the possibility of a life she recognized; he was tangible proof that her life would go forward from this hell. Other Kissi came to meet Tamba, a fourteen-year-old second son. Safua and her baby, Bessy, were also lucky. They met some of their country people who offered them a roof and food, a safe space to recuperate.

A Sherbro woman named Terro also heard that some of her people were in the cattle pen and hastened there. No records reach us, but there must have been scenes of unbounded joy and delight as Manay and Marray, who called each other sister, embraced her, relieved beyond words at this rescuer's arrival. Terro offered to share her home and her scanty food with them for they were all sisters.

Countrymen are also reported to have come to welcome two of the children. Seven-year old Bono went to live with a Loma family. Perhaps they hoped that somebody was taking care of their own children, from whom they had been stolen away, and through Bono saw hope that caring and sharing might extend to those they had lost. A seven-year-old who whose name had been written "Mano"—whether a rendering of her name or her attempt to give her people's identity—was also claimed.

At Freetown's arrival yard an entire continent of gods were praised in the elation of reunion and among the "suffering, moral and physical," were scenes of pure, life-affirming joy. Kayang, Safua and Bessy, Tamba, Manay and Marray knew that they had only to wait for their release from British authorities and they could leave their captivity. They were among the most fortunate of all the new arrivals.[16]

11

The Court Case

After a couple of days, white men arrived in the pen and asked questions about Robert Bostock and John McQueen. Tamba, Ball, and Yarra understood some of the words. Still, the wider implication, the intimations shrouded within those rounded British vowels, can only have been bewildering. Bostock and McQueen, and Charles Mason before he sailed away, had controlled their days and their nights, where they went, what they ate, and where they rested their heads. The men had tried to own their minds. Yarra was slightly older and was not captured until he was at least old enough to have Poro scars down his back, but Bostock had owned Tom for so long that he had grown up inured to his former owner's fantasies of omnipotence.

Tamba, Ball, and Yarra cannot have fully known it, but the request for their witness would have been strange almost anywhere around the Atlantic Ocean in the early nineteenth century. In many places it would have been anathema. Yet a couple of years earlier it had been decided that "the Negroes themselves should appear as parties . . . before the Court, in order to implead their right to freedom." Africans had testified at the court cases of Joseph Peters and William Tufft in June 1812. Even so, there had not been many Africans called. A potential roadblock was the issue of whether their testimony could stand if they did not pledge an oath, and it was a remarkably broadminded decision for the times that had allowed that they could swear to tell the truth in the manner of their own countries or however they so chose. Those who had bravely gone before them and those would come soon after used not only the Old and New Testaments and the Koran but had also recited prayers in their own languages, sworn on their mother's lives, invoked direct hits from God, kissed the earth, and performed other solemn rituals: "he rubbed his two forefingers on his forehead and applied the dust to his tongue."[1]

It is not clear why Tamba did not give evidence. Possibly he was too con-flicted about his own role, or not yet able to psychically distance himself from his former owners. Perhaps this was also an acknowledgment that the British knew another truth, one that they could not afford to spell out in the legal record for fear of blurring their fantasy of a clear line between sinful trader and sup-plicant African awaiting their divinely inspired assistance. Likely they knew that Tamba was not simply a captive awaiting sale but also a man said by other African slave traders to have been "in the slave trade."

Tom Ball and Yarra agreed to give accounts of what Bostock and McQueen had been doing: of the captives and the ships, the minutiae of their own hor-rific jobs guarding and feeding and loading aboard slave vessels. Whether they believed they had any choice or not we cannot know, but nonetheless it showed remarkable bravery. Ball and Yarra had no way of knowing whether Bostock and McQueen still claimed ownership over them and might wreak revenge for having testified. Ball also could not have known whether Charles Mason, his old master from the Gallinas factory, would come back for him. For some, the risks of testifying were just too much. Another slave trading trial fell apart because the main witness refused to appear, not wanting to incur any-body's wrath.[2]

On July 9, Yarra gave his evidence before Judge Robert Purdie and Purdie's assistant. There is no record of whether Purdie wore formal court dress as required by the Lord Chamberlain, and so presented himself sweating in the intense humidity in a dark-colored frock coat and breeches with white silk stockings and a wig.

Yarra was asked about his owner. He replied that he had previously be-longed to another white slave trader and after that man's death John McQueen had bought him. That had been twelve moons before, Yarra related, and since then he had been held at Mason and Bostock's factory. Next they turned to questions of his work. By the time his answer was noted down his original words were transformed into English: "I have been taking care of the slaves, putting them in Irons and looking after them. I put many slaves into boats and in Irons and sent them on board Vessels that have taken them away." He was asked to clarify that this had been under the direction of Bostock and McQueen, and he concurred. Yarra was then questioned about the people in the barracoon, but instead of speaking of those who had arrived in Freetown he talked of others who had not. Of those who had been held captive at the factory "about half a moon ago, when the Man of War came," he claimed that only around half had been brought to Sierra Leone. Yarra was given the metal-nibbed quill to make a mark under what they had written, and he made two lines, carefully crossing them. It was done.[3]

Next Tom Ball sat before the elderly white man. He was asked to make his own promise that he would tell the truth and did so in the manner of his own country, remembering back to the times he had seen men do this before he had been stolen away. His years of enslavement to Robert Bostock were far longer than Yarra's, and there was so much to tell.

"I hath been a slave of Robert Bostock since I was a little boy," Ball stated, "living with him first at Gallinas then came with him to St. Paul's Mesurado on the setting of that factory." He was the only one of the factory slaves to speak of Mason: "A year and a half ago Mason a white man with whom Bostock lived at Gallinas came in a Brig to Mesurado and filled her belly with slaves whom he took away with him."

Asked about the last time a slaving vessel called at their factory, the one prior to the *Fénix*, Ball replied: "about four months ago was the last time a Vessel took slaves from Bostock, she was a schooner and she carried away a great many." Questioned about John McQueen, Ball recalled how McQueen had lived with Bostock for two years, and "has helped Bostock to buy and send off Slaves and when Bostock was absent about a year ago McQueen had charge of the factory." They asked him about his own work: "I kept them when kept at the factory in Irons," he replied. He too was handed the quill and signed with a cross.[4]

Three days later, a week after having set sail from Cape Mesurado, their case was decided. Sierra Leone's courthouse was one of only six stone buildings in the town, used as a church on Sundays and every other day as the girls' school. Classes halted for the occasion, and Judge Robert Purdie got down to the business at hand. Having invoked "the name of Christ and having God alone before his eyes," Purdie decreed that the freedom of the 233 men, women and children who had been brought from Charles Mason and Robert Bostock's barracoon was legal under British law. One half of them were said to be the property of Robert Bostock, forfeited because he was a British citizen caught slave trading illegally. The other half of the captives were deemed the property of Charles Mason, who as an American lost this property as prize of the War of 1812. With that they were legally free.[5]

The news was conveyed to them back in the cattle pen in best king's English, a language they did not understand. The Britons making the grand declaration believed that they were performing an act of God and that the Africans' futures were now all rosy. It sometimes became such a sanctimonious performance of pomposity that one observer derided it as "mummery." It was nevertheless an escape by the slimmest of margins from enslavement in perpetuity.[6]

On July 11 Bostock and McQueen had decided to plead guilty, apparently convinced that if they admitted their crime and begged for forgiveness they would walk free. Edward Scobell wrote, "no denial . . . was attempted." They admitted slave trading but mentioned the length of time they had been involved in the business, hoping that having entered the trade before it was outlawed would ameliorate their guilt.[7]

The following day word reached them that their former captives had been declared free. It was a financial setback as significant as the loss of their inanimate goods and buildings the week before. Yet there must also have been a glimmer of satisfaction in the news, since the manner of their loss dealt a blow to those who had destroyed them. For the crews of HMS *Thais* and the *Princess Charlotte*, the decision to decree half of their former captives to have been the property of Charles Mason instead of Robert Bostock had been a disappointment. By 1813, "head money" of £60 for each man, £30 per woman, and £10 for every child was paid for those who rescued captives from slave ships, divided among all of those involved down to the lowliest cabin boy. The naval men had been expecting that this sum would be paid out for all of those saved from Bostock and Mason's barracoon. Collectively, the worth of the 233 Africans brought from the St. Paul River would have amounted to £8,410. But Purdie's decision meant that head money would not be paid for the half considered to have been Mason's property. They were instead prizes of war, and prize money usually came from the sale of the ship, cargo, armaments, and whatever else had been captured. But here at the sharp end of the abolitionist canon there was no question of half of those rescued being sold to line the naval men's pockets. Instead of the £8,410 they had been expecting, Maxwell, Macaulay, Edward Scobell, and the men of the *Thais* and *Princess Charlotte* shared £5,790.[8]

Ten days later, Bostock and McQueen were led to court. They hustled past wattled huts along Westmoreland Street, named for the Maroons' Jamaican home. The Nova Scotians had named the side streets they passed for Generals in the American War (Rawdon and Howe) or members of the Royal Family

(Gloucester, Charlotte, and George). The girls' school was again halted for this occasion.[9]

The case before theirs was the theft of a blue jacket and £9 in £1 notes, for which the defendant was found guilty and sentenced to five years' hard labor. It was a sideshow: it was Bostock and McQueen's trial that had drawn the crowd, their prosecution a hotly debated topic and quasi entertainment in this tiny colony where everybody lived and died by the fight against the slave trade.

They were tried under the 1811 Slave Trade Felony Act, also known as Mr. Brougham's Act, first used the year before in Samuel Samo's case. Just like Samo's trial, Bostock and McQueen's promised to be a spectacle, a theater of sin, sanctity, and possible redemption all under one roof. Samo's trial had involved tales of shackles, chains, captives branded on the right thigh. When he was found guilty, all in court had heard Judge Robert Thorpe assail Samo, "human beings made and created in God's image you have stolen," and then sentence him to a "penalty of law that is not death, but it is worse, for it reduces the convict to the most infamous degradation of life" where he would do hard labor with "a fetter or a log appended to some limb."[10]

Issuing a reprieve, Thorpe had invoked Samo to persuade his fellow dealers to abandon their trade so that "it be shattered to atoms in a storm of benevolent charity to mankind—it will be an immolation acceptable to the deity." Later, reading the King's Mercy to the prisoner, Thorpe had been so impassioned that one Englishman attending "wept almost the entire time."[11]

But there was bad news for Bostock and McQueen. It was Judge Thorpe who had convinced Governor Maxwell to recommend a pardon for Samo, and Thorpe had since returned to England. Presiding over Bostock and McQueen's trial, just as he had freed their former captives a week earlier, was Judge Robert Purdie, the colony's former surgeon, who lacked any legal training as well as Thorpe's histrionic streak. Just three weeks previously he had written to Governor Maxwell acknowledging that he was "very little acquainted . . . with the laws of England."[12]

This was not uncommon in faraway colonies where few people had legal training. A few years earlier, a storekeeper had been the colony's judge. It was actually more unusual that until a short time earlier Robert Thorpe, a trained barrister, presided over the Sierra Leone courtroom. That had happened only because Thorpe was sent to Sierra Leone as penance after being banished from Upper Canada for "violence and indiscretion." Nevertheless, in Freetown he had become "a devoted abolitionist," vigorously prosecuted cases against slave traders. In 1812, he had boasted to Governor Maxwell that between them they were stopping the slave trade, having "closely bound up the

Portuguese . . . crippled the Americans, and put flight to the Spaniards."
Thorpe believed that "immortal fame" rested in these deeds and that he and
Maxwell were "at the vanguard of social and legal change." But, needing a
break so that he could improve his health, he had sailed for England a few
months before Bostock and McQueen arrived in Freetown. Purdie had taken
over, supposedly temporarily.[13]

The same jury who had judged the guilt of the jacket thief remained on,
and however much Bostock and McQueen had prepared themselves for this
moment, it must still have been a shock. Kenneth Macaulay, a Briton who was
superintendent of captive Negroes, was in the jury. James Carr, an accountant
for the African Company who had left the colony at one point to go slave trading,
was also there. These were the only feint glimmers of hope for them.[14]

Also sitting among the jury, waiting to pass judgment, were Nova Scotians Joseph Jewett and Pompey Young. Representatives of the Maroon community were even more numerous. John Ellis was the Maroon preacher of the
Huntingtonian Church, and William Libert was a clerk and carpenter. Barney
Baily, John Morgan, and William Thorpe were all Maroons, and James Williams
was the son of a Maroon.[15]

Bostock and McQueen had traded alongside African men and sometimes
women, lived with African women, and had mixed-race children, but having
their fate in the hands of this multiracial jury, in which black men were a very
distinct majority, can only have seemed a perversion, a parody of all that they
believed themselves to be. Racial designations might not have been quite as
hardened as they would later become, but by the turn of the century an august
Englishman would be scandalized and incensed to discover that in Freetown a
white man could be sued by a local man, "with the damages assessed by a
coloured jury." Others alleged that they have been unfairly treated simply
because the jury was black.[16]

Bostock and McQueen learned that two of their former slaves had given
evidence against them. It was most likely a shocking development on two
fronts. A year earlier, Samo had been convicted more or less entirely on the
testimony of Africans, and Joseph Peters's sentence came at the word of his
former captive. Just the idea of Africans having this sway over white men had
been inflaming to many. Equally confronting, however, was to learn which of
their former slaves had testified. Yarra was a recent arrival at the factory, but
like so many American plantation masters who thought that their domestic
slaves were loyal and reasonably content, Bostock and McQueen surely believed
Tom Ball to be the most reliable of their bondsmen.[17]

Yet they had to sit and listen to Ball's statement that related how he had been enslaved as a "small boy" and had grown up as the personal property of Robert Bostock. He had told of their Gallinas factory and Charles Mason and the *Fénix* and other earlier slave ships. Both he and Yarra had revealed details of their factory and the captives they had bought and sold. It was one of the rare times that former African slaves ever testified before a court in the English-speaking world about the circumstances of their captivity.[18]

Bostock and McQueen also heard the confessions of John Sterling Mill and Philippa Hayes that they too were slave trading and had bought and sold from Bostock and McQueen. Whether they smiled sardonically upon hearing their solemn promises to quit the slave trade, or were angered, or were even coolly aware that they would have done the same, we cannot know. There seems little doubt that they knew that the pledges were hollow.[19]

After the testimonies of a few crewmen aboard the *Thais*, Purdie, with little idea of how to proceed, followed his learned predecessor. Thorpe had found Samuel Samo guilty, so Purdie did the same, "with confidence." He proclaimed the two men guilty and quickly passed sentence. Both were banished to Australia, Britain's prison colony founded back in 1788, for fourteen years.[20]

It caused them great distress, certainly. But they cannot have given up hope at this point. Samuel Samo had been convicted but then quickly pardoned. Now he was happily back slave trading in the Rio Pongo, despite his pledge to help it be "shattered to atoms in a storm of benevolent charity." Bostock and McQueen likely clung to the faith that a similar fate would meet them.[21]

Not long after that trial, Judge Purdie adjudicated another case. It was the final strand of the events that had seen the demise of Mason and Bostock's St. Paul enterprise. John Roach and the men of the *Kitty* claimed the slave ship *Fénix* as their rightful prize. Purdie declared the capture legal since one captive, Za, had been found aboard. Legally captured slave ships were usually sold in order for captors to receive their share of the prize money. Instead John Roach decided to keep the *Fénix*, or as he called it, the *Phoenix*.[22]

He also kept aboard Za, now called Jack Phoenix. Freedom for the young recaptive boy was to be the servant/apprentice of Captain John Roach.[23]

12

Becoming Soldiers, Cabin Boys, and Wives

At best, it was baffling. Even once they knew that they were not now captives, it was mysterious. Before enslavement they had been in the safety of their family and kin group, where human life stood tall. Then had come the hell of the coffles and the barracoons. What happened next was a blank slate.

The British believed that they had given them a priceless gift, and that escaping the barracoon can only have been an immense relief. Those enslaved in the Americas would doubtless have agreed overwhelmingly that to be suddenly deemed free was an inestimable windfall. But these men and women lacked clear insight into these alternatives: the endless toil of generations in the cane fields versus liberty. They had not come from nations that had recently adopted freedom as an all-encompassing aim, shouting huzzah for Liberty or Death, guillotining aristocratic necks in the name of *liberté* or proclaiming that the air of their country so pure that all must be free. They had not been longing for this thing the white men called *freedom*, at least not in the sense of individuality of action and autonomous decision making. The culture shock must have been monumental. Within a week they went from white men's merchandise chained in a stinking barracoon to experiments in enlightenment theory.

Many of them wanted more than anything to go home, which as one observer noted, was their idea of "genuine liberty." Children wanted parents, and husbands longed for wives. They had been snatched from a jigsaw puzzle of extended family and community that stretched back to the ancestors and reached out to the ones not yet born, where each person had established roles that anchored the earth to the sky and morning to night. No one piece, one person, told the whole story of that intricate puzzle, and only whole would it reveal the image entire. Liberty as the British perceived it was indecipherable. Worst, isolation and desolation were close kin. Humanity was found through society; life was in and through others.[1]

But going home was hardly ever a possibility, since the distances they were away from their homelands meant impossibly long journeys. Even if a route were known, they would be at immense risk of being re-enslaved. Some had been away for years and had received no news of their people. The circumstances of Tom Ball's and Tamba's appropriation from their families years earlier are unclear: perhaps they had no homes to which they might return. Some of the smaller children from the barracoon had no idea where their homes even were and could hardly travel there alone. They had little choice but to try and re-create some semblance of normality in this new place.

The British had little idea what rescued men, women, and children would do. Abolitionists had not anticipated this constant, and very much increasing, flow of recaptives because they had optimistically believed that the slave trade would be quickly wound up after 1808. Beyond that, they wavered about becoming too involved in the lives of the rescued Africans, since to them the slave trade was a matter of sin and abrogation of divine law, it was not a humanitarian matter per se.

When the slave trade had first been illegalized by the British five years earlier and Royal Navy ships sent out to catch those breaking the ban, almost all of the attention was on the actual business of slave trading and on prosecuting those found breaking the new laws. One solitary clause in Britain's law illegalizing the slave trade mentioned the captive humans they might find aboard the illicit slave ships. It would have been quite remarkable to them that it would ever be called "an early and bold judicial experiment in humanitarian intervention." There was no admission made among the abolitionists that captives, having been freed, were really their concern.[2]

Most Britons, including the abolitionists, imagined that Liberated Africans would be put to work in some way that contributed to imperial progress. They could be kept in various degrees of nonfreedom as long as they were not held in outright slavery. Apprenticeship for a term up to fourteen years or enlistment into His Majesty's army and navy were thought the most appropriate types of liberty. These were the sorts of thing that many young British boys had to choose between.

Yet the abolitionists did not believe that Africans could be expected to fully understand these options. So, a proviso that each was to be treated "as if he had voluntarily so enlisted or entered," revealed the abolitionists intentions to treat them along the lines of British boys and yet displayed that some would not actually have made a deliberate decision at all. Officers "appropriated" Liberated Africans for military service because they were not thought capable of making an informed choice. This is one of the reasons that Marcus Wood has argued acerbically that "emancipation [was] a mean-spirited and highly efficient plan for the continued exploitation of the African body as both commodity and resource." Tellingly enough, throughout decades of the campaign against the slave trade, the British termed the freed *Captured Negroes*, with the terms *recaptive* and *Liberated African* only used later.[3]

In March 1808, when two American slave ships had first arrived in Sierra Leone, having been captured by the naval patrol, nobody knew what to do with those aboard, nor had any money to pay for their upkeep. Believing that these would be rare cases rather than the start of a torrent, Governor Ludlam enlisted forty of the "ablest men" into the military, and the rest he "sold" as apprentices to Freetown's citizens for $20 each, the proceeds being paid to the naval men for their rescue. Ludlam claimed that he imposed the fee to secure a better sort of master for these "apprentices." But the captives were still wearing iron shackles, and most buyers thought they were purchasing chattel slaves whom they would own in perpetuity.[4]

Though Ludlam and the other abolitionists always hotly denied any wrongdoing, this was cutting things a bit too close. Zachary Macaulay admitted that the $20 should not have gone to the men of the naval patrol since "it tells ill, because it looks something like a sale." Thomas Perronet Thompson, who became governor in July 1808 a few months after this sale, had been horrified. He had declared all apprenticeships signed before he had arrived to be void, believing, as he wrote to his fiancée, that the scheme "introduced actual slavery." William Wilberforce and his fellow antislavery "saints" had "at last become slave traders with a vengeance" because of their support for apprenticeships, raged Thompson.[5]

Thompson had hoped to turn the Liberated Africans into a "free and hardy peasantry," but with no budget to do so he had been forced to go on apprenticing many of the newly arrived recaptives to Maroons and Nova Scotians. Advertisements in the *African Herald* reveal something other than the hearty farmers for which he hoped. In November 1809, Moses Grief had advertised a $60 reward for the return of his three "New Negro Fellows" who had gone off with abolitionist literature in their pockets. The following week's paper had advertised for the return of Cupid (tellingly, the fugitive called himself Osman, not Cupid), who had been rescued from a slave ship a few months earlier. He had run off, "in consequence of the light whipping given to his wench."[6]

There had been no more open sales of Liberated Africans after 1808, but in place of outright sale came negligence. When Edward Columbine replaced Thompson as governor, there had been allegations that Liberated Africans were given insufficient food and had been forced to go around the town "begging &

stealing for subsistence." Columbine, despite being an abolitionist and member of the African Institution, had remained unapologetic, apparently declaring on one occasion, "Tis enough that we give them liberty." They could "earn their bread by labour," he believed.[7]

Charles Maxwell had taken over from Columbine by the time Bostock and Mason's captives arrived, but there was little change with Maxwell "bidden to continue Columbine's regime of economy." A visitor in 1811 had watched HMS *Thais* bring in some other recaptives and wrote, "if the settlers wish to have any of them, to employ them in their houses, or on their farms, they make application to the Governor specifying the number they want." Maxwell then wrote out an indenture, the greater aim of which was "to inure them to the habits of industry, and teach them the arts of the civilized life." Yet by July 1813, even apprenticeships were not widely used.[8]

The only man among the *Thais*'s arrivals who knew what to do was Joshua, the Kru man who had been trying to make his status obvious. Near the harbor, not far from where they had landed, was Kroo Bay. Since the very earliest days of the colony Kru men had established their own place with "loosely wattled sheds," a village where the skilled seafarers could live while they were working in the colony. Three years later Kroo Bay would become the first parcel of land within the Sierra Leone colony alienated for a specific ethnic group. At least six hundred to seven hundred of Joshua's kinsmen were there and could offer him a place to sleep and a plate of food while he found work.[9]

So Joshua hastily headed for Kroo Bay, slaking off the embarrassment of having been erroneously brought in as a recaptive. He could look for seafaring work and earn as much as three or four dollars per month. But Kroo Bay was famously a "bachelor village"—even a reward of £5 5s to any Kru man who brought his wife and children to the colony had failed—so there was no place for the Kru children Bassa and Saree.[10]

The others had little idea what to do. They were given a blanket and a piece of cloth long enough to wrap around their body. Each child got a smaller bit of fabric and shared the blanket with another boy or girl. And that was virtually all the help they got.[11]

They were hungry, traumatized, and away from everybody who could offer support. Worse, perhaps the most immediate threat for those not ailing from disease was the man officially in charge of them, twenty-one-year-old Kenneth Macaulay. Stories flew back to London that he was "in the constant habit of debauching numbers of the captured negro girls." He was said to treat the girls and young women as his personal harem and later kept "a seraglio of half a dozen women" with whom he lived "in the most libidinous and profligate manner." Nobody ever asked his alleged victims for their stories: they were young girls recently wearing chains, unable to understand him, and he was a white man in a position of almost unmitigated power.[12]

The boys and men might have escaped his more lascivious attentions, but Macaulay was said to "shamefully coerce and chastise" them. He paid little attention to their well-being or fate, and in this laxity was room for people to re-enslave them or otherwise exploit their need for help. Only one of them, eleven-year-old Paway, was indentured. The rest had no idea what to do.[13]

This white man's gift called freedom may well have seemed to possess some very strange features.

As morning dawned over their first day after the strange ceremony, the meaning of which was still opaque, men in uniform appeared at the pen. The adult males and teenage boys were told to line up. Limb touching limb, they likely stood dignified and unflinching as they had learned in the Poro bush. They had come so far, they would not break at this. They knew that to reveal any emotion was to give their tormentors a tool with which to unstitch them. The sick perhaps harnessed their might, standing as tall and straight as they could manage because this might be an audition for life. A show of health and vitality might prove their worth, might be the difference between life and death.

The white men looked, examined, and discussed. They made notes. Then they pointed at Konbah, probably a Kono; Fallee, perhaps a Kissi man; Miah, a Mende man whose serried row of cicatrices had been drawn in the arrival book; and Bala, one of the Gbande men. They motioned to the tallest of them all, Canaba, and one of the shortest, Kangaree. "The most muscular"—those who had managed to fight off the worst of the diseases and starvation—were separated from the rest. They had come together, now some of them stood apart.[14]

For Kerricure it was seemingly all too grave. Nineteen years old, she saw her countryman picked and knew that her last consolation, the last thread that led back to the other life before, would be lost. Distraught, too overwhelmed to shroud her pain behind an impassive veil, she apparently clung to the man who embodied all that had been stolen from her. Perhaps the other women looked on, unsure if Kerricure was plucky or crazy. Yet somehow it worked. Alone of the women, Kerricure stood with the chosen men.

There were more white men wearing different uniforms. More were singled out, a cut deeper than the last. Soon forty-two more stood apart. Mamaroo, a proud Muslim man of sixteen, Nacoi, Gumboo, Blaman, Woorie, Panday, and Fouray with scarification on his cheeks and forehead. Tom Ball, listed under his African name, was one of those taken. The youngest were only nine years old, surely too young to be soldiers and perhaps wanted as servants or porters. Whole groups of those from the muster roll chose to go or not go, as if they had stood with their countrymen and fellow language speakers when they had arrived and now together selected their fate.

The British declared that anybody who resisted could stay behind, but how to chose when so little was known? Tom Ball might have understood that they were being chosen for military service. He, or African clerks who were earlier recaptives, may have been able to explain. But it is far from certain. It is entirely possible that many of them had no idea what was happening, much less that they had a sliver of choice. The only experience they had with white men was enslavement, and many believed that they had been purchased by the white men in Sierra Leone, in the form of the head money given to their rescuers. It was a view shared by many of the people living around the colony who thought that the Liberated Africans belonged to the white men who governed. For what other purpose would the white men have brought them to the colony? Decades earlier, aboard the slave ship leaving Africa, Olaudah Equiano had been told by his countrymen that they "were to be carried to these white people's country to work for them." It probably seemed to some that this was simply coming true.[15]

There was even some justification behind these apparent misconceptions, since the law provided that recaptives were "for the sole use of His Majesty, his heirs or successors." It was a provision intended to prevent their being re-enslaved, but it nonetheless spoke of a bigger picture in which their labor was not entirely their own. Since November 1811, when a "Black Company" had been added to the Royal African Corps (RAC), the collector of customs in Freetown had been required to turn over any newly rescued men fit enough for military service. Edward Scobell carried instructions to look among those he liberated from slave ships for "a supply of recruits to complete the Black Regiments."[16]

In Westminster, where they were agonizing about war on several fronts — there were fears that Britain itself might be invaded — and suffering an acute shortage of recruits, this forced recruitment of released captives made perfect sense. Britain itself had already been driven to try both ballots and a system whereby each parish had to provide a certain number of men for the army. It did not seem too much of a stretch to enlist Liberated African men to fill the ranks of faraway corps. The British also thought that military service was a way that Liberated Africans could repay them for their freedom. Having convinced themselves that they were now moral giants for their stance against the slave trade, many Britons thought that those liberated from slave ships should, at bare minimum, be appreciative.[17]

For the captives, it was a glimpse of the largely unquestioned notions of superiority held by the British. It was far from the worst racism that they and their descendants would face, but it showed that equality was not even imagined. Most of the abolitionists saw Africans as unlucky children in need of teaching and improving. Civilization was the mantra of the age, and it was hoped that Africans might be shown the way forward, and so be manifestly improved, if only the British taught them how to be the proper sort of human being. How exactly this would happen given that their white comrades-in-arms in the RAC were men "of the worst description," profligate drunks who were too dangerous to be "set at large," was obscure even to those watching on. Clearly proximity to even the lowest of Britons was thought to be a step-up for Africans.[18]

Yet, even for those recaptives who did know something of their choice, who loathed everything to do with white men, and who had perhaps begun to discern and abhor the patronizing zeal of this new set, there were likely positive reasons to enlist. Men who had endured capture, chains, and whipping, who had been powerless to protect their families, probably found the idea of carrying weapons tempting. Some of them had been warriors in their homelands. In military service might be dignity and honor, a future way to defend themselves and their people.

By the end of the day, the first twenty-two men were enlisted into the RAC, and the second forty-two were destined for the recruiting depot of the West India Regiment (WIR). For British men the RAC was a convict corps, a punishment for those who had committed some crime or deserted from another regiment. The white man's punishment was the black man's liberation. In 1813, it was one of the better options available for men of African origin no longer in their homelands.[19]

They marched out of the cattle pen under a "strong escort" of sickly looking men in red and green, carrying muskets. Robert Thorpe spoke of government men "driving a terrified Being to the fort, who knew not what was said to him, nor what was to become of him." They were led to one of the few stone buildings where wooden benches were lined up. Only a handful of days before a clerk had attempted to write down their names. Now they were told a new name, unlike any they had known.[20]

Twenty-two appeared as soldiers in the RAC's muster. Their African names, or rather the approximations of them that had been written down by the British clerk, were no more. Kangaree, Fallee, Baloo, Nacoi, and all the others had, by unknown alchemies, become David Neptune, Isaac Newton, John Nero, and Tom Parrott. Rather than letting his imagination roam free, the clerk obviously decided not to mess up his alphabetization and so gave all twenty-two men surnames beginning with the letters *N, O,* or *P.* Who was who no longer mattered.[21]

They were handed a strange array of items. Some coins—later they would discover that it was barely half the amount given to white recruits—and a variety of "gifts." Some got "Barley Corn Beads assorted" and a tambourine; others got amber or coral, panpipes, tobacco, and a snuffbox with an image of a black man in uniform on the top. They were the type of gewgaws that dealers had tried to trade for slaves for hundreds of years. Some received iron bars. They were also given a red jacket, grey pantaloons, and a hat. The jacket had "trifling lace cord" that the new masters had requested especially for them, believing that it would make them feel important.[22]

They were herded back to the harbor and loaded aboard small boats once more. At last freed from their shackles, they saw for the first time the swaying, stirring splendor of Sierra Leone's harbor, the picture postcard emerald idyll sliced through with cobalt waters below a lucent sky. For twenty miles they traveled upriver, a scene acclaimed for its "exquisite and peculiar beauty" with "nodding palms uplift[ing] their heads above umbrageous groves," "the whole canopied by a sapphire sky."[23]

At a small island they were gestured to disembark. A chilling sight met them: a "formidable" building, "about one hundred feet in length, and thirty in breadth . . . under which are commodious large cellars and store rooms." Laid out in front was an apron of forbidding cannons, beckoning seaward, though the embrasures from which they had formerly peeped out lay in ruins. They were at Bunce Island, once the main slave trade factory in Sierra Leone where fifty thousand Africans had been forced into exile, bound as beasts of burden. Freedom had been a headlong leap into a far more conventional slave trading fort than that from which they had been rescued.[24]

In its heyday in the mid-eighteenth century Bunce Island had boasted fine lodgings for Europeans, a conference hall, a Tradesmen's Gallery where up to ninety visiting merchants could display their wares, a rice house, a meat house, and a bakery. There had even been a two-hole golf course complete with African caddies wearing tartan loincloths imported from Glasgow. Now there were just some British men trying to run a recruitment depot among the decaying buildings. The same buildings that had formerly held slaves were thought particularly suitable for the new recruits because escape was all but impossible.[25]

Even the directors of the African Institution in London admitted that the plan was far from perfect. At Bunce Island, they admitted, new recruits suffered "great hardships." Two former employees had, after all, already stood trial for slave trading. Punishments and chastisements were brutal, and though the same could be said for white recruits' training, when mixed with bigotry and thrown into a slave trading context, the results were grim.[26]

Tom Ball, his feet never before shod—so recently padding the rust earth from the pens to the cookhouse—forced his toes into military boots. He tried on the green jacket with red cuffs, three lines of metal down the front, over blue pantaloons. He had grown up with Robert Bostock and knew the correct way to cover the body with these items. Perhaps he helped the others with the shiny buttons, fiddling with the lace trim to meet their superior officers' demands, and try to drag them back from the precipice of trouble. But there was an element of the absurd. It was so unlike their usual dress.[27]

There was rudimentary training with muskets. *Prime and Load!* was shouted, and they had to learn to load cartridges, pull back the hammer to half-cock, and load powder. The ramrod had to be used to ram the powder to the breech of the barrel. There was a right way to stand, an exact sequence of maneuvers that had to be followed in order not to be yelled at or beaten. It all had to happen so quickly before the shout of *Fire!* was heard.

A few weeks later, Tom Ball and some of the others enlisted in the WIR embarked aboard ship. Ball had been saved from an ocean voyage when Bostock had purchased him as a small boy. Now he was going after all. He was a soldier in His Majesty's Army.[28]

For those in the RAC it was less of a journey to their new homes. They recrossed the harbor and went to the side of Fort Thornton, where they were allowed to build huts. They took over garrison duties for the town, surely a vast upturn in their situation no matter the harshness of the discipline.[29]

Meanwhile, those still waiting back in the cattle pen made their first forays into the colony. Freetown was unlike anything they had seen before. Its broad thoroughfares were set out in a grid pattern in a way that promoted regularity and distance, rather than the sense of community derived from having homes clustered. The buildings not made from stone were rectangular frame and shingle topped with thatch, all so different from the round mud brick and mangrove wood buildings of their homelands. Each had a small garden laid out with, "orange plantations, paw paw, apples, pepper, ginger." The Nova Scotian and Maroons' clothing was nothing they had ever seen Africans wear. Freetown's women wore long skirts and sleeves to their wrists, head ties with a hat atop that. Many of the men wore "very respectable" trousers and shirts. Even in its earliest days Freetown aspired to Englishness and a sort of European gentility.[30]

Many of them saw the town as they were marched across the city eastward to where Governor Maxwell had a plantation, Belle Vue. By some reports an overseer or "director of some public work" came for those not enlisted into the army or navy the morning after they were declared free. "The sanction of the poor ignorant captured negro the moment he landed a freeman" was cause for many complaints about their treatment. They were "marched off in small lots, under the care of some white man commonly a soldier on fatigue duty." Several decades later, a visitor would note that "Africans recently liberated" did all the work that in other countries was performed by "beasts of burden." Governor Maxwell's estate grew "yams, Indian corn and other produce" as well as coffee, which had first been noticed growing in the colony in the 1790s by Nova Scotian Andrew Moore, who had grown up on a slave plantation in Georgia. It had since been widely planted and was seen as a potential export crop for Sierra Leone.[31]

Some of the recaptives rescued from Mason and Bostock's business worked among the coffee plants, watching for pests. Belle Vue, twenty-eight years later, was "much cooler and more pleasant in every way" than Freetown, "birds of every colour are for ever flitting past." By then it had "the side of a hill . . . cleared and planted with coffee [that] rises like a wall."[32]

Ironically enough, it was the work that many of their brothers and sisters transported to Cuba were doing on the other side of the ocean. There, coffee was the secondary crop to sugar throughout the era, employing at least as many bondsmen in the 1810s. Liberated Africans in Sierra Leone were not kept in "prison-like quarters" and watched constantly, but they similarly received no pay since they were already considered to be in debt to the British for their rescue, food, and the blanket.[33]

The women were not taken to do this work. Ideas about what female Liberated Africans might do were based on ideas of femininity prevalent in Britain. They were to be kept away from all but the lightest agricultural labor. This was both a blessing and a curse, protecting them from the type of backbreaking labor that was carrying away many of their sisters in the Caribbean, but narrowing the ways that they might feed and clothe themselves and care for the small children from their kin groups who were with them in the pen. For those trying to ward off Macaulay's attentions, they also needed to find a way to protect themselves.

The only options open to them were domestic service or finding a male settler to live with in something approximating marriage. The latter was by far the more attractive option for those who had been initiated into womanhood, since living with a man in some sort of mutual arrangement was what they expected from life. Learning the delights of ironing a settler's breeches with a large stone was not, and left them little more than "domestic slaves" who lacked rights over their own children. If respectable citizens came to ask for their service, however, they could hardly refuse. Macaulay let them be used as cheap labor. Fifteen-year-old Coree was sent to live with the Reverend Charles Wenzel—by this time "deaf, lame and sometimes blind from opthalmia caught from recaptives"—and his Nova Scotian wife as a domestic servant.[34]

Kayang had gone with her countryman now known as Mulberry, and Kerricure was with her countryman who had joined the RAC, but some of the others had no choice but to hastily marry men in the colony. Under a later governor, newly arrived recaptive women had only three months to find themselves a husband before being summarily cut from the government's food allowance. They were shipped around for display in various villages where there might be willing men. They had to agree to marry any man who came looking, wrote one observer, painting a picture of them being "carried off to joy by liege lords, who assume their unasked consent." But in mid-1813 there was not even a three-month leeway. They had to find a man, find some other way to feed themselves, or starve.[35]

Twenty-seven-year-old Blango went to live with John Davidson. Sixteen-year-old Banga found a man named Harry Zuanill willing to take her as his wife. How these deals were struck, their longevity, much less the women's thoughts about their fate, is lost to history.

For the girls not yet initiated there were fewer choices still. One of those who came to know many of them well would later say that no one suffered as much in the slave trade as girls aged ten to twelve. There were not many girls rescued from Bostock and Mason in this category, but two who were, Yatta and Faylay, stayed behind in the pen, presumably taking safety with adults from their people who were there with them. Eleven-year-old "Jenny" went to live with Governor Maxwell, either at Belle Vue or at his stone house at the top of the wharf steps. The governor also took younger girls: nine-year-old Pessay and eight-year-olds Zo and Dee, while Reverend Wenzel took care of a nine-year-old girl named Fo, perhaps a countrywoman of Coree, and Lieutenant Dodds took Sewa, whose noted name was that of a river that flowed through the colony's hinterland.[36]

13

Leaving Africa

Robert Bostock and John McQueen were expecting a reprieve, some grand chastisement like that handed down to Samuel Samo, at which they could hang their heads and look suitably abashed. They could have been planning to go back to slave trading as Samo had done as soon as backs were turned, though with the destruction of their barracoons rebuilding would be harder.

Days blended together as they waited. Then, confounding hopes, they were told that they were to be re-embarked aboard HMS *Thais*. They were allowed the privilege of saying their last goodbyes, visiting people in Freetown to bid them farewell.[1]

Back aboard ship they were in new territory, their punishment going further than Samuel Samo's. They were being sent to England for their sentences to be actuated. The *Thais* was the first ship bound for home, and its crew was priming the vessel ready to return and rest from their tropical fevers. It was much needed, with more added to the sick list each day and some thrown to a watery grave.

Back in the pen where the rest of the recaptives were languishing, the British imperial project came to see which of the boys might be put to work. Some of the *Thais*'s men arrived, perhaps faintly recognizable. Following a long tradition of taking African boys as sailors, they were looking for likely lads for the crew. Rules and regulations made African seamen less common aboard Royal Naval vessels than merchantmen, but all sailors were used to their employment. No vessel in the antislavery squadron sailed without Africans. "Peter Romney, Black Boy" had died from a fall aboard HMS *Thais* near Cape Mesurado in May 1813. A Kru man named Ben Freeman had also recently been employed on the *Thais*, and its sailors had carved into an elephant tusk powder horn the endorsement: "Ben Freeman born at Krew Cetra Honest Man has sailed in HMS *Thais* from Sierra Leone to Ambriz to the Satisfaction of the officers."[2]

Manee, aged around eleven, with "twenty scars above his right elbow," got the signal. Sarwae, the Kru boy, was an obvious choice. Then two boys named Gurra, both about ten. Famoi and Nacoi, about nine years old. Jongo, Wossay, Coomah, and Gombo, perhaps a year younger. The *Thais*'s Lieutenant Watkins, who had led the party in the boats to attack Bostock and Mason's factory, took the small boy whom he had made his servant during the voyage, the eight-year-old boy he called Prince. The last picked was Sessay, the Mende boy stolen from his parents two years earlier and forced to walk for more than an entire moon to the sea. As at the original muster he had tried to hold back, had not been one of the more brazen boys pushing forward. His reticence had not brought invisibility. He was earmarked to go.

The enemies of Sierra Leone decried the summary enlistment of boys aboard naval ships as "slavery under another name," not least as they were apparently unpaid and given scantier rations. But others disagreed, believing naval service to be an excellent way for them to contribute to imperial progress. Edward Scobell wrote that the twelve boys taken aboard the *Thais* "might be useful on board HM ships." With "excellent materials afforded in the African nature" they would save English sailors from death in tropical climates. Afterward, Scobell believed, they would go home and tell their fellow Liberated Africans about the wonderfully munificent British.[3]

They were loaded back aboard the vessel that had brought them from their captivity. Again they lined up before a man standing making shapes in a book but this time they were told a new name. Now they were New Ben of Liverpool—soon shortened to Ben Liverpool—Black Andrew, Boy Jack, New Tom, Ben Williams, William Coff, George, William (Bill) Williams, Jack Bew, Sam Freeman, and Samuel Davis. Strangely, not even Prince, Lieutenant Watkins's servant, got to keep this name. The only boy who managed to register his own non-Anglo-Saxon name on the hallowed paper of a naval muster was the Kru boy Sarwae or Sarwae Tetee—a suffix meaning "son of"—who was listed as "Sarititee."[4]

Back at the pen other naval men sized up the boys who remained. Eleven more of them were selected. Paway and Boi, almost old enough for Poro initiation. Six eight-year-old boys, their names originally rendered as Wona, Ghema, Corree, Coona, Yorrow, and the two Mano boys named Paye. Mende boys Boi and Sessay. Fangha, a Kono child who had become separated from his twin brother and had sustained a large scar down his temple. His large eyes, swollen with fear, had already been written down as one of his distinguishing features.

Together this group of eleven more also retraced their steps to the harbor. They had been ashore a mere handful of days, and now they were marched aboard another of the huge water beasts. On its side was written, though it is unlikely any of them could read it, HMS *Albacore*.

On the *Albacore's* muster they were listed separately from the white crewmen as "black boys from the colony of Sierra Leone," but there were no longer eleven of them. What happened to the others—whether they were judged unsuitable and returned to the cattle pen, were assigned elsewhere, or if they passed away from hunger, diseases, and mistreatment—was not recorded. Those who stayed became Tom Handyman and John Cardigan (both thought to be eleven years old, these were possibly Paye and Boi, who had earlier been recorded as being older than the others); Roderick Random, John Junk, Jerry Pounce, James Marlin, Timothy Chipps, and William Warwick.

HMS *Thais* set sail on August 4, 1813, exactly one month after they had departed Cape Mesurado. As Bostock and McQueen sailed out of Freetown's "exquisitely beautiful" harbor they must have suspected what would turn out to be the truth. Neither of them would ever again set foot in Sierra Leone.[5]

They were listed among the *Thais's* supernumeraries aboard, given two-thirds of the sailors' allowance of food and grog. Scobell later said that he and his men treated them "with every possible indulgence." Needless to say, Bostock and McQueen did not agree. They complained bitterly of their "heavy irons." In their minds anything that made them felons was wrongheaded, reasoning that was bolstered when the *Thais* headed southward to visit Accra before sailing for England, and they passed Elmina and Cape Coast Castle. Bostock and McQueen can only have marveled at the change in morality seeing these monuments that lay bare the centuries when European powers traded in slaves with hardly a blush. Sailing from there on September 3 they saw several slaving vessels including the *Bom Caminho*, which would deliver 503 captives from Benin to the slave markets of Bahia, Brazil, and at Sao Tome the *Whydah*, an unapologetic Portuguese slaver. Their situation must have seemed all the more unjust.[6]

None of those taken aboard the *Thais* or the *Albacore* as cabin boys and servants ever had a chance to record what they made of these first days aboard ship. Many of them came from communities where waterways were crucial to trade and survival, where they had learned to handle canoes in a way far more skillful than their new crewmates from the time they were tiny children. But, other than Sarwae Tetee, they had no tradition of going out onto the big water and leaving sight of the land. Sarwae, the young Kru boy of around nine years old, was the only one who would have grown up hearing about this work from his father, grandfather, and uncles. He was the only one who had likely known that seafaring work was his destiny even before these strange events.[7]

We must hope for them that they found the *Albacore* and *Thais*'s crew to be as amenable as, half a century earlier, Olaudah Equiano had found the men with whom he shared his first berth. They "used me very kindly," Equiano wrote, "quite contrary to what I had seen of any white people before." It was this that made Equiano wonder whether "they were not all of the same disposition." Even then, the seamen tormented Olaudah, teasing them that they were about to kill him and eat him.[8]

The white men from the slave factory were aboard the vessel too, but they rarely saw them between the hauling, carrying, helping, cleaning. The boy known as Prince continued as servant to Lieutenant Watkins, but for the others there was the more wide-ranging role of being a "3rd class boy" in the British Navy. Hardtack riddled with worms, salted meat from an animal they cannot have identified, deafening noise, and terrible grime became their lives.

They arrived in the land of the white man in November. A handful of those liberated from Mason and Bostock's barracoon, including William Williams and Sam Freeman, were still aboard and found themselves part of the Royal Navy's vast operations, at the mercy of distant legislators to know where they would be sent next, whether they would stay aboard the *Thais* or whether, like many in their situation, they were simply to be paid off in this strange land. Then HMS *Albacore* also arrived from Sierra Leone, bringing with it a few more of those liberated with them. They too were assigned berths on other vessels as necessitated by the Royal Navy. Both William Warwick, aged ten, and Timothy Chipps who was even younger, were sent from the *Albacore* to HMS *Prince*, a veteran of the Battle of Trafalgar then reduced to a receiving ship, on Christmas Eve of 1813.[9]

These children found themselves in a world they cannot possibly have understood. Within the dockyard at Portsmouth were "immense store-houses, handsome residences for the principal officers, a spacious mansion for the Commissioner, an Academy of naval instruction, a neat chapel, mast-houses,

&c." There were two steam engines, vast piles of timber ready for use, a three-story rope house for making cables, a gilt statue of Richard III wearing a toga, and most fearful of all the Anchor Forge, where the conflagration of flames, smoke, and incessant din of smashing hammers created "Cyclopean scenes."[10]

Another boy found himself alone in the United Kingdom. For James Marlin, not yet ten years old, freedom was to be left alone on the docks in Portsmouth on December 21, 1813. What happened then to the poor, lost boy is not known. Among other, far more horrific problems, he must have been freezing. It was not until 1815 that a captain in the navy raised the alarm about the "extremely distressed state" of African sailors being dismissed from ships in Britain, and an agreement was reached to feed them until they could be returned to Africa. Likely, in this time of national emergency, Marlin was again swept up into the navy's grasp or taken perhaps into the merchant marine.[11]

Scobell was unsure what to do with Bostock and McQueen. He had been told that Governor Maxwell had sent on the paperwork from their trial, but it had not yet arrived. Along with two of their former captives, they were sent aboard HMS *Prince* at Spithead to be held prisoner.[12]

As 1813 turned to 1814, Robert Bostock and John McQueen were rowed into Portsmouth and handed over directly to the town jail, a newly opened building on Penny Street where modern ideas of incarceration were in use. No more of the "promiscuous throng" that had existed at the old jail, now prisoners could be "properly classed." Bostock and McQueen would not have to associate with the lower sort.[13]

Sessay stayed aboard HMS *Thais*. Captain Scobell was soon gone, replaced by Captain Henry Weir, but Sessay found a home for himself, growing up between decks. He was still there when they set sail a few months later "with secret orders": they were heading to Hellevoetsluis in the Netherlands to collect £450,000 in French coins and then sail for Bordeaux to take them to Wellington's forces.[14]

14

A Village
of Their Own

In the hills outside of Freetown beyond Leicester village a small footpath led higher up the slopes away from the town. Two hours' walk down that track laid a tiny place, more of a notion than a reality. Four years earlier Governor Thomas Perronet Thompson had laid the first stone and named it Kingston-in-Africa, but his high hopes for the place had not been realized. It was mostly abandoned and generally known as Hogbrook after the creek in its center that was a common drinking spot for pigs.[1]

Only a matter of weeks after their arrival in Sierra Leone, Kenneth Macaulay dispatched most of the *Thais* recaptives left behind by the army and navy recruiters to this remote place. It was so deserted that later they—noted in the records as "people brought by a slave ship from Mesurado," which was almost true—would be credited with having "formed" the village in July 1813.[2]

It seems possible that some of them were happy enough to be sent into the hills because Freetown offered few opportunities to feed themselves if they had failed to find a countryman or woman offering assistance. Most of the inhabitants of the tiny colony—the handful of original settlers who still remained, the Nova Scotians, and the Maroons—were struggling despite having been there for a decade or two. A few were very successful, but most had "nothing but the labour of their own hands" and were far from secure enough to build up any capital or begin enterprises that might employ a large workforce. A new customs house had been completed the previous year, but only the former factory slaves knew this type of business.[3]

There was nowhere in Freetown where it was easy to build homes and begin farming. Many of the recaptives came from rice-cultivating people and were highly skilled cultivators, but there were few places around town that they might attempt this, even in the new settlements being laid out around the edges of the original settlement. Some of the *Thais* recaptives taken as soldiers in the

RAC would soon live in these newly created places, but for others this was not an option. They could not simply claim land and were not given any either.[4]

They may also have felt unwelcome in town. The numbers of Liberated Africans was overwhelming the Nova Scotians and Maroons, who were resentful and scared of this growing influx. Two years earlier, a census of Freetown had listed 1,917 settlers—roughly split between the Nova Scotian and the Maroon communities—plus 22 white men, women, and children. Those numbers had risen in the two years since, but the number of babies born into these communities was nothing like the numbers of recaptives arriving. Dee, the last of those arriving from Mason and Bostock's aboard HMS *Thais*, was the 4,570th Liberated African to arrive in Freetown. Not all of them were in the city and many had died, but they still far outnumbered the other populations of the city added together.[5]

It was not simply a matter of numbers. There were many in the Nova Scotian and Maroon communities who were resentful of each other, never mind the growing influx of hungry, sick recaptives whose cultures were utterly different from their own. The newcomers posed a huge risk that they would unmoor the advances that both communities felt they were making. They were clinging by their fingertips to the tenets of "civility" as the British parochially judged these things. Each act that united everybody of African origin too closely was a step backward for the Maroons and the Nova Scotians. The Nova Scotians, at least according to Governor Ludlow, had been horrified when the Maroons had arrived in Freetown, because their "savage warlike appearance struck them with dismay." It would take generations for those feelings to completely heal, and just prior to the arrival of HMS *Thais* from Cape Mesurado Governor Maxwell had lamented "the invidious distinctions of Maroon and Settler."[6]

The newly arrived recaptives were much more threatening still. In each new batch were so many examples for any bigots (and there were plenty of them) who wanted to illustrate that Africans were uncivilized. The newly arrived recaptives were near naked whereas the British saw dress as central to polite society; they were considered mostly to be nonbelievers whereas Christianity was the pivot of civilization; they ate with their fingers whereas the British viewed this as one short step from anthropophagy. What had they done to contribute toward enlightenment and human progress, such as these things were judged in Europe? In January 1813, *Pride and Prejudice* was published in Europe, and in December Beethoven's Seventh Symphony in A premiered. It was these things that the British, and indeed the majority of Europeans and white Americans, saw as progress. For the Nova Scotians and Maroons, urgently clinging to modes of respectability brought with them from the New World, their status as vaguely "civilized" was far too precarious to withstand being associated too closely with these hungry, semi-clad illiterates. In the recaptives they saw writ large everything that they were accused of by the white world. Getting too close meant losing their status, and that was terrifying.

There were other reasons too that the original settlers felt aggrieved by the influx of recaptives. The new arrivals were starving, and because they were not provided for by the government, they begged for assistance and even grabbed what food they could. The Maroons and Nova Scotians, struggling themselves, accused the recaptives of "despoiling their land of its crops, cutting down their cinnamon and coffee-trees for firewood." They believed that the recaptives watched where they planted crops and then dug up the seeds at night and ate them. Some Maroons even left the colony, believing themselves at risk from the newcomers.[7]

These divisions would continue for decades. In the 1830s, British visitor Frederick Harrison Rankin observed, "the haughty black Settlers sneer at the new importation of savage Captives." The settlers derisorily calling them "Willyfoss [Wilberforce's] niggers," and there were reports of "guns . . . fired all night," thefts, the burning of property, destroying planted crops, and the savage beating of a Liberated African who married a settler. One old lady settler, apparently agitated that the Liberated Africans had their own hospital, said, "it is only my wonder dat we settlers do not rise up in one body and kill and slay."[8]

Nor was the British government willing to help the newly arriving recaptives to any great extent. It was not simply a matter of economy, though that was certainly an anxious issue given the wartime privations back home. In 1813 the Liberated Africans cost Britain £4039, an amount that was printed with dismay in newspapers. More than that, the type of evangelical uplifting that had provoked the abolitionist campaign did not include the British government assisting the recaptives in any material way. The abolitionists assumed that they would teach recaptives the glories of the Protestant work ethic and then the newly liberated would be fine. The abolitionists felt that Africa's biggest problem was that the slave trade had buoyed idleness. Able to sell enemies, passers-by, and other miscreants, the abolitionists supposed that Africans simply sat back luxuriating in their ill-gotten gains. "Indolence" was "a disease which it is the business of civilization to cure," they believed. They hoped to "excite . . . a spirit of industry among them," which would also have the happy advantage of "improv[ing] their morals." Handing out food and clothes, beyond a bare minimum to make them decent, would send out the wrong message entirely. It was in some ways an even more pitiless type of freedom than emancipation without the forty acres or the mule—albeit many of them were not owed life-times' worth of back pay—since the recaptives did not know the land and the language or have any family with them.[9]

In line with this philosophy, and clear now that the influx of recaptives was not about to end, the British had adopted a scheme to have the recaptives per-form agricultural labor in the hills around the city. It fit with British hopes that they would soon be able to support themselves and the long-standing concern that not enough Maroons or Nova Scotians had turned to productive agricul-ture. It also meant that they would be further away from the Nova Scotians and Maroons who resented them. Leicester, around three miles from Freetown, had already become a "neat village," with ground cleared for planting crops. Now Governor Maxwell offered seeds and simple tools to settlers prepared to go to "the west of Leicester Mountain." Placing the liberated into small, free villages was an idea that would be followed extensively in Jamaica when slavery came to an end.[10]

The only report by any of the newly liberated comes from the Bassa child who would take the name David Noah. Later he would recall, "after we had staid [sic] one month in Freetown, we were sent to Regent—then called Hog-brook." But they were not inanimate parcels to be sent around, and there was likely more decision making than that. It is not hard to imagine Boi, Dogua, and Fangha, the elders among them; Tamba, clearly making himself into a leader; the Kono twins named Fangha and others sitting together to discuss their options, summoning common words and ideas to make plans. A group of fourteen men, listed one after another on the arrivals list, all chose to move to the mountains, indicating that they were kinsmen who spoke the same language and had stood together in the cattle pen. Yarra was the first among another group of nine men who all chose to go to the hills, suggesting that perhaps he had a group of his country people following him, looking to him for advice and help because he could speak some of the white men's language and was one of their people.[11]

They needed to find a way to survive, and quickly. Their needs were urgent. Beyond the piece of cloth, the blanket that Macaulay gave to each of them, and the food they ate in the pen, only the most seriously sick or disabled recaptives were given any assistance. They were desperately traumatized, suffering from myriad illnesses and injuries from their horrific experiences. They understood very little about this new colony in which they found themselves. Three-fifths of them were children, who were at particular risk of being re-enslaved if they re-mained in Freetown, where the kidnapping of children remained a lucrative business for decades. Yet British authorities expected them to immediately start

fending for themselves. We cannot be too surprised if they looked to the villages
being settled in the hills, hoping for space to make the necessities of life for
themselves, the time and distance to regroup and find the space to negotiate
some middle path. For all the remoteness, for all that there was very little in the
way of infrastructure, it was the land beyond the town that offered this potential. There they could live away from the white men, who came to appropriate
them for all kinds of tasks they little understood, but close enough to Freetown
to not be troubled by slave raids.[12]

One hundred and eleven of those who arrived from Mason and Bostock's
barracoon at the St. Paul River took seeds, hoes, shovels, and rakes and set out
from the town to their new home. There were thirty-eight men and fifteen boys
aged between eleven and sixteen. Forty-six boys aged ten and younger were
also with them, presumably simply following men and women whose languages
and ways of life they could understand. They could help with the simpler tasks
but would also need care and teaching.

Only six adult women were with them, as well as six girls aged fourteen and
younger. There had been fewer of them to begin with, and now some had gone
to be wives to settlers. Again the women are less visible in the records, and it
is harder to imagine the choices they believed they had. Yet one of the girls,
seven-year-old Zenee or Zeenee, gives us some insight. Zenee was marked out
in the census of the colony that would soon be taken as being specifically under
Yarra's protection. It is only a glimpse of what was obviously a much bigger
story, but it seems that Yarra had found one of his country people, a small girl,
and had kept her with him. Those who had arrived aboard the *Thais* and *Princess Charlotte* were bound together now by experience, but their old loyalties to
kin and country remained strong.[13]

There were enough of them to begin again, though few records exist of these
earliest days when they must have been a group of traumatized, hungry, sick
people dropped onto a hillside above the town. They were met at the site of the
village by Macaulay and a man named as Captain William, but then left to
their own devices. The first necessity was to put up some kinds of rudimentary
shelters to protect themselves because the rains were beginning, which would
bring sickness as the rains did each year. They were "surrounded by nothing
but bushes." Fortunately wood and leaves for thatch were plentiful, as was mud
to fill the walls. They also had to begin the heavy work of clearing the ground
for planting. In the shorter term there was hunting to supplement the leaves,

fruits, and herbs that the women gathered. Their British rulers believed the land to "abound with lions, leopards, hyaenas, musk-cats, weasels, porcupines, wild hogs, squirrels, antelopes and various species of monkey," and for those that were real rather than imagined, they offered potential for bush meat.[14]

It was unbearably tough. They were a group of people who had little in the way of common language and worldviews, some of them were traditional enemies of others, and they arrived with nothing but diseases and suffering. David Noah would later remember that they had been there for more than a year before they had any help: "we lived in a wretched way," he wrote, "without hope in the world." He described the village as "a desert . . . surrounded by bushes. "It had been so bad, he reported, that they had wanted to leave but had been "forced" to stay. Whether they had literally been impelled or had few other options he did not make clear.[15]

They were joined at Hogbrook by a group of mainly Igbo captives, brought in on an illegal slave vessel. Forty of them had initially been sent into the army at Bunce Island but had been "discharged as intractable" and moved to Hogbrook. British authorities did not know, much less care, that these people were utterly different to those who arrived aboard the *Thais*. Igbo land was almost two thousand miles from that of the Mende and the others, a similar distance as London to Fes or St. Petersburg. The Igbo were from places far beyond those that knew of the Poro and Bundu societies.[16]

There were reports that the people argued, that the Igbo stole from the others, killing dogs and pigs. Although observers would later declare that "the greater number were not, indeed, sunk into a state of degradation as low as that of the Ebos," all of them were considered by British authorities to be savages, incapable of "proper" behavior. When put to work with an African who spoke some English operating as their overseer, he "exercised what appeared to him unavoidable severity." We cannot know, but it was quite possibly Tamba who, as well as speaking some English, had been raised to oversee other workers in a slave factory and guard captives awaiting sale and would likely have ideas of labor control different from the devout man who would later write of this event.[17]

And yet things did get better. The men from Bostock and Mason's were mostly Mende, Kono, Kissi, and Gbande, and standing side by the side as they constructed homes and made shelters, they began the process of learning each other's ways. They needed to develop common names for tools and household items. They heard each other's stories and traditions. They began to look after pigs and chickens.[18]

Others arrived in the colony who were far easier to understand than the Igbo. The *NS das Dolores*, which had purchased its captives at Gallinas, possibly even at Bostock and Mason's other factory, was brought in not long after their arrival. The next year the *Volador, Golondrina,* and *NS de Belle*, all of which had loaded their captives at Cape Mount, weighed anchor in the harbor. Which of these captives were sent to live in Hogbrook is not entirely clear, but they would certainly have heard of this village where other Windward Coast peoples were living. It was likely one of these vessels that delivered the man who would become William Davis, soon Tamba's closest colleague.[19]

Together they began to build a village. While in some communities one language predominated, in mixed villages like Hogbrook, settlers "speedily learn[ed] a broken kind of English as a common medium of intercourse." It was from such interactions that eventually, much later, they would all become Krio, making a culture and language by assimilating what they had carried with them and melding it onto that brought over the seas by the Nova Scotians and the Maroons.[20]

As agricultural tasks were gender specific among the ethnic groups from which they had come, the women must have struggled to cook and wash for so many men even before the land was cleared for them to plant and later harvest. But bending at the brook to wash their clothes against the stones was at last a glimpse of normality. After the unspeakable horrors of the coffle, the barracoon, the voyage to Freetown, and the cattle pen, here was something routine. Just as their brothers and sisters did on plantations across the Americas, they began learning words of other languages, and as the months spread ahead they developed common terms for things that spanned different language groups. They combed the hair and washed the clothes of all the children who were not theirs but for whom they now had some kind of responsibility. They began to plant seeds.

15

A Murder, and an Appeal
to the Prince Regent

As Robert Bostock and John McQueen began what turned into a lengthy wait in jail, they wrote home to their families in Liverpool and Glasgow telling of their terrible news. A dark cloud of infamy hung over them. Fourteen years transportation to the end of the world, far from their families, friends, and businesses, seemed to them absurdly harsh. Their crime, only a few years previously, had been no crime at all.

As the weeks became months they began to learn how greatly the nation they had left behind a decade before had changed. A sense that slave trading was immoral as well as illegal, that that it was so *un-British* as to be verging on traitorous, had taken firm hold. Abolitionism was such a force that it was changing the social landscape of Britain. It was now extolled as the height of mercy toward lesser people, a dazzling example of British virtue. Things might not have been going well in other spheres—war in Europe seemed interminable, the popular king was quite mad—but lo, it was majestic to be British.

Bostock and McQueen had missed a sea change. At a meeting in March 1808 to celebrate the first anniversary of their parliamentary victory, the "Friends to the Abolition of the Slave Trade" had begun with toasts to the king and queen, progressed smoothly through salutes to the British Army and those "hearts of oak," the Royal Navy, and then moved on to the speeches. Rising to address the crowd of five hundred, the Duke of Gloucester had not restricted himself to thanking their supporters but also fulsomely praised his own dedication to the cause. He was a better man, he intimated, and his nation an altogether greater one, because of its ending of the slave trade.[1]

By 1811, when Charles Mason had been sailing off aboard the *Dos Amigos* to Cuba, to stand against the slave trade had become as integral a part of the collective British persona as tea drinking. In August of that year, the *Times* of London had published an article claiming that British subjects were no longer

engaged in the slave trade, "or at least, comparatively, in a very trifling degree."
Just the dastardly Spaniards and Portuguese were continuing, the *Times*
claimed. The following year, when it was admitted that some British men were
still involved in the trade, Lord Brougham stated that they were "derogatory to
the interests and honour" of the nation. That same year, when Bostock and
McQueen were supplying the *Zaragozano* and numerous other ships with
human cargoes, a writer named W. Davis in Bath linked the abolition of the
slave trade to efforts to "civilize the Indian tribes," educate poor children and
introduce the bible across the tropics, bracketing them all as "Divine Providence," examples of British benevolence, and things for which future generations would owe a debt to his own.[2]

By the time Bostock and McQueen were firmly established at the St. Paul
River, back in their homeland it was believed that Britain's antislavery stance
was well on its way to saving the whole continent of Africa, perhaps the entire
world. The news that penalties for anybody caught slave trading illegally had
been extended was published from Chester to Cheltenham with the heading,
"we sincerely congratulate our countrymen and the world at large on this
signal example of Justice." That year, the British Parliament heard that the
continuation of the slave trade by other nations was the "great hinge on which
the future welfare of Africa turns." Meanwhile, the actions of the British and
Americans in outlawing the slave trade were reported by one "expert" to have
"tranquilised the Natives in some degree, and given them a turn for agriculture,"
while another opined that it had "rendered the Natives more industrious, and
less disposed to seek occasions for disputes."[3]

In the space of a few short years, while Bostock and McQueen had been
busy at their slave factories, opposition to the transatlantic slave trade had become a glowing mark of self-acclaim for Britons. Abolitionism was being transformed hastily into a way in which they would, in their own self-regarding
rhetoric at least, somehow "save" the world's second largest continent. It was
this, Bostock and McQueen learned, that they were pitted against, just as much
as the laws and statutes.[4]

By the end of 1813, the news filtered back from Cape Mesurado to Havana.
Slaving merchant Antonio Escoto learned that John Roach and the *Kitty* had
captured his vessel *Fénix*. Escoto was outraged and knew exactly to whom he
should turn. William Gould Page, a Briton based in Havana, had permission
from the Spanish consul to take to Lord Castlereagh appeals from slave traders

whose ships had been captured. The capture and sale of the *Fénix*, Page claimed, involved, "Grievances Nullities Inequities Injustices Injuries and Errors in the Proceedings."[5]

In the meantime, Escoto apparently made other, far less legal, plans to punish Roach and the rest of the *Kitty*'s crew. Six months after the destruction of Mason and Bostock's St. Paul business, Roach and his crew—including the rescued child Jack Phoenix/Za—spotted another slave vessel off Gallinas. In hopes of more prize money they planned an attack. But before they could fire the first shot there was a covert approach. Five men from the slaver rowed over to the *Kitty*, shouting that they wanted to join Roach's ship. They were told that the *Kitty* had a full crew but Roach was presumptuous. He allowed them aboard, believing that he would soon need extra men to sail the slaver to Freetown as his prize.[6]

For a few hours all seemed normal. But that evening, as Roach and his first and second mates sat down to dinner in the cabin, the five men made their move. Captain Roach, cutting into his food, only had time to yell "No!" as he jumped up to fight before he was stabbed "through the heart." The first mate, also stabbed, managed to run from the cabin trailing blood and was chased to the fore-rigging, where he threw himself overboard. The second mate, cut with a handspike, jumped from the port window. Flailing in the sea he found the *Kitty*'s Kru sailors already in the water, one dying from a shark attack.[7]

The first mate dragged himself back on deck, finding Roach breathing his last. By the time the second mate got back aboard, the attackers had control of the whole brig, and the crew were defeated. The ship was lost. An African woman cook named Venus Murray saw Captain Roach's body thrown overboard and his belongings plundered. The *Kitty*'s ivory, gold, cloth, "bottles of Lavender," bedding, dollars and doubloons, "six pigs . . . one Bull, one Sheep . . . six Goats, thirty ducks, three coops Fowls . . . a number of Parrots . . . a Crown bird," and a "walking stick which changed into a spy glass" were all looted.[8]

The following morning the victors put the *Kitty*'s surviving white sailors into a small boat with some bread and water. The Africans aboard were not released; with value as saleable merchandize, they became part of the prize. "Nineteen Kroomen [Kru men] coming to Sierra Leone," Venus Murray the cook, the infant son of a trader from Cape Coast Castle who was a passenger, and Jack Phoenix were all held aboard the ship.[9]

Venus Murray somehow escaped to tell her tale, but Za/Jack Phoenix was not heard from again. The British believed that Za and the others were taken to Havana and sold into slavery. The ship after which he had been named, the *Fénix* or *Phoenix*, was also sold at Havana. For Za, the respite from slavery had been only a few brief months. The child who first had been a token of trade, had been liberated, and had then become a sailor was condemned to the auction block.[10]

By the time that the legal protest instigated by Escoto and penned by Page reached London, John Roach was no longer alive to answer for his actions. It was left to his widow, Constance, to testify that he had been in a "very considerable Line of Business" and had owned a lot of property in Africa at the time of his death.[11]

In Portsmouth jail, as 1813 turned into 1814, Bostock and McQueen still waited and hoped for the king's mercy to be granted. The months ticked monotonously by with the aggravation of knowing that the costs of their incarceration were growing. News arrived of the events of the War of 1812, the conflict that had somehow damned them. They were in prison when the British burned Buffalo, New York, and were still there the following August when British troops occupied Washington, DC. Rumors in February that Napoleon was dead were later proven to be a hoax, and more news from the wars on the continent flooded in. They were there for so long that they became friendly with their jailer, even getting him to help shape their pleas for clemency. Bostock's mother and McQueen's father wrote in their children's favor, begging that they be given mercy.[12]

Eventually Bostock and McQueen decided to go right to the top. They wrote to the prince regent, who had taken over from his increasingly mad father George III under the Regency Act of 1811. They wrote of their "broken constitutions" after their years in Africa and how they were "sinking under the heavy sentence which has been passed upon them." They had, they lamented, been, "Dragged from Africa as Felons" but obviously having quickly deduced how things had altered in their absence, argued that the example set them by Britain, "this most humane, great and united Kingdom," had already been "most beneficial." They lurched between toadying *mea culpa* and a sense of furious entitlement to forgiveness as if somewhere in the bonds of the two might be their salvation.

Unclear if they were being insulted racially or in a class-based manner, they insinuated both. The way that they had been shipped to Britain aboard the *Thais* had been "disgraceful," they wrote, since they had been made to wear "heavy irons." Without irony, they claimed that this was surely "insulting to the munificence of Britain," a country whose "Philanthropy and Protection so powerfully comforts the humble African." "Confined with the Dregs of Society with Felons of the worst description," in Portsmouth jail, they signed off with a hyperbolic flourish: "death will be a welcome visitor."[13]

Their hopes for a pardon remained high as other convict transports set sail for Australia, and they were not ordered aboard. Two sailed in January, another in March, and then a forth during August. Still they remained in jail. Then their luck ran out. They were sent to the *Retribution* hulk and in October 1814 loaded onto the transport *Indefatigable*. Convicts were regularly sung aboard convict ships, sent away with chains clanking to the ditties and ballads of defiance. It was the only way that many, usually poor people who had committed paltry thefts of food and clothing, could endure being sent away from their family and friends. But there was no such recourse to impudence for men like Bostock and McQueen. They can only have been mortified.[14]

Their new shipmates were 198 other convicts, the youngest three only thirteen years old and another two aged fourteen. They were mostly petty thieves (among their collective loot: "custard cups," a cruet set, a bed headboard, a pair of sugar tongs, some pantaloons, and a teapot). There were also three men caught in possession of forged bank notes, two highwaymen, eight soldiers court-martialed for desertion, and a man who had received stolen goods in the form of three asses belonging to Lord Ellenborough.[15]

As they stepped aboard it was Bostock's and McQueen's social class, rather than the nature of their crime, which set them apart. Bostock considered himself a gentleman, and McQueen was certainly aspiring to middling status. Their crime might, to modern eyes, have been far more serious than that of the three teenage boys aboard who had together stolen one solitary handkerchief, but that was certainly not the way that they viewed such things. The British class system being what it was, Bostock, and probably McQueen, considered themselves gentlemen wrongly done by, whereas the three handkerchief thieves were riffraff, nuisances to the honest men of the kingdom like themselves.[16]

They waited and hoped, growing ever more indignant, desperate for a last minute reprieve. It was not to be. They sailed in convoy with the *Sydney Packet*, heading out across the Atlantic to catch fair winds rather than sailing down past their old home. They were, as it turned out, the only slave traders who would make the long journey to Australia in captivity.[17]

16

Experiments in Civilization and Liberty

In Hogbrook, homes were strengthened with extra wood nailed across, more thatch heaped atop to better protect those inside. Better places to hunt meat were found and new sources of fruit located. Clouds grouped and darkened over the hills and the rains fell, water cascading down the laterite spindle pathways that ran through their mountain valley. More recaptives arrived in the colony and were sent to join them, skeletons shocked through with the worst of human experience. Those who had arrived earlier had so little, and their homes were "in a rather miserable condition," but they opened their doors to the newcomers. Then, as the rusty trails between their homes dried into parched earth, the first crops they had planted began to reap returns.[1]

Just as they were digging in, changes were coming from outside to ease their lot. When they had been in the colony for a year Governor Maxwell resigned and left for a quieter post in Dominica. After some uncertainty, Charles MacCarthy was installed permanently as his replacement. A Catholic of Jacobin heritage, son of a Frenchman and an Irishwoman (MacCarthy was his mother's name), MacCarthy was a very different man to those who had gone before.[2]

He was shocked by the state of the Liberated Africans. Determined to do better, he instituted a plan that once recaptives had been declared free they would be provided with basic household items and, for the men, tools to grow foodstuffs. They would also be given daily provisions of rice, beef, and vegetables until they could afford their own. For those who arrived after 1814 things would not be as desperate materially as they had been for the men and women aboard the *Thais* and *Princess Charlotte*. Yet MacCarthy's distress at the state of most of the Liberated Africans puts into perspective the scale of the achievements of those in Hogbrook, those led by the men from Bostock and Mason's business. Somehow, with little more than togetherness and sweat, and with virtually no help, most of them were surviving, recouping, and rebuilding.[3]

MacCarthy's leadership provided opportunity to build on this start. Fields were planted with rice and cassava. The road to Hogbrook from Leicester was said by visitors to be a marvel to behold, with vast cultivations lining the sides of the still-rugged path. In this new world, the people of the *Thais* and *Princess Charlotte* were holding their own.[4]

Yet their lives would not be entirely their own, at least not within the world-view of the British Empire. Praises began to be lavished on Hogbrook, but they reveal as much about the hopes and expectations of the British as the lives and achievements of the Liberated Africans. In 1815 it was said that "the conduct of the settlers is said to differ very little from the generality of English Villagers," an accolade that was considered to be the highest praise. The recaptives exhibited "every shade of improvement," it was claimed.[5]

"Improvement" meant much more than simply planting crops and providing for themselves. As much as Tamba, Yarra, the twins named Fangha, and all the rest doubtless felt they were struggling to survive, they were actually test cases. Sierra Leone had always been the petri dish of free labor, but after the first recaptives landed in 1808 expectations were heightened. Liberated Africans were human experiments in the battle between slavery and free labor, between Africans as beasts of burden or as brothers. If they could prove themselves industrious without slavery, on what grounds would Caribbean planters argue that enslavement should continue ad infinitum?

"Improvement" also meant becoming more refined, more civilized, all together more British. Achieving this was a central pillar of the abolitionist campaign since it would crush many of the pro-slavery arguments and simultaneously fit in with their brand of Evangelicalism. But, only a decade past the final shockwaves of the Haitian Revolution, this was a tall order. Images of white women and children being murdered by rampaging gangs of blood-thirsty African assassins remained far more in the public conscience than any notions of Africans in suits and ties reading the Bible.[6]

To the African Institution, Africans were as capable as anybody else of achieving progress and enlightenment, given the right guidance and succor from the more advanced peoples of the earth, by which of course they meant those of European origin. Africans were redeemable given the right influences and training; they might currently be lesser, but they were not inherently so, merely less fortunate in their upbringings, teachings, and surroundings. This idea was entirely at odds with that of most planters in the Caribbean, for whom Africans' debasement was inherent and insurmountable. To the pro-slavery faction, anybody of African origin could never ascend to the high standards of intellect, culture, and morality displayed by those of European heritage.

Meeting back in 1807, just as they were winning the campaign against the slave trade, the Committee of the African Institution in London had spent a long time arguing about the posited negative qualities of black men and women. They concluded that some of these were simply figments of planters' imaginations. Those that they thought had some basis in fact, such as Africans' "indolence," were "by no means an incurable defect." They just needed to be shown the right way.[7]

A few months after the London meeting, Governor Ludlam noted that the abolition of the slave trade would not "prevent the Africans from still remaining a savage and uncivilized people." Nevertheless, he hoped that without the slave trade, they would now "exert themselves, in the way of regular industry." If British authorities could "introduce the blessings of a civilized society among a society sunk in ignorance and barbarism," then the recaptives might become "civilized." In 1810, the directors of the African Institution had written: "Africans are as susceptible of intellectual and moral culture as the natives of any other quarter of the globe." It was a view far ahead of its time, if also a long way from acknowledging alternative notions of intellect or morality.[8]

One of the central ways in which such improvement was to be activated was through teaching Africans, presumed wildly slothful, the protestant work ethic. For those not enlisted into the army or navy, it was felt that an appropriate sort of regular labor was agricultural production. This was in part because the colony needed not only to feed its people but also to prove itself financially viable in order to counter pro-slavery arguments that the affluent Caribbean islands would fall into devastation without an enslaved workforce. Agricultural exports that could contribute to the imperial juggernaut would help immensely.

Schools in Sierra Leone had long taught not only reading and writing but also agricultural skills. Long periods of the African Institution's meetings were taken up in the earliest years, before they truly acknowledged the scale of the illegal slave trade, with discussions of crops and how best to plant them in African soils. All manner of produce was suggested. In 1809, the African Institution had even established a system of rewards of fifty guineas each for the first people importing crops such as cotton, coffee, indigo, and rice from Sierra Leone into Britain. The plan was abandoned after the only winners were the firm of Anderson of Philpot Lane, the slave traders from Bunce Island.[9]

So the rice and cassava being cultivated up at Hogbrook, those fields laid out by Bostock and Mason's former captives as a means of survival, became something much more. Tamba, Yarra, the Kono twins named Fangha, and all the others thought that they were feeding themselves and making new connections. To the British abolitionists they were also disproving centuries of ingrained misinformation and bigotry. Hogbrook was taking the first steps being a model village. At the head were Tamba and others from Bostock and Mason's.

With the Liberated Africans clearing and cultivating the land, the other pillar of the civilization plan began. The word of the Lord had to be sown. Governor MacCarthy put education throughout the tiny colony in the hands of the Church Missionary Society (CMS), which had been founded in 1799 by William Wilberforce and other prominent abolitionists. They were ideally suited to taking over Sierra Leone's education, not only to save the government a great deal of money, but also because education was believed to comprise not just letters and numbers but also morality, civility, and the Bible. The CMS received its first land grant on the side of Leicester Mountain and began a school.[10]

Hogbrook got a schoolteacher, Thomas Hirst, who, in the absence of any other Europeans around, also acted as superintendent of the Liberated Africans. There was a hospital, which had ten sick boys in 1815. Hirst called meetings to talk of God. The young Bassa boy who had escaped from John Sterling Mill's barracoon was one of those to whom Hirst tried to teach the Lord's Prayer. A chapel and a schoolroom were planned. Even Sierra Leone's enemies would soon agree that "one very excellent settlement has been made at the Hogbrook."[11]

More missionaries flooded into the colony, and all manner of improvements were witnessed among this most experimental flock. They began to form the Krio language as a way to communicate and to learn this new religion. As Christopher Fyfe wrote, "Amid the Babel of tongues English became not only a lingua franca but a Pentecostal interpreter."[12]

As early at 1814 Liberated Africans were even perceived to "express gratitude for their mercies" and "lament the misery and degradation of their African brethren." This was a major development as far as their rulers were concerned, since British visitors only three years earlier had claimed that "many of these men are insensible of the services that have been done to them." They were not sufficiently aware of their "obligation" to those who "snatched them from the horrid grasp of their tyrants." Now the Africans were at last considered to be showing more of the required appreciation.[13]

17

Prisoners
in New South Wales

It is such an intriguing image to draw: two men who had sold tens of thousands of Africans now themselves below decks, ironware around their ankles. Whether Bostock and McQueen sensed the reparative, Old Testament-style appropriateness in their punishment we cannot know, but many of their contemporaries saw the links. Analogies were drawn relatively often between Britain's mode of criminal punishment and the slave trade. In earlier times, British slave traders had fought the abolitionist movement by citing convict transportation as a parallel, arguing that if Britain deemed it acceptable to send its criminals across the seas then it should be legal for Africans to send captives, some of whom were surely convicted of crimes, over the Atlantic. A few years after Bostock and McQueen's banishment the abolitionists would turn that contention on its head, hoping that the "celestial ray" of benevolence that had fought the slave trade would now be cast on convict transports.[1]

In truth, the analogies were more in the perception than the detail. Bostock and McQueen's voyage was very much longer than the transatlantic Middle Passage, yet only two of the two hundred convicts aboard the *Indefatigable* died. This was nothing approaching the 10–20 percent mortality rates on slave ships. The convicts survived because conditions were far better with less confinement, more air, better food, and medical care. A slave vessel the size of the *Indefatigable*, even allowing for the troops that slavers did not carry, would have packed aboard somewhere in excess of a thousand Africans during the years of the illegal slaving trade, five times the number of convicts aboard the *Indefatigable*. In fact, if convict transportation seeped too close to slavery, it caused an outcry. Not long before the *Indefatigable* sailed, another transport used slave shackles on some of the convicts aboard, provoking uproar.[2]

Ultimately, the difference between convict transportation and the transatlantic slave trade cannot be found in statistics. The real gulf was in the realms of human perception and sentiment. For captive Africans their voyage was into an unfathomable, gaping unknown. Whether they survived or not, and what they would be if they did survive, was terrifyingly unclear. By contrast, in the 1810s the British and Irish knew quite a lot about the penal colony at New South Wales. They sang ditties about it. Transportation was almost always a permanent departure from family and friends, which was utterly traumatic, but there were many who hid their distress in a show of defiance toward the society that was throwing them out. It sometimes became a ghoulish festival of counter-culture, "a party of pleasure," since it was their only chance to mock a society that was sending them away for what were mostly very petty crimes.[3]

So while slaves looked at sailors and wondered if they were cannibals about to eat them alive, convict men (more than a few of whom had been seafarers) tried to befriend them. Many convict women began flirting madly. The convicts' actions were born of desperation certainly: these were survival tactics of the powerless. Nevertheless, they molded the rules of engagement in a way that most African captives simply could not.[4]

If Bostock and McQueen wanted to compare firsthand their fate with that of those they had sold into bondage—and likely no such thing, other than as a rhetorical device, would ever have crossed their minds—they had a chance when the *Indefatigable* made an unscheduled five-week stop at Rio de Janeiro, home to around twelve thousand slaves of African origin. Arriving in Rio's resplendent harbor, they sailed past Ilha das Cobras with its slave prison and then passed the customhouse with newly arrived slave ships reeking and creaking alongside. An American visitor a few years later wrote that the water of Rio's harbor was "covered with the bodies of blacks" who, he believed, had thrown themselves overboard from arriving slave ships. When the tide went out, their drifting bodies washed up "on the strand."[5]

On Rio's docks, the two former slave traders could see enslaved stevedores milling around loading and unloading cargo. Slave canoemen rowed sick convicts to shore. Enslaved porters delivered food and water casks to the ship. Ashore they may have seen the slave warehouses at Valongo, public pillories for whipping slaves set alongside the imposing cathedrals in elegant squares, and African slaves doing every kind of labor conceivable. In this city, wrote one visitor, slaves "take the place of horses." There were so many enslaved Africans on the streets of Rio that arriving foreigners sometimes thought themselves in Africa.[6]

Leaving Rio, the *Indefatigable* recrossed the Atlantic, sailing around the Cape of Good Hope and across the Roaring Forties where the wind sent the vessel flying. Finally they reached the Pacific Ocean and then steered northward. Almost five months after leaving England, they sailed through the heads into

Sydney from the North Shore, ca. 1817. Joseph Lycett, courtesy of the Mitchell Library, State Library of New South Wales.

Sydney's harbor, famously considered by the earliest colonizers from Britain to be "the finest and most extensive harbour in the universe, and at the same time the most secure, being safe from all the winds that blow."[7]

We know nothing of Bostock's and McQueen's first impressions of the town perched besides the grandeur of the coves and inlets, but for many convicts it was relief. Appearing at long last in the distance, Sydney looked "a place so very like my own native home," wrote one convict upon arrival. Further reassurance paddled up as higgledy-piggledy craft swarmed alongside, settlers coming aboard armed with welcomes, fruit, and invitations. Aboriginal elders in their *nowies* arrived to greet them too, and if others aboard were unsure of what to make of such an act, it was not the first time Bostock and McQueen had come face to face with a culture not their own.[8]

The *Indefatigable*'s passengers finally set foot ashore at Sydney Cove in late April 1815. They were at what is today Circular Quay, where the coastline warps between the Sydney Opera House and the southern end of the Harbour Bridge. It was almost two years after the slave ship *Fénix* had arrived at their factory in Africa, bringing the wrath of the Royal Navy in its wake.

The *Sydney Gazette* wrote that the *Indefatigable*'s prisoners looked healthy and "of particularly clean appearance." There was perhaps something of an echo of a slave ship's arrival in the *Gazette*'s comment, the prisoners' potential for labor being the real, if tacit, point of interest. But such echoes were extremely faint. While in the seventeenth century there had been some overlap in the status of African slaves and British and Irish convicts in the Caribbean, this had waned long before with the rise of racial stratification. Before the American Revolution there had been a racial divide that separated black slaves from white convicts, and in New South Wales there was not even a sale of convicts' labor as there had been in the American colonies.[9]

The *Indefatigable*'s convicts were allotted as private servants to existing settlers or sent to labor on the colony's public works. Many went to the outlying settlements at Windsor, Parramatta, and Liverpool, but Bostock and McQueen remained in town. They were about to discover that things would not turn out nearly so badly as they must have feared.[10]

When Bostock and McQueen arrived in 1815, Sydney was still figuring itself out. It had been founded as a convict colony, a city of damned outcasts, and was in fact Sierra Leone's twin, the two colonies having been started at the same time. But it was also Sierra Leone's inverse: a nonfree white colony (the Indigenous people were not considered) in contrast to the free black community in Africa. In 1787, as ships had bobbed in the harbor being victualed for both settlements, it had seemed very clear to black men aboard the First Fleet destined for the South Seas that Sierra Leone was the better option.[11]

There had been hard times, but by 1815 Sydney was more than a vast prison camp. It was moving far ahead of its supposedly more advantaged African coeval. While Sierra Leone was struggling, Sydney was on the cusp of being an extraordinary success story.

The fillip was deliberate policy, coming not from London but instigated by Governor Lachlan Macquarie. Launching a grand scheme of stately buildings and decorous parkways, the fifty-four-year-old set about reinvigorating the colony. He dreamed of making Sydney into an imposing city of shipping and commerce, modeled on the opulent grandeur he had witnessed during an earlier posting at Bengal.

Macquarie modeled this dream using convicts and former convicts. In the process he created many prospects and lucky breaks for criminals whom Britain had condemned to suffer. Macquarie, himself a self-made man, determined to allow New South Welshmen to make their own fortunes as best they could. He became famously generous with pardons.[12]

The opportunities Macquarie offered to convicts were so controversial that in 1819 Britain sent out Commissioner John Thomas Bigge to investigate what on earth was going on. A former chief justice of Trinidad, Bigge was horrified by what he found: lax rule and little of the intensive agriculture he had seen slaves performing in the Caribbean. Before Bigge's arrival, however, New South Wales was the ideal environment for convicted men to start again.[13]

Macquarie's vision of building the city on seaborne trade meant that Bostock and McQueen's expertise was immediately marketable. Everything in the small colony revolved around business. It can only have been a welcome sign to Bostock, who had grown up around the vast docks and trading offices of Liverpool. The Commissariat, the agent for government supplies, remained the largest trader in the colony, but the private sector was growing rapidly. There was huge demand for imported goods, even luxury items that would have been rare treats in Britain. Rumor had it that in Sydney the most ignorant man could earn "a few thousand" simply by "merchandising." The deputy commissary flounced around town sporting a feather in his hat.[14]

If one could overlook the illicit character of the "goods" they had previously bought and sold, Bostock and McQueen were just the type of men that Sydney needed. Fortunately for the two former slave traders, overlooking previous transgressions was something at which Sydney excelled. In fact, many of the colony's elite had arrived in chains. The wealthiest man in Sydney was Simeon Lord, a thief turned shipbuilder, sealer, auctioneer, and entrepreneur. Samuel Terry, known as "the Rothschild of Botany Bay," was a former stocking thief. James Underwood, once sentenced at Maidstone, had become a very wealthy boatbuilder, sealing merchant, the owner of St George Coffee Lounge and a Regency-style house.[15]

Fresh off the *Indefatigable*, Bostock and McQueen should have been given out as servants to a free colonist or employed on Macquarie's growing list of public works. Perhaps they were in the short term, but no records survive of their immediate fate. In fact, their exact status, and even how far their bondage extended, was an intriguingly blurred issue. Even the idea that convicts were attainted had waned, and neither those who arranged their transport nor their employer had any property rights over them. Into the 1820s, newspapers in the colony debated the issue of transportation: was bonded labor part of the deal, or was the sentence simply banishment? This was largely a notional argument for those distributed as servant laborers to colonists, but there were checks and balances and recourse to complaint for anybody treated excessively badly. The argument that New South Wales was a slave society seems, at least from a point of view looking out to sea from Cape Mesurado over the Atlantic to Cuba, to be stretching a point.[16]

Far away in the Atlantic, while his former captives, his business partner, and their assistant had all been forced to make new lives for themselves, Charles Mason was busy working in the slave trade. He had lost one of his factories but had other ventures ongoing, including the Gallinas operation and his business in Cuba.

On November 13, 1815, Charles Mason—or Masson/Massón as he was sometimes called in Cuba—again took to the seas. He had purchased a former privateer called *Commodore Perry* and refitted it as a slaving vessel called *Rosa*. Following the usual path, they sailed to Cuba and installed a Spanish-Cuban captain, Bartolomeo Mestre, and papers suggesting a Cuban origin. They carried rum, tobacco, and gunpowder to trade for slaves in Gallinas.[17]

After a halt in Matanzas to wait out a storm, they made a quick crossing of the Atlantic. On January 4, 1816, Charles Mason was back at his old factory. Soon he had 277 slaves aboard the *Rosa*, and they were ready to set off on the adrenalin-fueled sprint back to Cuba. It was all or nothing, great wealth if they escaped the patrols or utter disaster if they were captured.

Six hours later, Mason and the crew realized to their dismay that an English schooner, the *Mary*, had spotted them. It was an unbearable moment, described colorfully by a slave trader the following decade: "I cannot describe the fretful anxiety which vexes the mind under such circumstances. Slaves below; a blazing sun above; the boiling sea beneath; a withering air around; decks piled with materials of death; escape unlikely; a phantom in chase behind; uncertainty everywhere; and, within your skull, a feverish mind, harassed by doubt and re-sponsibility, yet almost craving for any act of desperation that will remove the spell. It is a living night-mare [*sic*], from which the soul pants to be free." The *Rosa*'s crew raised Portuguese colors in a desperate attempt to stop the *Mary* attacking, but the effect was only temporary. The *Mary*'s crew launched a barrage of fire, killing four of the *Rosa*'s men.[18]

The *Rosa* was sizeable for an illegal slave vessel and was mounting twenty guns. It was not beaten, but it struck its ensign as if in surrender. The *Mary* dis-patched a boarding party. As soon as it was within range the *Rosa*'s crew fired at the boats.

Exasperated and furious, the *Mary*'s crew stood off. But the next morning they again sighted the *Rosa* and now also HMS *Bann*, which they signaled for help. The *Rosa* repeated the trick, fooling the *Bann*'s crew into thinking all was calm enough for them to send a lieutenant to investigate. The *Rosa*'s guns again opened fire as the boat approached. HMS *Bann* and the *Mary* lost patience and unloaded their weapons onto the *Rosa*. A lucky strike sent a twelve-pound shot right through the *Rosa*'s mainmast.[19]

The world of illegal slave trading around Gallinas and Mesurado was a small one. The slave traders all knew each other. Often their pursuers were on first-name terms with them too. Given the scale of devastation and repercussions that their actions have wreaked, it is easy to imagine a huge web of men, but actually in any narrow time period the number of people slave trading between, say, Havana, the Windward Coast, and the United States was small. Unpicking their networks turns up the same names again and again. The British naval patrol was only too aware of whom HMS *Bann* had finally caught. *The Twelfth Report of the Directors of the African Institution* wrote that a slave ship named *Rose* [*sic*] had been captured, and aboard was an old slave trader from Mesurado. The Americans, relying on an account from Sierra Leone given to Viscount Castlereagh, reported that the *Rosa* was "fitted out and manned with Americans" and that one of the captured had been once "partner of Boostock [*sic*] at Mesurado."[20]

By the time it arrived in Freetown nine days later, the captured *Rosa* had only 262 slaves aboard, another sixteen having died. The survivors were taken to the Liberated African yard, where they were added to the growing numbers of recaptives in the colony.

The *Rosa*'s crew, excepting the injured boatswain, took accommodation in Freetown. Mason wandered around the town where some of his former captives were living, alongside a few of his former slaves that he knew much better, like Tamba. Then reports swirled that the *Rosa*'s men were planning a daring escape, stealing their vessel back and making off across the ocean. It must have been terrifying for Tamba and the others in Hogbrook, for surely they feared that he was planning on taking them if he fled illegally with his vessel.

Taking no chances, authorities put the *Rosa*'s men in jail. They remained there on February 3 when the vessel was condemned for illegal slave trading. The ship was purchased by the government and pressed into service to relieve the ailing *Princess Charlotte*, the vessel that had helped raid Bostock and Mason's factory in 1813.

Two and half years after his former partner Robert Bostock was incarcerated there, Charles Mason found himself in Freetown's jail. But his situation was not nearly as dire as Bostock's had been. Since at least 1810, Mason had claimed to be an American, and most people around the region believed him to be a citizen of the United States. This was an era in which the divide between these nationalities was still in some dispute, and the British held that anybody born in Great Britain was incontrovertibly British, regardless of what citizenship they claimed. But in this case most of those involved seemed to be in little doubt that Mason was American. After the War of 1812, Britain no longer pursued Americans for slave trading.[21]

So although the capture and seizure of the *Rosa* and its captives was another financial blow, Mason's freedom was not in jeopardy in the way that Bostock's and McQueen's had been. Rather than being hauled up before Freetown's court, Charles Mason was only tangentially involved in the case over the *Rosa*. Authorities were unsure how to divide up the prize money between the crews of the *Mary* and the *Bann*, so Charles Mason and Bartolomeo Mestre appeared in court to state which vessel they considered their captors.[22]

There were other captured slave ships alongside the *Rosa* in Freetown harbor: the *Guadeloupe*, the *Rayo*, the *Eugenie*, and the *Augustina*, all along with their crews. Freetown's authorities could not endlessly hold so many disaffected sailors, so the local authorities released one small vessel, the *Bella Maria* of Cadiz, to carry some of them back to Havana. Charles Mason was free to go, once more sliding back to the world of illicit slave trading. He embarked on the *Bella Maria* along with twenty-one other Americans and Spaniards/Cubans, including six others from the *Rosa*'s crew as well as men from the *Guadeloupe*, *Rayo*, *Eugenie*, and *Augustina*.[23]

They set out in April. It should have been a straightforward trip westward to home, but six weeks out and with the shoals of the Bahamas and Turks and Caicos nearly in sight, the weather started to look ominous. The clouds darkened and waves deepened as the storm closed in. Suddenly concerns about returning to Havana without slaves and without money must have seemed trivial. Returning to Havana at all was the best they could hope for. Then, at the worst possible moment, the pilot made a fatal mistake. Two of the sails were furled, "completely capsizing the ship."

The ship started to break up, the sea bulging over the decks. Five men abandoned ship. The former captains of the *Eugenie* and *Rayo*, the third pilot of the *Augustina*, and two American sailors reached a small boat and cast off. For Mason and the rest there can only have been dread, the seas swallowing the vessel before they could reach the safety of the small boats.

The five men who had managed to get away did not have to wait long for salvation. The *Bella Maria* was sinking around thirty leagues from Abaco in the Bahamas, and the survivors were drifting in a busy shipping channel. The *Fame* from Providence, Rhode Island, bound to Havana, spotted them. It was all the rescued men could do to tell their story. The *Fame* made the wreck as quickly as possible, but these efforts were in vain. The weather was too rough, and darkness approached. The rest of the men were lost.

Among the roll call of the dead was Charles Mason. Not quite three years after the loss of his slaving enterprise on the banks of the St Paul's River, Charles Mason was gone.[24]

18

Christianity
at Hogbrook

Jolted awake, Tamba realized that in a trancelike state he had climbed from his bed and was on his knees. Clinging to the bedframe like a shield, his cheeks were streaming with tears that he had no memory of crying. He had endured a nightmare of "a man coming into his cottage and making in the middle of it a large fire." The malevolent man had then dragged two people into the home, then "he bound . . . [them] in chains and put them into the fire." The prisoners had not burned quickly, forcing Tamba to watch while they were "howling with anguish," the fire so hot that the nails fell from their fingers and toes. Next the murderer came for Tamba and tried "to thrust him also into the fire." Fortunately another man intervened at the last moment, arguing, "Let him alone; he belongs to me." It had launched Tamba from his bed, seeking sanctuary.[1]

The dream had been so intense, so lacerating to Tamba's psyche, that even realizing that the events were not real—or at least not happening then—and that he was safe at home in Hogbrook did not soothe him. His wooden home was better made than some, but still the cool mountain air of the night puffed through the planks as he stayed on his knees, bereft. As morning dawned he was still disturbed by what he had seen in the dark corners of his mind.

Nobody can see into another man's dreams, much less across centuries and cultures, but today, should Tamba have experienced such night terrors, he would surely be evaluated for post-traumatic stress disorder. It is impossible not to raise the question of whether Tamba was reliving the horrors of his past, the events of his liberation in 1813 when Bostock and Mason's Cape Mesurado barracoon had burned down with people still inside.

It seems highly likely that Tamba met with Charles Mason in late 1816, or at least heard of his old master's appearance in town, and that this in some way proved to be the catalyst for his night terrors. By the time Mason was in Freetown promenading around the streets, Tamba had married and was Hogbrook's butcher. Tamba and his wife, like many others in Hogbrook, walked frequently, even daily, down to Freetown, setting up open-air markets around the capital to sell their produce. Freetown was a tiny place where news of fresh arrivals spread quickly, and those caught aboard illegal slave ships were spicy gossip. It seems impossible that they would not have heard that Charles Mason was in town, and while many who had been held captive in his barracoons would not have known his name, Tamba certainly did. A new fear could well have taken hold since Mason's presence raised the specter of re-enslavement, that Tamba would be compelled to return to his earlier life, especially after the rumors that Mason was going to steal his ship away from under the nose of British authorities.[2]

None of these causes were really explored at the time: psychology as a separate field of study was still decades away. The devout European who recorded the event, William Augustine Bernard Johnson, saw the dream as a typical vision of hellfire, a representation of what Satan had in mind for nonbelievers. Yet even Johnson intimated that there were links between this most distressing nightmare and Tamba's former life, that his visualization of hellfire was all the more striking because of what he had seen and done. Tamba was "like the jailer of old," Johnson wrote, while another narrator changed this to "like the Philippian jailer." Clearly they saw links between the biblical jailer at Philippi who despaired when his prisoners escaped during an earthquake and Tamba, who had lost half of the prisoners he was charged with keeping when HMS *Thais* attacked.[3]

The morning after the nightmare it was Johnson from whom Tamba sought counsel and comfort. Johnson, a former London sugar refiner born in Germany, and his wife had arrived in Sierra Leone the previous year, with Johnson taking over from Thomas Hirst as Hogbrook's schoolteacher. Where Hirst had struggled with illness and a flock utterly uninterested in his teachings, Johnson's style and passion were having more of an effect. Though still in his twenties, he was becoming their guide, the conductor of a Liberated African ensemble. The Reverend Johnson, as he was soon ordained, was their leader.[4]

When Johnson took the post at Hogbrook, it was considered among the most challenging and deadly of all in the CMS's realm. All of West Africa was believed to be "pre-eminently reigned over by the Evil One," but within that, Hogbrook was a place where "mingle wickedness, woe, and want," its people "the degraded race of Ham." Despite these warnings, when Johnson arrived he was aghast. "Natives of twenty two different nations" were living crowded into the hillside huts, he wrote, and "some of them [were] so hungry they were 'skeletons.'" More died each day. To Johnson's mind it was not just "the brutalizing cruelties of the slave trade" that had created this situation. These were "poor heathens" with "naturally depraved hearts." The recaptives at Hogbrook were "the off-scourings of Africa," Johnson grieved, "some of the wildest cannibals in Africa." Tamba, Yarra, and all their former shipmates aboard the *Thais* were not considered as degraded as the Igbo, who had arrived soon after them, but this was hardly promising. Things were so bad that Johnson's nerve wavered. "I think I shall be of no use among so wild a race as that at Hogbrook," he wrote home to the CMS.[5]

Johnson soon rallied. By as early as July 1816, he led Sunday services that lasted all day, attendance obligatory for all of those living in the mountain valley. An impassioned public speaker, he thrilled them with dramatic renderings of Noah's Ark, prodigal sons, David versus Goliath, and the children of Israel finding the Promised Land after four hundred years of slavery. He exhorted them to accept the word of God, or they would burn in hell forever more.

With his wife's help, Johnson also set about feeding the hoards of hungry people, distributing food given by Governor MacCarthy. He arranged for the local doctor to inoculate them against smallpox. A school for boys took shape, using Bell's method, by which the smartest boys were taught first and then they led groups of less gifted boys.[6]

For some these might have been purely matters of faith, but it is also easy to see how many who were not believers, those who held onto their native religions, came to see Johnson as their savior. He commanded life and death, and winning his favor and approval could mean substantial gains. Visiting their farms, he determined whether they were showing the requisite industry to be worthy of the food and clothing distributed by Governor MacCarthy. Fascinatingly, he was believed to have supernatural powers, striking a backslider lame through the sheer power of his invective. This was likely more of a reflection of many of his congregation's native belief systems, where the mystical was an unquestioned part of life, than he was prepared to admit. Small wonder that with magical powers, distributing food and clothing that showed his wealth and prestige, and his compound filled with dependents, he was the biggest of big men in their traditional worldviews. That this fitted neatly into a Christian narrative they were now being taught was a happy concurrence.[7]

Soon Hogbrook's people, along with some volunteer soldiers from the RAC (possibly some of their old friends from Bostock and Mason's), lined up to start digging the foundations of what would become the colony's first stone church. It was on the rise just at the top of the main pathway through the cottages, the boys' and girls' schools sitting beside it.[8]

Church and Missionary House in Regent, Sierra Leone, 1850. From Thomas Poole Eyre, *Life, Scenery and Customs in Sierra Leone and the Gambia*, vol. 2 (London: Richard Bentley, 1850).

All of these developments were undoubtedly very positive for many. They had more food and clothes, some semblance of governance, and an arbitrator to whom they could look to rule between their many misunderstandings and conflicts. The children were in school and could look to a brighter future than when they were kidnapped, stolen, traded, and walked vast distances across Africa in coffles.

Yet this also marked a point when the achievements of the *Thais*'s captives were subsumed into a European-led narrative. Some of Johnson's claims about the state of Hogbrook upon his arrival were not just the first impressions of a European man in Africa for the first time, but a more conscious account of Christianity setting out to find a path through the dense jungle of heathenism. Johnson finding the village initially destitute made the transformation he was determined to bring about all the more spectacular. So the immensely hard work the men and women had already put into clearing the land and planting crops, all the rice and cassava fields laid out, was disregarded. In Johnson's narrative they were living in "a complete wilderness," surviving only by plunder, grabbing chickens and then eating them raw. The fact that they had built homes and welcomed large numbers of new arrivals into them translated to a condemnation of the lack of "female purity" because "in some huts ten of them were crowded together, and in others even fifteen or twenty."[9]

Similarly at the time of Tamba's distressing nightmare of burning to death, Johnson claimed that Tamba and his wife were "weeping for hunger." Yet other sources suggest that by this point Tamba was "entirely independent" of government resources, no small achievement in an era when most Liberated Africans remained completely reliant on the government for food. He had a small farm, owned a bullock and a goat, and as well as being Hogbrook's butcher he burned charcoal for the blacksmith. At the time of his formal conversion he was already successful enough to tithe half a crown weekly to the church. Many were certainly hungry, but Tamba does not seem to have been one of them.[10]

Tamba's official conversion, in Johnson's narrative, was at the time of his nightmare of hellfire. But that was something of a gloss on a more complex story. In 1816, before the nightmares, when Johnson became ill with fever, he had written that he could "lay down his head without a care," knowing that "the faithful Tamba" was taking care of things. Whatever the exact sequence of events, Tamba was certainly "one of the first fruits of that mountain valley." Tamba began taking classes in English reading and writing in the mornings before the rest of his work and in the evenings attended the first of the classes led by Johnson.[11]

With Johnson at the helm, Hogbrook was converted "to a smiling village," its formally "savage" people now "tame and civil." It now had 1,100 people, and huts built on both sides of the creek led down to the brook where hogs still drank.[12]

Johnson's successes were reported in British and American newspapers as early as 1816. "Here the triumphant influence of Christianity," they trumpeted, "in rapidly civilizing and blessing rude and ignorant men, is remarkably displayed." Hogbrook was no longer considered a respectable enough name for such a village. Governor MacCarthy renamed it Regent in honor of the Prince Regent, the man of whom Bostock and McQueen had begged pardons.[13]

19

The End
of Their Punishment

For almost ten months Bostock and McQueen had been walking Sydney's George Street and strolling across the Domain where Mrs. Macquarie loved to ride, lately Bostock promenading with his new belle on his arm. It probably seemed not so bad after all, that the conditions of their banishment were certainly endurable. Then, not long after they had marked their first antipodean Christmas and seen in the New Year, wonderful news arrived. The ship *Fanny* sailed into harbor carrying a dispatch that set the colony alight. The *Sydney Gazette* hastily printed a "Gazette Extraordinary" to broadcast the news. Napoleon Bonaparte, "the Faithless Disturber of Europe and Destroyer of the Human Race," had surrendered. And there was something more important for Bostock and McQueen snuggled amid the curled papers carried in the *Fanny*'s chests. Alongside news of Wellington's victory were their pardons. They had been written in June 1815 but had taken seven months to reach them.[1]

That night, by happy coincidence, a ball for the queen's birthday was already planned, so the town's worthy danced across a floor "painted with emblems of martial glory . . . the figure of Fame, in the center of the floor, sounding her trumpet, and holding in her right hand a scroll, whereupon were inscribed 'WATERLOO, WELLINGTON AND VICTORY.'" Whether Bostock, perhaps even McQueen, was there is not clear, but they both were almost certainly present on Saturday when Sydney honored the Duke of Wellington with a Grand Salute from the Battery of Dawes Point, followed by a *feu de joie* from the 46th Regiment in Hyde Park. As Union Jacks waved in a patriotic flurry, Bostock and McQueen had their own news to celebrate.[2]

Three days after the celebrations, a mere five days after the *Fanny*'s arrival, Robert Bostock married fifteen-year-old Rachael Rafferty at St. Phillip's Church. The daughter of an Irish convict woman and a ship captain who had sailed away long before, Rachael had been born free in New South Wales and was a renowned beauty. It seems likely that Bostock had been awaiting free-dom to marry her, eager to not harm her status as a freeborn woman through marriage to a convict. It was no small matter to attract a wife in a colony where there were more than three men for every woman, rarer still to win the hand of a free girl. Whatever Bostock had been working at during his months of convict servitude he was clearly making waves. His African wives were forgotten.[3]

The following week Bostock patriotically joined the committee collecting donations for "relief of the sufferers at the . . . glorious battle of Waterloo." Bostock's donation was £5 5s, the same amount given by Simeon Lord, Sam-uel Terry, and even colonial grandees like William Balmain and D'Arcy Wentworth.[4]

Later that month their pardons were officially transmitted. Robert Bostock was listed as being from Liverpool, thirty years old, 5 feet 4 inches tall, with a "Fair ruddy" complexion, hazel eyes, and "Flaxen" hair. John McQueen was recorded as being a native of Glasgow, twenty-four years old, 5 feet 6¾ inches tall, with pale skin, brown hair, and blue eyes. It was two and a half years since their arrest in Africa. Now they were "restored to all the rights and Privileges of a free Subject."[5]

Three days before this official documentation was delivered, Robert Bostock placed an advertisement in the *Sydney Gazette*. He had for sale "ladies and chil-dren's straw bonnets, and dress caps, slops of all kinds, blankets, damask table cloaths [*sic*], queen stuffs, dimity, chintz, black bombazeen [*sic*] &c. Cognac Brandy and Hollands' Gin." Robert Bostock, respectable colonial merchant, had set up shop.[6]

It was a good moment to start a business, as the recession of the previous few years was receding. Bostock's soon became a well-known emporium at 14 Hunter Street, at the corner of Bligh Street, where Sydney's first church had once stood. John McQueen worked as his assistant, just as he had in the old days at Cape Mesurado. Now their merchandise spanned everything from furniture to food-stuffs; beer, wine, and liquor; apparel of all kinds including hats, umbrellas, and parasols; all manner of ironmongery; a vast assortment of cloth; tobacco and snuff; stationery, trunks, and even grand pianos and bird cages. Soon Bostock owned homes on both Hunter and Blight Street.[7]

At the end of 1816, Bostock received a first grant of land from Governor Macquarie. He and Rachael also became parents. Into the next year Bostock bought and sold, placing regular advertisements in the *Sydney Gazette*. Bostock was almost certainly receiving letters and news from England via the ships that pulled into harbor, and likely he already knew that not long after he and McQueen had sailed aboard the *Indefatigable*, Robert Thorpe, formerly Sierra

Leone's judge, had published a book in the form of an open letter to William Wilberforce. Barred from returning to Sierra Leone after a public spat with the abolitionists, Thorpe had turned vehemently against them. Thorpe's book argued that Bostock's and McQueen's convictions were illegal.[8]

Then by late 1817 more exciting news still arrived for Bostock, possibly sailing into Sydney in the letters aboard the convict ship *Larkins*. It was not only that three slave dealers arrested in 1814 had won their cases to have the convictions overturned; one of them had been awarded £20,000 compensation from former governor Maxwell for his losses. Another was claiming £50,000. Robert Bostock decided that he would make his own case. At worst he could have his conviction expunged. At best he might gain a vast sum in recompense for his losses and sufferings while a convict.[9]

Astonishingly, Bostock had already earned enough for the usually prohibitively expensive passage back to Britain. Very few convicts ever afforded to return, but Bostock embarked aboard the *Harriet*, paying for his wife and baby daughter to accompany him. Like adventurers, they carried antipodean curios for show-and-tells they would perform in England.[10]

The *Harriet* set sail a few days before Christmas in 1817. Before they could even get into the southern ocean they discovered some convicts had stowed away on board. They sailed into harbor at Hobart, Van Diemen's Land, to offload the stowaways. They were there only a few hours, but long enough for Bostock to see a bit of a town that would play a big part in his future. Evidently it took his fancy.[11]

20

A Model Village

By 1817, things were getting better for those in Sierra Leone. The population of the tiny colony was now nine to ten thousand people, more than double that of only three years earlier, and positive signs could be seen everywhere. The jail was finally finished, "a three story stone building" to replace the houses formerly used. The town hall had been built, and the first stones of St. George's Church in Freetown were laid to the reading of Psalm 100. The wharf had been reconstructed with new steps leading down. Arriving in 1817, the new chief justice wrote home that he was *"well content"* with the state of the colony. A man calling himself "a Lover of Truth" boasted in the *Royal Gazette*, "in 1814 we had six Stone Houses . . . we have now nearly sixty."[1]

Amid all of this development, Regent, as Hogbrook had been renamed, was indisputably the colony's jewel. Once considered a place of "heathen barbarity and darkness," it was now known far and wide as "a most romantic spot." Rivers cascaded down the mountains into the brook, a meadow for cattle was fenced beyond the homes. In Britain it was reported that they were "making very great progress" in growing crops. Reverend Garnon, making his first visit in February 1818, wrote of Regent: "The first view which you have of it, in going from Leicester Mountain, is as you emerge from a thick wood and are descending into a valley. There, on a small eminence, stand the Church, the Parsonage House, and the Schools. In all directions are seen the houses of the Liberated Negroes. The whole is surrounded with 'cloud-capt mountains,' covered with an almost impenetrable forest."[2]

Garnon attended one of Johnson's preaching marathons—three rounds of divine service and two prayer meetings—and declared himself "well satisfied with the conduct of these dear Negroes." There was a considerable population crowded into Regent's church, the village now containing 790 Liberated African adults and 565 children, along with four Europeans. Some of those who were rescued from Bostock and Mason's barracoon had built homes on the main street, now called Christian Street.[3]

By December 1818 the local *Royal Gazette and Sierra Leone Advertiser* printed a celebratory article about Regent. "The young men settled there," it enthused, "have furnished an example which will long be admired, and not easily surpassed." Among the Liberated Africans' achievements were "two excellent stone bridges," roads built remarkably "solid and level," and the construction of a hospital. Clearly, said the journalist, people just rescued from the holds of slave ships had only achieved these things with the help of "the hand of Heaven."[4]

At the center of these developments, working as Johnson's right-hand men, were Tamba and another Liberated African named William Davis. At this time only around twelve people in Regent took communion, but Tamba and Davis were among them. Their influence was quite extraordinary, and the idea that two African men, rescued from the transatlantic slave trade, had become such devout servants of Jesus was proclaimed reverently as some sort of miracle. At a general CMS meeting as early as 1817, following the speakers it was Tamba who led everyone in prayer, leaving reports to gush: "Not yet of two years old in knowledge, and yet how heavenly wise!"[5]

This was extremely beneficial to the abolitionist agenda, but Tamba was undoubtedly very useful to Johnson in other ways as well. He was an interlocutor between the Liberated Africans and the church, and Reverend Johnson regularly used him to intervene in cases of misunderstanding or backsliding. In 1817, Tamba was sent to talk to a man who professed the Christian faith but then feared he must leave the church when told that his marriage was not recognized. Johnson told him to speak to Igbo women about the Lord, showing his lack of understanding since Igbo was not among the many languages Tamba spoke.[6]

Many of the Regent recaptives apparently looked to Tamba in the role of interlocutor and, wrote Johnson, "seem to be very fond" of him. This might just have been Johnson's interpretation, wishful thinking, but it likely also reflected the rare insight Tamba had into the white world. Tamba had grown up around the Caulkers and Clevelands, who themselves had learned to belong to both the African and European worlds. Unlike the overwhelming majority of the Liberated Africans, Tamba knew long before he arrived in Regent how to speak, dress, eat, and generally live in a way familiar enough to Europeans to be considered "civilized."

Having this kind of cultural intermediary was invaluable to many of those trying to survive in a society so very alien. There was plenty of scope for misunderstandings even when the intention was good. In nearby Gloucester village, some Liberated Africans feared that Reverend Düring was helping them while they were sick so that they would be worth more when sold. Even at Regent a small girl howled with horror when first taken into the church, thinking it a slave market. That many Liberated Africans struggled to trust white men was hardly surprising; their fears were more than understandable given the traumas bestowed upon them by their experiences.[7]

Having a go-between not only helped recaptives understand more of the missionaries' motives; it was particularly important because the kind of Christianity being proselytized by Johnson was one considered visible. Christianity and civilization went hand in hand so that faith was almost one and the same as adopting outward English culture. Dressing in European-style clothing, cultivating fields, building a "better" home, and eating with knives and forks was a requirement. Respectability could be found through the ownership of sofas and cupboards with crockery.[8]

Sierra Leone's British rulers were unquestioning about this. Although word was sent out to Sierra Leone to "not mistake civilization for conversion," the adoption of British modes of behavior, in addition to devout faith, was required. Few Britons questioned whether their own way of life was at the very pinnacle of civilization and progress. A visitor from Britain wrote, "I find myself perfectly satisfied to find a solid foundation of British pre-eminence" in Sierra Leone. The only things that disturbed him were the Africans' failings in manners and "social tact." Vigorous interventionism was unchallenged. Having experienced a world in which one was bought and sold as a human commodity, having to learn to eat with a knife and fork was doubtless a much better option.[9]

But it was alarming nonetheless. The CMS allowed Britons who made a donation of £5 to name a Liberated African child as if he or she were an exotic pet. Some of those who did so were wealthy individuals like Miss Harriet Newbiggin who gave £10 to name a child Henry Palmer; whole congregations also clubbed together to name a recaptive child for pastors and other revered elders. Donors requested that the CMS publish reports of "the behaviour and character" of each these namesakes. With Tamba taking a leading role in Regent's affairs, it seems very likely that some of the children rescued from Mason and Bostock's were among those receiving a British name from a sponsor in this way. It is not possible to prove, however, since original African names were not recorded alongside their new Anglo ones. Their motivations might not have been the same, but the CMS was carelessly stripping people of their identities, and by extension their original ethnicities, just as planters in the Americas did.[10]

At around this time Tamba added the Christian name William to his own, presumably after the Reverend Johnson's first name (though Johnson was more commonly referred to as Augustine). In those lessons with Johnson, he learned to sign himself William Tamba. William Davis perhaps took his surname from Reverend Davis, a Methodist minister who had been one of the first two men to welcome Reverend Johnson to Freetown. Many who, at least outwardly, adopted the Christian faith of their new leaders took wholly Anglicized names, albeit retaining their African names too. Tamba's old colleague Yarra became John Reffell after the superintendent of the Liberated Africans, Joseph Reffell, a close friend of both Governor MacCarthy and Reverend Johnson. Other Liberated Africans took names like Waterfall, Sea Breeze, Rose Bush, and Rose Bud. Whether they adopted these themselves, even perhaps taking the equivalent term for one of their original names in some cases—Waterfall was the meaning of the Kissi name Balloo, for example, the name of one of Bostock and Mason's former captives—or were given them by some British clerk, is unclear.[11]

Johnson's fervor included substantial pressure to relinquish their former ethnic identities—something rarely pushed in parts of the colony with less zealous missionary leadership—in favor of now being simply brothers and sisters in Christ. When Johnson proposed that they found a Benevolent Society in Regent, one unnamed recaptive stood up in church and declared, "Dat be very good ting, Broders! we be no more of plenty country: we belong to one country now—Jesus! Suppose one be sick, all be sick: suppose one be well, all be well!" It was a fine sentiment in many ways, and a move toward their later inclusion as Krio peoples, but it nevertheless demanded an impracticable severing of all that they had known, and it was far beyond what was expected of most Liberated Africans who lived in their ethnic groups for generations to come. To abandon these identities in the middle of their ongoing recovery from serious mental and physical damage can only have caused further instability. It was not just their time as captives and slaves that had been a travesty, they were now taught, but rather their entire previous lives. Those who had opened their homes to them, shared food and succor despite having so little themselves, those with whom they had shared understanding based on experiences that stretched back before their captures and enslavements, were supposed to be no more important than those previously considered enemies. It was a lot to take in and most never would.[12]

More troubling still was the implication that the recaptives had to distance themselves from their families from whom they had been taken, everything in fact that they had known before. The type of muscular Christianity preached by Johnson and followed by Tamba allowed no scope for inclusion of traditional African religious beliefs, which were derided as merely "deplorable superstitions." Unable to perceive the rich wealth of ancestral guides, myriad tutelary spirits, and supreme deities, much less the expansive diversity between the many different African religions found in the colony, all nonmonotheist places of worship were simply denounced as "chapels in honour of the evil spirit." Syncretism was judged akin to devil worship. The white man would settle for nothing less than control over their entire minds, demanding that they abandon not just their deities but also the ancestral spirits that had stayed with them in this strange new land. Even their drums were considered most unacceptable. Johnson would later crow proudly to London that there were no more drums left in Regent. Most startlingly of all, Johnson considered amulets as disfiguring as slave chains, as if all of their former lives with their families had been as destructive as their periods of enslavement.[13]

This relentless preaching to abandon so much of their former worldview, belief system and entire way of being was desperately disturbing to some. Already stolen from their families and deeply wounded by the events that had led to Regent, many now came to the horrible realization that if they adopted the religious beliefs of Johnson, Tamba, and the CMS, they were in effect damning to hell their families and friends back in their homelands. One young woman admitted to Johnson that in prayer her mind wandered back to her own country. Life was always a two-way pull, because when she thought of her lost home and family she feared that, not knowing Jesus, they were doomed to hell's fires. Another woman revealed how she always cried when she thought of her father because, "poor man, he no sabby [know] anything about Jesus Christ." Even Tamba was troubled by this implication, writing, "I remember my country people, which are far from the word of God."[14]

As if none of these things were difficult enough, the recaptives were also supposed to show gratitude to their British rulers. Governor MacCarthy, who by this time lived with Philippa Hayes's daughter Hannah as his common-law wife, believed that the recaptives were in debt to Britain, and the least they could do was show abject thankfulness. They "owed to Great Britain," MacCarthy wrote, "under the blessing of God, every thing that could dignify man: they were emancipated from Slavery; and, above all other benefits, they were educated in the principles of Christianity." Recaptives were required to be devout enough to disown all their previous religious beliefs, forsake their ethnic identity in favor of a newly created one, take a different name, adopt new ways of life, speak a new language, and then be grateful to those who demanded these things from them.[15]

Some of the Liberated Africans accepted this, becoming loyal members of the church. They included some of those who arrived aboard the *Thais*, who as early arrivals and associates of Tamba had heard the teachings more than most. One child admitted that he played and laughed when Hirst first taught them about God, but after Johnson's arrival he had a severe case of smallpox, commonly fatal, and remembered again the teachings about eternal life. He decided to follow the Christian faith and remained a member of the church. Yarra too, now John Reffell, was a member of the church, though nothing much is known about his decision to follow this path.[16]

The tricked, traded Bassa boy once purchased by John Sterling Mill and handed over as one of those he had been hiding for Robert Bostock, also became a member of Regent's congregation. David Noah, as he now called himself, just a boy when they had arrived aboard the *Thais*, had taken a longer path to the church than Tamba. He admitted that he had caused Hirst problems when the schoolteacher had tried to teach him the Lord's Prayer. Even after Johnson's arrival he had played up, with Johnson later admitting, "He was a very dull lad when I came hither." When he went to stay briefly in Freetown with Joseph Reffell, superintendent of the Liberated Africans, Reffell had grown mad with Noah's waywardness and had sent him away. He returned to Regent and went to stay with Reverend Johnson, who put him in charge of the rice store. Staying at Johnson's home, he had no choice but to attend divine service.[17]

By 1817, things had begun to change. In Johnson's words: "it pleased God to open his eyes about the beginning of 1817." Noah believed that in 1817 "Jesus first began to work on my heart," and he would later write that he had been called from darkness into light. Having made the decision to follow the Christian teachings, Noah showed himself to be a brilliant and dedicated scholar. "He then began with all his might, to learn to read," Johnson wrote. Soon he had "outstripped all the others." Noah became an usher in the church, and he and Johnson became extremely close. "I do not know what I would do without him," Johnson recorded. For Noah, his rescue from "temporal slavery" by the "government" and his deliverance from "the slavery of the Devil" by the CMS were one and the same.[18]

Even for the less devout than Tamba and Noah, there were reasons for the recaptives to follow the path that the CMS advocated. Church attendance brought a degree of acceptance, food and clothing when times were tight, education for them and their children, and a role in a tight-knit supportive community to partially replace that which they had lost. Ideas of God's love may well have been soothing and a warm embrace after times of such biting uncertainty. As the years moved forward, the incentives to join the church would become more pressing still to many of their children and grandchildren whose ties to their ancestral homelands thawed into their identity as Sierra Leonean Krios. Embracing European, Christian modes of life would bring opportunity, and they hoped for the material ease of the Europeans in the colony. The ideas of liberty and the aim of property ownership became compelling to those so nearly traded as merchandise.[19]

Others, however, not withstanding Tamba's, Davis's, and Noah's exhortations or the material gains on offer, were less certain. Some mixed their traditional ways into this newly learned faith. These could be simple misunderstandings, perfectly understandable attempts to interpret what Johnson and the others were telling them as seen through their own grasp of the world. One child, for example, believed that his financial contributions to the church would allow him to buy his non-Christian family a path to heaven. His people's lack of Christian faith had been troubling him, and he was "glad too [i.e., so] much" to hear that his donations to the church might somehow facilitate his being reunited with them. When a white man told him, "perhaps, through the coppers which we give" in church, he might see some of his countrymen again on Judgment Day, he seized the idea literally. A couple of decades later, liberated slaves in Jamaica similarly misconstrued missionaries when tickets proving church membership were believed to be fetishes, rewards for payments and "passports to heaven." It seems likely that Reverend Johnson's posited power to physically strike down doubters was an amalgamation of what the congregation heard preached from the pulpit filtered through their own understandings of the world.[20]

Often, too, this mixing of the old and new was more conscious and deliberate, a means to survive. Many Liberated Africans adopted two ways of being, one that they performed in public to satisfy the missionaries and government officials, and another wholly more African persona that they could be in private. Perhaps this was why Yarra was also still known as Yarra, despite taking the name John Reffell. The two names lived on, side by side. Culturally and spiritually, the newly preached ways would never totally supplant the old. "The customs of their country" were often practiced when no Europeans were around to see.[21]

Johnson and Tamba were aware that many of their congregation professed to follow their faith and yet also kept some of the ways of their homelands. Rather than seeing any richness in this, or even benevolently hoping that the new ways would eventually come out on top, they saw hypocrisy and duplicity. They preached against those who "have been baptized and now call themselves Christian: they think because they come to church, and say Lord! Lord!

they are going to heaven, while they have no heart-religion." These people who "only put Jesus Christ in their mouths" were still going to hell, they scolded their listeners.[22]

This duality was not always intentional. Some Liberated Africans were genuinely struggling between Christianity and their native beliefs, unsure which way their heart truly lay. They were drawn to the idea of eternal salvation and terrified by Johnson's preaching about hell's flames, yet they longed for the families and places from which they had been so cruelly stolen. "Suppose me pray, my heart run to My Country," one woman confessed to Johnson. This troubled her greatly, since in recalling her homeland she was also thinking about things "me no want to remember." She confessed that she did not know what to do, ending her sad tale by admitting, "Me think me sometimes have two hearts."[23]

For all those who followed Johnson's and Tamba's lead, whether as "heart-religion" or "mouth-religion," many others refused resolutely to follow the British Christian path at all. Some of these were Bassa people who had "built houses in the woods" outside of Regent. This was particularly troubling to William Davis and David Noah, who were themselves Bassa. When they tried to convince the Bassa to convert, one old man declared, "I think I and the Devil should do very well together. Me tall fellow, I could help the Devil cut wood to make fire good." Davis in particular was very dispirited by this. This Bassa group claimed that they lived outside of Regent because of sickness in the town, but Johnson's comment that they wanted to live not just outside of the Christian teachings, keeping their own gris-gris, but also wished to live "without society," suggests that it was British culture and control that they were rejecting as much as their faith. They were one of several groups that refused to conform.[24]

Johnson's dreams of a New Jerusalem in Africa extended far beyond the confines of Regent. In 1818 he made Tamba and Davis an extraordinary offer. He asked them to accompany him and British schoolteacher John Brereton Cates on a "circuit of the colony." The two men can only have been honored, if also a little apprehensive. With his ability to speak many of the "uncultivated" languages in the region, Tamba was an essential part of the undertaking and was delighted with this new role.[25]

The four men and their team traveled by canoe, fording streams where they were "obliged to pull off shoes and stockings, and walk through the mud." Near Tombo, the people all gathered around Tamba, "some on stools, and some on country chairs; forming a motely [*sic*] group" as he read the Bible. They saw sharks in the rivers, and in the vivified account that was told back in England they slept among leopards, elephants, and heathens who decided to murder them. Despite it all, "Tamba consecrated one native dialect after another by declaring in them, for the first time, the wonderful works of God."[26]

As soon as they returned, "a Second Journey was in contemplation," this one wholly more ambitious. It would take them far beyond the relative safety of Sierra Leone, to Sherbro Island and then down through the lands of the Vai and Dei peoples where Tamba had spent years working for Mason and Bostock, and to the Bassa country, which was Davis's home. A meeting was held before they left Regent discussing the true objectives of this peculiar mission. Cates was armed with an initiative to either found a new colony, or perhaps extend the existing one as far south as the St. John River. On February 1, 1819, Cates, Tamba, and William Davis again left Regent, venturing out of the lands of the abolitionists and into the domain of the slave traders.[27]

It was their first trip so far beyond the tiny colony, and it wasn't long before Cates went into deep shock. Barely beyond the boundary of British governance, the people's "drumming and dancing" infuriated him. He was soon uttering the non-too-Christian opinion that he was glad they would not convert since they were so heathen to be beyond help. Poro initiations incensed him, since he believed them simply to be the devil's work. What Tamba and Davis made of it is less certain; probably they were trying to interpret Cates's message to the people they met, a burden that would have fallen more heavily on Tamba during the first part of trip since he could speak Mende and Sherbro. There were certainly many reminders of his former life as they sailed close to the Plantain Islands and saw the village where he had once lived.[28]

Word of their exploits went ahead of them. As they walked through the country not far north of Gallinas, they encountered a man coming to greet them. He reported that he was one of Chief Siaka's sons, and that all in Siaka's camp had heard that "a White Man was walking through the country, who spoke against selling Slaves." Rather taken aback, Cates told him why he thought all types of slavery were indeed wrong. The man "seemed astonished," Cates wrote, "and said he thought that Black Men never would consent to life as I would have them: they must have plenty of Wives and plenty of Slaves."[29]

Undeterred, on February 15, 1819, Tamba, Cates, and Davis reached Gendema, Siaka's bastion, which they found "strongly defended: there are many cannon of different sizes, some mounted and others not; with a quantity of arms and spears." They thought that the town comprised about 150 houses and had around 600 inhabitants, "but, in time of war, they amount to 1000." It was an altogether strange place for the British abolitionist and the two former slaves. They met a man who had once lived in London and two European sailors left behind from a slaving vessel. Cates was more disturbed by the sight of "a fine healthy-looking boy, about four years of age, the child of some White Man who is either dead or gone away, and who left him to be brought up in all the wretchedness and superstition of an African. He was quite naked, and running about with other children." Cates believed that if the "Sons of lust and debauchery considered the misery which they frequently entail on their unfortunate offspring, they would restrain their licentiousness."[30]

Siaka was sick with yaws, but that evening the visitors went boldly to his home. Cates read the third chapter of Acts, focusing on the parts that exhorted Siaka to "repent, then, and turn to God" and turn "from your wicked ways." Siaka was unmoved. Later Tamba read the third chapter of St. John to some of the King's people who came to see them.[31]

Departing the next day, they went to visit Charles Gomez at Mano, another of the most powerful slave traders on the coast. Then, heading southward, they ventured from Cape Mount down to the banks of the St. Paul River. So Tamba, the former slave who had worked in the slave trade, arranged to hold a meeting on the banks where Bostock and Mason's enterprise had once stood, where he had once guarded captives, bought and sold those he now held as brothers. A message was sent to John Sterling Mill, once an acquaintance of Tamba and owner of their colleague David Noah, asking permission.[32]

Unfortunately an account of this extraordinary event comes only through the diary of Cates, who seems to have been largely oblivious to Tamba's connection to the place. They preached to thirty or forty people from Matthew chapter 25: "For I was hungered, and ye gave me no meat: I was thirsty, and ye gave me no drink: I was a stranger, and ye took me not in: naked, and ye clothed me not: sick, and in prison, and ye visited me not."[33]

Then crossing the St. Paul River two miles upstream to a small place named Sheppo, they began walking the six miles to the Mesurado River. For Tamba it must have been bittersweet and perhaps terrifying, for he came equipped with only righteousness and Bible versus where he knew all too well the arms Mill owned. Cates wrote little about their stay at Dazoe Island, not even referring to Mill by name until they were on their way back to Freetown at the end of their trip, so we are left to imagine the scene as Tamba and Davis tried to convince the slave trader of his sins. They also visited "Mrs. Phillipa"— Philippa Hayes—in whose compound they held morning worship and preached Psalm 96. At night they dined with her. Cates wrote only that Tamba met "many an old acquaintance," whom he believed looked with wonder into the eyes of a man who was now "new-born, even to their apprehension."[34]

Heading even further south, they next stopped at the St. John River and began walking inland. Davis preached from the second verse of Isaiah: "And it shall come to pass in the last days, that the mountain of the Lord's house shall be established on the top of the mountain." They were looking for a headman called John White but went instead to King John's town, where houses were circular with conical roofs, "better built than any we have seen lately," and there was plentiful grass to support the "numerous cattle." Cates was received "very cordially" by the Bassa King John, who wore long robes made of country cloth, "a blue scarlet cloth cap, ornamented with a van dyke and tassels," and who could only walk with the aid of a "staff." Cates offered to read "the book" to his people if King John would gather them together, to which the King "cheerfully assented." At this meeting one Bassa man was said to be so astonished at Cates's appearance, and the news that he had arrived from Sierra Leone, that he instead "stated it to be his opinion, that I came down from heaven, which he thought, of course, to be a shorter journey."[35]

Davis's appearance was more startling still. There had never before been an instance of a person sold into slavery returning to visit, Davis believed, so that it was as if he had returned from the lands of the dead. For those who had sold him into slavery, his reappearance was even more stunning. They tried to hide from him, Davis reported, because they were so ashamed, although "the mistress of his late master . . . ran towards him and fell on his neck and wept." Davis learned that his mother too was still alive, and though she was too far into the interior to be visited, he sent her a gift.[36]

After all of these challenging encounters, Tamba, Davis, and Cates were provided with a house for the night and given a meal of beef. Cates could not bear the palm oil, but Davis and Tamba were delighted by the dinner. They tried to hold a prayer meeting afterward but were rather disturbed by the Bassa "howling and dancing in an extravagant manner" with "drums and horns."[37]

The next morning King John, by now attired in a crown of "an enormous amount of leopard's teeth tied together," asked them to preach. Cates read from Matthew 18 while Davis translated. Afterward the King offered a bull to Cates, which he tried to refuse: it being Sunday he did not want the men to carry out the work of killing it. We can only imagine whether Davis was madly trying to negotiate a way through this cultural impasse since to refuse a gift was very bad form, but in the end Cates was prevailed upon to take the bull. King John was evidently perplexed, asking at this point if Cates's "great knowledge" had been acquired through a particular diet.[38]

Afterward Cates stood before a great meeting reading from the nineteenth Psalm and then the second chapter of Genesis, all of which Davis was tasked with not just translating but also explaining. When he criticized the people for killing many for the crime of one man, "the whole congregation, which had hitherto been silent, set up two or three loud shouts, as if they had been electrified." There were more prayers, more Bible readings, but also more of the drumming and dancing that so tormented Cates. Eventually the king asked if Davis could be sent to live among them to teach, and an agreement was made that some of the king's land would be available to the colony. The three Regentonians believed they had seen the urgent necessity of sending Davis to teach them when, on their final morning, they saw the masked spirit, undoubtedly a society mask, "turn into all sorts of postures . . . uttering a noise like that occasioned by blowing water through a pipe."

> A garment of dried grass or rushes covers him, and reaches to the ground. His arms and feet are concealed. A white country cloth covers his shoulders. Round his head, and tied under his chin, are two or three cotton handkerchiefs. The face is frightful. The mouth and nose are black. Two large teeth project far beyond the lips. A row of coarse shells is bound round, above the eyes. On the head is a red cap, which reaches four or five feet in height, and is surmounted by a plume of feathers.

It was alarming enough that they were happy to be returning to the safety and piety of their mountain home.[39]

A reward for this hard labor awaited them upon their return. Back in Regent, both Tamba and Davis were appointed "messengers of salvation in native districts." It was a remarkable achievement, a sign of how Liberated Africans might, in the 1810s and 1820s at least, push through the cracks of the British protestant facade that generally had so little scope for Africans. They were treated as children certainly, but there was room for them to grow up and attain the status of adults if they showed the requisite "civilization" and Christian devotion. Later, David Noah would become only the third man to be formally accepted into the CMS.

The timing of Cates, Tamba, and Davis's trip is slightly mysterious. They left Regent, armed with aspirations to expand the Sierra Leone colony or begin another, just before two American missionaries arrived in Sierra Leone hoping to found a new settlement of their own. It is possible that the American plan had reached Regent by letter in advance of the Americans' arrival, spurring the plans of Cates, Tamba, and Davis, but this is not certain. Perhaps Johnson had his own hopes of pushing the British government to expand their sphere of influence, and this would later conflate into the American plan.

Reverend Samuel Mills and Ebenezer Burgess arrived in Sierra Leone as agents of the American Colonization Society, which hoped to found an American free settlement. President James Monroe, after whom Monrovia would later be named, was a supporter of the scheme. But in spite of this high-profile support, the whole plan was riven to the heart with a welter of contradiction and anomaly. A handful of white American supporters hoped to create a promised land for African American ex-slaves. They hoped that the colony would be a buffer against the slave trade and a new hope for Africa, just as British abolitionists had imagined at the time of Sierra Leone's first steps. Allied to this, a handful of the white Americans supported the idea of colonization in the hope of redeeming their nation for its role in the slave trade. Elias B. Caldwell, a clerk of the Supreme Court, believed that the settlement of a free American colony in Africa would be "a national atonement for the wrongs and injuries which Africa has suffered."[40]

But for other white Americans, some liberal and enlightened people among them, it was more a matter of exporting a population they did not want. If the nation's slaves were to be freed, then they wanted them to go away, preferably far. Thomas Jefferson favored an end to slavery, but he also wanted "expatriation," writing, "Let an ocean divide the white man from the man of color."[41]

Leaving all of these schisms behind, Burgess and Mills had arrived in Sierra Leone in March while Cates, Davis, and Tamba were visiting Siaka. The Americans were impressed with Freetown's schools, where they heard boys read and watched them spell and saw "about 100 neatly dressed little girls, many of whom could read and sew." At the "very decent appearance" and "prosperous condition" of the town Burgess wrote, "It causes my heart to pant for the day that America shall have a foot hold on the continent."[42]

Some in Sierra Leone were less impressed with the Americans' plan, however. Two citizens wrote anonymously to the editor of the *Royal Gazette*, worrying that America would "behold" such a colony "in that light, Great Britain does now, New South Wales." In other words, they were concerned that the home country would not consider the settlers to be truly free. Above and beyond those philosophical concerns were also worries that a huge increase in the population of freemen near Sierra Leone would affect the colony's prosperity.[43]

Not dissuaded from their mission, and sure that concerns about potential settlers' freedoms were unfounded, Burgess and Mills headed up to Regent for Sunday service a week after their arrival. There they found "children once destined to foreign slavery; now fed, clothed, governed and carefully taught in the Christian religion." The sight of them in church was "a spectacle of grateful admiration." It was sufficient impetus for Mills and Burgess to leave the following morning, intent on founding a similar place for African American freed people. Mills died on their way home, but Burgess returned safely "and reported favourably on their Mission."[44]

Not long after this visit, two British schoolteachers, Mr. and Mrs. Jesty, also arrived in the village. In a letter to her sister written a few days later, Mrs. Jesty proclaimed herself so amazed by "our dear black brethren" that she hoped "all Africa may become as Regent's Town." Her husband was similarly impressed by the sight of people "once led captive to the will of Satan" who were now dressed decently and singing hymns. He was so delighted with the village that he was overcome with "wonder, love and praise."[45]

In Britain, however, doubts were mounting about Johnson's methods. The main criticism leveled was that he was placing too much trust in Liberated Africans. The CMS wrote to him expressing concern that "the peculiar character of your people" left them susceptible to the will of Satan. "Their judgements are imperfectly formed," the CMS wrote, "while their constitutions render them remarkably susceptible of having their feelings strongly wrought upon." Nor was their exuberance godly enough to English eyes. Rather than having a stiff upper lip they showed "violent excitement to the feelings." Johnson was ordered to be endlessly watchful and to exert an "inflexible firmness" on "his" "peculiar" people.[46]

Soon these doubts came to greatly affect Tamba and the handful of other Liberated Africans assimilated into the CMS. The arrival of the Jestys in the colony allowed roles to be shifted around to give Johnson and his wife an opportunity to return to Europe for a break. Johnson's departure was a time of worry in Regent, and many walked down to Freetown with him. When his ship sailed they were said to proclaim, "Massa, suppose no water live here . . . we go with you all the way, till no feet more!"[47]

Whatever their fears as they watched their leader and protector sail away, they could hardly have imagined what happened next. Tamba, Noah, or Davis wrote explaining to Johnson what had happened:

> That time Mr Cates sick, and Mr Morgan sick; and poor Mr Cates die. Then
> Mr Collier get sick, and Mr Morgan get sick again; and one friend said, "God

soon leave this place" and I said, "I trust in the Lord Jesus Christ: He Knows his
people: and, He never left then, neither forsake them"—and next Sunday Mr
Collier die about eleven o'clock—Then Mr Morgan sick—Mrs Morgan sick—
Mr Bull sick. Oh! that time all Missionaries sick! We went to Freetown,
Monday, and bury Mr Collier; and we come home again and keep Service in
the Church. Oh, that time trouble too much in my heart. Nobody to teach me,
and I was so sorry for my poor Country-people. Mr Cates died—Mr Collier
died—Mr Morgan sick—Oh, what must I do for my Country-men! but I trust
in the Lord Jesus Christ: He know what to do; and I went to pray, and I say, "O
Lord, take not all the Teachers away from us!"[48]

Mrs. Jesty had not survived long either: "delivered of a still-born child," it
was written, "she departed in a triumph of faith." Cates's death was blamed on
the trip to Grand Bassa, with Tamba and Davis admitting, "the journey . . . too
much for him, the land so long to walk and the sun so hot."[49]

All the sickness and death left Tamba, Davis, and Noah in positions of
great trust. But it was a marginal role, balancing between those in Regent who
wanted to live according to their own more African ideas of life, and those in
the CMS who believed that Africans were not to be trusted. Tamba heard
rumors that he, Davis, and the others were to be thrown out of the CMS for
behaving badly, and that Johnson would not return because of their disrespect.[50]

The truth was quite different, though the ambiguous feelings of the CMS
were real enough. All three men wrote letters to Johnson and, eager to show
how far Africans had been "civilized" and become pious Christians, they were
printed in American newspapers under the heading: "from Christian Negroes."
Left alone in Regent and unaware of the reach his letters were having, Tamba
tried desperately to keep the Benevolent Society and other Christian organiza-
tions alive, clinging to these life rafts that seem to have allowed him to make
some peace with his former life.[51]

While Johnson was away, some of the former Bostock and Mason captives who
had been drafted into the West India Regiments returned to Sierra Leone.
While those mustered into the Royal Africa Corps had been living nearby,
many of them in Soldier Town on the outskirts of Freetown, some of the forty-
two drafted into the West India Regiment had been far away. Among them
was Mamaroo, only sixteen when he arrived aboard the *Thais*. It was probably
at this time that Tom Ball also returned.

They and their fellow conscripts had been in the Caribbean, seeing at close quarters the lives of enslaved Africans and their descendants. Some of them were in Barbados in 1816 when they were ordered to help suppress the island's biggest ever slave revolt. After the abolition of the slave trade in 1808, some slaves apparently came to believe that "the island belonged to them and not to the white man whom they proposed to destroy." Bussa, an African-born man among a slave population that was over 90 percent Caribbean-born, led the revolt.[52]

What the Liberated Africans made of facing rebel slaves in battle is not easy to know. There were reports that the rebels thought that "the King's troops would join them." Upon seeing the black soldiers of the West India Regiment approaching, the rebels were said to be "confused," perhaps believing that they were Haitians come to help. The troops of the West India Regiment were attacked by slaves "armed with Firelocks, Bills, Pikes, Hatchets, &c" who gave "three cheers," believing that the black soldiers would not fight back. Their commander ordered them to load their muskets, however, and in the firefight forty rebel slaves were killed and another seventy taken prisoner. The rebels then made a stand at a nearby plantation house, where many more were "killed and wounded jumping from the windows & rushing from the doors," then being chased across the cane fields by the soldiers. The whole rebellion was quashed in three days but only after indiscriminate murder and the wanton burning of slave huts with immense loss of live among the enslaved. It was claimed that up to one thousand died in the fighting or were later executed.[53]

Now that their services were no longer required, the Liberated African soldiers were returned to Sierra Leone. Their arrival off the coast of Sierra Leone caused raucous celebrations. Hearing that their ship had docked, those in Regent were ecstatic, urgently looking for "parents, brothers and friends" among those who years earlier had been sent into the forces. "Glowing hope" was found on the faces of most at Regent.[54]

Tom Ball apparently went to Waterloo, a former Temne village once known as Jack Ryan's Town. He and the other soldiers were given land and farming tools, along with 5d a day allowance, a sum that allowed them to live reasonably well. Some of the returning soldiers married Bullom women, and others married women from the recaptives. It might have been around this time that Ball married a woman named Sophia (or Safi) and built a home on Robbin Street, Waterloo.[55]

In February 1820, Tamba was inordinately relieved to hear that Johnson was back. Regent again turned into a festival of celebrating and worship. David Noah recorded the scene as Regent's faithful heard that Johnson's ship had arrived: "[H]e come! he live in Town! And the people began to make noise. Some could not get through the door, but jumped out the window—they so full of joy. Some went to Freetown the whole night; and some people sing the whole night through!" They soon learned that Johnson carried with him news that pertained to Tamba, Yarra, and their shipmates: Robert Bostock was back from exile and demanding compensation for wrongful arrest. Authorities in Sierra Leone, including Johnson, were tasked with finding anybody who had been rescued from Bostock's factory to testify once again to the events of 1813. Far from escaping into a new world of Christianity and British-style civilization, Tamba and his fellow former *Thais* and *Princess Charlotte* arrivals learned that they would have to revisit their old lives as factory slaves and captives.[56]

21

The Appeal

It must have been the most happy and unexpected of family reunions. Convicts banished to New South Wales hardly ever returned to Britain, let alone only three years after they had left dripping with chains and shame. Yet here was Robert home and free, with a new young wife and baby daughter he had named for his mother and oldest sister, and the prospect of apology and compensation. They were welcomed back into the family that now comprised Elizabeth, the matriarch, brother Charles, and sisters Elizabeth, Maria, and Margaret. While they were in England the family was expanding, with both Charles and Maria having children, and two sons born to Robert and Rachael. Maria and her husband lived in Kent, but the others were still in Bootle, to the north of Liverpool, and at some point around then the road where they lived became known as Bostock Street.[1]

The Britain Robert returned to had changed. When he had been convicted in Freetown and then sailed for New South Wales, Britain had been at war with both Napoleon and the United States and desperately stretched on both fronts. Now those conflicts were memories, even the victories tainted by the famines and extreme unemployment that followed. While Bostock was in Britain preparing his case, anger gathered into demonstrations in favor of parliamentary reform, culminating in the Peterloo Massacre in Manchester when the cavalry charged protestors. In early 1820, a few months before he took the case back to court, news of a plot to murder the prime minister rocked the nation, and the subsequent hanging, drawing, and quartering of the conspirators was a public spectacle.

The abolitionist seascape had also changed completely since Bostock's original conviction in 1813. Hopes that the slave trade would quickly come to an end once it became illegal had been confounded. The abolitionists now knew that they were engaged in a long fight. Rulings of dubious legal standing had been overturned and new laws and regulations passed.

Most of all, the end of the wars had affected the abolitionists' campaign. In 1813, the British had believed that the Portuguese and Spanish would go along with Royal Naval attacks on their slave ships because they needed their help to force Napoleon out of the Iberian Peninsula. With the end of the war those ideas quickly died. Similarly, while the United States had not protested the capture of its slavers by the British before the War of 1812, afterward they were adamant that this was unacceptable, vehemently criticizing any incursions on their trade.

The case of the French slaver *Louis* in 1816 had been a turning point in anti-slavery tactics. The *Princess Charlotte*, the same vessel that had accompanied HMS *Thais* to Mason and Bostock's premises three years earlier, had captured the *Louis* offshore from Cape Mesurado and carried it into Sierra Leone for adjudication, where it was condemned. But the French had appealed the capture to the High Court of the Admiralty, and Sir William Scott ruled that British ships did not have a right of search over foreign ships in peacetime. The navy therefore could no longer board vessels suspected of slave trading if they belonged to another nation.

British policy had to change. The Treaty of Vienna had condemned slave trading, and Britain increasingly sought to make treaties with the nations who persisted. The government paid £400,000 to the Spanish government as compensation for lost shipping (or bribery) on agreement that the slave trade would be abolished. The Portuguese had received £300,000 to make the trade illegal north of the equator. To regulate things further, Freetown now had a Court of Mixed Commission with a judge earning one and a half times the salary of the governor.[2]

More than any of this, it was the pique of Judge Robert Thorpe, a personal crusade of ill will and frustration that had revealed the flaws in the antislavery laws, which brought Bostock back to court. Thorpe, the man who had stood so firm against slave traders while sitting on the bench in Freetown, was now Bostock's loudest supporter. Removed from his post in absentia and never allowed to return to the colony, Thorpe had become an avid advocate for slave traders.[3]

Thorpe was busy accusing the abolitionists of all manner of wrongdoing even where he had previously been involved. He did have some grounds for grievance. While in Freetown he had written continually to London asking that the laws against the slave trade be clarified. After Lord Liverpool had written back in 1812 ensuring him that his scope was wide, he had been left alone to piece together what he could. He had argued that slave ships were legal prizes based on his reading of British law and treaty laws, and more generally on common ideas about humanity. It was only in October 1815, after Thorpe had been sacked and was beginning to vent his anger against the abolitionists, that a judge in the High Court of the Admiralty wrote to the British foreign secretary advising him that the rule of law instituted by Thorpe in Sierra Leone was invalid.[4]

If Thorpe had been content to claim mistreatment at the hands of the British government based on the lack of instruction, he would have made a sympathetic case. But he was an angry man bent on revenge, and in his rage he moved full circle to support the slave traders. It was a position that was not entirely logical.

Thorpe had published the polemic *Letter to William Wilberforce* about the conviction of merchants like Bostock and McQueen. It was as abstruse, as overstated, as those original vague laws that had brought him down. His reading of the antislave trade law was as confused as the government's had been. He quoted the Slave Trade Felony Act: "if any British subject, or any person residing in the united kingdom, or any island, colony, dominion, fort, settlement, factory belonging thereto" was caught slave trading, they were breaking the law. He used this to declare that Bostock and McQueen (or Bostwick and M'Quin as he called them) were wrongly charged because Cape Mesurado was not British territory. Yet surely the quoted law intended that the suspect had to be *either* British *or* in British territory for the law to be invoked, not necessarily both. Certainly the attorney general's opinion was that the Royal Navy could arrest slave traders who are either Britons *or* in British territory.[5]

Thorpe's reading of this was not even backed up by the cases of other slave traders whom he had already supported. James Dunbar, George Cook, and Malcolm Brodie, arrested at Rio Pongo in 1814, had taken their suits to court, supported by Thorpe. James Dunbar, demanding £50,000 from Governor Maxwell for his losses, did so on the grounds that not only was Rio Pongo not British territory but that he was an American citizen (or alternatively, covering all bases, that he was Spanish and that his real name was Santiago Dunbar). George Cook also stated unequivocally that he was not British, having been born in South Carolina. His testimony in July 1817 had begun, "the Plaintiff in this Case is a subject of the United States of America," before launching into a plea about having been reduced from comfort to "absolute beggary" by Maxwell's actions. Maxwell had overstepped his bounds, there being no "Law so absurd as to affect to bind the subjects of foreign Nations" if they were not in British territory.[6]

Dunbar had died sometime around then, but Cook had won compensation. The attorney general stated that although Maxwell thought Cook was an

Englishman, he was ultimately wrong to prosecute him, as Britons could not punish Americans for acts in neutral territory. Cook was awarded £20,000. If Charles Mason had still been alive, he would have been in line for a significant payout.[7]

It was left to Bostock alone to make his case, however, which was far less clear, as had been the claim of the third of the Rio Pongo slave traders, Malcolm Brodie. Brodie, like Bostock, was British. The fact that he had been pardoned alongside his American colleagues was less an aspect of the government admitting wrongdoing than what was thought to be practical mercy. By the time his appeal was heard in London, Brodie had been grossly disfigured, "A Species of Cancer having attacked his face, eaten away his entire mouth, and part of his right Cheek." He was so sick by the time he appeared in court "as to appear a being not of the Human Race . . . foetid and noxious." Brodie's plea was to be respited from transportation not because of his innocence but because he was "a dying man." He was believed to be far too sick to survive the voyage to Australia, and mercy was shown.[8]

The case of Samuel Samo, the Dutchman whose case had been in many ways the forerunner of Bostock and McQueen, had also shown forcefully that these cases depended upon the nationality of the alleged slave trader as well as the claims to the territory in which they did business. Before a packed courtroom, Samo had claimed to be a Dutchman born in Amsterdam and flourished his passport for travel from Suriname to New York. He spoke fluent Dutch. Faced with this evidence, authorities had performed some extraordinary twisting to make sure of his guilt. There had been the extra-legal claim that the Rio Pongo was British territory and the improbable declaration that Samo's surname was actually "very common among the Jews born in the neighbourhood of Duke's Place [in London]."[9]

It was far from clear, therefore, whether Bostock had a case for wrongful arrest if solely based on the grounds, as Thorpe claimed, that Cape Mesurado was not British territory. Initially, the British government's legal advisers were unimpressed with Bostock's case. "Bostock being a British Subject," they opined, "though his crime was committed in the territory of an African prince [he] is as fully amenable to the operation of that Law as if the crime had been committed in Westminster." They backed up their case by referring to the recapture of the *Bounty* mutineers, the first of whom had been arrested and taken aboard HMS *Pandora* at the decidedly un-British location of Tahiti. (In fact, this too was stretching the point, as the original crime of mutiny had been committed aboard the *Bounty*, a Royal Navy ship and therefore British territory.)[10]

But, rattled by the successful suits brought by Cook and Dunbar as well as the expensive claims from a whole host of slave ship owners, they could not afford to act hastily. They decided to contest Bostock's case and made a surprising decision. They sent word to Sierra Leone to find anybody who had been enslaved, bought, or sold by Bostock and McQueen and to again have them testify.

As the request headed out to Freetown, officials set about tracking down other people involved. Robert's brother Charles testified that they were both British citizens. Francis Hopkins, whose relation to the case is unclear, claimed to have letters from Bostock in which he confessed his guilt. Even George Clarke, the jail keeper in Freetown, was sent for.[11]

Men from the *Thais*'s crew in 1813 were tracked down. Lieutenant Watkins, in charge of the boats that had gone into the St. Paul River, had died in the intervening years, but others from the crew were found. William Winsley, who had been whipped as they made their way to Cape Mesurado, William Chambers, and William Matthews were all among the marines who had been in the boats. Winsley told of the "heavy fire of small arms" they had faced and recounted how Bostock and McQueen injured two of his crewmates. Chambers stated that John McQueen had been remorseful over the wounded marines, but when he had asked the Scotsman about the burning of the factory, McQueen had allegedly admitted, "our people set fire to it before yours came." Matthews was perhaps the strongest witness of the three, since he was the man who had been injured when Bostock and McQueen opened fire, but unlike his fellow victim he had lived to tell the tale.[12]

One of the most damning testimonies was from the quartermaster aboard the *Thais*, Thomas Lovekine. Although he was not one of the landing party, he remembered incriminatory details. He claimed that the men admitted firing on the marines and that McQueen had claimed that bribery would ensure their freedom.[13]

It was another of the *Thais*'s crewmembers who gave by far the most remarkable evidence, however. Sessay, once a boy taken aboard the vessel by Edward Scobell, was now a grown man. He had led a remarkable life in the Royal Navy. Since he appears to have remained aboard or rejoined HMS *Thais*, he seems to have visited the Caribbean, glimpsing a version of the life of endless toiling as a slave that he had so narrowly escaped. He must have been involved in the dramatic capture of enemy vessels. He had perhaps visited Penang, Madras, and Bengal and seen China. Had he been at St. Helena when Bonaparte was held there? The Mende boy taken from the slave factory of

Bostock, Mason, and McQueen had grown into a man who had seen the world. He was no longer Sessay, nor even whatever British name he had been given when first entered into the muster roll in 1813. Now his name was Lawrence Summers.[14]

Faced with remembering the horrific details of his earlier life, he made a detailed statement. He had been "stolen from his parents," he told the clerk, and "driven down the country." He cast his mind back to how it had shocked him to see the four boats arriving at the slave factory with white men on the day that the *Thais* attacked, and how he had been there when Bostock and McQueen had started firing. "The factory was set on fire before the White Men came to it." "Bostock and McQuin [*sic*] ran away," he recalled. This last, stating clearly that the premises were destroyed deliberately and inferring some rather cowardly fleeing, was a significant statement. Of those testifying it was only Sessay, already at the factory rather than arriving on the boats, who had seen what had happened.

At first he had struggled with the chalk stick in his hand, struggling to form it into English words. Tamba had been visiting William Johnson in the early mornings for a few years, going to the vicarage before he started butchering meat and burning wood for charcoal. Then in the evenings, after a full day's work and sometimes the ten-mile round trip walk to Freetown, he would join a class. He and the others would sit and roll the words around their mouths and then try and scratch them onto the slate. They read the Bible, struggling over so many words that were not phonetic.

Then, a few months earlier, when Reverend Johnson returned to Regent from England, he had presented Tamba with an extraordinary gift. Paper-making, other than that laboriously handcrafted from old rags, was in its infancy, but Johnson had procured some of this newly available material for Tamba. Quills were still the commonest type of writing implement in use, and they were easy enough to come by. Johnson encouraged Tamba to start keeping a journal. It would be yet another proof of an African man's ability to progress.

Tamba had taken up the challenge diligently and had begun recording his wandering and preaching. He traveled the area speaking to some of those who had come from the *Thais* and *Princess Charlotte*. Presumably he had also been talking to those in Regent, but in his journals he wrote only of those who had left the settlement to live elsewhere.

Likely he was attempting to get others to testify, especially since in Free-town authorities were not trying very hard to track down those who had once been owned by Bostock. No public announcement appeared, nor was anything published in the newspaper requesting their assistance. Seven years had passed, and some had died, victims of anguish and loss, disease and dismay. Others, like Sessay and some of those drafted into the armed forces, were no longer in the colony. Authorities simply did not know where to look for those still around, a puzzle that spoke of administrative muddle as well as the fact they were at liberty to go wherever they pleased. And again there was the troubling part of it all, that some of them had not been Bostock and McQueen's captives at all. David Noah, now a devout servant alongside Tamba, could hardly testify with-out muddying the waters since he had been counted among the 233 rescued from them but had actually belonged to John Sterling Mill.

Despite these setbacks, Tamba was seemingly trying to get others to give evidence. He wrote in his diary, "I went to see my country people first" and then traveled to "Calley place," probably referring to the man whose name the British had written as "Cauley," who was now in his late thirties. At Nebyo's Place—likely the man listed by the British in 1813 as Nibea—he met five men and four women who had moved away from Regent, again speaking as if at least some of them had arrived with him from Mason and Bostock's.

Those who heard the summons Tamba was issuing had more reasons for fearing it than for answering. It can only have been mysterious and rather terri-fying. Why were they wanted? What strange notions had these inexplicable white men come up with now that might single them out? Rumors swirled that if they raised their hands and admitted that they had been rescued from Bostock and Mason's compound, they would have to go to London to give evidence. It was petrifying to contemplate. It would mean traveling across the water where so many had departed and not returned. They would face their former owners in a foreign land, judged by laws they little understood. Surely the risk was per-petual bondage once more. It was safer to say nothing.[15]

On the eve of his testimony about the events at Bostock and Mason's factory, Tamba wrote nothing about it. It seems that it was on his mind, however. A few weeks before he had preached from Exodus 20: "I am the Lord thy God, which brought thee out of the land of Egypt, out of the house of bondage." Then as he rode home to Regent from Leicester village the evening before he gave his testimony, an uncharacteristic doubt filled his mind. When he reached home he sat down and wrote: "While I was going my mind told me, mind your-self every Day; you told the people to pray to God, and to leave of [sic] their country fashion, and perhaps you are not in the right way." He consoled himself with how sweet Jesus's name was to him when he first heard it and prayed hard, yet wrote that his "heart is the house of hell."[16]

While for his shipmates there were plenty of reasons not to give evidence against Bostock, for William Tamba it was an opportunity. Perhaps it was an act of repentance for his own part in the sufferings of those who were now friends and neighbors, and a way to damn Robert Bostock, whose actions had left him so deeply distressed. It was also a way to show his devotion to his Christian beliefs, allied as they were to the abolitionist movement. Tamba had spoken to Johnson of his former life, relating how he had been "the jailor" at Bostock and Mason's factory. He had been around the region begging his former acquaintances to give up their slave trading ways and was making peace with his own actions through the Bible. Since William Johnson was one of those collecting evidence, there was little doubt that Tamba would make a statement.[17]

Tamba testified that Robert Bostock had owned him since he was young, a pitiable story similar to the one Tom Ball had once told. While Bostock and McQueen would occasionally buy ivory or wood if a trader offered it, Tamba was unequivocal that their chief business was in human flesh. He recounted once more the arrival of the *Fénix*, the appearance of the Caulkers' canoes to warn Bostock, and how he, Tamba, was subsequently ordered to take the captives and go and hide. He claimed that he did not know what caused the fire at the factory, but he did offer that the houses of the Kru sailors were too far away for the conflagration to have begun there. Tamba also revealed that those who were brought to Freetown were only a fraction of the original number held at the factory. He told of how that had happened: he had been told to guard them at a nearby chief's compound, but more than half had escaped.

Tamba and Johnson also prevailed upon Yarra, now John Reffell, to give an account. He testified before Johnson that he had worked for Bostock and McQueen at Mesurado, stating, "Slave trading was their principal business and the means by which they supported themselves." At the time of the raid, Yarra recalled, Bostock had just bought the cargoes of two Spanish ships and was waiting to send the slaves from his barracoon as payment. But after Captain Roach arrived with the *Kitty*, followed later by HMS *Thais*, he and Tamba were sent away with slaves. Yarra told how he was hiding in the bush when fighting had broken out. He could not give any evidence as to whether Bostock and McQueen set fire to the factory deliberately to hide their crime or whether it was an accident. He also made another claim to back up Tamba's. Only about half of the slaves owned by Bostock and McQueen were recaptured and liberated in Freetown. The rest had mysteriously disappeared.

Tamba's and Yarra's statements revealed the influence of their years in Regent and of the British. Although Yarra (John Reffell) still endorsed his statement with the cross of the illiterate, William Tamba was now highly articulate and literate, all those years of study with Johnson obviously having paid off. Similarly, whereas Tom Ball had in 1813 been "sworn after the manner of his Country," Yarra and Tamba were now "duly sworn on the Holy Evangelists." (Summers, testifying before a different justice of the peace, does not appear to have been asked to swear or sign, although it might be that this was simply not noted.)[18]

None of this raised any doubt that Bostock and McQueen had been illegally slave trading when they were arrested. In fact, Bostock himself never denied it. Nor was there much debate about the principal matters of the case: Bostock was a British man, as even his own brother avowed, and Cape Mesurado was not British territory. The case did not, as Robert Thorpe had intimated, fall apart solely on those grounds.

Yet Bostock and McQueen had been wrongly convicted, and the British government knew it. The problem at the heart of their case was jurisdiction. The court in Sierra Leone only had jurisdiction over recaptured slave ships and crimes committed within its boundaries. Bostock and McQueen were captured not aboard a slave ship but on land at Cape Mesurado, beyond Sierra Leone's borders. As it had been put in the case of the French slaver *Louis* captured there in 1816, Cape Mesurado was "as much removed from the local jurisdiction of Great Britain [as] the middle of the Atlantic or the Baltic." It was an exaggeration but a valid point.[19]

Bostock and McQueen's wrongful conviction hinged not on the matter of their nationality, like that of Cook and Dunbar, nor even on whether their crimes were committed in British territory. What actually led to their conviction being overturned was an oversight on the part of the British government. Before their arrest in 1813 the British Government had failed to send out a new commission to Sierra Leone to allow them to try those captured for slave trading if they were beyond British boundaries and on land rather than at sea. Without such a commission, Bostock and McQueen should have been shipped back to England for trial.

Bostock had not been convicted in error so much as tried in the wrong location. This would actually have been an even stronger case had Charles Mason still been alive to press the issue, as the court in Sierra Leone had no jurisdiction whatsoever to make prizes of war. As William Wilberforce had earlier said when he stood in Parliament to discuss the cases of Dunbar, Brodie, and Cook, it was "a mere point of law not upon the merit of their case, that they got off." Another honorable member put it another way: "the defect was only in those persons not being tried by a proper commission; but . . . there was nothing else, either in the law or in the evidence, which was in their favour." They were "criminals" who had escaped "from merited punishment."[20]

So despite having gone to the extraordinary lengths of finding and interviewing William Tamba, John Reffell, Lawrence Summers, and any number of former crewmen from HMS *Thais* and various other relevant parties, and having taken the trouble of revisiting the words of Tom Ball and Yarra from years earlier, the British government had little choice but to overturn Bostock's conviction. Much more than the free pardon that arrived in New South Wales, this made Bostock a free man with no past convictions on his record. His slave trading past was expunged.[21]

With this in place, Bostock claimed £50,000 damages, the same sum claimed by James Dunbar. Supposedly this sum included compensation for four years imprisonment (an exaggeration, since he had actually been a convict for about two and a half years and for a large part of even that had been all but free) and the value of every inanimate item held at his slave factory when the *Thais* had arrived plus the buildings. He even included the cost of the three handkerchiefs he had owned at the time.

Bostock could hardly launch this suit against Governor Maxwell, as Dunbar and Cook had done, as Maxwell was already financially embarrassed after Cook's victory. Robert Purdie, the judge who sentenced McQueen and him back in Freetown, had died some years earlier. Bostock and Thorpe therefore launched the suit against Edward Scobell, former captain of HMS *Thais*. It must have been rather a shock to him since he had long before ceased to be leader of the antislavery squadron. After delivering Bostock and McQueen to England, Scobell had resigned his command, saying that he was "giving up the *Thais* for the renovation of my health." Like half of his crew, he had been unable to fully recover from the "lassitude and enervation" (probably recurrent bouts of malaria) that their time in Africa caused. He would pass away five years later at the age of forty-one.[22]

Already smarting from having to pay countless claims by wronged slave ship captains and having bailed out Governor Maxwell after Cook's £20,000 win, the government agreed to settle out of court. Since the settlement was hidden behind closed doors, there is no record of what Bostock received, and no amount is entered into treasury ledgers as having been paid to him at this time. Since he was not a foreigner like previous slave traders who had won compensation, his case was unchartered territory.[23]

Quite possibly, Bostock had already given the government a way to get rid of him with minimal financial damage. Around this time he applied to the secretary of state for a free settler certificate for Van Diemen's Land, the place he had seen from the decks of the *Harriet* for a few hours two and a half years earlier. It was about as far away as it was possible to go, a place Britain continued to send its dirty secrets. Why argue the finer points of the law if Bostock was happy with a free settler certificate and perhaps what might have been a quite small amount in cash?

22

Helping to Found Liberia

For all his devotion to Christianity, the first words that Tamba had written in his journal when he received it from Reverend Johnson revealed that he was still very much a Kissi man. His understanding of kinship networks remained West African, filtered through the lens of somebody who had been through the nightmares of the slave trade. His first entry had been about his shipmates, those who arrived with him aboard the *Thais*. He wrote of them as his "countrymen." They had arrived together, he wrote, and so must remain united together. Tamba may have brothers in Christ, fellow brethren in his church and faith, but he never conceived of giving up his other comrades.

But these connections troubled him. Just like those who worried that their families back home were condemned to hell because they had never heard Christian teachings, Tamba was desperately worried when his "countrymen" from Bostock and Mason's refused to convert to Christianity. He felt ties to them that he wanted to maintain, yet part of the teachings of the church were, as William Davis said, to "be a separate people," apart from non-Christians. Davis was "afraid that some did still keep company, improperly, with people of worldly minds."[1]

When Tamba had ventured to the tiny settlements of those who had left Regent, intent perhaps on having them testify against Bostock, the bigger aim was to speak about the state of their souls and their Christian beliefs. This at least was how he wrote about these encounters in the journals, which would later go to the CMS. At "Calley place," he asked Calley and his people if their hearts were good. They claimed that they were since they "Do No bad to any body." But Tamba harangued them, "God said every one of us is bad because God said thieves are fornicators, murderers, and adulterys, and liers, and such ascursed and mark the Lord's day." They would all go to hell, Tamba told them. The fact that he had told them of Jesus's words, but they had not accepted Him into their hearts, "Shall be a witness against you in the Day of Judgement." At Nebyo's Place he informed the people there that if they died that very night they would spend the rest of eternity in hell. They scoffed at his words. He had to leave without reaching any resolution and wrote that his "heart is full of sorrow for my country men."[2]

Mamaroo, returned from the West India Regiment, was also refusing to live in Regent and so warranted a visit from Tamba. Mamaroo's experiences over the six years since they had been rescued from Mason and Bostock's had been profoundly different from those whom he had left behind in Freetown's recaptive pen when he enlisted. While they had been in Regent, beginning farming and listening to entire Sundays of Christian teachings, he had been in the Caribbean and had likely witnessed the retribution after Bussa's rebellion. Who could wonder if he now chose to live away from white control?

It is also likely that it was his own Islamic beliefs that Mamaroo wished to hold onto. Like Indigenous belief systems, Islam was little accepted in Regent, and Tamba was combative when faced with Muslims and the Koran. Seeking to have autonomy, Mamaroo had formed a small hamlet outside Regent with five other men and three women, at least some of who had also come from Bostock and Mason's place.

"The Lord send me to clean myself from blood," Tamba announced, a mixing of the idea of Jesus's blood washing away sins with what was perhaps an intimation of his own guilt about events back at the slave factory. He then barked that hellfire was going to be their destination if they did not repent of their sins. One of the men tried to argue, claiming, "we no do bad," but Tamba chastised them, maintaining that they were going straight to hell for thrashing rice on a Sunday. They can only have been astonished by Tamba's rhetoric, this man whom they had once known as one of their enslavers in an entirely different world.

The words Tamba used in this exchange reveal that he too was still more an African than a British man with dark skin, as Johnson and the CMS aspired. Having called them countrymen, Tamba launched into a speech that spoke to the idea of "shipmates," common between the enslaved throughout the Americas. "The Lord brought us from a long country," he implored them. "Many of us come together." It was an ordeal that, at least in Tamba's telling, bound them together no matter their origins or their different experiences since that day.[3]

St. Charles Church Regent, 2017. Courtesy of Lansana "Barmmy Boy" Mansaray.

In Regent, where St. Charles Church was ever expanding and the pressure to attend was intense, others who had arrived aboard the *Thais* were among the most faithful. A couple of months before Tamba's and Yarra's testimony about Bostock's past actions, a number of the Liberated Africans had spoken in church of the events that had led to their captures, winding their enslavement stories into a Christian narrative of darkness and light, of bondage and freedom. David Noah was one of those who testified, speaking of his capture, of his fears when he was seized and then his terror aboard the naval vessel. He concluded that he was glad to have heard the word of God and hoped that his countrymen in this homeland might also hear the news.[4]

Others from the Liberated African community followed in piety. No names were given when this was reported back to Britain: they had become merely Christian Africans in the CMS's rhetoric. But their statements indicate that nearly all of them were in Regent, then called Hogbrook, before Johnson's arrival, revealing that more of the *Thais* arrivals, their Igbo neighbors, and other of the earliest settlers were among them.

One woman told how her mother died when she was young, and then a dreadful sickness had afflicted her people. Fearing this disease, her father took her away, but they were caught on the road. Her father begged and pleaded for her to be released, crying as her captors refused. She had been walked for days, sold hand to hand, all the time getting sicker and weaker until she was just skin and bone. As the woman related these events, she broke down and could speak no more.[5]

The tales they told made clear that the type of Christianity promoted in Regent was intended to replace not just their former religious and spiritual beliefs but also their cultures and ways of life. Woven into their stories were hints to the listening missionaries that they now disapproved of all manner of "native" behaviors, including drumming and gris-gris, which were thought akin to devil worship. Everything before their arrival in Regent was to be condemned in toto, the family life that many of them yearned for and missed terribly had to be denounced as forcefully as their time in coffles and barracoons. One woman outdid the others, telling an overblown tale of native savagery that she obviously believed the church leaders wanted to hear. She was captured along with all of her brothers and sisters, who were murdered and put into a pot, boiled and eaten, she related.[6]

Undoubtedly they were revealing trauma and hellish experiences. Yet there was something else too, discord between longings for their families and the lives the missionaries were promoting. "When I was a little boy, no done suck, fight come to my country," one young man revealed, continuing, "Mammy run away; and, when she run, she throw me away and a man come and pick me up, and I no see my Mammy again, bye and bye they sell me for a bundle of tobacco." The man was intimating that his mother, whom he could surely hardly remember if he was as young as he claimed, was what the missionaries would consider a bad woman because she was not a Christian. Since it was these events that had caused him to be saved and have found the light, his mother seems to have been cast into the darkness as his condemner, at least in this narrative told before the church. Jesus had now replaced their heathen parents. "Some white man take me and sell me," revealed one man, declaring, "I know not my father and mother, but God is my father and mother."[7]

Another man's story revealed that he had come to know that one of the commonest forms of rebellion, of liberation at their own hands, was believed a sin. He told of those who had jumped from the slave ship he was aboard, a common enough practice since many supposed that if they did so they would go home in death. Watching "plenty people jump into the water . . . I want to do the same," he revealed. Now, however, the man was clearly uneasy about these people's choice. "Suppose I been die that time," he grieved, "I go down to everlasting condemnation."[8]

Another man's story reflected the long-held problem that it was his capture and enslavement that had led him to God. He confessed before Regent's congregation that in some sense he must feel glad about everything that had happened to him, since it was this that led to his being in Sierra Leone and therefore that had ultimately allowed him to be saved in Christ.

Many who made the Middle Passage shared these mixed sentiments. Phillis Wheatley had made one of the most eloquent statements some fifty years earlier:

> 'Twas mercy brought me from my Pagan land,
> Taught my benighted soul to understand
> That there's a God, that there's a Saviour too:
> Once I redemption neither sought nor knew.[9]

The irony is that these viewpoints came close to arguments made by apologists for slavery. Before the slave trade had been illegalized, those advocating its continuance had promoted the idea that Africans were better off being enslaved to a Christian master than left alone without the Bible's teachings in Africa. Africans were barbarous and savage, the pro-slavers had posited, arguing that the trade advanced the cause of civilization by leading them to a place where they might learn the advantages of Christian society.[10]

It was an argument that still mattered after the British legal battles over the slave trade were won and the fight shifted to the institution of slavery itself. A man who sailed on the British antislavery squadron in the 1820s hated Sierra Leone and its liberated people passionately, finding them "wretched, naked and disgusting." Africans were clearly better off in the Caribbean as slaves than left on their home continent, he wrote, since in the Americas they could learn through Christianity to be men and not brutes.[11]

It was not solely the slave trade and slavery that Tamba, Wheatley, and so many tens of thousands of others on both sides of the Atlantic were fighting. The racism so inherent to, and reinforced by, the slave trade and slavery had created a world in which Africans' intelligence, aptitudes, and even ability to feel complex sentiments was in question among those not of African origin. Their ability to reason was generally thought greatly inferior to that of a white man. In showing that Africans could be Christians, learned, and well-mannered, Wheatley helped redefine the meaning of "civilization" to potentially include those with dark skin. The fact that a woman born in Africa—her gender, race, and place of birth confounding the doubters—could produce beautiful poetry challenged existing racial designations. In a world in which Africans' entire place as humans was called into question by philosophers, thinkers, and governments, Wheatley was "auditioning for the humanity of the entire African people."[12]

So too were Tamba, Davis, and David Noah. In those private lessons each morning and classes every night, learning to swirl the *T* when he wrote what was now his surname, neatly copying out catechisms and the psalms, Tamba was doing far more than learning to keep a journal and write letters to the CMS. He, Davis, and Noah, along with so many others who played smaller roles, were fighting for their right to be seen as fully fledged people in the Atlantic world, to throw off their image as uncivilized, naked cannibals and prove that they could equal anybody else given the right circumstances.

Yet it was a steep mountain to climb, with even some missionaries who supposedly assisted the Liberated Africans believing them to be desperately inferior. One noted, "the extreme ignorance, and the ridiculously absurd prejudices of the African, are beyond all conception." Another, John Morgan, wrote, "I had in England read, heard and thought much on the African character, or rather given into some prejudices against the mental endowments of the negroes, and lean[ed] rather still to the side of uncharitableness." It was only working with Tamba and other Liberated Africans that caused Morgan to change his mind.[13]

What the abolitionists, and their allies Tamba, Davis, and Noah, thought that they were working toward was the improvement of the entire African race, which they believed could only be attained through Christianity, education, learning to cultivate the land, and other acts that comprised "civilization." For the abolitionists, Africans were not *yet* on the same level as those of European origin, but there was nothing innate stopping them from leaping forward with the right assistance and training. It was an idea that would continue for the next decade or two before being smothered by fogs of bigotry. In the 1820s, Hannah Kilham, a missionary and educator based in Sierra Leone, thought that Liberated African children would soon do as well in school as their British equivalents. Governor Sir Neil Campbell, although holding Liberated Africans in "deep disgust," nonetheless thought that they "possess the same faculties and propensities as white people." The ultimate outcome of these ideas was that Africans might become darker-skinned Englishmen and women if provided with the right conditions. Every Liberated African was either a sunbeam for Jesus or well on the way to being one.[14]

The stakes extended far beyond Tamba and the other *Thais* and *Princess Charlotte* freedmen. They would matter even more in the years that followed. The abolitionists, having won the war to have the slave trade illegalized, were now focusing on outlawing slavery in Britain's Caribbean possessions. Sierra Leone was a proving ground. So it was trumpeted widely when some of the Liberated Africans of Regent were considered so "civilized" that they were called for jury service in Freetown. By the mid-1820s, no fewer than one in three people living in Regent could read and write, a huge achievement by any standard. Most of the children were in school, learning not just to read and write but dressmaking in the case of the girls and woodwork for the boys.[15]

British authorities were so keen to show that Sierra Leone was progressing along very British lines that at times the colony was in danger of being a parody. In 1819, Freetown Fair began with "an elegant dejune a la fourchette" for the colony's "gentry" and included a pony race and a ten-guineas cup. By 1820, the local *Royal Gazette* had progressed to a "Fashionable Memoranda" column that reported the doings of the elite. In one week there was a choice of "a petite fete champetrè" at the chief justice's "elegant chauniere," a dinner party on a visiting naval ship, a trip on the governor's barge, a "grand dinner party at the Pavilion," a small dinner at the Masonic lodge, and two smaller dinner parties at Government House. The newspaper also thought that its readership might appreciate tidbits such as poems by Lord Byron and a story about a man who, scandalously forgetting propriety, touched the queen's daughter on the arm. Liberated Africans were all taught to give rousing renditions of "God Save the King."[16]

They could not overstep the mark, however. They were supposed to be becoming black Englishmen, but few seemed to have really thought through that they might then consider themselves equal, much less that they would use the religion they were being taught to make that case. When Tamba dared to preach against "swearing, and cursing, and Drunkenness," warning that "every one who Dose these things shall go to hell," a white man in his congregation, Dr. Bell, "looked at me very sharp," he wrote. Afterwards the two men had "words." Being reprimanded for their conduct by an African was evidently not what many had in mind when they had taken jobs in Sierra Leone, and the next time Tamba visited Leicester to preach he found that "Doctor Bell was in his Room, he wished not to hear me talk." The visit after that, Bell took his horse and rode off down to Freetown in order to escape hearing Tamba's message. Recaptives were supposed to learn to be pious British Africans but always remember to defer to actual Britons regardless of their piety.[17]

Tamba's role was more difficult than most. If he failed to understand some of the dislocation inherent in the Christian teachings—their unattractive implication that enslavement and subsequent liberation was the only pathway for most Africans to being saved—it was perhaps because he still witnessed slave trading. This was highly unusual. He was even more exceptional in that he met those with whom he once was involved in slave trading several times after being liberated. He was a former slave, grabbed from his family before adulthood, who sat down to dinner with those still slave-trading like Philippa Hayes, John Sterling Mill, and the Caulker family. To Tamba, the very real alternative of the Christian faith was the bloody world of slave trading. Small wonder that he was such a devout servant of Jesus.

Tamba spent weeks traveling around the region speaking about his new beliefs, exhorting people to respect the Sabbath day and not use amulets. His most serious altercations came when people heard him speak but questioned his words. One man argued that the Bible was to white men what gris-gris were to black men, concluding that although he was glad to hear Tamba's words he would carry on with the "women, and greegrees." Then he defiantly claimed: "nor will I leave off selling slaves, for whom will work for me when I get old?" Another man, a Manding, challenged Tamba, saying that "God's book," the Koran, came from the East, not the West, and that Tamba's Bible was "devil's book." Angered by Tamba's assertion that Mohammed was a thief and that polygamy was sinful, the man cursed Tamba in a language he did not understand.[18]

His frequent short journeys to preach the word came to a temporary halt in late 1820 when Tamba embarked on a longer mission. A few months after testifying about Robert Bostock's former activities, Tamba was asked to join a major proselytizing mission with Johnson and six African youths from the seminary. They appeared to be "the white missionary and his seven negro sons!" one writer commented, though Tamba was Johnson's contemporary.[19]

There was a short journey from Freetown, during which they were so scandalized by the canoemen's language that they felt the need to stop for a cleansing prayer. Then, having already escaped being eaten by sharks, they were in danger when Johnson sank to his knees while attempting to wade across a creek. Tamba pulled him out.

Soon they reached the Banana Islands, where they met George Caulker, himself a convert to Christianity who had begun translating the Bible and some hymns into Sherbro. By this time Caulker had ceded the Banana Islands to Britain and was in the process of handing over power to them. When Johnson began introducing his party, Caulker immediately recognized Tamba, recalling that he had known him "when in the slave-trade on the plantains." Johnson told them that Tamba was now a Christian, and an arrangement was made that he would travel again around the whole area visiting each village to teach the word of God in Sherbro. William Tamba had become a sort of African John Newton, a sinner who had engaged in the slave trade but was now among the most devout.

The group then traveled on to Tamba's old home at the Plantain Islands. Johnson reported that the place had "much the appearance of a European residence." He noted that Tamba, "who had lived there," knew most of the people. Leaving the island, Tamba again showed his boating skills and his local knowledge, saving them all when they were in danger of being wrecked, and their pilot did not know what to do. Tamba's "calm unruffled spirit, his firm hand, and his steady eye" were what saved them.[20]

Almost as soon as he returned from this trip, Tamba left again, making good on his promise to return to the Banana and Plantain Islands to teach the word of God. If testifying against his old slave owner was courageous, the new venture was equally brave since he would be away from Johnson and his protectors. He risked re-enslavement daily, going straight to "his old acquaintances," who were utterly astonished to hear him "reason of righteousness, temperance and judgment."[21]

Tamba eventually returned to Regent at five in the morning on Christmas Eve, a Sunday, in time for the earliest of morning worship.

In February 1820 a vessel called *Elizabeth*, better known as the *Mayflower of Liberia*, weighed anchor in New York. Less than a month before the Missouri Compromise, the eighty-eight settlers aboard were leaving to form a free black republic. The high hopes transmitted back to America by Mills and Burgess less than two years before had resulted in a scheme to form a colony on Sherbro Island. The intending colonists were full of optimism, determined to found their own land and live on their own terms.

They arrived in Sierra Leone and waited to move to Sherbro. While there they met with John Kizell, the man who had once exhorted Charles Mason to stop slave trading. Kizell moved with the settlers to Sherbro, where they founded a new settlement, but it was not long before things started to go wrong. One of the leaders, Reverend Samuel Bacon, died from fever, and soon their settlement was all but deserted, even the church bell stolen in a miasma of tropical quarreling.[22]

A few months later Ephraim Bacon and Joseph Andrus, two more white Americans, arrived in Sierra Leone ready to join the new colony. Instead they learned the bad news about Sherbro, and Ephraim learned that his brother, Samuel, had passed away. Speaking with survivors, they decided not to restart the Sherbro plan but rather to find a new site for their colony and begin again. Reverend William Johnson met them and provided advice.[23]

Before they departed Freetown to find a spot, Johnson invited Bacon and Andrus to visit Regent. They gratefully accepted his hospitality and rode up into the hills to visit this renowned wonder. Andrus performed Holy Communion for no less than four hundred of Regent's people. They had heard that Grand Bassa was perhaps the best place for their settlement, but after "an interview with Tamba and Davis on the subject," they were slightly less certain; Cape Mesurado and other nearby locations apparently added to the mix. Johnson offered them some practical help: two translators to go along with them on their journey to find land for their new settlement. The translators would be Davis and Tamba. Tamba and Davis's inclusion on the mission "excited a lively interest among the people" at Regent, "who offered up many prayers for the success of the undertaking." The plan that Johnson had tried to put into motion two years earlier, when Cates had gone south to claim land at the St. Paul or St. John River, was reinvoked.[24]

Arrangements were made for Charlotte Bacon to stay with Johnson and his wife in Regent while her husband was away, and on March 19 the four men were ready to depart. Immediately they hit upon a problem, discovering that they could not sail because half of their sailors were drunk on shore. Captain Martin too was making "unnecessary delays" and causing trouble, alleged Bacon, who added rather cynically, "but I expected to find trouble in Africa."[25]

On March 25, as they "made land," Tamba was unsettled. "I remembered what I should speak to the people," he wrote, "and what I should Do for myself; and that made me feel afraid and made me more sick, and I could not sleep, but was full of fear, and trouble." What exactly he had to do "for himself" is unclear; the implication is that he was being encouraged to make some repentance for his former actions while a slave of Bostock and Mason. He took heart in the biblical message that Jesus had come not for the righteous but for sinners, and begged: "O Lord have mercy upon us" and "forgive all our sins and teach us to know more and more."

It was March 27 when they reached Cape Mount, and Tamba was "much cast down" and was so troubled that he could not pray. "When I prayed," he would write in his journal, "I could only say Lord Do what thou wilt with me; I am a great sinner: take away this stony heart and give me a new heart."[26]

Andrus and Bacon had been forewarned that King Peter, ruler of this whole stretch of coast, was "powerful and warlike" and "more deeply engaged in the slave trade than any of his neighbours." They did not attempt to meet with him but sailed on. They passed the St. Paul River and soon arrived at the mouth of the Mesurado River. Reverend Bacon wrote in his journal: "we came to anchor the next day, before two small islands, owned by John Mills [sic]."[27]

Bacon described Mill as a "yellow man" and denounced his establishment as "mere slave markets." They went on shore to meet "a dependent of King Peter," only to be turned away, even their present of trinkets rejected.[28]

Behind the rather scant recordings of Ephraim Bacon there are faint traces of two men with a mission. Within the United States the colonization plan was divisive, and later Liberia would come to have many problems, but from Tamba and Davis's perspective it was clear that they should help the Americans in what looked like a very worthy project. In 1819, the United States had passed a law allowing its navy to take anybody captured aboard illegal slave ships and return them to Africa, and there was hope among the British that this meant that the burden of suppressing the trade would be shared. Bacon and Andrus described their proposed colony as a place that would protect those brought in by American naval ships, much as Sierra Leone was a colony of the "recaptured." The prospect of an American colony equivalent to Sierra Leone seemed very real. Even before leaving Sierra Leone, Andrus and Bacon had two hundred recaptives who would join them if judged to be legally free. A new colony at the Mesurado or St. Paul River would be an act of redemption for Tamba and a huge victory. The place that anguished him would be reimagined as the beacon of freedom.[29]

Bacon's journal says little about Tamba and Davis on this journey, and in a sketch of the occasion they are standing to the side. Yet despite the fact that Mill was evidently fluent in English, Tamba played a bigger role than Bacon's journal suggests. William Tamba's recording of the affair was much more personal than Bacon's, since of course he knew Mill well and had visited him only the year before. He already knew that Mill had not kept to the "Recantation and Abjuration of the Slave trade" that he had made before the British at the time of Bostock's arrest. So instead of an outside observer commenting on a stranger, Tamba recorded a meeting between old acquaintances turned adversaries. "John Mills and Barky were there," he wrote, giving no further explanation of their roles; "I told them that we had come to get some land for the Missionaries to sit Down on." Barky, recorded by Bacon as "Baha, a black and native African," was Philippa Hayes's successor at Balli Island.[30]

In Bacon's journal, they were turned away and then simply left without another word. Tamba, however, gave a different version of events. Mill tried to dodge the Americans' demand, stating that the matter was not in his hands. He claimed to be unable to make a decision without consulting King Peter, who was too sick to be asked. Tamba stood his ground, demanding that Mill answer for himself rather than hiding behind a smokescreen of subjection. "The King has given you liberty to say to us about that what you like, I know that," harangued Tamba, intimating that perhaps he had even been negotiating behind the scenes. "And again," he added, "will you wait for the King when a ship comes for Slaves? Will you wait for him before you sell them?" A French slave schooner soon sailed into view, making his point, but it was a Pyrrhic victory.[31]

They had no choice but to sail on. But the area around Cape Mesurado had impressed the Americans. "The natural growth is luxuriant and abundant," enthused Bacon; "many of the trees attain to a large size, and present every indication of a strong and fertile soil."[32]

Soon they reached the St. John River, Bassa country, where they met with the local headmen. The old King John, who had made a deal with Cates, had died, and the new King Ben was unwilling to cede land even when the prior agreement was flourished. Instead he called a palaver. There a Kruman called Brown argued that the Americans were "emissaries from some slave ship" come to harm them, an accusation that Tamba could not let slide by. He interrupted Brown, cutting into his fiery speech to deny the charges. Eventually, after retiring to discuss under the "shade of a large silk cotton tree," the Bassa returned and offered a deal. King Ben agreed to their plan if the Americans made a written agreement not to interfere with the slave trade, and to in no way assist the antislavery patrols. Tamba wrote nothing of this condition, which surely must have appalled him, noting instead the price agreed for the land, "Two Cask of Rum, Two of Tobacco, one Box of Pips [pipes], 20 pieces of cloth, and many more things I forgot."[33]

Although dismayed by the condition imposed by the Bassa chief, Reverend Bacon nevertheless believed that he had secured land for an American colony, especially since King Ben sent his son back to Regent with Davis. The land was said to be thirty or forty miles square, "healthy and fertile—lying high—and producing rice of excellent quality, and all kinds of tropical grains and fruits and very good coffee, cotton and tobacco." The river itself, they enthused, "furnishes the best fish and oysters." It was a slice of paradise that would cost the Americans only "an annual supply" of items worth around $300.[34]

Back in Regent, the arrival of the Bassa king's son caused great rejoicing. David Noah learned that his father and siblings were alive and well, and others too heard news from home. But "the questionable contract with the Bassa tribe" was far from settled, no matter what the men liked to pretend, and was said to have "haunted those pious minds like malignant ghosts" that even prayer would not appease. Exactly what happened next is mired in myth and distortion, not least because Reverend Andrus died not long after his trip, and Ephraim and Charlotte Bacon were both very sick. Even the Bassa king's son soon passed away. Ultimately, the American colony would not be founded at Grand Bassa.[35]

According to one account, some Krumen were stuck aboard an American vessel that could not land because of a storm, and found themselves in America. They returned to Africa on a vessel captained by twenty-five-year-old Robert Stockton and also carrying Dr. Ayres, new agent of the Colonization Society. The Krumen apparently recognized Cape Mesurado as they pulled near and recommended the place. Stockton, Ayres, and some of the Krumen then went to salute King Peter, a meeting at which Stockton was harangued: "He be master of gunboat. He take ship with goods we sell. I be steward. He make masters wear iron. He break our trade." Stockton defiantly agreed that this was true; he was "an annoyer of the slave trade" by profession, and in the ensuing fight he pulled his gun.[36]

By some embellished accounts, Stockton held his gun to King Peter's head, and a "shaft of golden sunlight appearing" at that moment, the Americans took it to mean that God esteemed their plan. By more sober reckoning it was John Sterling Mill who sent a young boy as a messenger, telling Stockton and Ayres to return. A small bull was offered to them as apology. The palaver began again, and finally, on Christmas Eve 1821, it was agreed that a strip of the coast 120 miles long, stretching 40 miles wide, and to include the islands owned by John Sterling Mill and Barky (formerly Philippa Hayes) could be had for six muskets, powder, a barrel of rum, clothes, four umbrellas, three walking sticks, four hats, ten iron pots, soap, and some shoes.[37]

Relieved at last to have a place to found their colony, prospective settlers in America began to prepare for their new lands. Unfortunately for them, by the time they arrived King Peter had changed his mind. The only place they could disembark was on the small island owned by John Sterling Mill. He had "sold" his tiny island, plus his house upon it, to the American agents for "the consideration" of a barrel each of rum, bread, beef, and port, a tierce of tobacco, and a piece of cloth. They renamed the island Providence. The Reverend Lott Cary, one of the earliest settlers who had been born a slave in Virginia and purchased his own freedom, wrote of Cape Mesurado, "It is a delightful spot . . . here I expect to spend my days." "Our work is almost like building the walls of Jerusalem."[38]

Was there some destiny perhaps, some attempt at deliverance, in Tamba being part of a plan that refashioned the slave barracoons he knew so well into an island of freedom? Tamba's and Davis's roles in these events are underplayed, yet the accounts read as if somebody had been pushing firmly for Cape Mesurado, perhaps even for Mill's island specifically, as the perfect place for the American colony. The Americans had been told that Grand Bassa was the most likely spot before they met Tamba, but after this meeting Bacon wrote, "The neighbourhood of Cape Mesurado" had "been indicated as a part of the coast favourable to our purpose." Tamba and Davis might have been largely airbrushed from the common accounts of Liberia's founding, left a role as little more than boatmen and translators, but it seems that they were much more than that. They had an objective in view and determined that the place that Tamba had once hidden Bostock and Mason's captives, the place that others of the kin that they had formed in Regent, like David Noah, had once been held chained and "treated like brutes," would be the frontline of a new nation of African liberty.

23

Van Diemen's Land

Following his trip back to Britain, at the end of February 1821 Robert Bostock arrived in Hobart, Van Diemen's Land. It was three years and two months since he had departed Sydney as an emancipated convict. Now he carried a certificate from the secretary of state for the colonies declaring that he was a free settler. Rather than a convict who had been freed, a common enough status in Britain's Australian colonies, it was as if he had never been a convict at all.

Bostock never revealed much about his decision to again sail for the colonies rather than remain in Britain, but clearly the ease with which he had made considerable wealth in Sydney appealed to him. Since the end of the Napoleonic Wars Britain had suffered a severe economic downturn, so there was little beyond family to keep him in England. But returning to Sydney, where John McQueen was still faithfully running their businesses, was not appealing. People there knew only too well that he had been a convict. To make a new start he needed to go somewhere that his past was not known.

Not long before he left Britain, Charles Jeffreys's book *Van Diemen's Land* was printed, recommending the island in the glossiest of terms. According to Jeffreys, Van Diemen's Land was "El Dorado . . . pregnant with every essential article of human necessity." In postwar Britain it "arouse[d] a mania." The more extreme of Jeffreys's claims were not actually true; the book had been plagiarized from a stolen manuscript. ("Lieutenant Jeffreys . . . sometimes deals in the marvellous," claimed the writer whose manuscript he had bootlegged, in what must be considered a model of restraint.) But it mattered little to intending emigrants who believed they would make money in the colony "by hook or by crook." Jeffreys's book created "ship-load after ship-load hurrying to their distant and eagerly adopted homes."[1]

The climate may also have played a role in Bostock's decision. Contemporary writers always mentioned Van Diemen Land's weather when writing about the island, praising its very English coolness. Charles Darwin, visiting Hobart in 1836, wrote in his diary of the temperature making the land fertile and abundant. Others trumpeted that Van Diemen's Land climate was "the most salubrious and congenial of any in the known world," "more congenial" to a European's "constitution" than the sunshine of Sydney.[2]

This mattered for reasons far beyond a personal preference for showers and mist. Climate was considered to have a direct link to race by way of the darkening effects of the sun. Notions of inherent superiority and inferiority were tied up with climate. James Ross, who arrived as a free settler in Van Diemen's Land in 1822, wrote that he chose it because he believed that in Sydney's climate a man "must content himself with having his future progeny . . . as dark and swarthy as a Spaniard, or a Tawny Moor." It was, said Ross, "to resign the complexion if not the constitution of an Englishman." Whether this was a consideration for Bostock, who now had three children with Rachael, we cannot know, but it might well have mattered more to a man who had once been the father of a mixed-race family than it did to men like Ross, for whom such concerns were more notional.[3]

When the Bostock family arrived, Hobart was so rough and ready it was known as "the Camp." Another settler who docked just after Bostock wrote that the settlement was "in a very embryo state." Its population of about two to three thousand people lived in wattle-and-daub huts, and the "old market place" was little more than an "impassable mud hole" that the tide washed over. The jail was so flimsy that just before Bostock's arrival some thieves rather inventively broke *into* the jail to steal from the jail keeper. "Open concubinage" was said to be rife, and rumor told of wives sold for fifty ewes or £5 plus a bottle of rum. Even the lieutenant governor, William Sorell, was a "base and treacherous seducer" living openly with another man's wife.[4]

For all that, it was a very good time to arrive in Van Diemen's Land. A weekly market was just beginning, new roads were being built, and a mail service was starting. The worst of the bushranger terror seemed to be behind them. Looking back some twenty years later, one writer claimed that Van Diemen's Land's "virtual nativity dates with 1820," as before that time it was "little better than an extensive penitentiary." That year marked the date when Hobart "sprung up with a celerity worthy of Aladdin and his redoubtable lamp."[5]

Bostock had carried an assortment of merchandise with him from England, and soon he placed an advertisement in the *Hobart Town Gazette* for brandy and gin, cloth and clothes of various kinds, plus "a few dinner services of elegant china."[6]

Then he set off for Sydney to sort out his affairs with John McQueen. His old business partner had been running their business under the name "Bostock and McQueen," but now bought him out completely, one sign among many that McQueen too was doing well. He had just applied for an auctioneer's license and acted as agent for prominent men whose businesses took them out of town. This soon proved to be exceptionally lucrative when one client left him an incredible bequest: the schooner *Endeavour*. McQueen had it refitted and began trading with Van Diemen's Land and Robert Bostock. McQueen also now had a common-law wife, Catherine Ryan, and two children.[7]

On his return to Hobart, Bostock applied for a land grant. Normally these were made in June, but it was July 2, 1821, when Bostock put his case before Lieutenant Governor Sorell. Sorell was handing out grants of land on a scale never before witnessed: 47,180 acres were allocated to settlers just in 1821, obviously with no regard whatsoever for the diverse populations whose ancestors had lived there for at least forty thousand years. The amount of land given depended upon the amount of money a settler had, or rather what he claimed to have, a figure generally inflated, so Bostock listed his assets. He professed to have £1800 "Merchandize & Cash on Hand," the houses in Hunter Street and Bligh Street in Sydney worth £1200 and £300, respectively, and another £1800 from the proceeds of the business with McQueen. (This more than anything suggests that his payout from the British government had not been more than the cost of his family's voyages and the goods that accompanied them.)[8]

Sorell allotted Bostock a prize plot of land by the waterfront—today the site of the twelve-story Hotel Grand Chancellor, formerly the Sheraton—where he built a new store. He sold all manner of items: a Brussels carpet with a chintz pattern, a mahogany footstool, and a silk sash. There was a demand for these things because, just as in Freetown, the population was socially aspirational and trying to re-create Anglo-Saxon culture. There was only a tiny middle class, but these few tried to outdo each other. Settlers held dinners with new ingredients adapted to mimic the old: kangaroo pies, roast kangaroo, and kangaroo soup. Soon Hobart had regular regattas, cricket matches, and horse races. The Bostocks were at the forefront of dignified colonial society, and Reverend Robert Knopwood made polite social calls where they drank tea and discussed the weather.[9]

Bostock remained utterly silent about his past. Rachael, having traveled back to England with him for the court case, must surely have been aware of his conviction, but his children were never told of their father's earlier career.

Despite the overwhelmingly abolitionist sentiment in Britain, it was not just his slave trading past that he was hiding. He was extraordinarily anxious to dissociate himself from the "convict stain." Free settlers held themselves aloof from convicts and emancipists, religiously laying claim to their moral superiority. Van Diemen's Land was said to be "a caste-based society, with an untouchable majority barred from almost all contact" with the free. As a free settler who had once been a convict, Bostock needed all the distance from the convict and ex-convict world he could get.[10]

Socially this was critical. It was not just a matter of his and Rachael's hopes of entertaining the better sort at dinner. His children's chances depended on his ability to protect them from the convict stain that he had avoided by the merest of margins. There were stories of children thrown out of schools when it was discovered that their long-dead mother had once been a convict. Bostock understandably wanted nothing of the kind for his growing family.[11]

24

Liberty
in White and Black

Tamba did not return to Regent with the two American missionaries and Davis. As they sailed past the Banana Islands he disembarked, following the earlier request from George Caulker to spend time at the islands. As he went about preaching the word he diligently recorded in his journal his successes and the problems he ran into. Returning to one village two years after his first visit, he found that they had miscalculated the days of the week and so had been resting on Saturdays instead of Sundays. One man demanded to know what he should do with his other wives if he was now to just have one. Another said that he would rather Tamba had brought clothes from the white men instead of more orders. Despite all this, the whole visit was so successful that George Caulker wrote a letter to the CMS asking if they could "spare him [Tamba] again before the rains, before the people are lulled again to sleep?"[1]

Tamba hoped to be a missionary among the Sherbro, but it was not to be. Instead he was sent to St. Mary's, today Banjul, at the mouth of the Gambia River. The CMS's first preacher sent there had died, and the second departed, so Tamba was sent to fill in, showing the high standing he had attained. A small settlement of 1,845 people, St. Mary's had a small courthouse, a barracks, and a hospital and was home to a Wesleyan mission as well as the CMS mission. The Wesleyans' Reverend John Morgan should have been an ally for Tamba, but it was not that simple. Morgan wanted to escape back to England, believing that "the brutal wretchedness of the natives" meant that they were "inferior to the human species, and incapable of benefitting from his labours." It must have been unimaginably difficult for Tamba, with his friends eight hundred miles away in Regent and his only likely ally believing him not just unequal but less than human. Nevertheless, Tamba went about his work, holding services twice a day and working as the settlement's schoolteacher. He even had some success,

it being reported that "the people under his care do certainly improve" and
that the schools were now in "good order."[2]

Tamba sailed back to Regent in 1822, critically ill with pleurisy (possibly a
complication of pneumonia). He survived and returned to his usual rounds of
preaching and prayer meetings, actually in better health than many as ophthal-
mia then yellow fever swept the colony. When Reverend Düring had to leave
due to illness, Tamba was placed in charge of Gloucester Village, and soon
after William Davis took control at Bathurst. That Christmas Day, Tamba
walked with his entire congregation over the hill to Regent, making what Johnson called "the largest congregation I ever saw in Africa."[3]

By this time David Noah had become the schoolteacher at Regent. Johnson wrote of him:

> David Noah is employed from daybreak till ten o'clock at night, a continuance
> of exertion which no European could endure in this climate. He conducts
> entirely the day and evening schools; besides this he issues rations for about
> 1,200 people, keeps the provision-lists and returns, and school-lists, measures
> out all the lots, and sees that the houses and fences are regularly built; prays
> with the sick, receives the stores every Thursday in Freetown, enters marriages,
> baptisms &c. and does the duty of a parish clerk; in short, he is every thing at
> Regent's Town.

Noah did all of this "with great pleasure," enthused Johnson, "and never thinks
that he can do too much." Perhaps most astonishingly of all, Johnson wrote to
the CMS: "I would not exchange him for a European school master."[4]

Noah attended Bible classes morning and night with his wife, and in the
second of a new set of classes in late November 1822 he spoke so well that his
message was conveyed back to England. Reading from Ephesians II, he took
especial note of verse eight: "For by grace are ye saved through faith; and that
not of yourselves: it is the gift of God." He spoke to the group about how he
found in this passage "a view of the slave trade, how God had brought good
from evil."[5]

So close was their bond, so deep the admiration, that in late 1822, when
William Johnson again asked permission from the CMS to travel to Britain
since his wife was sick, consent was sought for David Noah to accompany him.
Noah had been "begging hard," Johnson wrote, noting that he would travel as
his servant and so incur little expense. In early 1823 the CMS replied granting
Johnson authorization to take a break, but they wrote, "Respecting David

Noah, the Committee came to a different decision. We have seen so much evil arise, with hardly an instance to put into the opposite scale, from Africans coming to this country." Fearing the "temptations and snares to which he would be exposed, and the spiritual injury he might receive," it was decided to "decline to authorize his coming with you." They had written to him to "soften the disappointment."[6]

Noah stayed behind, and along with Davis and Tamba he was left in charge of the CMS's entire endeavor in Sierra Leone. It was testament to their abilities and was truly an amazing achievement: only a decade from enslavement, having recently learned to read and write English, they temporarily took over the venerable body's activities in the region. In March 1824, Noah traveled to Kissy and on the anniversary of the CMS mission there courageously told his story, recounting how he had been a child sold into slavery while on a trading mission. The wrongs done to him he attributed to the lack of faith beyond the colony. Before the Kissy crowd, he explained: "As there was no Christian Religion there; there was no pity so I became a slave." "My African brethren I beseech you to be thankfull," he preached, adding, "you know what we were once."[7]

The problem they would face without a man as open to African brotherhood as Johnson was already very clear. Just before Johnson left, Tamba had caused a scandal by preaching, "both white and blacks, dying in their sins, would be cast to hell." When he spoke these words, the one white man in the congregation, named only as Mr. S, "was enraged, and has ever since hated Tamba," wrote Johnson. As earlier with Dr. Bell, any intimation that everybody would be equal before the eyes of God on Judgment Day was obviously pushing things too far for some. Tamba was unrepentant and, supported or at least not chastised by Johnson over the matter, boldly refused to apologize for his words.[8]

After Johnson sailed away, the CMS also discounted Tamba, Noah, and Davis, overlooking their leadership, which they considered to be naturally inferior. African leaders were akin to no leader, and Regent's people were now "like sheep without a shepherd." Tamba came as close as he would to chiding them for this attitude, as well as censoring those like Mr. S, on Christmas Day 1823, not long after Johnson's departure. Writing from Gloucester, Tamba wrote rather pointedly, "I am put a poor Black Man, but God is no respecter of persons." He was equal, he asserted, in the eyes of the Lord, whatever they chose to believe. It was a brave and bold comment, couched in terms that made it difficult to rebuke.[9]

Not long after Johnson's departure, news arrived that Governor MacCarthy had been killed in conflict with the Ashanti. It was a terrible blow to the whole colony. In March 1824, all seemed to be well, with Tamba reporting, "morning and evening prayers is kept regular," though Noah wrote of a smallpox outbreak that had carried away twenty of their pupils. By April, Tamba reported to the CMS: "its gone very ill with us." He took solace in the words of St. Matthew's Gospel, "blessed are ye when men shall revile you, & persecute you" and prayed, "the Lord knows what he intends to do with poor Africans."[10]

Then in the first week of September disastrous news arrived. Reverend Norman, who was standing in for Johnson at Regent, revealed it first to his closest confidantes. Johnson had passed away not long after his ship sailed, some of his last words apparently reserved for Noah, whom he wished to be told to "go on steadily in his duty." Noah was devastated, but Norman simply told him and all the others that they had to bear "the trial with Christian meekness and patience." That evening Norman broadcast the news to Regent's entire congregation. "I spoke to them," he wrote, "and begged them not to make any noise, as I knew it was an African custom to cry aloud when they had lost a friend. I told them that the Christian manner of bearing a trial was with patience and silent submission. Nevertheless, the CMS would report, "A general cry of weeping (as only Africans can make) enveloped the town." Even in mourning they were simply too African.[11]

Noah wrote to the CMS that it had "pleased the Lord to try us on every side, in taking away our Spiritual Father." Tamba would record these losses with the simple remark, "it go dark sometimes with us." By December things had settled down. When Reverend Düring returned he was very pleased with Tamba's progress. "William Tamba has conduced the whole to my entire satisfaction," Düring wrote, "and the people seem to like him very much, for, as yet, I have not heard a single individual complain of him; but, on the contrary, all speak of him with respect." But with the congregations dwindling and revenues declining, the CMS was less than happy. The Liberated African preachers were rebuked for not inspiring their people to donate enough money to the missionary cause, considered the "spiritual barometer of any Christian community."[12]

By the standard of his times, Tamba was wildly successful. Yet he struggled with his racial origins, no matter his valiant defenses against bigotry. His letters and journals give a privileged view into his life and opinions and reveal that despite his triumphs he was inevitably affected by the culture of white degradation toward people of African origin that prevailed all around the Atlantic world.

Despite Tamba living where Africans were the overwhelming majority, his skin color seems have been a source of some shame to him, or at least very ambiguous esteem. Spending his youth as a slave in the transatlantic slave trade can hardly have left him unaware of the implication of his skin color to Europeans, even before confrontations with men like Mr. S. Then in Regent he was taught that he was also the color of sin. "I am but a poor Black man," he wrote in 1824, referring to spiritual rather than material poverty. More than three years later he wrote, "Though the world may call me black; yet the Lord is able to make me white by the blood of his Son Jesus Christ."[13]

Johnson and MacCarthy's deaths heralded the beginning of cutbacks and reductions. After 1824, the CMS no longer administered Regent, Gloucester, and the other villages, and expenditures were severely cut.

In some ways the years that had gone before had been a golden age in terms of support the liberated would get from Britain. The colony was failing economically, and Britain increasingly looked to cut costs. Farming was fruitful enough at Regent: in 1820 Liberated Africans there sold "near 7,000" bushels of rice to the government to feed those less productive. But the majority of farms were nowhere near that fruitful, and as a whole the recaptive community did not support itself, unlike the liberated populations in Cuba and Brazil. Nor had Sierra Leone found a staple crop for export. The amount that the colony cost Britain was repeatedly raised in Parliament and would matter much more by the following decade when there were calls to abandon it all together.[14]

Regent never really got back its status as a model village after Johnson's departure. Norman, his successor, stayed only a year, and his replacement died after only a short time at his post. In 1826, Noah wrote, "as fast as the Lord is sending us his faithful servants among us, so fast he remove them from us by death." Noah admitted, "sometimes I incline to think the Lord intends to leave us entirely to punish us our sins on account of our wickedness." The Liberated African faithful had to fill in, with the CMS dispatching them to the various villages, whether they wanted to go or not. First, David Noah was appointed native teacher at Kissy. He admitted to the CMS that leaving Regent was "a trial" for him, and later Tamba declined to follow an order from the CMS to also move to Kissy and take control. This led to Tamba being suspended for "contumacy." He was forced to beg for forgiveness for the "inward Sickness" that had caused him to disobey this "order." He would not make the same mistake again and seems to have gone about his work quietly from them on, aware that his days of negotiating with Johnson were over. From the mid-1820s, Tamba lived in Regent but moved throughout the Krio villages, working for periods in Gloucester and Wellington and regularly visiting Kissy, Kent, Hastings, and Waterloo. Noah also traveled around to teach and preach, writing in 1826, "there are not people enough belonging to the Society to fill every station."[15]

To some extent Tamba internalized the idea that his own leadership was inferior to that of white Europeans, or at least he was prepared to intimate this to the CMS. He longed for more white people to be sent out to Sierra Leone and must have desperately missed the heyday of Johnson's leadership. Writing to the CMS in 1827, he prayed that "the Lord send more faithfull people to come & preach the Gospel of Christ among poor black people." Without them, his congregation "fell back into the world, by the sin whoremongers & adulterers." Noah too wrote to the CMS begging that they "pray for the poor sons of Ham," referring to the idea that Africans were the descendants of the biblical Noah's son, punished by the curse of Canaan for an evil deed.[16]

Tamba remained a devout servant through periods of debilitating sickness. In March 1828 he described his routine: "On Monday evening we keep prayer meeting. Tuesday I visit the school only Boys, no Girls school, afternoon I visit the Sick. On Wednesday I visit the hamlets between Hastings & Allans Town, evening I speak to the people when about seventy attend. On Thursday I visit the hamlets of the Town between Hastings and Waterloo; Friday I visit the school evening I speak to the people." David Noah had similar duties, traveling throughout the hills and to Kissy.[17]

Then in 1829, David Noah made a decision to "leave the missionary work of this colony for the purpose of returning to my Native Country to settle." He wrote of his "benighted Countrymen, whom I can see no longer without a hope in the world." The CMS granted him six weeks' leave to travel to Bassa and report back on the feasibility of his plans.[18]

He sailed in February for the new colony at Liberia that now lay between Sierra Leone and Bassa country, attending a church service and visiting Governor Randall. Then he sailed on to Bassa. Setting foot ashore, he wrote that he was "surrounded by many of my Countrymen." "I appeared to them just as one who arose from the dead," he wrote, noting that some were too afraid to approach him, thinking him some kind of ghost. With great sadness he learned that a slave vessel had only recently carried away a great number of captives.

King Tom sent for Noah, and a fatted goat was killed to celebrate the return of his lost Bassa son. Some of Noah's family arrived and cried "in their country fashion" with joyfulness. Noah told them not to cry, speaking of how the Lord had blessed him since he had been stolen away. "I cannot fully express with pen," he wrote, "the joy and gladness which possessed us while we were together."

Noah began preaching to his countrymen, reporting that they were astonished to hear the Bible in the Bassa language. Noah chastised them for wearing
fetishes, to which they answered that it was their custom and that his own ways
were merely "whitemen's fashions." Although he was welcomed by many local
chiefs and believed that they would support his returning to live in Bassa country,
he found it tough, reporting that many thought his instruction to rest on the
Sabbath was mere "foolishness." Nor could he persuade them to stop sacrificing
chickens to their "greegrees," and he lamented one Sunday, "we were obliged
to have Divine Service by ourselves." Attending a funeral, he hated the drumming and dancing and wrote, "Nothing but heathenism is carried on among
them." It was all so dispiriting that soon Noah was ready to return to "my
Christian friends."

He did not speak of any fear that he might be re-enslaved, but throughout
his visit he was extremely disheartened to see the arrival of slaving vessels. "Oh
when shall this horrible traffick of human blood be done away?" he implored
in his journal. Then on his way back to Regent he took passage aboard the
schooner *Susan*, which found itself surrounded by slave ships when they reached
Cape Mount. The slavers launched musket fire and cannon at them, and only
by luck did he escape unharmed. Taking refuge on shore, Noah saw "no less
than about 3 or 4 hundred slaves." He returned to Regent dejected, sad that his
homeland was still so badly afflicted by the slave trade, and arrived to the devastating news that his wife had passed away in his absence.[19]

Far away in Van Diemen's Land, in 1826 Bostock received another grant of
land. It was to the north of Hobart on the South Esk River. It was frontier land
but a very beautiful spot. Within a few years he had another adjoining 1,800
acres granted to him. He began to build a grand home as well as a barn, granary,
yards, and stables and soon owned 63 cattle, 2,500 sheep, and 8 horses. He was
allotted a whole coterie of convict servants—mostly petty thieves—to work for
him both in the fields and in the house. His family had three pianos including a
grand, and they played backgammon and shot possums.[20]

He was part of Australia's burgeoning wool industry. Once merino sheep
were found to flourish in Australia, the colonists had a product that was in huge
demand on the world market and that could be transported relatively cheaply
for long distances. The number of sheep owned by settlers skyrocketed from
sixteen thousand in 1816 to sixteen million by 1850, an expansion driven by the
fact that "land was not only abundant but essentially priced at zero." Wool

proved astonishingly profitable, becoming the main force behind Australia's economy—soon providing some of the highest standards of living in the world—until it was outshone by the gold rushes of the 1850s. Funded also by "enormous subsidies" from the British government, life was very good for those among Australia's pastoral businessmen.[21]

Bostock's daughters were part of the exclusive set who attended boarding school at Ellenthorpe Hall, hand-picked by the redoubtable headmistress Hannah Maria Clarke as being suitable objects for her lessons in refinement. Board and tuition was £40 a year and included lessons in French, decorative needlework, and dance. Instruction on the harp cost extra. One frequent visitor to Bostock's (he was enamored of one of Bostock's daughters) wrote, "the view from . . . the residence of Mr. Bostock is very beautiful. The river winding through the valley, its course marked by long times of the Tea Tree, and old Ben Lom[o]nd a lofty mountain in the distance."[22]

Africa must have seemed far away; John McQueen was his only real tie to the past, and even he was 650 miles away in Sydney. Even for McQueen, the past was being left far behind as he was making extraordinary business advances. He opened a store near the King's Wharf, branched into the seal trade, and bought shares in the Bank of New South Wales. He increasingly left the day-to-day running of his business to others, as befitted a gentleman.[23]

Then suddenly John McQueen was dead, still only in his late thirties, passing away at his home in Princes Street. He was buried on March 21, 1829, at St. Phillips Church, "the ugliest church in Christendom," where Robert and Rachael had married. McQueen's obituary in the *Sydney Gazette* called him an "enterprising and upright Merchant of this Colony."[24]

When Tamba had written of being a "poor black man" he was not generally referring to his economic situation—Tamba was far from poor when compared to the many recaptives who struggled to feed themselves—but the type of wealth rapidly being accumulated by his former owners in Australia was far beyond his reach. He tried to be accepting of his lot, writing in 1826, "the world may count me poor, I need no more."[25]

By 1829, a handful of Maroons and Nova Scotians had well-paid positions in the government, but even they were usually mixed-race men born to European fathers. A few sons of Maroons and Nova Scotian fathers did gain government work, but they were paid significantly less than their mixed-race colleagues. Such opportunities simply did not exist for Liberated Africans. They were not only damned by their blackness but also regarded as "corporate objects rather than individuals," like other former slaves unable to shake off their former status as merchandise.[26]

The land grants seen in the Australian colonies were unknown in Sierra Leone. Even the land that Tamba, Yarra, and all the others cleared and cultivated when they first reached Regent would be mostly lost. When Sir Neil Campbell took over as Sierra Leone's governor in 1826, he announced the seizure of all informally held land. A British visitor in 1834 saw that land grants given to recaptives were "limited to about half a rod" around the "square shed" in which they lived, a situation he compared unfavorably to Liberia, where recaptives had land grants of fifty acres.[27] But even the Liberian example was tiny compared to most land grants in Australia.[28]

In Van Diemen's Land, Bostock had eight thousand acres allotted to him by the government, and he had earlier been given the land on Bligh Street in Sydney where his shop stood. John McQueen was only just starting to build his holdings when he passed away but had already been granted four hundred acres in 1821. In Sierra Leone, recaptives had tiny plots to grow a few vegetables for their own sustenance, similar to the strips cultivated by the enslaved in the Americas. In Australia land was "the most important resource during much of the nineteenth century, and access to it was the principal route to acquiring private wealth." Land meant wealth and status, and Bostock and McQueen still had far more than those who had been rescued from them.[29]

Sierra Leone's economic strife—its failure to find a staple crop that would make it valuable to Britain—was an ongoing problem. By 1830, there were moves before the British Parliament to withdraw from the colony altogether. Even Thomas Fowell Buxton, leader of the abolitionists, admitted, "the experiment of Sierra Leone has failed." An 1832 *Dictionary of Commerce* condemned Sierra Leone as "the most pestiferous of all pestiferous places."[30]

By Sierra Leonean standards, nonetheless, Tamba was doing very well. By the late 1820s, Tamba's son, also named William, enlisted at Sierra Leone's Fourah Bay College, the first Western-style university in West Africa. Mark Joseph Tamba, who assisted in church duties, may have been another son.[31]

As Tamba went around the villages of Sierra Leone, he was not simply preaching from the Bible but was engaged in melding the people into communities that cut across language and ethnic ties. They were beginning to be Krio. Tamba himself came to write of those who were not Kissi nor his shipmates from the *Thais* and *Princess Charlotte* as countrymen. Mende, Kono, and others might be included in this term as the years went by, forming the kind of regional affiliation that enslaved Africans often made on the plantations of the Americas.[32]

The Regent house of the Reffells, the descendants of Yarra, alias John Reffell, who was enslaved by John McQueen in 1813. Possibly on the same land their ancestor first built his home. Note St. Charles Church in the background. Courtesy of Lansana "Barmmy Boy" Mansaray.

Tamba's own shipmates, those who arrived with him, remained part of his life. It is unlikely that Sessay, now called Lawrence Summers, ever returned to Sierra Leone, and nor is it clear whether men like Mamaroo and Nibea ever returned to live in Regent.[33]

Tom Ball's whereabouts also remain ambiguous. He and his family appear to have lived for some time at Waterloo, where former soldiers from the West India Regiment were sent, but he had close ties with his former shipmates at Regent. One of his grandchildren apparently married one of Yarra's. Perhaps at some point he did move to Regent, though this is far from certain. The colonial chaplain, Thomas Eyre Poole, visited Regent in the 1840s and stayed with a man named "Old Thomas," one of the earliest settlers, whose house was filled with English furniture and who dressed in English clothes. It is fanciful to think this could be Tom Ball, but in the absence of evidence other than his grandchildren's activities, we can perhaps imagine an echo of Tom Ball in the gray-haired, bright-eyed and sprightly "Old Thomas," respected elder in Regent.[34]

David Noah and John Reffell were also there, living out their lives. Both were members of the church, and Reffell owned one of the oldest homes in Regent, where "in final touch of fairyland, the stream . . . actually flowed under the house."[35]

With McQueen's death, Bostock's ties to Africa were gone. But we cannot quite leave him yet, because his engagement in another affair is worth briefly recounting. The slave trade's coagulation of a racial divide based almost entirely on skin color had a long and painful range. It easily reached Tasmania, feeding into British xenophobia toward the Indigenous peoples. In the late 1820s and into the 1830s, we see Bostock one final time, at home on the South Esk River, then a frontier in the Black War between settlers and Indigenous inhabitants of the region.

Not long after the Bostocks' move to the South Esk, the real push of the Black War began. The traditional inhabitants of the land were fighting for survival as their access to food evaporated. The settlers were intent on proclaiming the land theirs. They aimed at nothing less than the complete removal of Indigenous people from the island.

This was hardly unrelated to the "global colour line." In 1826, the *Hobart Town Gazette* wrote of the Aboriginals as the lowest form of humanity, noting that they wished that these "Oceanean Negroes" were related to Africans, as then they might be able to be tamed into docility and suitable for hard labor. Observers at the time wrote of Indigenous peoples of Van Diemen's Land as "a fragment of a world strangely riven from the coast of Africa."[36]

So Robert Bostock, now in his late thirties, was required to stand on what became known as the Black Line. "A truly immense and desperate operation," it involved "a mass mobilisation of all able-bodied men to defend the colony— *a levee en masse*." They would stand together to form a chain across the island and walk toward the sea, capturing all the native people who were still living. The "chain of posts" showing the lines to be marched passed straight through Bostock's land. The plan was an utter failure, but nevertheless here at the end of the world we find a baffling but related image, a final glimpse of the man who had once been a fair-haired boy hearing his father's stories of slave trading in Africa. Now the former slave trader and his sons stood with rifles in an attempt to rid his new land of dark-skinned people.[37]

By this time Robert Bostock seems to have been a model citizen, as some of his descendants today are keen to point out. His life was an exemplar of what middle-class men with entrepreneurial talents and vast amounts of luck could achieve. But if viewed from a perspective that stretches far beyond Australia's shores, it is also clear that he was the recipient of heady doses of white privilege, one of the many legacies his former trade bestowed upon the world.

He passed away in 1847, a year of great bushfires and a jubilee to celebrate the end of convict transportation, at his grand house on the South Esk River. His obituaries lauded him a pioneer settler and gentleman whose "kindness of heart" had won many friends. It was a story he had willed into being.[38]

Tamba passed away just over seven years earlier than Bostock after a long illness. His former congregation were just singing the last bars of evensong when a messenger ran through the door with a message that Tamba was gone. He had died, "free from fear," his friends said, having "fought a good fight." In truth, he had done so much more than that.[39]

Epilogue

I lay no claim to having "discovered" the story of Robert Bostock, slave trader turned proud Australian pioneer. Professor Cassandra Pybus first told me the rather astonishing news that a mansion built by a convict transported for slave trading still existed in Tasmania. Later the house would appear in the coffee table book *Country Houses of Tasmania*, and one snowy day fellow historians Hamish Maxwell-Stewart and Kirsten McKenzie would kindly indulge my curiosity and drive with me to see it. It sits majestic on high ground with an iron lacework Victorian veranda on three sides from which to take in the vast grounds and charming view of Ben Lomond.[1]

The Bostock family sold the house immediately after Robert's death. He left his estate to all of his Australian children who outlived him rather than keeping it in the hands of his eldest son, meaning that the grand home had to be sold for all to get their share. And so when I met Thelma Birrell, née Bostock, a great-great-granddaughter of Robert Bostock and a genealogist extraordinaire, she was eager that I know that she does not come from money. Her father grew up in an orphanage, and everything that she and her husband Matt have has been hard won. Thelma tells of being in awe when the then-owners allowed her to visit the old house. Its grandeur is far from the life of struggle she knew as a child, growing up a Bostock in the mid-twentieth century. A narrative of the Bostocks as dashing pioneers and settlers is one of which she is extremely proud.

Thelma very generously let me use her private archive, where I gained rare insight into the world of the early Bostocks in Australia, such as the schoolbooks of Bostock's sons and old family photographs. It is churlish therefore, I admit, for me to suggest that an alternative point of view comes into being if the lives of those rescued from Bostock are also taken into account. In some ways, I believe, the old house can be seen as a distillation of the gross inequality at the heart of this story. It is not just that Bostock grew wealthy enough to build such a home despite his conviction and transportation. Among its many bedrooms, music room, stables, and all the rest is a glimpse of the security, education, and privilege that his sons and to a slightly lesser extent his daughters had, enabling them to grab hold of the myriad opportunities available to them.

Not long after Bostock died, Tasmania became a self-governing colony. With land in Tasmania becoming increasingly scarce by comparison to what had gone before, most of Bostock's children became settlers in the newly opened mainland areas, today in the west of Victoria, and became local worthies. George Bostock was on the board of trustees of Christ Church in Warrnambool, Thomas exhibited vegetables at the Warrnambool show, Augustus sat on the Warrnambool Hospital Board, and youngest brother James manned the Fish Protection Society. They all donned their whites and turned out for the town cricket team. They would leave behind large Victorian families; the name Bostock is today relatively common throughout Australia.[2]

Without taking anything away from all of that hard work and entrepreneurial spirit, it is problematic not to acknowledge another story that lurks beneath. Bostock and his children and (white) grandchildren in Australia were able to use hard work and entrepreneurial spirit to build, sure that their banks were safe, that their government was to some extent representative, and knowing that, provided they did not fall foul of the law, they would be treated as upstanding men and women. The antislavery impetus that had entrapped Bostock did not fight against racism but rather increased it, mutating into the dreams of imperial expansion and economic domination that benefited his descendants.

As scientific racism cut swathes through the later century, they were beneficiaries of its bogus findings. They may have struggled: undoubtedly conditions for many were very hard. But they were nevertheless always regarded as men and women capable of progress, while in Sierra Leone Bostock's former slaves were considered unable to experience complex emotions. Hoping to find out more, Surgeon Clarke of the Liberated African Hospital (who actually had comparatively progressive ideas about Africans' capabilities) collected forty-three skulls from Liberated Africans. This happened within the lifetime of many of Bostock's freed captives.[3]

A few decades later, when Fourah Bay College (Tamba's son's alma mater) affiliated with Durham University in the United Kingdom, the London *Times* was provoked to enquire whether Durham was thinking next of an alliance with London Zoo. By the end of the century segregation came to Freetown. Africans might visit the white community at Hill Station in the day to do cleaning, gardening, and childcare, but by nightfall they and their deadly diseases were banned. Even those earlier claims of possible civility somewhere down the decades, if they displayed the requisite signs of progress, were betrayed. By painful contrast, three of Robert's children would live to see the federation of the Australian colonies into one independent country within the British Empire. The new nation declared itself—proudly, stridently—to be a white man's country.[4]

In fact race, and the privileges accorded to those deemed white, very much mattered in Australia too. While Britons had got behind antislavery en masse, they "largely shunned" its later incarnation, the Aborigines' Protection Society, leaving white men in Australia considerable leeway to act as they saw fit. When Thelma's grandfather Robert was born at Eumeralla West in 1850, his father, George Bostock, and his fellow settlers were in the midst of the Eumeralla Wars against the Gunditjmara people. The settlers had to be armed even if they were going only to their own milking shed. George Bostock's part is unknown, but his brother-in-law John Cox was part of a group who "opened fire upon the tolerably large body of blacks," with Cox recalling, "I distinctly remember knocking over *three* blacks, two men and a boy."[5]

And so it went on. As Robert Bostock's sons opened up the territory to the west of Melbourne, so a few of his grandsons headed north in the great pastoral boom. In what is today the Northern Territory, grandson George Bostock had children Peter and Fanny with a Jingili woman named in the records only as "unknown F/B [full-blood] Aborigine," and according to the family he had more children by other Indigenous women. The nature of these relationships is highly contentious. There is no evidence that Bostock was involved, but near to his property three white men started a "slavery racket," kidnapping young Aboriginal women and girls and selling them to white men for £10 each. Wakaya men, whose women had been taken, then murdered these slavers. In retaliation, Bostock's partner and a gang of other settlers set off to seek revenge. One member of the avenging party bragged afterward that "a Wagai [Wakaya] warrior bit the dust" for every bone in the dead men's bodies. Other men did not buy women but simply kidnapped them, with one writer noting, "Sex with black women was part of the bushman's identity." As elder Riley Young Winpilin succinctly noted, "White man did big cruel."[6]

In 1907, in a time of drought, George Bostock got tired of the "colourless" life, "absolutely devoid of human interest," as some anthropologists who met him wrote, and sailed back to Victoria. But there was a real problem for the children he left behind. In 1911, the Commonwealth passed a bill for the Northern Territory entitled the Aboriginals Ordinance Act. This allowed the authorities to "remove" mixed-race children from their "full-blood" Aboriginal mothers because under the prevailing mores of the era the children's "superior" white genes would somehow be damaged by such mothering. Separation was considered imperative. Throughout the early part of the twentieth century, Aboriginal communities posted lookouts to watch for men coming for their children, sending them into the bush when strangers approached, and even blackening the paler-skinned ones with boot polish.[7]

In the 1920s, Dr. Cecil Cook—the "enlightened" chief protector of Aborigines in the Northern Territory—announced that the solution to mixed-race people was to "breed them out." As eugenicist ideas grew, mixed-race people were considered to be a risk to the country's development because "hybridized people are a badly put together people," a "pathetic, sinister third race," or "the sad futureless figure[s] of this lonely land." By 1931 Cook decreed that "all illegitimate half-castes . . . under sixteen years" would be forcibly institutionalized.[8]

Those taken away became "semi-enslaved and disenfranchised domestic and rural workers." Children were sometimes given new names and even birthdates, meaning that there was little chance they could ever be reunited with their family or even trace their ethnic origin. Between one-tenth and one-third of Australian Indigenous children, principally those of mixed racial heritage, were forcibly removed from their families from 1909 into the 1970s. They are known as "the stolen generations."[9]

George Bostock's son Peter, born to the unnamed Indigenous woman, went on to have a daughter named Bessie, who was around ninety years old when I had the privilege of meeting her in Elliott, in Australia's Northern Territory. She was with her daughter Mona, whom Bessie battled to get back after Mona was taken away at the age of four to be an "inmate" at St. Mary's Hostel in Darwin, some 450 miles away. This was far from Bessie's only life achievement. Bessie fought for sixteen years to get an "Aboriginal community living area of 25 square kilometres [10 square miles]" from some of the land grabbed from her Jingili ancestors by George Bostock and his mate Harry Bathern to make Beetaloo Station. Bessie declared proudly to me, "I am a Bostock." She was also one of the last of the native Jingili speakers and named her land Jingaloo, going there for corroborees, where they spoke the old language, performed their old rites, and sang their own songs.[10]

While George Bostock was in the Northern Territory, his cousin Augustus John Bostock had moved to the Tweed River, today on the border between

New South Wales and Queensland, and had children with at least one Bund-jalung woman. In the family memory this relationship was far more freely entered into than many between Indigenous women and white men, but never-theless their children and grandchildren were mixed-race in a world that de-cried being any such thing. They would grow up on missions where they were supposed to be learning "civilization" and the protestant work ethic, a painful echo of Britain's earlier attempts at "improving" and proselytizing to Africans.

Among Augustus John Bostock's descendants are the Indigenous campaign-ers Lester, George, and the late Gerry Bostock and renowned artist Euphemia Bostock. Lester has been Aboriginal elder of the year four times and awarded an Order of Australia medal; Gerry was among the most prominent Aboriginal rights activists of his era; George Bostock has fought for recognition of Indige-nous men who have fought in Australia's armed services. In Australia, the name Bostock is perhaps best associated with these Indigenous men and women who have fought so hard against the ravages of racism.

Shauna Bostock-Smith, George's youngest daughter, is today writing her own account of her astonishing family history. Like Bessie Bathern, she too is very proud of being a Bostock and believes that it is wonderful to have in a way "reclaimed" their name as a symbol of racial justice. Yet speaking about Indige-nous history in Australia, she says, "If you think it's over . . . it's not over yet. . . . I wonder if we will ever put it behind us totally." "The recovery is only starting now," she argues, because Australia's Indigenous people are only just starting to gain the things that "everybody else takes for granted."[11]

None of this is to cast blame on those alive today, to suggest that those— like Thelma Birrell, and Annette Hurdis, John McQueen's descendant, who also kindly spoke to me—whose bloodlines descend from Robert Bostock and John McQueen are in some way culpable for the deeds of the past. But while guilt is not transmissible down the generations, power, wealth, opportunity, edu-cation, social standing, and so much more certainly are, and not to acknowledge that seems to be acting out the pretense that the actions of Bostock and the thou-sands of other slave traders have left no mark on our world, or at least none that stretches to Australia. This is simply not the case.

There are no families in Sierra Leone with the surnames Tamba, Reffell, and Ball with spare rooms full of genealogical data that trace their origins back to other nations, or at least none of which I am aware. When I asked about families named Tamba, I was firmly told that this name is a "native" name and does

Nafisatu Deen, descendant of the Ball family, outside on the land in eastern Freetown where her forebears lived, 2013. Screen grab from filmed footage in author's own collection.

not exist in the Krio community, in which many older members still cling firmly to their British identities. At some point in the past, they suggest, a family named Tamba would have taken a more Anglo name. As more and more "native" people were included in the colony of Sierra Leone when the protectorate was declared in 1896, the Krio were ever more determined to mark their difference, and names like Tamba were abandoned.

I had more luck with the Ball family, however. Having spent months tracing them, I had discovered that while the surname Ball is unknown today in Krio Freetown, into the 1950s Tom's descendants had lived on Lucas and Clark Streets in the east of Freetown. Then Mrs. Cassandra Garber of the Krio Descendants' Yunion kindly invited me to her home to speak to a group of Krio elders, and a man named Solomon Abiodun Parker remembered something nobody else had. A well-known Krio family called Sanusi had once had the surname Ball. The Krio community is small, and a phone number was traced within minutes. The Sanusis invited me to their home. They were a two-minute walk away from Lucas Street, around the corner where its east end runs into Savage Square, still there but with a new surname. Mrs. Raila Sanusi-Ball (as she afterward asked me to call her) became teary speaking of how her grandmother always cried when she related how her own great-grandfather, Tom Ball (a first name I had not revealed to her), had been a slave.

Mrs. Sanusi-Ball went on to tell me of their ties to another family whose ancestor, as it turns out, was seemingly Yarra (a name they had not known), once a factory slave owned by John McQueen. I had known that Yarra took the name John Reffell, but this is one of the most common names in the Krio community and finding the correct descendants was tricky. Raila Sanusi-Ball told me, reaching back into the family's oral genealogy she learned from her grandmother, that one of Tom Ball's grandchildren had married one of John Reffell's. This then, most likely, was the John Reffell once named Yarra. It is a connection the two families still hold dear.

Raila also told me that Tom Ball's grandson Matthew was one of the many Krio in Sierra Leone who traded with Abeokuta, in what is today Nigeria. In the late 1830s, some Krio bought a condemned slave ship at auction in Freetown and sailed to Badagry, in the Gulf of Guinea, determined to spread Liberated African civilization along the coast. They founded Abeokuta and another town called Olowogbowo as refuges from the raids and wars that made captives of so many. By 1840 Abeokuta had a population of almost forty thousand. The descendants of those rescued from Mason and Bostock's factory fought the transatlantic slave trade just as had their forebears.[12]

Things have not been easy for the Sanusi-Balls and their compatriots. It was 1961 when Sierra Leone gained its independence, a sixty-year delay after Australia that spoke of perceived racial difference. Democracy lasted only a handful of years before a dictatorship took hold. In 1991 one of the most brutal civil wars the world has seen swept in from Liberia. In 1997, St. Charles Church in Regent, once the pride of William Tamba and David Noah, was used as a sanctuary when the village was attacked. Some of those hiding within its walls, singing hymns, could easily have been—more than likely were—the descendants of those who arrived aboard HMS *Thais* and the *Princess Charlotte*. When the war was over a decade later, the country had no hospitals, no electricity, no schools functioning, the biggest percentage of amputees in the world, and a huge number of former child soldiers and child "bush wives" who were victims of gang rape, forced drug addictions, and severe mental trauma.

Many feared that Sierra Leone would never recover, questioning how former child soldiers would grow into peaceful, able adults. Yet the country picked itself up and carried on. The benchmark of recovery from civil war is the decade mark: make it there, and a country's hopes are good. Sierra Leone made it, peaceful and booming, with elections deemed free and fair. Two short years beyond that came the Ebola crisis and its resulting severe economic downturn.

Raila Sanusi-Ball, whose face lit up when she told me that the Reffells of Regent were family—"our grandfathers were cousins"—explained simply,

"Everything is struggle for we." They were the same words Rueben had used on the banks of the St. Paul River. When we look for the reasons for the struggles faced by Reuben and Raila Sanusi-Ball today, the transatlantic slave trade may seem just a whisper behind much more acute sociopolitical challenges. The sources of Raila's and her country's problems might not lead us directly back to the transatlantic slave trade, but if we stand at the ruins of Hotel Africa and look out, I believe we can see one of its major tributaries gushing down the river.

Acknowledgments

A few colleagues have been involved in this book in unanticipated ways. As mentioned in the text, Cassandra Pybus told me about Robert Bostock's house in Tasmania years ago, inadvertently setting off this project. Kirsten McKenzie and Hamish Maxwell-Stewart later drove by the house with me, while Clare Smith was a central part of the fantastic Tasmanian weekend that followed. I am grateful to all of them for being better friends than I deserve.

Suzanne Schwarz's part in this story did not make the final cut but is nonetheless a treasured memory. Almost a decade ago, before they became part of a British Library Endangered Archive project, she and I were both working on the Liberated African Letterbooks in the Sierra Leone archives. I had been looking for the arrivals from Bostock's factory for some time when she came across them and cheered, calling me over. It is only because of that finding that any detail about the captives rescued that day could be deduced. Beyond that, my searches through the interior of Sierra Leone looking for information about the names was aided first of all by Joe Alie and his suggested connections in Freetown, and then by the inestimable Lansana "Barmmy Boy" Mansaray. I would never have found so much, gone so far, nor had nearly so much fun without Barmmy, and our ever-wonderful driver, Abu Bakr Bah. Barmmy also saved me much embarrassment by gently pointing out that one of the names on the Liberated African list, if pronounced in a certain way, is today a very colorful word in Sierra Leone and nothing I should perhaps be blithely saying in front of all sorts of chiefs and elders. Suzanne Schwarz also put me in touch with her former student Denise Jones, who I was lucky enough to meet with in Liverpool and who shared with me her own research into the Liverpool Bostocks.

I am grateful to Deirdre Coleman twice over: once for arranging with Starr Douglas to send me an image from the Cleveland papers, and then again for having some of David Noah's letters sent when my university library could not get them. Beyond that, she has been a faithful supporter of this project and has welcomed another Australian writing about Sierra Leone. Marilyn Lake has also provided great encouragement, and Marcus Rediker's and Joseph Miller's words of support have been both very helpful and immensely encouraging. I am truly grateful. Randy Sparks and an anonymous reviewer for University of Wisconsin Press provided feedback that much improved the final work. Penny Russell, Robert Aldrich, and Andrew Fitzmaurice were all astonishingly tolerant of my frequent absences while they variously occupied the chair of history at the University of Sydney. Dennis Lloyd at the University of Wisconsin Press has been supportive of the whole project since first reading the manuscript. Elise Collie and Sarah Hill both helped immensely with proofreading and providing feedback. Many thanks to them both.

I'm very thankful I had Oilda Hevia and Jorge Felipe González as research assistants in Havana. Jorge in particular was the most knowledgeable person anybody might wish for, and helped re-create the complex events around both the murder enacted in revenge for the loss of Bostock and Mason's factory and the subsequent events aboard the *Bella Maria*. Manuel Barcia, María del Carmen Barcia, Reinaldo Funes Monzote, and Marial Iglesias Utset also helped in many ways with connections and information about the Cuban part of the research. It was Manuel whom I originally emailed to ask about Liberian legacies in Sierra Leone because of this story, leading to one wonderful day that he and I drove out of Havana on what became the first of many trips to the Gangá-Longobá casa in Perico, Matanzas. That meeting did not prove useful to this project but set me off on the entirely unexpected journey of making the documentary *They Are We*. While that distracted me so much that this book has taken around five years longer than it would otherwise have done, it is nonetheless something for which I am exceptionally grateful. I cannot even begin to unpick how different my life might be had Manuel and I not visited Perico that day and been welcomed by the late, great Magdalena "Piyuya" Mora Herrera.

A few people whose ancestors were part of this story have also been very helpful and gracious. Thelma Birrell, née Bostock, her husband Matt, and her cousin Les Watters very kindly welcomed me and let me discuss with them the legacy of their forebear Robert Bostock. Thelma has done a remarkable job collecting documents and records about the Bostock family in Australia, and I am very appreciative for her input and willingness to let me use her private archive. Annette Hurdis, a descendant of John McQueen, generously agreed to be interviewed about her family history.

I was lucky enough to meet Shauna Bostock-Smith, along with her husband Allan Smith and daughter Brenna, through researching this story and am now lucky enough to call them friends. She is writing her own story of the Bostocks, focusing on the Indigenous Australians, and I very much look forward to reading it. I encourage readers to do the same.

In Sierra Leone, Raila Sanusi-Ball poignantly told stories of her ancestor Tom Ball and put me in touch with Joseph Reffell, apparent descendant of John Yarra, whose family house still sits near St. Charles Church in Regent. Paramount Chief Reverend Doris Lenga-Koroma, née Caulker, tried valiantly to help me discover who Bostock's Caulker wife had been.

None of this could have happened without the generous funding provided by the Australian Research Council through the University of Sydney. A five-year fellowship allowed the research for this project to be completed. I also benefited immensely from a short-term fellowship at the Gilder Lehrman Center at Yale University.

As usual, my greatest thanks are for my family. My parents were as endlessly supportive and encouraging as ever. I cannot thank them enough for always believing in me and listening. This book, however, is dedicated not to them this time but to my husband, Sergio Leyva Seiglie, who helped in an incalculable number of ways. I am much happier finishing this book, having him in my life, than I was at its start, many years ago, when I did not. So this is for him, with love and gratitude.

Notes

Abbreviations

ANC   Archivo Nacional de la República de Cuba
BHPS   Bristol [Rhode Island] Historic and Preservation Society
CMS   Church Missionary Society
LRO   Liverpool Record Office
NASL   National Archives, Sierra Leone
NSWSRA   New South Wales State Records' Authority
RAC   Royal African Corps
TNA UK   The National Archives, United Kingdom
WIR   West India Regiment

Prologue

1. Rodney D. Sieh, "Feuding over Liberia's Debts: Ghosts of OAU '79 in 2011 Political Play," www.focusonliberia.wordpress.com/2010/07/05.

2. Ellen Johnson Sirleaf, *This Child Will Be Great: Memoir of a Remarkable Life by Africa's First Woman President* (New York: HarperCollins, 2009); Helene Cooper, *The House at Sugar Beach: In Search of a Lost African Childhood* (New York: Simon and Schuster, 2008), 145; obituary, President W. Tolbert, *Times* (London), 14 April 1980, 17.

3. Peter Beaumont, "How a Tyrant's Logs of War Bring Terror to West Africa," *The Observer* (London), 27 May 2001.

4. Visiting a few years later, George Robertson implied that Bostock and Mason's factory had been at Providence Island, but this must be wrong. The original agreement Bostock and Mason signed was to construct a factory at "St Pauls Monserada"; the *Thais*'s captains' and masters' logbooks report that his factories were on the banks of the St. Paul River, as do Bostock's own letters, the *Fénix* records, and the court documents. G. A Robertson, *Notes on Africa: Particularly Those Parts Which Are Situated between Cape Verd and the River Congo* (London: Sherwood, Neely and Jones, 1819), 34; letter to Robert

Bostick, "Africa. Gallinas. Slavery. Sierra Leone. Letter, 1813," www.worthpoint.com /worthopedia/africa-gallinas-slavery-sierra-leone-letter (as at April 2010); Special Court of Oyer and Terminer, and Gaol Delivery Held at Freetown on the 22nd Day of July 1813, Robert Bostock vs. Edward Scobell, TS 11/826/2732, The National Archives, UK (hereafter TNA UK); "Appeal No. 983, Captured Ship: Phoenix," HCA 42/488/983, TNA UK; "King vs. Robert Bostock and John MacQueen," ADM 1/1647, TNA UK; captains' logs, HMS *Thais*, ADM 51/291451/2914, TNA UK; masters' logs, HMS *Thais*, ADM 52/3462, TNA UK.

Introduction

1. Special Court of Oyer and Terminer, TS 11/826/2732, TNA UK; Liberated African Letterbooks, National Archives of Sierra Leone (hereafter NASL).

2. Evidence of Tom Ball in Special Court of Oyer and Terminer, TS 11/826/2732, TNA UK.

3. Maria Louisa Charlesworth, *Africa's Mountain Valley; or, The Church in Regent's Town, West Africa* (London: Seeley, Jackson and Halliday, 1856), 189; Robert Benton Seeley, *A Memoir of the Reverend W. A. B. Johnson* (New York: Robert Carter and Brothers, 1853), 245.

4. William Tamba journal in William Tamba, Original Papers—Missionaries, Church Missionary Society archive (hereafter William Tamba papers, CMS).

5. The term *factory* historically meant a place where "factors"—merchants— worked and was widely used for slave trading enterprises. It does not imply any actual production was carried on there.

6. Slave barracks, from the Spanish *barracón* and the Portuguese *barracão*.

7. Norman Robert Bennett and George E. Brooks, eds., *New England Merchants in Africa: A History through Documents, 1802–1965* (Boston: Boston University Press, 1965), 86–87.

8. Interviews with the author, recorded interviews in author's collection, Voinjama, Balahun, and Foya, Liberia, 2010 and 2013; Liberated African Letterbooks NASL; "Register of Disposal of Captured Negroes," CO 267/38, TNA UK.

9. Evidence of Lawrence Summers, in Special Court of Oyer and Terminer, TS 11/826/2732, TNA UK.

10. Liberated African Letterbooks, NASL; "Register of Disposal of Captured Negroes," CO 267/38; David Eltis, "Welfare Trends among the Yoruba in the Early Nineteenth Century: The Anthropometric Evidence," *Journal of Economic History* 50, no. 3 (September 1990): 521–40; Gareth Austin, Joerg Baten, and Bas Van Leeuwen, "The Biological Standard of Living in Early Nineteenth-Century West Africa: New Anthropometric Evidence for Northern Ghana and Burkina Faso," *Economic History Review* (26 September 2011): 1–23.

11. Eya was very likely Aiah, the third-born son of Kissi and Kono women. Sarae was really Sarwae, a Kru child. Famai's name is more difficult to pin down definitively.

I have decided to use the names as rendered by the British in order to facilitate discussion of who these people were, with the exception of the men named "Boy" by the British—really Boi—since this is pejorative and can be reasonably clearly attributed as Mende.

12. This paragraph is based on the oral evidence of their hometowns and villages. Interviews in author's collection.

13. Kenneth Little, *The Mende of Sierra Leone* (Oxford: Routledge, 1951), 221–23; Sylvia Ardyn Boone, *Radiance from the Waters: Ideas of Feminine Beauty in Mende Art* (New Haven, CT: Yale University Press, 1986), 129–32; George Schwab, *Tribes of the Liberian Hinterland* (Cambridge, MA: Peabody Museum, 1947), 306–7. Evidence regarding Bostock and McQueen's physical appearance is in Pardon, 4/4472, pp. 9–11, New South Wales State Records' Authority (hereafter NSWSRA).

14. The higher figure, in today's prices, would be approximately a quarter of a million dollars in real terms, or more than six million dollars in income value.

15. Evidence of Tarra/Yarra (see below) in Special Court of Oyer and Terminer, TS 11/826/2732, TNA UK; Slave Trade Cases, Admiralty Miscellanea, ADM 7/606, TNA UK; Evidence of Brodie in George Cook vs. George William Maxwell, TS 11/823/2712, TNA UK. The main evidence given in 1813 is by a man whose name is written as Tarra, but since nobody gave the name Tarra when they arrived into Freetown and the stories overlap, I have assumed that they were one person and not two.

16. Linda Colley, *Britons: Forging the Nation, 1707–1837* (New Haven, CT: Yale University Press), 351; "Evidence of Thomas Lovekine," in Special Court of Oyer and Terminer, TS 11/826/2732, TNA UK.

17. Helmut Tuerk, *Reflections on the Contemporary Law of the Sea* (Leiden: Martinus Nijhoff, 2012), 74; Special Court of Oyer and Terminer, TS 11/826/2732, TNA UK; "King vs. Robert Bostock and John MacQueen," in Special Court of Oyer and Terminer, and Gaol Delivery Held at Freetown 22 July 1813, enclosed in George Collier to John Wilson Cook, Letters of Captains, ADM 1/1674, TNA UK; Liberated African Letterbooks, NASL.

18. Entry for 25 June 1813, captains' logs, HMS *Thais*, ADM 51/2914, TNA UK.

19. Brantz Mayer, *Captain Canot; or, Twenty Years of an African Slaver* (New York: Appleton, 1854), 94.

20. Sessay is a common name throughout the region and popular among the Mende. Za, spelled Saa or Sahr, is the name given to firstborn sons in Kono and Kissi.

21. Journal of Rev. S. Mills in *The Royal Gazette and Sierra Leone Advertiser*, 19 August 1820.

22. Henry Louis Gates, *Faces of America: How Twelve Extraordinary People Discovered Their Pasts* (New York: New York University Press, 2010), 7.

23. This is an ongoing debate. The major works remain Eric Williams, *Capitalism and Slavery* (Chapel Hill: University of North Carolina Press, 1944); Seymour Drescher, *Econocide: British Slavery in the Era of Abolition* (Pittsburgh: University of Pittsburgh Press, 1977), and more recently books such as Edward E. Baptist, *The Half Has Never Been Told:*

Slavery and the Making of American Capitalism (New York: Basic Books, 2014), and Sven Beckert, *Empire of Cotton: A Global History* (New York: Knopf, 2014).

24. Nathan Nunn, "The Long-Term Effects of Africa's Slave Trades," *Quarterly Journal of Economics* 123, no. 1 (February 2008): 139–76; Nathan Nunn and Leonard Wantchekon, "The Slave Trade and the Origins of Mistrust in Africa," National Bureau of Economic Research Working Paper Series, no. 14783, March 2009.

25. Gad J. Heuman and James Walvin, "General Introduction," in Heuman and Walvin, eds., *The Slavery Reader*, vol. 1 (London: Routledge, 2003), 8; Herbert S. Klein, *The Atlantic Slave Trade* (Cambridge: Cambridge University Press, 1999), 138–39; Baptist, *The Half Has Never Been Told*, xxiii; Barbara L. Solow, "Capitalism and Slavery in the Exceedingly Long Run," *Journal of Interdisciplinary History* 17, no. 4 (Spring 1987): 711–37.

26. William Hague tells us what Wilberforce ate for breakfast in *William Wilberforce: The Life of the Great Anti-Slave Trade Campaigner* (San Diego: Harcourt, 2008), 7.

27. Randy J. Sparks, *Africans in the Old South: Mapping Exceptional Lives across the Atlantic World* (Cambridge, MA: Harvard University Press, 2016), 1, 3–4.

28. Philip R. Misevich, "The Origins of Slaves Leaving the Upper Guinea Coast," in David Eltis and David Richardson, eds., *Extending the Frontiers: Essays on the New Transatlantic Slave Trade Database* (New Haven, CT: Yale University Press, 2008), 157.

29. Tiya Miles, *Ties That Bind: The Story of an Afro-Cherokee Family in Slavery and Freedom* (Berkeley: University of California Press, 2005), xiii–xv; and more generally on historical silences Michel-Rolph Trouillot, *Silencing the Past: Power and the Production of History* (Boston: Beacon Press, 2015), 26–27.

30. General Notices, *Sydney Gazette and New South Wales Advertiser*, 7 December 1833, 2; Sydney Quarter Sessions, *Sydney Gazette and New South Wales Advertiser*, 1 February 1834, 2; Law Intelligence, Sydney Quarter Sessions, *The Sydney Herald*, 3 February 1834, 1; Tamba journal, March–June 1821, William Tamba papers, CMS; David Noah to Church Missionary Society, "Journal of a Trip to Bassa Country," in David Noah, Original Papers—Missionaries, David Noah, Church Missionary Society archive (hereafter David Noah Papers, CMS).

31. There was a boy named William Tamba who was sent to school in Clapham, England, in the early years of the nineteenth century. This seems a strange coincidence but likely not more than that: the boy in England was listed as the son of "Pa Tamba, trader at Bullom," a different history altogether to the William Tamba from Bostock's. Tamba is an extremely common name in the region, as every second-born Kono and Kissi boy's name as, of course, was William in the nineteenth century Anglo-sphere. William Tamba, rescued from Bostock and Mason, was apparently taught to write by Augustine Johnson, and it is very unlikely that Johnson would not have mentioned it if he had known that Tamba visited England at some point. The possibility that Tamba was feigning a slave past among the Liberated Africans remains, of course, but I have found no evidence to suggest that. See Bruce L. Mouser, "African Academy—Clapham, 1799–1806," *History of Education* 33, no. 1 (January 2004): 87–103.

32. For a broader understanding of antislavery and racism, see Richard Huzzey,

Freedom Burning: Anti-Slavery and Empire in Victorian Britain (Ithaca: Cornell University Press, 2012), 6, 185.

Chapter 1. Son of a Liverpool Slave Dealer

1. Quoted in Ray Costello, *Black Salt: Seafarers of African Descent on British Ships* (Liverpool: Liverpool University Press, 2012), 11; Thomas Clarkson, *The History of the Rise, Progress and Accomplishments of the Abolition of the African Slave Trade* (London: John W. Parker, 1839), 375–77; Richard Brooke, *Liverpool as It Was during the Last Quarter of the Eighteenth Century: 1775–1800* (Liverpool: J. Mawdsley and Son, 1853), 37; Jon Stobart, "Culture versus Commerce: Societies and Spaces for Elites in Eighteenth-Century Liverpool," *Journal of Historical Geography* 28, no. 4 (October 2002): 471–85.

2. Kenneth Morgan, "Liverpool's Dominance in the British Slave Trade, 1740–1807," in David Richardson, Anthony Tibbles, and Suzanne Schwarz, eds., *Liverpool and Transatlantic Slavery* (Liverpool: Liverpool University Press, 2001), 14–20; *Gore's Liverpool Directory 1790*.

3. Gomer Williams, *History of the Liverpool Privateers and Letters of Marque* (1897; repr., Cambridge: Cambridge University Press, 2010), 598.

4. Denise M. Jones, "The Business Organisation of the Liverpool Slave Trade in the Eighteenth Century: A Case Study of Robert Bostock" (master's thesis, University of Liverpool, 2006), 11–12; *Voyages: The Transatlantic Slave Trade Database*, www.slavevoyages .org, voyage numbers #91581, #92478, #80587; Williams, *Liverpool Privateers*, 234–35; "Sales of 307 Slaves Import'd in the Ship Bloom," 1:123, Robert Bostock Letterbooks, 387 MD 54–55, Liverpool Record Office (hereafter LRO).

5. Bickerton Papers, 942 BIC 1, LRO; Richard B. Sheridan, "The Guinea Surgeons on the Middle Passage: The Provision of Medical Services in the British Slave Trade," *International Journal of African Historical Studies* 14, no. 4 (1981): 601–25; W. N. Boog Watson, "The Guinea Trade and Some of Its Surgeons," *Journal of the Royal College of Surgeons* 14 (1969): 203–14; Emma Christopher, *Slave Ship Sailors and Their Captive Cargoes, 1730–1807* (New York: Cambridge University Press, 2006), 33–34, 39.

6. Thomas Winterbottom, *An Account of the Native Africans in the Neighbourhood of Sierra Leone* (London: John Hatchard, 1803), 137; Anna-Maria Falconbridge, *Two Voyages to Sierra Leone during the Years 1791-2-3* (London: printed for the author, 1794), letter 8; George E. Brooks, *Eurafricans in Western Africa: Commerce, Social Status, Gender, and Religious Observance from the Sixteenth to the Eighteenth Century* (Athens: Ohio University Press, 2003), 299; Linda Day, "Afro-British Integration on the Sherbro Coast, 1665–1795," *Africana Research Bulletin* 12, no. 3 (1982): 82–107, 92; A. P. Kup, *Sierra Leone: A Concise History* (Devon: David and Charles, 1975), 103; Imodale Caulker-Burnett, *The Caulkers of Sierra Leone* (Bloomington, IN: Xlibris, 2010), 56; Walter Rodney, *A History of the Upper Guinea Coast, 1545–1800* (New York: Monthly Review Press, 1970), 220; G. R. Collier, Sir Charles MacCarthy, et al., *West African Sketches* (London: L. B. Seeley and Son, 1829), 137–38.

7. Elizabeth Cleveland's story is told in Sparks, *Africans in the Old South*, chapter 1, quote on 12. On racial designations see Roxann Wheeler, *The Complexion of Race: Categories of Difference in Eighteenth-Century British Culture* (Philadelphia: University of Pennsylvania Press, 2000); Kathleen Wilson, *The Island Race: Englishness, Empire and Gender in the 18th Century* (London: Routledge, 2003); Colin Kidd, "Ethnicity in the British Atlantic World, 1688–1830," in Kathleen Wilson, ed., *A New Imperial History: Culture, Identity and Modernity in Britain and Empire, 1660–1840* (Cambridge: Cambridge University Press, 2004); Dror Wahrman, *The Making of the Modern Self: Identity and Culture in Eighteenth- Century England* (New Haven, CT: Yale University Press, 2004).

8. G. E. Brooks, *Eurafricans*, 299; C. B. Wadström, *An Essay on Colonization* (London: printed for the author, 1795), 2:15. James's half-brother John Cleveland apparently had a somewhat more humane reputation: Sparks, *Africans in the Old South*, 22.

9. For example, Elizabeth Donnan, *Documents Illustrative of the Slave Trade to America* (Washington, DC: Carnegie Institution, 1930–35), 4:497–99; Richard Drake, *Revelations of a Slave Smuggler* (New York: R. M. DeWitt, 1860), 200; William Smith, *A New Voyage to Guinea* (London: John Nourse, 1745), 213, 251; Nicholas Owen, *Journal of a Slave-Dealer* (London: G. Routledge, 1930), 85; Nathaniel Uring, *A History of the Voyages and Travels of Captain Nathaniel Uring* (1726; repr., London: C. Cassell, 1928), 97; John Newton, *Journal of a Slave Trader, 1750–1754*, edited by Bernard Martin and Mark Spurrell (London: Epworth Press, 1962), 15, 23–24, 37, 68, 76–79, 88.

10. D. M. Jones, "Case Study of Robert Bostock," 58–59; Robert Bostock to James Cleveland, 10 August 1789, vol. 2, 23; 13 November 1789, vol. 2, 52; 20 January 1790, vol. 2, 68; and 9 June 1790, vol. 2, 94; all in 387 MD 54–55, LRO. There is little evidence that Cleveland did name a son Robert, but he may have been the son that Adam Afzelius mentioned in 1795 as being "a boy of 6 years" who owned three slaves; Adam Afzelius, *Sierra Leone Journal, 1795-6* (Uppsala: Almqvist und Wiksell, 1967), 8.

11. Robert Bostock to James Cleveland, 6 May 1790, vol. 2, 90, 387 MD 54–55, LRO.

12. D. M. Jones, "Case Study of Robert Bostock," 58–59; Kenneth Morgan, "James Rogers and the Bristol Slave Trade," *Historical Research* 76, no. 192 (May 2003): 189–216; Robert Bostock to James Cleveland, 10 August 1789, vol. 2, 23, 387 MD 54–55, LRO; *Voyages*, slavevoyages.org, #82173.

13. David Pope, "The Wealth and Social Aspirations of Liverpool's Slave Merchants of the Second Half of the Eighteenth Century," in Richardson, Tibbles, and Schwarz, *Liverpool and Transatlantic Slavery*, 168–80, 208; Brooke, *Liverpool as It Was*, 253; Robert Bostock to James Fryer, 25 July 1790, vol. 2, 109, 387 MD 54–55, LRO; D. M. Jones, "Case Study of Robert Bostock," 38.

14. The equivalent of approximately £129,000 or US $207,000 today, although many times even this in the "prestige" value of the sum.

15. Afzelius, *Sierra Leone Journal*, 9; Morgan, "James Rogers," 199; S. G. Checkland, "Economic Attitudes in Liverpool," *Economic History Review* 5, no. 1 (1952): 59; Robert Bostock to William Cleveland, 16 August 1791, vol. 2, 138, 387 MD 54–55, LRO.

16. Much has been written on this subject. I have drawn especially on Kenneth

Morgan's account in *Slavery and the British Empire: From Africa to America* (Oxford: Oxford University Press, 2007). See also Seymour Drescher, *Capitalism and Antislavery: British Mobilization in a Comparative Perspective* (Oxford: Oxford University Press 1987).

17. Francis E. Hyde, Bradbury B. Parkinson, and Sheila Marriner, "The Port of Liverpool and the Crisis of 1793," *Economica* 18 (November 1951): 363–78; Kenneth Morgan, "James Rogers," 189–216; Paul Mantoux, *The Industrial Revolution in the Eighteenth Century: An Outline of the Beginnings of the Modern Factory System in England* (London: Rutledge, 2006), 254.

18. Thelma Birrell, *Mariners, Merchants — Then Pioneers* (self-published), 8.

19. Vere Langford Oliver, *The History of the Island of Antigua* (Antigua: Mitchell and Hughes, 1894), vol. 1, letter 10.

20. Averil Mackenzie-Grieve, *The Last Years of the English Slave Trade, 1750–1807* (London: Frank Cass, 1941, 1968), 69; *Voyages*, slavevoyages.org, #82274; David R. Green and Alastair Owens, "Gentlewomanly Capitalism? Spinsters, Widows, and Wealth Holding in England and Wales, c. 1800–1860," *Economic History Review* 56, no. 3 (August 2003): 510–63; Leonore Davidoff and Catherine Hall, *Family Fortunes: Men and Women of the English Middle Class, 1780–1850* (Abingdon, Oxon: Routledge, 2002), 283–84; Birrell, *Mariners, Merchants*, 13, 16.

21. Birrell, *Merchants, Mariners*, 7, 13, 17; Bostock Letterbooks, vol. 2, 165, and vol. 2, 168, 387 MD 54–55, LRO. I am unsure who the "Mr Bostock" at the Rio Nunez was, if any relative. See Bruce Mouser, "The Nunez Affair," *Académie Royale des Sciences to D'Outre Mer* (1973–74): 697–98, at http://www.tubmaninstitute.ca/sites/default/files/file/Nunez_Affair.pdf (accessed October 2017). At the helm of one of the vessels leaving Liverpool was Captain John Roach, the man who would eventually cause Bostock's downfall, but I have not found any evidence that it was Roach's ship that Bostock sailed aboard. See Muster of the *John*, Registry of Shipping and Seamen, Agreements and Crew lists, Series 1, BT 98/62, TNA UK.

22. D. M. Jones, "Case Study of Robert Bostock," 39.

Chapter 2. A Kissi Child Caught in the Slave Trade

1. George W. Harley, "Notes on the Poro in Liberia," *Papers of the Peabody Museum* 19 (Cambridge, MA: Peabody Museum, 1941); Caroline Bledsoe, "Political Uses of Sande Ideology," *American Ethnologist* 11, no. 3 (August 1984): 455–72; Richard M. Fulton, "The Political Structures and Functions of the Poro in Kpelle Society," *American Anthropology* 74, no. 5 (1972): 1218–33.

2. Sahr John Yambasu, *Between Africa and the West: A Story of Discovery* (Bloomington, IN: Trafford, 2013), 18; Elwood D. Dunn, Amos J. Beyan, and Carl Patrick Burrowes, *Historical Dictionary of Liberia* (Lanham, MD: Scarecrow Press, 1995), 270–72. There is much controversy about the extent to which rice cultivation techniques, like those of the Kissi, were transferred to the Americas by bondsmen and women. Useful starting points in this discussion can be found in Judith A. Carney, *Black Rice: The African Origins of Rice*

Cultivation in the Americas (Cambridge, MA: Harvard University Press, 2001), and for a different viewpoint, David Eltis, Philip Morgan, and David Richardson, "Agency and Diaspora in Atlantic History: Reassessing the African Contribution to Rice Cultivation in the Americas," *American Historical Review* 112, no. 5 (December 2007): 1329–58.

3. Harley, "Notes on the Poro"; Bledsoe, "Political Uses of Sande," 457; Fulton, "Poro in Kpelle Society."

4. Alexander Gordon Laing, *Travels in the Timannee, Kooranko, and Soolima Countries in Western Africa* (London: John Murray, 1825), 327–28.

5. Rodney, *Upper Guinea Coast*, 255.

6. Dunn, Beyan, and Burrowes, *Historical Dictionary*, 270–72.

7. Kenneth C. Wylie, "Fountainheads of the Niger: Researching a Multiethnic Regional History," in John P. Henderson and Harry A. Reed, eds., *Studies in the African Diaspora: A Memorial to James R. Hooker* (Dover, MA: Majority Press, 1989); P. E. H. Hair, "An Account of the Liberian Hinterland c. 1780," *Sierra Leone Studies* 16 (1962): 218–26.

8. Djibril Tamsir Niane, "The War of the Mulattos (1860–1880): A Case of Resistance to the Slave Trade on the Rio Pongo," *Black Renaissance/Renaissance Noire* 3, no. 3 (Summer 2001): 117; Sylviane Diouf, "Devils or Sorcerers, Muslims or Studs: Manding in the Americas," in Paul E. Lovejoy and David V. Trotman, eds., *Trans-Atlantic Dimensions of Ethnicity in the African Diaspora* (London: Continuum, 2003), 139–57, 141; Sylvester Corker and Samuel Massaquoi, *Lofa Count in Historical Perspective* (n.p. [1972?]), 1–2, 3, 6, 10; Nester H. Duncan, *Family Life in Lofa County, Liberia* (n.p. [1970?]), 1:8–9; Laing, *Travels*, 280–81.

9. James H. Sweet, *Domingos Álvares, African Healing and the Intellectual History of the Atlantic World* (Chapel Hill: University of North Carolina Press, 2011), 33; Charles Piot, "Of Slaves and the Gift: Kabre Sale of Kin during the Era of the Slave Trade," *Journal of African History* 37, no. 1 (1996): 31–49; Benjamin G. Dennis and Anita K. Dennis, *Slaves to Racism: An Unbroken Chain from America to Liberia* (New York: Algora, 2008), 77; Benjamin G. Dennis, *The Gbandes: A People of the Liberian Hinterland* (Chicago: Nelson-Hall, 1972), 135, 143.

10. Michael F. Kallon, *Idols with Tears* (Bloomington, IN: AuthorHouse, 2005), 19, 26; E. Dora Earthy, "The Impact of Mohammedanism on Paganism in the Liberian Hinterland," *Numen* 2, no. 3 (1955): 206–16; Boone, *Radiance*, 8–9; Kenneth Little, *The Mende of Sierra Leone: West African People in Transition* (Abingdon, Oxon: Routledge, 1967), 217–26; Kenneth Little, "The Function of Medicine in Mende Society," *Man* 48, no. 142 (1948): 127–30; Corker and Massaquoi, *Lofa County*, 30–33; Dennis, *Gbande*, 6, 88.

11. Harley, "Notes on the Poro," 8.

12. Michael D. Jackson, *The Palm at the End of the Mind: Relatedness, Religiosity, and the Real* (Durham, NC: Duke University Press, 2009), 10; Michael D. Jackson, *Life within Limits: Well-Being in a World of Want* (Durham, NC: Duke University Press, 2011), 160.

13. Kumba Kemusu Solleh, *The Damby Tradition of the Kono People of Sierra Leone, West Africa* (Bloomington, IN: AuthorHouse, 2011), 96–97.

14. F. W. Butt-Thompson, *West African Secret Societies* (London: H. F. Witherby, 1929), 148–49; Daniel Flinkinger Wilberforce, *Sherbro and the Sherbros; or, A Native African's*

Account of History Country and People (1886; repr., Charleston, SC: BiblioBazaar, 2010), 16–17; Schwab, *Tribes*, 212–13.

15. Elizabeth Tonkin, "Jealousy Names, Civilised Names: Anthroponomy of the Jlao Kru of Liberia," *Man* 15, no. 4 (December 1980): 653–64; Gordon Innes, "A Note on Mende and Kono Personal Names," *Sierra Leone Language Review* 5 (1966): 34–38; Kumba Kemusu Solleh, *Kono Gold or Koine Gold: Onomastics, the Human Naming Tradition* (Bloomington, IN: AuthorHouse, 2009); E. Ralph Langley, "The Kono People of Sierra Leone: Their Clans and Names," *Africa* 5, no. 1 (1932): 61–67; Julie F. Nemer, "Phonological Stereotypes and Names in Temne," *Language in Society* 16 (1987): 341–52, 341.

16. Harley, "Notes on the Poro," 7, 13; Ruth B. Phillips, "Masking in Sande Mende Initiation Rituals," *Africa* 48, no. 3 (1978): 265–77.

17. Harley, "Notes on the Poro," 7, 13; Corker and Massaquoi, *Lofa County*, 15; Winterbottom, *Account*, 136; M. C. Jedrej, "Structural Aspects of a West African Secret Society," *Ethnologische Zeitschrift* 1 (1982): 133–42; Bledsoe, "Political Uses of Sande Ideology," 455–72.

18. Mark Hanna Watkins, "West African Bush School," *American Journal of Sociology* 48, no. 6 (May 1943): 666–75; Little, "Function of Medicine," 129–30; Bledsoe, "Political Uses of Sande Ideology," 457; Phillips, "Masking in Sande"; Boone, *Radiance*, 52; Butt-Thompson, *West African Secret Societies*, 126.

19. Harley, "Notes on the Poro," 10, 14–15; F. W. H. Migeod, "Some Observations on the Physical Characteristics of the Mende Nation," *Journal of the Royal Anthropological Society* 49 (1919): 270; F. W. H. Migeod, *A View of Sierra Leone* (London: Kegan Paul, 1926), 236–38; Schwab, *Tribes*, 23, 118; Little, *Mende*, 119–20; Dennis, *Slaves to Racism*, 93.

20. Butt-Thompson, *West African Secret Societies*, 148–49; Boone, *Radiance*, 63; Phillips, "Masking in Mende," 267; Innes, "Mende and Kono," 37; V. R. Dorjahn, "Initiation of Temne *Poro* Officials," *Man* 61 (February 1961): 36–40; Watkins, "West African Bush School," 666–75; Winterbottom, *Account*, 135; Wilberforce, *Sherbro*, 16–17; Michael A. Gomez, *Exchanging Our Country Marks: The Transformation of African Identities in the Colonial and Antebellum South* (Chapel Hill: University of North Carolina Press, 1998), 97; Butt-Thompson, *West African Secret Societies*, 148–49.

21. Bledsoe, "Political Uses," 457; Fulton, "Poro in Kpelle Society."

22. Boone, *Radiance*, 15, notes that Bassa women at one point joined the Sande society en masse, and Harley, "Notes on the Poro," states that among the Kru the Poro "exists in a somewhat modified form," 6, 17.

23. Liberated African Letterbooks, NASL.

24. Ibid.

Chapter 3. The Banana Islands to Gallinas

1. No record exists of Bostock in the Banana Islands. This account is adapted from F. Harrison Rankin, *White Man's Grave: A Visit to Sierra Leone in 1834* (London: Richard Bentley, 1836), ch. 15, and James Boyle, *A Practical Medico-Historical Account of the Western Coast of Africa* (London: S. Highley, 1831), 64–69.

2. Caulker-Burnett, *Caulkers*, 58–61; Deirdre Coleman, ed., *Maiden Voyages and Infant Colonies: Two Women's Travel Narratives of the 1790s* (London: Leicester University Press, 1999), 101; Christopher Fyfe, *A History of Sierra Leone* (Oxford: Clarendon Press, 1962), 81; *Third Report of the Directors of the African Institution, Read at the Annual General Meeting on the 25th of March, 1809* (London: J. Hatchard, 1814), 44.

3. Evidence of Yarra/John Reffell, in Special Court of Oyer and Terminer, TS 11/826/2732, TNA UK; Mayer, *Captain Canot*, 110.

4. Mayer, *Captain Canot*, 115–18; Deirdre Coleman, *Romantic Colonization and British Anti-Slavery* (Cambridge: Cambridge University Press, 2005), 33.

5. Mayer, *Captain Canot*, 112–14.

6. Special Court of Oyer and Terminer, TS 11/826/2732, TNA UK.

7. Henry Caswell, *Martyr of the Rio Pongas* (London: Rivingtons, 1857), 114.

8. John Newton, *The Select Works of the Rev. John Newton* (Edinburgh: Peter Brown and Thomas Nelson, 1831), 13.

9. G. Tucker Childs, *A Grammar of Kisi: A South Atlantic Language* (Berlin: Mouton de Gruyter, 1995), 333; John J. Grace, "Slavery and Emancipation among the Mende in Sierra Leone, 1896–1928," in Suzanne Miers and Igor Kopytoff, eds., *Slavery in Africa: Historical and Anthropological Perspectives* (Madison: University of Wisconsin Press, 1977), 418–19; Gustavus Reinhold Nyländer, *Grammar and Vocabulary of the Bullom* (London: Church Missionary Society, 1814), 10.

10. The same geographical factors led to slave traffic increasing in this era further north in Rio Nunez and Rio Pongo. See Kenneth G. Kelly and Elhadj Ibrahima Fall, "Employing Archaeology to (Dis)entangle the Nineteenth-Century Illegal Slave Trade on the Rio Pongo, Guinea," *Atlantic Studies* 12, no. 3 (2015): 317–35.

11. Testimonies of John McQueen and Robert Bostock in Special Court of Oyer and Terminer, TS 11/826/2732, TNA UK.

12. Thomas Norman DeWolf, *Inheriting the Trade* (Boston: Beacon Press, 2008), 45; Matthew E. Mason, "Slavery Overshadowed: Congress Debates Prohibiting Atlantic Slave Trade to the United States, 1806–1807," *Journal of the Early Republic* 21, no. 1 (Spring 2000): 59–81.

13. Anne Farrow, Joel Lang, and Jenifer Frank, *Complicity: How the North Promoted, Prolonged and Profited from Slavery* (New York: Ballantine Books, 2005), 111; "Bills for the Misses D'Wolf," vol. 1, 1821, D'Wolf Papers, Baker Library, Harvard University.

14. Box 2, folders 3, 4, 18, 41, D'Wolf Papers, Bristol, Rhode Island, Historic and Preservation Society (hereafter BHPS); Bruce L. Mouser, "Trade, Coasters and Conflict in the Rio Pongo from 1790 to 1808," *Journal of African History* 14 (1973): 45–63; *Voyages*, slavevoyages.org, #36849, #36840.

15. Box 9, folder 19, D'Wolf Papers, BHPS; George Howe, *Mount Hope: A New England Chronicle* (New York: Viking Press, 1959), 101; Jay Coughtry, *The Notorious Triangle: Rhode Island and the African Slave Trade, 1700–1807* (Philadelphia: Temple University Press, 1981), 145.

16. Hugh Thomas, *The Slave Trade: The Story of the Atlantic Slave Trade* (New York:

Simon and Schuster, 1997), 545, unnumbered note; Calbraith Bourn Perry, *Charles D'Wolf of Guadaloupe, His Ancestors and Descendants* (New York: T. A. Wright, 1902), 27–29; Farrow, Lang, and Frank, *Complicity*, 111.

17. Howe, *Mount Hope*, 107; Mark A. DeWolfe Howe, *Bristol, Rhode Island: A Town Biography* (Cambridge, MA: Harvard University Press, 1930), 13.

18. Testimony of Robert Bostock in Special Court of Oyer and Terminer, TNA TS 11/826, TNA UK.

19. Individual Petition: Elizabeth Bostock and John MacQueen, HO 17/1 f. 1, TNA UK.

20. Jane Humphries, *Childhood and Child Labour in the British Industrial Revolution* (Cambridge: Cambridge University Press, 2010), 168.

21. Testimony of Malcolm Brodie and George Cook in George Cook vs. Charles William Maxwell, TS 11/823/2712, TNA UK; Jane Landers, *Atlantic Creoles in the Age of Revolution* (Cambridge, MA: Harvard University Press, 2011), 129; Daniel L. Schafer, "Family Ties That Bind: Anglo-African Slave Traders in Africa and Florida, John Fraser and His Descendants," *Slavery and Abolition* 20, no. 3 (1999): 1–21; Drake, *Revelations of a Slave Smuggler*, 18, 46–48; Mouser, "Trade, Coasters, and Conflict."

22. Drake, *Revelations of a Slave Smuggler*, 18, 46–48; Mayer, *Captain Canot*, 95.

23. Canot, *Revelations*, 70.

24. Louisa Smith to Lydia S. Fales, 13 July 1806, Fales Family Papers, John Hay Library, Brown University, Providence, RI; *Voyages*, slavevoyages.org, #36883; advertisements, *Charleston City Gazette*, 10 and 17 July 1807; "Ship News," *Charleston City Gazette*, 19 February 1807 and 15 July 1807; Svend Einar Holsoe, "The Cassava-Leaf People: An Ethnohistorical Study of the Vai People with a Particular Emphasis on the Tewo Chiefdom" (PhD diss., Boston University, 1967), 120; *Sixth Report of the Directors African Institution, Read at the General Meeting on 25th March 1812* (London: J. Hatchard, 1812), 148–49; Collier et al., *West African Sketches*, 152–55; Loren Schweninger, ed., *The Southern Debate over Slavery*, vol. 2 (Urbana: University of Illinois Press, 2008), 84–87; Howe, *Mount Hope*, 124–25.

25. Legajo 44, Num. 3, Consulado 3572, Archivo Nacional de la República Cuba (hereafter ANC); Index to New England Naturalization Petitions, 1791–1906, M1299, 39, National Archives and Records Administration.

Chapter 4. Making Deals with Siaka, Selling to the DeWolfs

1. J. F. Ade Ajayi and B. O. Ọlọruntimẹhin, "West Africa in the Anti-Slave Trade Era," in John E. Flint, ed., *The Cambridge History of Africa*, vol. 5, *C. 1790 —c. 1870* (Cambridge: Cambridge University Press, 1976), 200–201.

2. See Emma Christopher, "'The Slave Trade Is Merciful Compared to [This]': Slave Traders, Convict Transportation, and the Abolitionists," in Emma Christopher, Cassandra Pybus, and Marcus Rediker, eds., *Many Middle Passages: Forced Migration and the Making of the Modern World* (Berkeley: University of California Press, 2007).

3. Mason was possibly working for, or allied with, the DeWolfs, though this is not entirely clear in the extant records.

4. Collier et al., *West African Sketches*, 109–12; James Sidbury, *Becoming African in America: Race and Nation in the Early Black Atlantic* (New York: Oxford University Press, 2007), 171–72; Kevin G. Lowther, *African American Odyssey of John Kizell* (Charleston: University of South Carolina Press, 2013).

5. Fyfe, *History of Sierra Leone*; Simon Schama, *Rough Crossings: Britain, the Slaves and the American Revolution* (London: BBC Books, 2005); Cassandra Pybus, *Epic Journeys of Freedom: Runaway Slaves of the American Revolution and Their Global Quest for Liberty* (Boston: Beacon Press, 2006); Stephen J. Braidwood, *Black Poor and White Philanthropists: London's Blacks and the Foundation of the Sierra Leone Settlement, 1786–1791* (Liverpool: Liverpool University Press, 1994); Alexander X. Byrd, *Captives and Voyagers: Black Migrants across the Eighteenth-Century British Atlantic World* (Baton Rouge: Louisiana State University Press, 2010); Maya Jasanoff, *Liberty's Exiles: American Loyalists in the Revolutionary World* (New York: Knopf Doubleday, 2012).

6. Granville Sharp, "A Letter on the Formation of a New Settlement at Sierra Leone," 13 October 1788, from Papers of Thomas Clarkson, Huntington Library, San Marino, CA; Fyfe, *History of Sierra Leone*, 97.

7. Jeremy D. Popkin, "Race, Slavery, and the French and Haitian Revolutions," *Eighteenth-Century Studies* 37, no. 1 (Fall 2003): 113–22.

8. A Portuguese slaver was reported to have sailed from Bostock and Mason's factory just before the arrival of the *Kitty*. On Portuguese ships at this part of the coast see Daniel B. Dominguez da Silva, "The Atlantic Slave Trade to Maranhão, 1680–1846: Volume, Roots and Organization," *Slavery and Abolition* 29, no. 4 (2008): 477–501.

9. Svend E. Holsoe, "Slavery and Economic Responses among the Vai," in Miers and Kopytoff, *Slavery in Africa*, 293–94; Tara Helfman, "The Court of Vice-Admiralty at Sierra Leone and the Abolition of the West African Slave Trade," *Yale Law Journal* 115, no. 5 (March 2006): 1124–56; Maxwell to Bathurst, 12 June 1813, Letters from Secretaries of State, ADM 1/4226, TNA UK.

10. Beverly Malin, "The Illegal Slave Trade, as Practiced by the De Wolf Family of Bristol, Rhode Island, 1790–1825" (master's thesis, Brown University, December 1975), 23; *Voyages*, slavevoyages.org, #36928, #36889.

11. *Voyages*, slavevoyages.org, #36927, #7539, #7541, #7521, #7542, #7543; Thomas Perronet Thompson Papers, 1809, DTH/1/11, University of Hull, UK.

12. Sir George Collier to Admiralty, 13 January 1820, Letters from Captains, ADM 1/1674, TNA UK; "Captain George Howland's Voyage to West Africa, 1816–1817," in Bennett and Brooks, *New England Merchants*, 90–91.

13. Paul E. Lovejoy and David Richardson, "The Initial 'Crisis of Adaption': The Impact of British Abolition on the Atlantic Slave Trade in West Africa, 1808–1820," in Robin Law, ed., *From Slave Trade to "Legitimate" Commerce: The Commercial Transition in Nineteenth-Century West Africa* (Cambridge: Cambridge University Press, 2002), 32–33.

14. W. E. B. Du Bois, *The Suppression of the African Slave Trade to the United States of*

America, 1638–1870 (New York: Longmans, Green, 1896), 102, 112–15; Charles Clarke of the *Little Watt*, 27 January 1808, DeWolf Papers, Box 3, Folder 19a, BHPS; Hugh Thomas, *Cuba: A History* (London: Penguin Books, 2010), 85–87.

15. *Third Report of the Directors of the African Institution*, 14; Thomas Perronet Thompson Papers, DTH 1/39, University of Hull; *Fourth Report of the Directors of the African Institution, Read at the Annual General Meeting on the 28th of March, 1810* (London: J. Hatchard, 1814), 2–3; *Fifth Report of the Directors of the African Institution, Read at the Annual General Meeting on the 27th of March, 1811* (London: J. Hatchard, 1811), 2.

16. "Edward Henry Columbine (1763–1811)," *Oxford Dictionary of National Biography*; *Fourth Report of the Directors of the African Institution*, 8–9; Fyfe, *History of Sierra Leone*, 105; Voyage to Africa in the ship *Crocodile*, 20 December 1809–2 March 1811, E. H. Columbine Papers, University of Chicago.

17. Anon., *Extracts from the Report of the Commissioners Appointed for Investigating the State of the Settlements and Governments on the Coast of Africa* (London: printed for the House of Commons, 1812), 101; *Voyages*, slavevoyages.org, #7551; Juan Luciano Franco, *Comercio Clandestino de Esclavos* (La Habana: Editorial de Ciencias Sociales, 1985), 144–46, 154; [First] *Report of the Committee of the African Institution*, vol. 6, 107–9. For evidence that this ship was trading with Bostock, see the letter to Robert Bostock, "Africa. Gallinas. Slavery. Sierra Leone. Letter, 1813," http://www.worthpoint.com/worthopedia/africa-galli nas-slavery-sierra-leone-letter (accessed April 2010).

18. Collier et al., *West African Sketches*, 109–12; Sidbury, *Becoming African in America*, 171–72; Lowther, *African American Odyssey*, 179.

19. Diary entry for 13 August 1810, EH Columbine Papers; Collier et al., *West African Sketches*, 112–17; Special Court of Oyer and Terminer, TS 11/826/2732, TNA UK; Donnan, *Documents Illustrative*, 2:658.

20. Thomas Fowell Buxton, *African Slave Trade and Its Remedy* (London: John Murray, 1811), 229; *Second Report of the Committee of the African Institution, Read at the Annual General Meeting on the 25th of March, 1808* (London: J. Hatchard, 1812), 22.

21. Djibril Tasmir Niane, "Africa's Understanding of the Slave Trade: Oral Accounts," *Diogenes* 45, no. 75 (1997): 84–85.

22. Benjamin N. Lawrance, *Amistad's Orphans: An Atlantic Story of Children, Slavery, and Smuggling* (New Haven, CT: Yale University Press, 2014), especially 7, 46.

23. Based on interviews in Gbande country and surrounding areas that a great many names on the Liberated African Letterbook list for those rescued from Bostock suggest a village or a close network of villages. Liberated African Letterbooks, NASL; *Voyages*, slavevoyages.org; Boubacar Barry, *Senegambia and the Atlantic Slave Trade* (Cambridge: Cambridge University Press, 1998), 134.

24. David Dalby, "Banta and Mabanta," *Sierra Leone Language Review* 2 (1963): 23–25; Schwab, *Tribes*, 29.

25. Holsoe, "Slavery and Economic Responses among the Vai," in Miers and Kopytoff, *Slavery in Africa*, 293–95; Migeod, *Sierra Leone*, 145–46; Svend E. Holsoe, "The Condo Federation in Western Liberia," *Liberian Historical Review* 3 (August 1966): 1–28;

Robert Selig Leopold, "Prescriptive Alliance and Ritual Collaboration in Loma Society" (PhD diss., Indiana University, 1991), 19–21.

26. *Sixth Report of the Directors of the African Institution*, 149–50; Adam Jones, *From Slaves to Palm Kernels: A History of the Galinhas Country, 1730–1890* (Wiesbaden: A. Schröder, 1983), 56–61, 65; "Captain George Howland's Voyage, 1816–1817," in Bennett and Brooks, *New England Merchants*, 88; "Captain George Howland's Voyage to West Africa, 1822–1823," in Bennett and Brooks, *New England Merchants*, 109; Collier, *West African Sketches*, 152–53. Mattier was possibly the "Boakei Kpana Matia" who sold an engraved ivory trumpet to a sea captain in 1826. It is now in the Peabody Museum at Harvard: see Adam Jones, "White Roots: Written and Oral Testimony of the 'First' Mr Rogers," *History in Africa* 10 (1983): 151–62; Fredrick Lamp, "Ancient Wood Figures from Sierra Leone: Implications for Historical Reconstruction," *African Arts* 23, no. 2 (April 1990): 50.

27. Emma Christopher, *A Merciless Place: The Fate of Britain's Convicts after the American Revolution* (New York: Oxford University Press, 2011), 315.

28. "Robert Bostock Documents Concerning the Slave Trade," James Marshall and Marie-Louise Osborn Collection, Beinecke Rare Book and Manuscript Library, Yale University (hereafter Robert Bostock Documents, Beinecke Library); A. Jones, *Slaves to Palm Kernels*, 28–31. The deed states that it would be at "the point of" Bance Island, Gallinas, and for obvious reasons this has led some to assume that the factory was at the well-known Bance Island, the notorious slave trading fortress of a slightly earlier era in the Sierra Leone River. Yet November of 1813 was rather too late to be slave trading there, and the local "chiefs" who signed the document—who logically must have had control over the land on which it was to be established—ruled in Gallinas. Tom Ball also named the place as Gallinas, and even the agreement itself states that the location was Gallinas River. While "Gallinas River" was an ambiguous term in 1810, at least to non-African visitors, since it was used for both the Kerefe and the Moa Rivers, both of these were far away from the Sierra Leone River where Bunce Island is located. See A. Jones, *Slaves to Palm Kernels*, 2.

29. The writing closely resembles that taught in American schools in this era and is very different to that of Robert Bostock. See George Fisher, *The Instructor, or American Young Man's Best Companion Containing Spelling, Reading, Writing, and Arithmetick* (Worcester: Isaiah Thomas, 1786); Tamara Plakins Thornton, *Handwriting in America: A Cultural History* (New Haven, CT: Yale University Press, 1996), 12, 20–21.

30. J.J. Crooks, *A History of the Colony of Sierra Leone, Western Africa* (1903; repr., London: Frank Cass, 1972), 87, quoted in Lowther, *Odyssey*, 179.

Chapter 5. A Cargo of Slaves for Havana

1. Copy of an Agreement between Bostock and Mason, in Special Court of Oyer and Terminer, TS 11/826/2732, TNA UK. Conceivably, the man left behind was Crawford, who would sell slaves from Gallinas to the NS *Das Delores* in 1813 and who was said to have been delighted, hugging the sailors, after the murder of John Roach.

2. Junta de Fomento, Leg. 86, Exp. 3506, ANC; Edward H Columbine, Voyage to Africa in the ship *Crocodile*, 20 December 1809–2 March 1811, Columbine Papers; Vice Admiralty Proceedings, Sierra Leone, HCA 49/97 f. 12, TNA UK; Vice Admiralty Court Returns, Sierra Leone, HCA 49/101, TNA UK; Christopher Lloyd, *The Navy and Slave Trade: The Suppression of the African Slave Trade in the Nineteenth Century* (London: Longmans, 1940), 61.

3. Special Court of Oyer and Terminer, TS 11/826/2732, TNA UK; MacCarthy to Bathurst, 15 September 1815, CO 267/40, TNA UK; *American State Papers, Foreign Relations*, 5:105; Bruce L. Mouser, *American Colony on the Rio Pongo: The War of 1812, the Slave Trade, and the Proposed Settlement of African Americans, 1810–1830* (Trenton, NJ: Africa World Press, 2013), 64.

4. Anthony Trollope, *The West Indies and the Spanish Main* (London: Chapman and Hall, 1860), 149; Robert Francis Jameson, *Letters from the Havana: During the Year 1820* (London: John Miller, 1821), 58–60.

5. Jameson, *Letters from the Havana*, 58–60; Manuel Moreno Fraginals, *The Sugarmill: The Socioeconomic Complex of Sugar in Cuba, 1760–1860* (New York: Monthly Review Press, 1976, 2008), 73; Manuel Barcia, *The Great Slave Revolt of 1825: Cuba and the Fight for Freedom in Matanzas* (Baton Rouge: Louisiana State University Press, 2012), 33; diary entry for 21 August 1810, Columbine Papers; Warwickhistory.com, General George D'Wolf (accessed 29 May 2014).

6. David R. Murray, *Odious Commerce: Britain, Spain and the Abolition of the Cuban Slave Trade* (New York: Cambridge University Press, 1980), 17–19; Manuel Barcia, "Sugar, Slavery and Bourgeoisie: The Emergence of the Cuban Sugar Industry," in Ulbe Bosma, Juan Giusti-Cordero, and G. Roger Knight, eds., *Sugarlandia Revisited: Sugar and Colonialism in Asia and the Americas, 1800–1940* (New York: Berghahn Books, 2010), 153; Matt D. Childs, *1812 Aponte Rebellion in Cuba and the Struggle against Atlantic Slavery* (Chapel Hill: University of North Carolina Press, 2006), 9, 37, 49; Louis A. Pérez, *Cuba: Between Reform and Revolution* (New York: Oxford University Press, 2011), ix; Laird W. Bergad, Fe Iglesias García, and María del Carmen Barcia, *The Cuban Slave Market, 1790–1880* (Cambridge: Cambridge University Press, 1995), 26; Robin Moore, *Nationalizing Blackness: Afrocubanismo and Artistic Revolution in Havana* (Pittsburgh: University of Pittsburgh Press, 1997), 16.

7. Jameson, *Letters from the Havana*, 60.

8. G. Aguirre Beltran, "The Rivers of Guinea," *Journal of Negro History* 31, no. 3 (1946): 290–316, 305. There are numerous other possible explanations for this name, but I am yet to be convinced that any of them are more compelling.

9. Pérez, *Cuba*, 105; Bergad, García, and Barcia, *Cuban Slave Market*, 73–75.

10. Leonard Marques, "Slave Trading in a New World: The Strategies of North American Slave Traders in the Age of Abolition," *Journal of the Early Republic* 32, no. 2 (Summer 2012); Thomas, *Cuba*, 161; Trollope, *West Indies*, 136.

11. Marques, "Slave Trading"; Wilfred H. Munro, *The History of Bristol, R.I.* (Providence: J. A. and R. A. Reid, 1880), 323; Lemuel C Richmond, Bristol, to Spalding,

Cuba, 16 December 1822, Edward Spalding Papers, Otto G. Richter Library, the University of Miami. The other serious contender is Antonio Escoto of Havana. See Tribunal de Comercio, Legajo 161, Exp. 17, ANC.

12. Howe, *Mount Hope*, 129–30, 202–5. Howe claims that the *Rambler* was one of the three ships, but at its capture in 1813 it was still listed as belonging to James DeWolf. See Prize Papers, Rambler, HCA 32/1308, TNA UK.

13. Special Court of Oyer and Terminer, TS 11/826, TNA UK.

14. A Correspondent, "Slave-Trade Felony Act," *Times* (London), 20 June 1811.

Chapter 6. A New Slave Factory at the St. Paul River

1. Mayer, *Captain Canot*, 420–21; Special Court of Oyer and Terminer, TS 11/826/2732, TNA UK.

2. Ephraim Bacon, *Abstract of a Journal Kept by E. Bacon, Assistant Agent of the United States, to Africa* (Philadelphia: Clark and Raser, 1822), 13–14; Jehudi Ashmun, *A Memoir of the Exertions and Sufferings of the American Colonists Connected with the Occupation of Cape Montserado: Embracing the Particular History of the Colony of Liberia from December 1821 to 1823* (Washington, DC: Way and Gideon, 1826), 7, unnumbered note; Evidence of John Sterling Mill in Special Court of Oyer and Terminer, TS 11/826/2732, TNA UK; Samuel Abraham Walker, *The Church of England Mission in Sierra Leone* (London: Seeley, Burnside and Seeley, 1847), 235.

3. Svend E. Holsoe, "A Study of Relations between Settlers and Indigenous Peoples in Western Liberia, 1821–1847," *African Historical Studies* 4, no. 2 (1971): 331–62; *Sixth Report of the Directors of the African Institution*, 110; Special Court of Oyer and Terminer, TS 11/826/2732, TNA UK; Tim Hetherington, *Long Story Bit by Bit: Liberia Retold* (New York: Umbrage Editions, 2009), 10.

4. Allen M. Howard, "Nineteenth-Century Coastal Slave Trading and the British Abolition Campaign in Sierra Leone," *Slavery and Abolition* 27, no. 1 (April 2006): 23–49; Bruce J. Mouser, "Îles de Los as Bulking Center in the Slave Trade, 1750–1800," *Revue Français d'Histoire d'Outre-Mer* 83, no. 313 (1996): 77–91; Philip Misevich, "On the Frontier of 'Freedom': Abolition and the Transformation of Atlantic Commerce in Southern Sierra Leone, 1790s to 1860" (PhD diss., Emory University, 2009), 56, 179–80; Ernest Obadele-Starks, *Freebooters and Smugglers: The Foreign Slave Trade in the United States after 1808* (Fayetteville: University of Arkansas Press, 2007), 6–8; Ted Maris-Wolf, "'Of Blood and Treasure': Recaptive Africans and the Politics of Slave Trade Suppression," *Journal of the Civil War Era* 4, no. 1 (March 2014): 54.

5. "Colony of Liberia," *Times* (London), 23 November 1840, 3; Mayer, *Captain Canot*, 333, 357.

6. Captain Denman's Trial, Gallinas, ADM 7/605, TNA UK; Slave Factories at Gallinas, 1840, TS 18/58, TNA UK; Liberation of Slaves by HMS *Alert* at Gallinas, TS 18/60, TNA UK.

7. Testimony of William Salter Saunders in George Cook vs. George William Maxwell, TS 11/823/2712, TNA UK; Kelly and Fall, "Employing Archaeology"; Information re the Claims of George Cook, Foreign Office Correspondence, Spain, FO 72/182 f. 81, TNA UK; Bruce L. Mouser, "Women Slavers of Guinea Conakry," in Claire C. Robertson and Martin A. Klein, eds., *Women and Slavers in Africa* (Portsmouth, NH: Heinemann, 1997), 326.

8. Captain Denman's Trial, Gallinas, ADM 7/605, TNA UK; Slave Factories at Gallinas, 1840, TS 18/58, TNA UK; Liberation of Slaves by HMS *Alert* at Gallinas, TS 18/60, TNA UK; Kelly and Fall, "Employing Archaeology"; Sidney De La Rue, *Land of the Pepper Bird: Liberia* (New York: Putnam, 1930), 210–11.

9. Information re the Claims of George Cook, Foreign Office Correspondence, Spain, FO 72/182 f. 81, TNA UK.

10. Special Court of Oyer and Terminer, TS 11/826/2732, TNA UK.

11. Testimony of José Cabez in Appeal No. 15: Ntra. Sra. De los Dolores, HCA 42/488/982, TNA UK; Testimony of Yarra/John Reffell in Special Court of Oyer and Terminer, TS 11/826/2732, TNA UK; Mayer, *Captain Canot*, 76–77.

12. Mungo Park, *Travels in the Interior of Africa* (Edinburgh: Adam and Charles Black, 1858), 159–60, 278.

13. Samuel Abraham Walker, *Missions in Western Africa among the Soosoos, Bulloms &c.* (Dublin: William Curry, 1845), 43; A. Jones, *Slaves to Palm Kernels*, 46; interviews at Blama, Sierra Leone, March 2010.

14. Testimony of Lawrence Summers in Special Court of Oyer and Terminer, TS 11/826/2732, TNA UK.

15. Interrogation of Jesse Porter of the *Penel*, Thomas Perronet Thompson Papers, DTH/1/42; *Edinburgh Review, or the Critical Journal* 21 (February–July 1813): 76. The spelling is variously given as *Penel, Pennel,* or occasionally *Penelope.*

16. Anon., *The Trials of the Slave Traders: Samuel Samo, Joseph Peters and William Tufft* (London: Sherwood, Neeley and Jones, 1813), 22.

17. "The Trials of the Slave Traders . . . ," *Edinburgh Review, or the Critical Journal* 21 (February–July 1813): 72–93.

18. Anon., *Trials of the Slave Traders*; George Cook vs. George William Maxwell, TS 11/823/2712, TNA UK; Fyfe, *History of Sierra Leone*, 120–22; "Notice: Charles Hickson, deceased," *Royal Gazette and Sierra Leone Advertiser*, 11 July 1818; Emily Haslam, "Redemption, Colonialism and International Criminal Law: The Nineteenth Century Slave-Trading Trials of Samuel Samo and Peters," in Diane Kirkby, ed., *Past Law, Present Histories* (Canberra: ANU Press, 2012), 7–22.

19. "Trials of the Slave Traders . . . ," 80; Fyfe, *History of Sierra Leone*, 120; Anon., *Trials of the Slave Traders*; Haslam, "Redemption, Colonialism," 13–14.

20. Testimony of Tom Ball in Special Court of Oyer and Terminer, TS 11/826/2732, TNA UK.

21. Eliga H. Gould, *Among the Powers of the Earth: The American Revolution and the Making*

of a New World Empire (Cambridge, MA: Harvard University Press, 2012), 169–70; Eliga H. Gould, "The Wars of 1812," *Journal of the Early American Republic* 34, no. 1 (Spring 2014): 109–14.

22. Greg H. Williams, *The French Assault on American Shipping, 1793–1813: A History and Comprehensive Record of Merchant Marine Losses* (Jefferson, NC: McFarland, 2009).

23. Scobell to Crocker, 18 March 1813, and Scobell to Croker, 24 April 1813, ADM 1/2536, TNA UK; Navy Board Head Money, 1813, ADM 43/64, TNA UK; captains' logs, HMS *Thais*, ADM 51/2914, TNA UK; Munro, *History of Bristol*, 311; *Eighth Report of the Directors of the African Institution, Read at the Annual General Meeting on the 23rd of March, 1813* (London: J. Hatchard, 1814), 15–16; *Voyages*, slavevoyages.org, #36848, #36880, #36915; Papers of the *Rambler*, HCA 32/1308, TNA UK; Robert Bostock Documents, Beinecke Library.

Chapter 7. In the Barracoon

1. William E. Allen, "Liberia and the Atlantic World: Convergence and Effects," *History in Africa* 37, no. 1 (2010): 7–49.

2. David Noah's Speech at the Anniversary of the [illegible] at Kissey, 1824, David Noah Papers, CMS; Seeley, *Memoir*, 198–99.

3. David Noah's Speech; Seeley, *Memoir*, 198–99; S. A. Walker, *Church of England Mission*, 234–35.

4. Testimony of Lawrence Summers in Special Court of Oyer and Terminer, TS 11/826/2732, TNA UK.

5. Schwab, *Tribes*, 93, 253; Liberated African Letterbooks, NASL.

6. William D. Piersen, "White Cannibals, Black Martyrs: Fear, Depression, and Religious Faith as Causes of Suicide among New Slaves," *Journal of Negro History* 62, no. 2 (April 1977): 147–59; John Thornton, "Witches, Cannibals and Slave Traders in the Atlantic World," *William and Mary Quarterly* 60, no. 2 (April 2003): 273–94; James H. Sweet, *Recreating Africa: Culture, Kinship and Religion in the African-Portuguese World, 1441–1770* (Chapel Hill: University of North Carolina Press, 2003), 162; Costello, *Black Salt*, 13; W. Jeffrey Bolster, *Black Jacks: African American Seamen in the Age of Sail* (Cambridge, MA: Harvard University Press, 1997), 57. See Rosalind Shaw's remarkable book *Memories of the Slave Trade: Ritual and the Historical Imagination in Sierra Leone* (Chicago: University of Chicago Press, 2002), especially 3, 55, 62–64, 93, 231, for how such ideas played out among the Temne, and Gomez, and *Exchanging Our Country Marks*, 146–48, on how similar ideas may have influenced West Central Africans.

7. Robert T. Parsons, *Religion in an African Society* (Leiden: Brill, 1964), 161; Little, *Mende*, 221–23; Boone, *Radiance*, 129–32; Henry John Drewal, "Mami Wata: Arts for Water Spirits in Africa and Its Diasporas," *African Arts* 41, no. 2 (Summer 2008): 60–83; Alex van Stipriaan, "Watramama/Mami Wata: Three Centuries of Creolization of a Water Spirit in West Africa, Suriname and Europe," *Matatu* 27/28 (2003): 323–37.

8. Schwab, *Tribes*, 306–7.

9. David W. Blight, "If You Don't Tell It Like It Was, It Can Never Be As It Ought to Be," in James Oliver Horton and Lois E. Horton, eds., *Slavery and Public History: The Tough Stuff of American Memory* (Chapel Hill: University of North Carolina Press, 2008), 27.

10. See Paul E. Lovejoy, "Impact of the Atlantic Slave Trade on Africa: A Review of the Literature," *Journal of African History* 30, no. 3 (1989): 365-94; Judith Hyde and Kevin Bales, "Physical and Mental Health Aspects of Rehabilitating Children Freed from Slavery," Free the Slaves, Washington, DC, final draft submitted to the U.S. Department of Labor, Bureau of International Labor Affairs, 12 May 2006; Sweet, *Recreating Africa*, 69; Liberated African Letterbooks, NASL.

11. Niane, "Africa's Understanding," 45, 75-90; A. Jones, *Slaves to Palm Kernels*, 51; Sharman Apt Russell, *Hunger: An Unnatural History* (New York: Perseus, 2005), 99-100, 114.

12. Earthy, "Impact"; Stephanie E. Smallwood, *Saltwater Slavery: A Middle Passage from Africa to American Diaspora* (Cambridge, MA: Harvard University Press, 2007), 58-60, 140-41.

13. Holsoe, "Slavery," 291; Kup, *Sierra Leone*, 95; Dennis, *Gbandes*, 14.

14. Benjamin Samuel Ngovo, "The Bandi of North Western Liberia: A Study of Continuity and Change in Bandi Society to 1964" (PhD diss., Western Michigan University, 2011), 57-59, 87; interviews in Voinjama, Kolahun, and Foya, Liberia, 2010.

15. Diouf, "Devils or Sorcerers," 146; Rodney, *Upper Guinea Coast*, 110-12; Benjamin Anderson, *Journey to Musardu* (New York: S. W. Green, 1870), 109.

16. Liberated African Letterbooks, NASL; Duncan, *Family Life*, 1:20; Kallon, *Idols with Tears*, 109; Parsons, *Religion*, 46; Langley, "Kono," 61-67.

17. Interview Kenema, Sierra Leone, 2010.

18. Interviews in Kolahun, Liberia, 2009; Kailahun, 2010 and 2012; Guékédou, Guinea, February 2010.

19. Innes, "Mende and Kono," 36.

20. William P. Murphy, "The Sublime Dance of Mende Politics: An African Aesthetic of Charismatic Power," *American Ethnologist* 25, no. 4 (November 1998): 563-82.

21. Boone, *Radiance*, 97, 176-77, 181.

22. Gomez, *Exchanging Our Country Marks*, 99-100; Margaret Washington Creel, *A Peculiar People: Slave Religion and Community-Culture among the Gullahs* (New York: New York University Press, 1989); Marcus Rediker, *The Amistad Rebellion: An Atlantic Odyssey of Slavery and Freedom* (New York: Penguin, 2013), 134; Butt-Thompson, *West African Secret Societies*, 138; *They Are We* (documentary), directed and produced by Emma Christopher (New York: Icarus Films, 2014).

Chapter 8. The Slave Ship *Fénix* and Setting the Factory Alight

1. Junta de Fomento, Leg. 86, Exp. 3506, ANC; Appeal No. 15: Ntra. Sra. De los Dolores, HCA 42/488/982, TNA UK.

2. Junta de Fomento, Leg. 86, Exp. 3506, ANC; Du Bois, *Suppression*, 104; *Sixth Report of the Directors of the African Institution*; Lowther, *Odyssey*, 171.

3. Special Court of Oyer and Terminer, TS 11/826/2732, TNA UK.

4. Bill of Lading of the *Phoenix*, HCA 42/488/983, TNA UK; letter from Bostock to William Young of Charleston, www.worthpoint.com/worthopedia/slavery-africa-south-carolina-shipping-bill (accessed 14 March 2017).

5. *Voyages*, slavevoyages.org, #80768, #80838, #82039, #82040.

6. "Case of the *Amelia*," *Sixth Report of the Directors of the African Institution*, 36, 40–41; *Voyages*, slavevoyages.org, #7659; Anon., "Hints for Improving the Colony of Sierra Leone," *The Philanthropist, or Repository for Hints and Suggestions Calculated to Promote the Comfort and Happiness of Man* (London: Longman, 1812), 2:41–56; Lowther, *Odyssey*, 198 and 268, note 64.

7. Case of the *San José Triunfo*: Jeremiah Vernice, *Jeremiah Vernice of the Island of Saint Thomas, Merchant, Claimant of the Cargo, as the property of Juan Bailey, of the island of Puerto Rico . . .* (London, 1812); *Voyages*, slavevoyages.org, #7577; Robert Thorpe, *A Letter to William Wilberforce, ESQ, MP, Vice President of the African Institution . . .* (London: Law and Gilbert, 1815), 57–59.

8. Appeal No. 15: Ntra. Sra. De los Dolores, HCA 42/488/982, TNA UK.

9. Special Court of Oyer and Terminer, TS 11/826/2732 TNA UK; King vs. Robert Bostock and John MacQueen, 1813, Letters from Captains, ADM 1/1674, TNA UK; Liberated African Letterbooks, NASL.

10. Special Court of Oyer and Terminer, TS 11/826/2732, TNA UK.

11. Robert Bostock Documents, Beinecke Library.

12. Ibid.

13. Entry for 8 June 1813, captains' logs, HMS *Thais*, ADM 51/2914, TNA UK. The two ships might actually have already spoken two days earlier.

14. Entries for 4 May and 5 June 1813, captains' logs, HMS *Thais*, ADM 51/2914, TNA UK; Sancreed Church Tombstone; Information re the claims of George Cook, Foreign Office Correspondence, Spain, FO 72/182 f. 79, TNA UK; Order of the Admiralty, W. Dennett, Joseph Yorke and Walpole to Edward Scobell, 5 October 1811, George Cook vs. George William Maxwell, TS 11/832/2712, TNA UK; John Burke, *A Genealogical and Heraldic Dictionary of the Landed Gentry of Great Britain and Ireland* (London: Henry Coulburn, 1847), 2:1197–98.

15. "Boys of the Third Class" and "Supernumeraries for Wages," Admiralty Ships' Muster: *Thais*, ADM 37/3341, TNA UK; Maxwell to Bathurst, 12 June 1813, CO 267/36, TNA UK; Maxwell to Bathurst, 12 June 1813, Letters from Secretaries of State, ADM 1/4226, TNA UK.

16. Maxwell to Bathurst, 12 March 1813, CO 267/36, TNA UK; Maxwell to Bathurst, 16 March 1813, and enclosed in letter from JW Croker to Admiralty, 30 August 1813, Letters from Secretaries of State, ADM 1/4226, TNA UK.

17. Testimony of Edward Scobell in George Cook vs. George William Maxwell, TS 11/832/2712, TNA UK; Liberated African Letterbooks, NASL.

18. Scobell to Croker, 18 March 1813, ADM 1/2536, TNA UK.

19. Paul Jolly to Colonial Office, 25 April 1813, CO 267/37, TNA UK; Appeal no. 680, Captured Ship *Juan*, HCA 42/455/680, TNA UK.

20. Entry for 25 June 1813, captains' logs, ADM 51/2914, TNA UK; Special Court of Oyer and Terminer, TS 11/826/2732.

21. Entry for Friday 25 June 1813, captains' logs, ADM 51/2914, TNA UK; entry for same date, masters' logs, ADM 52/4362, TNA UK.

22. Special Court of Oyer and Terminer, TS 11/826/2732, TNA UK.

23. Seeley, *Memoirs*, 198–99.

24. Entry for 26 June 1812, captains' logs, HMS *Thais*, ADM 51/2914, TNA UK; Special Court of Oyer and Terminer, TS 11/826/2732, TNA UK.

25. Special Court of Oyer and Terminer, TS 11/826/2732, TNA UK.

Chapter 9. Leaving, Never to Return

1. Bruce L. Mouser, "Trade and Politics in the Nunez and Pongo Rivers, 1790–1865" (PhD diss., Indiana University, 1971), 105–6.

2. David Noah's Speech; S. A. Walker, *Church of England Mission*, 235.

3. Evidence of Lawrence Summers, Yarra/John Reffell, Mill and Hayes in Special Court of Oyer and Terminer, TS 11/826/2732, TNA UK; entry for 1 July 1813, captains' logs, ADM 51/2914, TNA UK.

4. Evidence of Mill and Hayes, Special Court of Oyer and Terminer, TS 11/826/2732, TNA UK.

5. Entry for 2 July 1813, captains' logs, ADM 51/2914, TNA UK.

6. Seeley, *Memoirs*, 198–99; Nicholas Parry received thirty-six lashes of the cat-o'-nine-tails for saying that he would be "bugger'd before he would go in the boat" to fetch slaves, entry for 2 July 1813, captains' logs, ADM 51/2914, TNA UK; Olaudah Equiano, *The Interesting Life of Olaudah Equiano, or Gustavus Vassa, the African* (London: printed for the author, 1794), 48–49.

7. Entry for 2 July 1813, captains' logs, ADM 51/2914, TNA UK.

8. Entry for 4 July 1813, captains' logs, ADM 51/2914, TNA UK.

Chapter 10. Arriving in Freetown

1. William Brown died from his injuries on 27 June 1813, captains' logs, ADM 51/2914, TNA UK.

2. Testimony of Edward Scobell, Special Court of Oyer and Terminer, TS 11/826/2732, TNA UK.

3. Mayer, *Captain Canot*, 357.

4. Thomas Coke, *An Interesting Narrative of a Mission Sent to Sierra Leone, in Africa, by the Methodists, in 1811* (London: printed for the author, 1812), 39; Mary Church, *Sierra Leone; or, The Liberated Africans, in a Series of Letters from a Young Lady to Her Sister in 1833 and 34*

(London: Longman, 1835), 29; *Proceedings of the Church Missionary Society for Africa and the East, Twenty-First Year: 1820–1821* (London: L. B. Seeley, 1821), 240.

5. Bolster, *Black Jacks*, 49–50.

6. George S. Brooks Jr., "A View of Sierra Leone ca. 1815," *Sierra Leone Studies* 4, nos. 13–14 (1960): 24–31, 30.

7. *African Herald*, 25 November 1809.

8. Misevich, "Origins of Slaves," 157; John Peterson, *Province of Freedom: A History of Sierra Leone, 1787–1870* (London: Faber, 1969), 187.

9. Liberated African Letterbooks, NASL.

10. Ibid.; Leonard, *Records of a Voyage*, 57–58; interviews with Joseph Tugbah-Manneh and Chief Tuleh Davis, 1 March 2011, Kroo Town, Sierra Leone. A witness in the 1812 case of Joseph Peters had also, however, given his name as Tom Krooman, see Anon., *Trials of the Slave Traders*, 42.

11. Another Liberated African girl, Emily Augusta Gason, some years younger than this one, also gave her ethnicity as "Bassa Kroo." See Silke Strickrodt, "African Girls' Samplers from Mission Schools in Sierra Leone (1820s to 1840s)," *History in Africa* 37 (2010): 189–245, 206; interview with Kru Chief Tuleh Davis, who clarified: "It is from these people that all these people came from who went on the slave expeditions, who are manning the slave ships, from that seaside."

12. Fyfe, *History of Sierra Leone*, 98, 110; evidence of George Clarke, Special Court of Oyer and Terminer, TS 11/826/2732, TNA UK.

13. Akintola Wyse, *The Krio: An Interpretive History* (Madison: University of Wisconsin Press, 1989), 4; Hannah Kilham, *Memoir of the Late Hannah Kilham, Chiefly Compiled from Her Journal* (London: Darton and Harvey, 1837), 328; F. A. J. Utting, *The Story of Sierra Leone* (London: Longmans and Green, 1931), 117; S. A. Walker, *Church of England Mission*, xxxiv.

14. H. J. Ricketts, *Narrative of the Ashantee War: With a View of the Present State of the Colony of Sierra Leone* (London: W. Simpkin and R. Marshall, 1833), 218; *Proceedings of the Church Missionary Society for Africa and the East, Twenty-Second Year: 1821–1822* (London: L. B. Seeley, 1822), 63–64.

15. *Sixteenth Report of the Directors of the African Institution, Read at the Annual General Meeting on the 10th of May, 1822* (London: J. Hatchard, 1822), 346.

16. Evidence of R. Clarke, Assistant Surgeon at Sierra Leone, quoted in S. A. Walker, *Church of England Mission*, xxxiv; "Register of Disposal of Captured Negroes," CO 267/38, TNA UK.

Chapter 11. The Court Case

1. *Special Report of the Directors of the African Institution, Read at the Annual General Meeting on the 12th of April, 1815* (London: J. Hatchard, 1815), 55; Anon., *Trials of the Slave Traders*, 42–48; Emily Haslam, "Silences in International Criminal Legal Histories and the Construction of the Victim Subject of International Criminal Law," in Christine

Schwöbel, ed., *Critical Approaches to International Criminal Law: An Introduction* (London: Routledge, 2014), 181–95.

2. Haslam, "Silences," 13.

3. Testimony of Tarra/Yarra, Special Court of Oyer and Terminer, TS 11/826/2732, TNA UK.

4. Testimony of Tom Ball, TS 11/826/2732, TNA UK.

5. Vice Admiralty Proceedings, Sierra Leone, HCA 49/97, f. 9, 85, TNA UK; A Lover of Truth to The Editor, *Royal Gazette and Sierra Leone Advertiser*, 30 May 1818, 1–2; Fyfe, *History of Sierra Leone*, 134; Sheldon H. Harris, "An American's Impressions of Sierra Leone," *Journal of Negro History* 47, no. 1 (January 1962): 35–41; Robert Purdie, Decretal [*sic*] of Sentence, TS 11/826/2732, TNA UK.

6. G. S. Brooks, "View of Sierra Leone," 30.

7. Testimony of Robert Bostock, TS 11/826/2732, TNA UK; "King vs. Robert Bostock and John MacQueen," 1813, in Letters from Captains, ADM 1/1674, TNA UK.

8. 31 December 1809–2 March 1811, part 2 of 3, p. 162, Columbine Papers; Vice Admiralty Proceedings, Sierra Leone, HCA 49/97 f. 9, f. 85, TNA UK; *An Account of All Sums of Money Paid or Claimed under the Acts Passed for the Abolition of the Slave Trade, or under Any Orders in Council, as Bounties for Slaves or Natives of Africa, Condemned in Any Court of Vice Admiralty Navy Office, 28th June 1817* (London: printed for the House of Commons, 1817).

9. Fyfe, *Sierra Leone*, 99.

10. Bruce L. Mouser, "The Trial of Samuel Samo and the Trading Syndicates of the Rio Pongo, 1797 to 1812," *International Journal of African Historical Studies* 46, no. 3 (2013): 423–41; Haslam, "Redemption, Colonialism," 15–16.

11. Anon., *Trials of the Slave Traders*, 20, 33–35, 39.

12. Mouser, *American Colony*, 70–71; Purdie to Maxwell, 1 July 1813, CO 267/36, TNA UK.

13. Tara Helfman, "The Court of the Vice-Admiralty at Sierra Leone and the Abolition of the West African Slave Trade," *Yale Law Journal* 115, no. 5 (March 2006): 1133; Fyfe, *History of Sierra Leone*, 115; *Special Report of the Directors of the African Institution, Read at the Annual General Meeting on the 12th of April, 1815* (London: J. Hatchard, 1815), 109–10, 154–55; Maxwell to Bathurst, 16 March 1813, CO 267/36, TNA UK; Dr. Thorpe's Case, 1815–1827, CO 267/88, TNA UK.

14. Special Court of Oyer and Terminer, TS 11/826/2732, TNA UK; Iain Whyte, *Zachary Macaulay, 1768–1838: The Steadfast Scot in the British Anti-Slavery Movement* (Liverpool: Liverpool University Press, 2011), 209–10; Fyfe, *History of Sierra Leone*, 68, 74, 92, 115.

15. Fyfe, *History of Sierra Leone*, 140, 144, 177, 205, 319; James W. St. G. Walker, *The Black Loyalists: The Search for a Promised Land in Nova Scotia and Sierra Leone, 1783–1870* (New York: Africana, 1976), 273; Mavis C. Campbell, *Back to Africa: George Ross & the Maroons* (Trenton, NJ: Africa World Press, 1993), 31; Robin W. Winks, *The Blacks in Canada: A History* (Montreal: McGill-Queens University Press, 1997), 77; Suzanne Schwarz, "Reconstructing the Life Histories of Liberated Africans: Sierra Leone in the Early Nineteenth Century," *History in Africa* 39 (January 2012): 175–207.

16. Augustus Ferryman Mockler-Ferryman, *British West Africa: Its Rise and Progress* (London: Swan Sonnenschein, 1900), 30–31.

17. Haslam, "Redemption, Colonialism," 13–14; Haslam, "Silences"; P. E. H. Hair, "Africanisms: The Freetown Contribution," *Modern African Studies Review* 5, no. 4 (1967): 531–32.

18. Evidence of Tom Ball in Special Court of Oyer and Terminer, TS 11/826/2732, TNA UK; Haslam, "Silences."

19. Testimony of John Sterling Mill and Philippa Hayes in Special Court of Oyer and Terminer, TNA TS 11/832, TNA UK.

20. *Special Report of the Directors of the African Institution*, 98–99.

21. Mouser, *American Colony*, 82–83.

22. By some accounts there were two children already aboard the *Fénix* at the time of its capture. However, the crew recalled only one slave, and Za alone was entered onto the Liberated African list at Freetown.

23. "Register of Disposal of Captured Negroes," CO 267/38, TNA UK.

Chapter 12. Becoming Soldiers, Cabin Boys, and Wives

1. Leonard, *Records of a Voyage*, 143.

2. Maeve Ryan, "'A Most Promising Field for Future Usefulness': The Church Missionary Society and the Liberated Africans of Sierra Leone," in William Mulligan and Maurice Bric, eds., *A Global History of Anti-Slavery Politics in the Nineteenth Century* (New York: Palgrave Macmillan, 2013), 37–39, 42–43; Helfman, "Court of Vice-Admiralty," 1122.

3. *Special Report of the Directors of the African Institution*, 144–45; *Journals of the House of Commons*, 69:860; Joseph Marryatt, *Thoughts on the Abolition of the Slave Trade, and the Civilization of Africa* (London: JM Richardson and J. Ridgway, 1816); Marcus Wood, *The Horrible Gift of Western Freedom: Atlantic Slavery and the Representation of Emancipation* (Athens: University of Georgia Press, 2010), 14; Fyfe, *History of Sierra Leone*, 114–15.

4. *African Herald*, 25 November 1809, 2 December 1809; *Special Report of the Directors of the African Institution*, 49–54; Fyfe, *History of Sierra Leone*, 106, 143.

5. *Special Report of the Directors of the African Institution*, 54; Michael J. Turner, "The Limits of Abolition: Government, Saints and the 'Africa Question,' c. 1780-1820," *English Historical Review* 112, no. 446 (1997): 319–57; Peterson, *Province of Freedom*, 51–54.

6. Fyfe, *History of Sierra Leone*, 107; *African Herald*, 18 November 1809.

7. Samuel Swan's "Journal of a Voyage along the West African Coast, 1815-16," in Bennett and Brooks, *New England Merchants*, 72–73.

8. Fyfe, *History of Sierra Leone*, 116; Coke, *Interesting Narrative*, 35–36, 40; Utting, *Story of Sierra Leone*, 119.

9. "Register of Disposal of Captured Negroes," CO 267/38, TNA UK; Michael Banton, *West African City: A Study of Tribal Life in Freetown* (Oxford: Oxford University Press, 1970), 16; T. R. Griffiths, "On the Races Inhabiting Sierra Leone," *Journal of the*

Anthropological Institute of Great Britain and Ireland 16 (1887): 300–310; Coke, *Interesting Narrative*, 44–45; Harris, "American's Impressions," 35–41.

10. A. B. C. Sibthorpe, *A History of Sierra Leone* (London: Cass, 1970), 23; F. Harrison Rankin, "A Visit to Sierra Leone, in 1834," *Carey's Library of Choice Literature*, no. 41, part 2 (2 July 1836): 276–349 (Philadelphia: L. E. Carey & A. Hart; Leonard, *Records of a Voyage*, 55–56.

11. Ricketts, *Narrative of the Ashantee War*, 196.

12. "Register of Disposal of Captured Negroes," CO 267/38, TNA UK; Fyfe, *History of Sierra Leone*, 118, 146.

13. Fyfe, *History of Sierra Leone*, 115; *Special Report of the Directors of the African Institution*, 112–13; "Register of Disposal of Captured Negroes," CO 267/38, TNA UK.

14. Rankin, *White Man's Grave*, 2:107.

15. A. B. Ellis, *History of the First West India Regiment* (London: Chapman and Hall, 1885), 16–19. See also Rankin, *White Man's Grave*, 2:112; [First] *Report of the Committee of the African Institution, Read to the Annual General Meeting on the 15th of July, 1807* (London: J. Hatchard, 1811), 43; Coke, *Interesting Narrative*, 42; Equiano, *Interesting Life*, 48–49.

16. Quoted in Ryan, "'Most Promising Field,'" 39; Arthur T. Porter, *Creoledom: A Study in Freetown Society* (Oxford: Oxford University Press, 1963), 37; J. J. Crooks, *History of Sierra Leone, Western Africa* (London: Browne and Nolan, 1903; repr., London: Frank Cass, 1972), 87; Peterson, *Province of Freedom*, 58; Order of the Admiralty, W. Dennett, Joseph Yorke and Walpole to Edward Scobell, 5 October 1811.

17. Kevin Linch, *Britain and Wellington's Army: Recruitment, Society and Tradition, 1807–15* (London: Palgrave Macmillan, 2011), 31–33; Coke, *Interesting Narrative*, 41.

18. *African Repository and Colonial Journal* 7 (1831–32): 364.

19. Linch, *Britain and Wellington's Army*, 145.

20. Rankin, *White Man's Grave*, 2:107; Robert Thorpe, *A Reply "Point by Point" to the Special Report of the Directors of the African Institution* (London: F. C. and J. Rivington, 1815), 84; A. B. Ellis, *History*.

21. Liberated African Letterbooks, NASL; Register of Disposal of Captured Negroes, CO 267/38, TNA UK; Recruiting Accompt of a Detachment of the Royal Africa Regiment of Infantry, WO 12/10344 and WO 12/10345, TNA UK.

22. S. C. Ukpabi, "West Indian Troops and the Defence of British West Africa in the Nineteenth Century," *African Studies Review* 17, no. 1 (1974): 133–50; Brian Dyde, *The Empty Sleeve: The Story of the West India Regiments of the British Army* (St. Johns, Antigua: Hansib, 1997), 32; R. J. Wingfield to Col. Torrens, 18 November 1811, reprinted in *Miscellaneous Accounts and Papers*, vol. 10, 7 January–30 July 1812 (n.p.: preserved in the Bodleian Library, 1812), 113; Wingfield to War Office, *Journals of the House of Commons*, 69:856, 860.

23. Captain J. F. Napier Hewett, *European Settlements on the West Coast of Africa, with Remarks on the Slave-Trade and the Supply of Cotton* (1862; repr., New York: Negro Universities Press, 1969), 87–89.

24. Coleman, *Maiden Voyages*, 57–58; Butt-Thompson, *Sierra Leone*, 146.

25. David Hancock, *Citizens of the World: London Merchants and the Integration of the British Atlantic Community, 1735–1785* (Cambridge: Cambridge University Press, 1995), 1–2, 190–91; Coleman, *Romantic Colonization*, 50; Dyde, *Empty Sleeve*, 31.

26. *Ninth Report of the Directors of the African Institution, Read at the Annual General Meeting on the 12th of April, 1815* (London: J. Hatchard, 1815), 54; Anon., *Trials of the Slave Traders*.

27. Rene Chartrand, *British Forces in the West Indies, 1793–1815* (London: Osprey, 1996), 33.

28. Dyde, *Empty Sleeve*, 30–31.

29. Fyfe, *History of Sierra Leone*, 119.

30. Christopher Fyfe, "The Foundation of Freetown," in Christopher Fyfe and Eldred D. Jones, eds., *Freetown: A Symposium* (Freetown: Sierra Leone University Press, 1968), 1–8; A Lover of Truth, "Letter to the Editor," *Royal Gazette and Sierra Leone Advertiser*, 30 May 1818, 1–2; Fyfe, *History of Sierra Leone*, 134; Harris, "American's Impressions," 35–41; Francis B. Spilsbury, *Account of a Voyage to the Western Coast of Africa* (London: Richard Phillips, 1807), 29; *Special Report of the Directors of the African Institution*, 21.

31. Thorpe, *Reply "Point by Point,"* 84; G. S. Brooks, "View of Sierra Leone," 25–31; Leonard, *Records of a Voyage*, 47; "Register of Disposal of Captured Negroes," CO 267/38; Fyfe, *History of Sierra Leone*, 62.

32. Mrs. E. H. Melville, *A Residence at Sierra Leone* (1849; repr., London: Frank Cass, 1968), 39; C. H. Fyfe, "A View of Freetown, Sierra Leone," *Journal of Sierra Leone Studies* 1 (2016): 26–27.

33. Theresa A. Singleton, "Slavery and Spatial Dialectics on Cuban Coffee Plantations," *World Archaeology* 33, no. 1 (2001): 98–114.

34. *Fourth Report of the Directors of the African Institution, Read at the Annual General Meeting on the 28th of March, 1810* (London: J. Hatchard, 1814), 65–68; "Register of Disposal of Captured Negroes," CO 267/38, TNA UK; Fyfe, *History of Sierra Leone*, 130–31.

35. Sibthorpe, *History of Sierra Leone*, 38; Crooks, *History of Sierra Leone*, 131–32; Leonard, *Records of a Voyage*, 87; Rankin, *White Man's Grave*, 2:107–8, 125.

36. *Proceedings of the Church Missionary Society for Africa and the East, Twenty-Fourth Year: 1823–1824* (London: L. B. Seeley, 1824), 1823–24, 226.

Chapter 13. Leaving Africa

1. Evidence of George Clarke, Special Court of Oyer and Terminer, TS 11/826/2732.

2. Entry for 15 May 1813, captains' logs, ADM 51/2914, TNA UK; quoted in Costello, *Black Salt*, 41–42.

3. Scobell to JW Croker, 21 November 1813, ADM 1/2537, TNA UK; Marryatt, *Thoughts on the Abolition*, 11; Ships' Musters (Series 2), Ship *Thais*, 1 January 1812–30 June 1813, ADM 37/4430, TNA UK; Leonard, *Records of a Voyage*, 253–54; Lawrance, *Amistad's Orphans*, 168–69.

4. Ships' Musters (Series 2), Ship *Thais*, 1 January 1812–30 June 1813, ADM 37/4430, TNA UK; "Register of Disposal of Captured Negroes," CO 267/38, TNA UK; interview with Kroo Chief Tuleh Davis.

5. Voyage to Africa in the ship *Crocodile*, 20 December 1809–2 March 1811, EH Columbine Papers.

6. Admiralty Ships' Muster: *Thais*, ADM 37/3341 TNA UK; Mr. William Villacott and Mr. George Bartholomew, TS 11/832/2712, TNA UK; "The Slave Trade," *Times* (London), 30 November 1813, 3; captains' logs, ADM 51/2914, TNA UK; *Liverpool Mercury*, 17 December 1813; Marryatt, *Thoughts on the Abolition*; *Voyages*, slavevoyages.org, #7367.

7. Bolster, *Black Jacks*, 47.

8. Equiano, *Interesting Life*, 56.

9. Ships' Musters (Series 2), Ship *Albacore*, 1 August 1812–28 February 1814, ADM 37/4462, TNA UK; Ships' Musters (Series 2), Ship *Thais*, 1 January 1812–30 June 1813, ADM 37/4430, TNA UK; Ships' Musters (Series 2), Ship *Thais*, 1 July 1813–31 August 1814, ADM 37/4431, TNA UK; Costello, *Black Salt*, 35.

10. Edward Wedlake Brayley and John Britton, *The Beauties of England and Wales*, vol. 4 (London: Vernor, Hood, Longman, 1805), 320–22. Among the navy's imperfect mustering system and the profligate trading of names, where they went next is unclear.

11. Ships' Musters (Series 2), Ship *Albacore*, 1 August 1812–28 February 1814, ADM 37/4462, TNA UK; *Tenth Report of the Directors of the African Institution, Read at the Annual General Meeting on the 27th of March, 1816* (London: J. Hatchard, 1816), 37.

12. Edward Scobell to Bathurst, 3 December 1813, CO 267/37, TNA UK.

13. *Times* (London), 30 November 1813; Henry Slight and Julian Slight, *Chronicles of Portsmouth* (London: Lupton Relfe, 1828), 44.

14. Herbert H. Kaplan, *Nathan Mayer Rothschild and the Creation of a Dynasty* (Stanford: Stanford University Press, 2006), 89.

Chapter 14. A Village of Their Own

1. Fyfe, *History of Sierra Leone*, 107.

2. *Eleventh Report of the Directors of the African Institution, Read at the Annual General Meeting on the 26th of March, 1817* (London: J. Hatchard, 1817), 139; Collier et al., *West African Sketches*, 187; Fyfe, *History of Sierra Leone*, 119; Anon., "Sierra Leone" *The Friend: A Religious and Literary Journal*, 3:301 (Philadelphia: John Richardson, 1830); *African Herald*, 15 April 1809, 1; *Special Report of the Directors of the African Institution*, 112.

3. *Ninth Report of the Directors of the African Institution,*, 53–54; Sibthorpe, *History of Sierra Leone*, 26–27; *Third Report of the Directors of the African Institution, Read at the Annual General Meeting on the 25th of March, 1809* (London: J. Hatchard, 1814), 38–39; Marryatt, *Thoughts on the Abolition*, 48–49.

4. Fyfe, *History of Sierra Leone*, 134.

5. Ibid., 114.

6. Spilsbury, *Account of a Voyage*, 30; Maxwell to Bathurst, 15 June 1813, CO 267/36, TNA UK.

7. Sibthorpe, *History of Sierra Leone*, 25-26.

8. Rankin, *White Man's Grave*, 2:105; Leo Spitzer, *The Creoles of Sierra Leone: Responses to Colonialism, 1870-1945* (Ile-Ife: University of Nigeria Press, 1972), 11; Seeley, *Memoir*, 122; Melville, *Residence*, 240-42.

9. *Times* (London), 24 August 1814; [First] *Report of the Committee of the African Institution*, 24; *Eighth Report of the Directors of the African Institution, Read at the Annual General Meeting on the 23rd of March, 1813* (London: J. Hatchard, 1814), 16-17; Ryan, "'Most Promising Field,'" 43-44.

10. *Ninth Report of the Directors of the African Institution*, 57-59; Catherine Hall, *Civilising Subjects: Metropole and Colony in the English Imagination, 1830-1867* (Chicago: University of Chicago Press, 2002), 120-27.

11. David Noah's Speech; S. A. Walker, *Church of England Mission*, 235.

12. Ryan, "'Most Promising Field,'" 39-42; *Ninth Report of the Directors of the African Institution*, 53-54; Leonard, *Records of a Voyage*, 81-82.

13. "Register of Disposal of Captured Negroes," CO 267/38, TNA UK; Lawrance, *Amistad's Orphans*, 191.

14. David Noah's Speech; S. A. Walker, *Church of England Mission*, 235; Coke, *Interesting Narrative*, 2-3.

15. David Noah's Speech; S. A. Walker, *Church of England Mission*, 235.

16. S. A. Walker, *Church of England Mission*, 17.

17. *Proceedings of the Church Missionary Society for Africa and the East, Twentieth Year: 1819-1820* (London: L. B. Seeley, 1820), 89-90; S. A. Walker, *Church of England Mission*, 17.

18. S. A. Walker, *Church of England Mission*, 17.

19. It is possible that the *Dolores*, or *Dores*, was the "Portuguese" vessel that sailed off from Mason and Bostock's at the St. Paul River during the chaos with Roach and the *Kitty*. Since the *Dolores* reported that it did not get to the Windward Coast until July, however, and appears to have purchased its captives from Crawford and a Mr. Cross at Gallinas, this seems to have not been the case. The possibility remains that it sailed off to go to Mason and Bostock's Gallinas factory, of which Crawford may then have been in charge. See the "Appeal No. 15: Ntra. Sra. De los Dolores," HCA 42/488/982, TNA UK.

20. *Proceedings of the Church Missionary Society for Africa and the East, Eighteenth Year: 1817-1818* (London: L. B. Seeley, 1818), 167.

Chapter 15. A Murder, and an Appeal to the Prince Regent

1. Anon., "Abolition of the Slave Trade," *Times* (London), 26 March 1808.

2. Mercatoe, "Slave Trade Felony Act," *Times* (London), 17 August 1811; *Fifth Report of the Directors of the African Institution, Read at the Annual General Meeting on the 27th of*

March, 1811 (London: J. Hatchard, 1811), 4–8; "To the Editor," *Bath Chronicle and Weekly Gazette*, 20 February 1812, 4.

3. "Slave Trade," *Chester Chronicle*, 14 July 1811, 4; "Slave Trade," *Cheltenham Chronicle*, 6 June 1811, 4; Anon., *Extracts from the Report of the Commissioners Appointed for Investigating the State of the Settlements and Governments on the Coast of Africa* (London: Printed for the House of Commons, 1812).

4. Colley, *Britons*, 351; Srividhya Swaminathan, *Debating the Slave Trade: Rhetoric of British National Identity, 1759–1815* (Farnham, Surrey: Ashgate, 2009), 94; Jasanoff, *Liberty's Exiles*, 139–40.

5. "The Memorial of William Henry Gould Page," FO 72/182 f. 72–4, TNA UK.

6. Maxwell to Bathurst, 1 May 1814, CO 267/38, TNA UK; *Twelfth Report of the Directors of the African Institution, Read at the Annual General Meeting on the 9th of April, 1818* (London: J. Hatchard, 1818), 162; *Voyages*, slavevoyages.org, #14675.

7. Testimony of Michael Williamson and John Gustave, CO 267/38, TNA UK.

8. Testimony of Richard Blundell, Michael Williamson, and Venus Murray, CO 267/38, TNA UK.

9. Ibid.

10. Testimony of Venus Murray, CO 267/38, TNA UK; *Twelfth Report of the Directors of the African Institute*, 162; Junta de Fomento, Leg. 86, Exp. 3506, ANC; *Voyages*, slavevoyages.org, #81655, #81654.

11. "Appeal No. 15: Ntra. Sra. De los Dolores," TNA HCA 42/488/982, TNA UK.

12. Individual Petition: Elizabeth Bostock and John MacQueen [*sic*], HO 17/1 f. 1, TNA UK.

13. Petition of Bostock and McQueen to the Prince Regent, TS 11/826/2732, TNA UK.

14. *Historical Records of Australia*, series 1, vol. 8, 602–3.

15. *Journals of the House of Commons*, vol. 70, 1036. See oldbaileyonline.org, including the cases at t18140420–45, t18140420–72, t18140420–42, t18140525–33, t18130714–8, t18140525–14, t18130714–1, t18140525–68, t18140706–106, t18140420–124.

16. Oldbaileyonline.org, t18140706–106.

17. Marika Sherwood, "The Trade in Enslaved Africans and Slavery after 1807," in Fernne Brennan and John Packer, eds., *Colonialism, Slavery, Reparations and Trade: Remedying the Past* (Oxford: Routledge, 2012), 24.

Chapter 16. Experiments in Civilization and Liberty

1. "Mr Bickersteth's Report," in S. A. Walker, *Church of England Mission*, 4–5.

2. Fyfe, *History of Sierra Leone*, 123–24.

3. Ryan, "'Most Promising Field,'" 45.

4. *Tenth Report of the Directors of the African Institution*, 73.

5. *Missionary Register for 1816, Containing the Principal Transaction of the Various Institutions for the Promulgation of the Gospel*, vol. 4 (London: L. B. Seeley, 1816), 238.

6. David Brion Davis, *The Problem of Slavery in the Age of Emancipation* (New York: Knopf, 2014), 4, 47.

7. [First] *Report of the Committee of the African Institution*, 22, 30.

8. Marryatt, *Thoughts on the Abolition*, 18, 46; [First] *Report of the Committee of the African Institution*, 11; *Fourth Report of the Directors of the African Institution*, 24.

9. *Second Report of the Committee of the African Institution, Read at the Annual General Meeting on the 25th of March, 1808* (London: J. Hatchard, 1812), iv, 11; *Third Report of the Directors of the African Institution*, 10.

10. Fyfe, *History of Sierra Leone*, 127.

11. Ryan, "'Most Promising Field,'" 45; Bronwen Everill, *Abolition and Empire in Sierra Leone and Liberia* (London: Palgrave Macmillan, 2012), 22–23; *Tenth Report of the Directors of the African Institution*, 76–77; "Mr. Bickersteth's Report," in S. A. Walker, *Church of England Mission*, 5, 235; *Proceedings of the Church Missionary Society for Africa and the East, Seventeenth Year: 1816–1817* (London: L. B. Seeley, 1817), 171; Thorpe, *Reply "Point by Point,"* 83.

12. Fyfe, *Sierra Leone*, 127.

13. Anon., "A Brief Sketch of the State of Sierra Leone, in 1814, from the National Intelligencer," in John Edwards Caldwell, ed., *The Christian Herald* (New York: John E. Caldwell, 1816), 2:341–43; Coke, *Interesting Narrative*, 41.

Chapter 17. Prisoners in New South Wales

1. Christopher, "'Slave Trade Is Merciful'"; Thomas Reid, *Two Voyages to New South Wales and Van Diemen's Land* (London: Longman, Hurst, Rees, Orme and Brown, 1822), ix.

2. *Historical Records of Australia*, series 1, vol. 8, 553; Herbert S. Klein and Stanley L. Engerman, "Long-Term Trends in African Mortality in the Transatlantic Slave Trade," *Slavery and Abolition* 18, no. 1 (1997): 36–48; M. H. Ellis, *Lachlan Macquarie: His Life, Adventures and Times* (Sydney: HarperCollins, 2010), 395.

3. Ellis, *Lachlan Macquarie*, 395.

4. Emma Christopher, "'Ten Thousand Times Worse than the Convicts': Rebellious Sailors, Convict Transportation and the Struggle for Freedom," *Journal of Australian Colonial History* 5 (2004): 30–46.

5. "Sydney: Ship News," *Sydney Gazette and New South Wales Advertiser*, 29 April 1815, 2; Mary C. Karasch, *Slave Life in Rio de Janeiro, 1808–1850* (Princeton: Princeton University Press, 1987), 61; Gerald Horne, *The Deepest South: The United States, Brazil and the African Slave Trade* (New York: New York University Press, 2007), 13.

6. Horne, *Deepest South*, 25; Karasch, *Slave Life*, 55–58.

7. John White quoted in Tim Flannery, ed., *The Birth of Sydney* (Melbourne: Text, 1999), 48–49.

8. Grace Karskens, *The Colony: A History of Early Sydney* (Sydney: Allen and Unwin, 2009), 162, 177; Grace Karskens, *The Rocks: Everyday Life in Early Sydney* (Melbourne: Melbourne University Press, 1998), 16; Carol Liston, "Colonial Society," in James Broadbent and Joy Hughes, eds., *The Age of Macquarie* (Melbourne: Melbourne University Press, 1992), 30-31.

9. "Sydney: Ship News," *Sydney Gazette and New South Wales Advertiser*, 29 April 1815, 2; Christopher, *Merciless Place*.

10. Information regarding allotment of convicts, reel 6004, 4/3494, p. 66, NSWSRA.

11. Cassandra Pybus, *Black Founders: The Unknown Story of Australia's First Black Settlers* (Sydney: University of New South Wales Press, 2006), 68-69.

12. Karskens, *Colony*, 193.

13. M. H. Ellis, *Lachlan Macquarie*, 221-41, 465-66, 468-76, 488-96, 500-503; Hamish Maxwell-Stewart, *Closing Hell's Gates: The Death of a Convict Station* (Sydney: Allen and Unwin, 2008), 149-50.

14. Jane Elliott, "Was There a Convict Dandy? Convict Consumer Interests in Sydney, 1788-1815," *Australian Historical Studies* 26, no. 104 (1995): 373-92; entry for 13 July 1815, Joseph Arnold Journal, Mitchell Library, Sydney.

15. "Lord, Simeon (1771-1840)," "Underwood, James (1771-1844)," "Kable, Henry (1763-1846)," and "Terry, Samuel (1776-1838)," all in *Australian Dictionary of Biography*; E. C. Richmond, "Simeon Lord: A Merchant Prince of Botany Bay," *Journal and Proceedings of the Royal Australian Historical Society* 30, no. 3 (1944): 157-95; D. R. Hainsworth, *The Sydney Traders: Simeon Lord and His Contemporaries, 1788-1821* (Melbourne: Cassell, 1972), 39-40; James Broadbent, "Macquarie's Domain," in Broadbent and Hughes, *Age of Macquarie*, 6; Karskens, *Colony*, 170.

16. Bruce Kercher, "Perish or Prosper: The Law and Convict Transportation in the British Empire," *Law and History Review* 21, no. 3 (2003): 527-84; Michael Dunn, "Early Australia: Wage Labour or Slave Society," in E. L. Wheelwright and Ken Buckley, eds., *Essays in the Political Economy of Australian Capitalism*, vol. 1 (Sydney: Australia and New Zealand Book Company, 1975), 33-38; J. B. Hirst, *Convict Society and Its Enemies* (Sydney: George Allen and Unwin, 1983), 24-26, 81-82; David Neal, "Free Society, Penal Colony, Slave Society, Prison," *Historical Studies* 22, no. 89 (October 1987): 497-518; John Hirst, "Or None of the Above: A Reply," *Historical Studies* 22, no. 89 (October 1987): 519-24.

17. Letter from William Fisher of HMS *Bann*, Letters from Captains, ADM 1/1813, TNA UK; Bryan Edwards, *The History, Civil and Commercial, of the West Indies*, vol. 4 (London: G. & W. B. Whittaker et al., 1819), 493; *American State Papers, Foreign Relations*, vol. 5, 104-5.

18. Mayer, *Captain Canot*, 207.

19. Letter from William Fisher of HMS *Bann*, Letters from Captains, ADM 1/1813, TNA UK; captains' logs, HMS *Bann*, ADM 51/2180, TNA UK; Case of the *Rosa*, Vice Admiralty Court Returns, Sierra Leone, HCA 49/101, TNA UK; Case of the *Rosa*;

Apresamiento de la Rosa, 1816, Tribunal de Comercio, Legajo 30, Dossier 199, ANC; *Twelfth Report of the Directors of the African Institution*, 161; Franco, *Comercio Clandestino*, 168.

20. *Twelfth Report of the Directors of the African Institution*, 164; *American State Papers, Foreign Relations*, 5:106.

21. *American State Papers, Foreign Relations*, 5:106; James H. Kettner, "Subjects or Citizens? A Note on British Views Respecting the Legal Effects of American Independence," *Virginia Law Review* 62, no. 5 (1976): 945–76; James H. Kettner, "The Development of American Citizenship in the Revolutionary Era: The Idea of Volitional Allegiance," *American Journal of Legal History* 18, no. 208 (1974): 208–42; Alan Taylor, *The Civil War of 1812: American Citizens, Irish Rebels and Indian Allies* (New York: Vintage Books, 2011), 4, 102–5.

22. Case of the *Rosa*, Vice Admiralty Court Returns, Sierra Leone, HCA 49/101, TNA UK.

23. I am grateful to Jorge Felipe González for helping me put together the events surrounding the *Bella Maria*.

24. "Ship News," *Providence Patriot*, 25 May 1816, 3.

Chapter 18. Christianity at Hogbrook

1. Seeley, *Memoir*, 55–56; Arthur T. Pierson, *Seven Years in Sierra Leone: The Story of the Work of William A.B. Johnson, Missionary of the Church Missionary Society, from 1816 to 1823 in Regent's Town, Sierra Leone* (London: James Nisbet and Co., 1897), 63–64; Stephen H. Tyng, *A Memoir of the Rev. W. A. B. Johnson, Missionary of the Church Missionary Society, in Regent's Town, Sierra Leone* (New York: R. Carter, 1853; repr., Memphis: General Books, 2010), 26.

2. Kup, *Sierra Leone*, 153; William Singleton, "An Account of a Visit to the Gambia and Sierra Leone," in Anon., *Report of the Committee Managing a Fund Raised by Some Friends for the Purpose of Promoting African Institution* (London: Harvey, Darton, 1822), 54–55; Leonard, *Records of a Voyage*, 49–50.

3. Seeley, *Memoir*, 55–56; Pierson, *Seven Years*, 64.

4. Sibthorpe, *History of Sierra Leone*, 29; Tyng, *Memoir*, 3; *Eleventh Report of the Directors of the African Institution*, 139.

5. Tyng, *Memoir*, 207–8; Charlesworth, *Africa's Mountain Valley*, 37; Seeley, *Memoir*, 26, 32–34, 36; Pierson, *Seven Years*, 15–16, 37, 39, 41; Peterson, *Province of Freedom*, 107.

6. Seeley, *Memoir*, 32–33, 56; Padriac X. Scanlan, "The Colonial Rebirth of British Abolition: The Liberated African Villages of Sierra Leone, 1815–1824," *American Historical Review* 121, no. 4 (2016): 1085–113.

7. Fyfe, *History of Sierra Leone*, 129; D. M. Jones, "Business Organisation."

8. Fyfe, *History of Sierra Leone*, 129.

9. Scanlan, "Colonial Rebirth"; Anon., "Sierra Leone," 301; S. A. Walker, *Church of England Mission*, 16–17.

10. Seeley, *Memoir*, 17–18, 68, 86, 333; Kup, *Sierra Leone*, 153; S. A. Walker, *Church of*

England Mission, 71-72; *Proceedings of the CMS*, 1817-1818, 246; Pierson, *Seven Years*, 108; Tyng, *Memoir*, 33, 44; see also Tamba journal March-June 1821, William Tamba papers, CMS.

    11. Charlesworth, *Africa's Mountain Valley*, 57, 69; *Proceedings of the CMS*, 1817-1818, 247.

    12. Sibthorpe, *History of Sierra Leone*, 33-34; Charlesworth, *Africa's Mountain Valley*, 36-37.

    13. "Regent's Town, 1816," *Boston Recorder*, 1 May 1819.

Chapter 19. The End of Their Punishment

    1. Government and General Orders, *Sydney Gazette*, 20 January 1816, 1; Individual Petition: Elizabeth Bostock and John MacQueen [*sic*] HO 17/1 f. 1, TNA UK; *Historical Records of Australia*, series 1, vol. 8, 602-3; *Sydney Gazette*, 20 January 1816.

    2. "Sydney," *Sydney Gazette*, 20 January 1816, 2.

    3. Bigge Reports, A2130, Mitchell Library, Sydney; Birrell, *Mariners, Merchants*, 36; Alan Atkinson, "The Moral Basis of Marriage," *Push from the Bush* 2 (1998): 104-15. Transportation was often considered akin to divorce even for those who had left their legal spouses in Britain or Ireland, never mind for spouses left in Africa.

    4. "Names of Persons in New South Wales Who Have Subscribed to the Relief of the Sufferers at the Memorial and Glorious Battle of Waterloo," *Sydney Gazette and NSW Advertiser*, 3 February 1816, 1.

    5. Pardon, reel 772, 4/4472, pp. 9-11, NSWSRA.

    6. Sales by Auction, *Sydney Gazette and New South Wales Advertiser*, 24 February 1816, 2.

    7. Hainsworth, *Sydney Traders*, 101-5; "Announcements," *Sydney Gazette and NSW Advertiser*, 8 November 1817, 2; Piper Papers, vol. 1, p. 279, A254, Mitchell Library; Colonial Secretary's Office, 2648, reel Z1787, Archives Office of Tasmania.

    8. Re land grant, Fiche 3266, 4/438, p. 9 NSWRA; Bigge Report A2130, Mitchell Library; Maxwell to Bathurst, 25 October 1814, CO 267/39, TNA UK; Thorpe to Bathurst, 26 October 1814, CO 257/39, TNA UK; Index for CO 267/40, TNA UK; Fyfe, *Sierra Leone*, 121; Thorpe, *Letter to William Wilberforce*, xvii (original emphasis); Advertisements, This Day Is Published . . ., *Times* (London), 14 July 1815, 2.

    9. "Parliamentary Intelligence," *Times* (London), 15 April 1815, 2; Fyfe, *History of Sierra Leone*, 123.

    10. Hassall Correspondence, Mitchell Library, Sydney, A1677-74, vol. 4, 107-8.

    11. Hobart Town, *Hobart Town Gazette and Southern Reporter*, January 3 1818, 2.

Chapter 20. A Model Village

    1. *Eleventh Report of the Directors of the African Institution*, 34-35, 136; Fyfe, *History of Sierra Leone*, 133-34; A Lover of Truth to the Editor, *Royal Gazette and Sierra Leone Advertiser*, 30 May 1818, 1-2.

2. *Special Report of the Directors of the African Institute*, 112; "Memoir of the Late Rev. William Garnon," http://anglicanhistory.org/africa/sl/garnon1819.html.

3. "Memoir of the Late Rev. William Garnon"; "Register of Disposal of Captured Negroes," CO 267/38, TNA UK; Kenneth Macaulay, *The Colony of Sierra Leone Vindicated from the Misrepresentations of Mr. McQueen of Glasgow* (London: Hatchard and Son, 1827), 124; Seeley, *Memoir*, 72–73, 88.

4. "Freetown: Public Works and General Improvements," *Royal Gazette and Sierra Leone Advertiser*, 19 December 1818; Seeley, *Memoir*, 126.

5. *Sixteenth Report of the African Institution*, 353; Charlesworth, *Africa's Mountain Valley*, 66–67.

6. Charlesworth, *Africa's Mountain Valley*, 83, 104–5.

7. Kup, *Sierra Leone*, 151; Peterson, *Province of Freedom*, 195; Pierson, *Seven Years*, 160–61; Seeley, *Memoir*, 268–69.

8. W. Singleton, "Account of a Visit," 58.

9. *Proceedings of the Church Missionary Society for Africa and the East, Nineteenth Year: 1818–1819* (London: L. B. Seeley, 1819), 223; *Eleventh Report of the Directors of the African Institution*, 33–34.

10. *Proceedings of the CMS*, 1816–1817, 214, 269, 272; *Proceedings of the CMS*, 1818–1819, 79; Peterson, *Province of Freedom*, 70; Seeley, *Memoir*, 348; *Special Report of the Directors of the African Institute*, 150.

11. Tamba actually did what the British had imagined when the first recaptives appeared in 1808. *Fourth Report of the Directors of the African Institution*, 62; Tyng, *Memoir*, 31; Seeley, *Memoir*, 36; Utting, *Story of Sierra Leone*, 117.

12. *Proceedings of the CMS*, 1819–1820, 86.

13. Anon., "Sierra Leone," 301; *Proceedings of the CMS*, 1819–1820, 91.

14. Seeley, *Memoir*, 87, 202; Tamba journal, 1820, William Tamba papers, CMS.

15. Fyfe, *Sierra Leone*, 147; *Proceedings of the CMS*, 1818–1819, 61.

16. Seeley, *Memoir*, 198–99; interview with Joseph Reffell, Regent, Sierra Leone, May 2012.

17. S. A. Walker, *Church Missionary Society*, 39.

18. Ibid.; David Noah's Speech, 250.

19. Everill, *Abolition and Empire*, 9; C. A. Bayly, *The Birth of the Modern World, 1780–1914* (Oxford: Blackwell, 2003), 10.

20. Seeley, *Memoir*, 199; C. Hall, *Civilizing Subjects*, 155.

21. Hair, "Africanisms"; W. Singleton, "Account of a Visit," 54.

22. Seeley, *Memoir*, 200.

23. *Proceedings of the CMS*, 1818–1819, 246.

24. Ibid., 246, 253.

25. *Missionary Register for 1824, Containing the Principal Transaction of the Various Institutions for the Promulgation of the Gospel*, vol. 12 (London: L. B. Seeley, 1824), 135; *Evangelical Magazine and Missionary Chronicle*, vol. 26 (1818), 198; *Proceedings of the CMS*, 1818–1819, 239.

26. *Proceedings of the CMS*, 1818–1819, 241; Charlesworth, *Africa's Mountain Valley*, 109–12.

27. *Proceedings of the CMS*, 1818–1819, 76; Letter from Reverend Johnson, *Religious Intelligencer* 6, no. 28 (8 December 1821), 43.

28. *Proceedings of the CMS*, 1819–1820, 265–67.

29. Ibid., 275.

30. Ibid., 276–77.

31. Ibid., 277–78.

32. Ibid., 280, 285–86.

33. Ibid., 286.

34. Ibid., 297–99; Charlesworth, *Africa's Mountain Valley*, 131.

35. *Proceedings of the CMS*, 1819–1820, 291–92.

36. "An Abstract of the Journal of Rev. J. B. Cates," in Bacon, *Abstract of a Journal*, 67–73; Pierson, *Seven Years*, 152–53; Anon., "American Colonization Society: Purchase of Land for a Colony at St. John's River," *Quarterly Christian Spectator* 3, no. 7 (1821): 649–53; *Missionary Register for 1819, Containing the Principal Transaction of the Various Institutions for the Promulgation of the Gospel*, vol. 7 (London: L. B. Seeley, 1819), 491–92; Charlesworth, *Africa's Mountain Valley*, 205.

37. *Proceedings of the CMS*, 1819–1820, 292.

38. Ibid., 292–93.

39. Journey of Mr. Cates, in *Religious Intelligencer*, vol. 6, for the year ending May 1822 (8 December 1821), 438–40; *Church Missionary Paper* 18 (Midsummer 1820).

40. Quoted in Lowther, *Odyssey*, 207.

41. Marie Tyler-McGraw, *An African Republic: Black and White Virginians in the Making of Liberia* (Chapel Hill: University of North Carolina Press, 2007), 13–14, 75; James T. Campbell, *Middle Passages: African American Journeys to Africa* (New York: Penguin, 2007), 41.

42. Quoted in Macaulay, *Sierra Leone Vindicated*, 122.

43. Two Africans, "To the Editor of the Royal Gazette," *Royal Gazette and General Advertiser*, 25 April 1818.

44. Africanus, "To the Editor of the Times," *Royal Gazette and Sierra Leone Advertiser*, 29 May 1820; *Proceedings of the CMS*, 1818–1819, 72.

45. Seeley, *Memoir*, 41–45.

46. Ibid., 176–77.

47. *Proceedings of the CMS*, 1819–1820, 71, 96.

48. Ibid., 97; Pierson, *Seven Years in Sierra Leone*, 219–20.

49. *The Washington Theological Repertory*, vol. 1, 294; Seeley, *Memoir*, 172.

50. Seeley, *Memoir*, 182–83.

51. *Religious Reporter*, 30 September 1820; Seeley, *Memoir*, 181.

52. Quoted in Hilary McD. Beckles, "The Slave-Drivers' War: Bussa and the 1816 Barbados Slave Rebellion," *Boletín de Estudios Latinoamericanos y del Caribe* 39 (December 1985): 85–110.

53. Beckles, "Slave-Drivers' War"; Michael Craton, *Testing the Chains: Resistance to Slavery in the British West Indies* (Ithaca: Cornell University Press, 1983), 263; Cleve McD. Scott, "Bussa's Rebellion, 1816," in Junius P. Rodriguez, ed., *Encyclopedia of Slave Resistance and Rebellion* (Westport, CT: Greenwood Press, 2007), 1:90–91; Hilary McD. Beckles,

"Emancipation by Law or War? Wilberforce and the 1816 Barbados Slave Rebellion," in David Richardson, ed., *Abolition and Its Aftermath: The Historical Context, 1790–1916* (Abingdon, UK: Frank Cass, 1985), 81–82; Fyfe, *Sierra Leone*, 136.

54. "Mr. T. Morgan to the Secretary," in Seeley, *Memoir*, 225.

55. Fyfe, *History of Sierra Leone*, 136; birth certificates of the early colony, NASL.

56. *Proceedings of the CMS*, 1819–1820, 98.

Chapter 21. The Appeal

1. Birrell, *Mariners, Merchants*, 13–17.

2. Helfman, "Court of Vice-Admiralty," 1148–49; Marryatt, *Thoughts on the Abolition*, 40–41; Fyfe, *History of Sierra Leone*, 136–37.

3. *Special Report of the Directors of the African Institution*, 87–92, 95–97.

4. Helfman, "Court of Vice-Admiralty."

5. Thorpe, *Letter to William Wilberforce*, 18–20; George Cook vs. George William Maxwell, TS 11/823/2712, TNA UK.

6. Maxwell to Bathurst, 29 March 1815, CO 267/40, TNA UK; George Cook vs. George William Maxwell, TS 11/823/2712, TNA UK; Dr. Thorpe's Case, CO 267/88, TNA UK; George Francis Dow, *Slave Ships and Slaving* (Mineola, NY: Dover, 2002), 227.

7. George Cook vs. George William Maxwell, TS 11/823/2712, TNA UK; Africanus, "To the Editor of the Royal Gazette," *Royal Gazette and Sierra Leone Advertiser*, 20 June 1818; Fyfe, *History of Sierra Leone*, 123.

8. What actually happened to Brodie is unclear; by some reports he returned to slave trading. George Cook vs. George William Maxwell, TS 11/823/2712, TNA UK; MacCarthy to Colonial Office, 5 May and 8 May 1819, CO 267/49, TNA UK.

9. Purdie to Maxwell, 13 July 1813, CO 267/36, TNA UK; Fyfe, *History of Sierra Leone* 120.

10. Special Court of Oyer and Terminer, TS 11/826/2732, TNA UK.

11. George Clarke to Henry Goulburn, CO 267/55, TNA UK; A. Grant to Henry Goulburn, 26 December 1820, CO 267/51, TNA UK.

12. Proof of Winsley, Chambers, and Matthews in Special Court of Oyer and Terminer, TS 11/826/2732, TNA UK.

13. Proof of Thomas Lovekine in Special Court of Oyer and Terminer, TS 11/826/2732, TNA UK.

14. John Marshall, *Royal Navy Biography; or, Memoirs of the Services . . .* (London: Longman, Hurst, Rees, Orme, Brown and Green, 1824), vol. 2, part 1, 496; *Asiatic Journal and Monthly Miscellany* 2 (1816): 327, 637. I attempted to search through the muster rolls at ADM 37, TNA UK, but a definite answer to his various name changes and ships between 1813 and 1820 seems improbable.

15. In the event only the jail keeper went to London, although Lawrence Summers might have already been there. George Clarke to Henry Goulburn, CO 267/55, TNA UK.

16. Tamba journal, April 2, 21, 22, William Tamba papers, CMS.

17. Seeley, *Memoir*, 55-56.

18. TS 11/826/2732, TNA UK.

19. John Dodson, *A Report of the Case of the Louis, Forest, Master: Appealed from the Vice Admiralty Court at Sierra Leone* (London: John Butterworth, 1817), 7.

20. *The Navy List, 1814*, 130; TS 11/826/2732; "Parliamentary Intelligence," *Times* (London), 15 April 1815, 2; *Special Report of the Directors of the African Institution*, 97.

21. Special Court of Oyer and Terminer, TS 11/826/2732, TNA UK; Fyfe, *History of Sierra Leone*, 123.

22. Dr. Thorpe's Case, CO 267/88, TNA UK; Scobell to Irby, December 1813 and March 1814, copied in Marshall, *Royal Navy Biography*, vol. 2, part 1, 496-97; Marshall, *Royal Navy Biography*, Supplement, part 2, 351; see also the inscription of his tombstone at Sancreed, Lake's Parochial History, 1868, http://west-penwith.org.uk/sancreed2.htm.

23. Checks in the Treasury Papers of TNA UK failed to turn up any information on this question.

Chapter 22. Helping to Found Liberia

1. *Proceedings of the CMS*, 1818-1819, 151.

2. Tamba journal, beginning 13 February 1820, William Tamba papers, CMS; Liberated African Letterbooks, NASL.

3. Ibid.

4. Seeley, *Memoir*, 199.

5. Charlesworth, *Africa's Mountain Valley*, 168-69.

6. Seeley, *Memoir*, 254-55.

7. Ibid., 196-97.

8. Ibid., 195.

9. Quoted in Henry Louis Gates Jr., *The Trials of Phillis Wheatley: America's First Black Poet and Her Encounters with the Founding Fathers* (New York: Basic Civitas, 2003), 70.

10. Swaminathan, *Debating the Slave Trade*, 31; Dale Herbert Porter, "Defense of the British Slave Trade, 1784-1807" (PhD diss., University of Oregon, 1987), 85-86.

11. Frederick Chamier, *The Life of a Sailor by a Captain in the Navy* (New York: J & J. Harper, 1833), 1:111, 31.

12. Mary McAleer Balkun, "Phillis Wheatley's Construction of Otherness and the Rhetoric of Performed Ideology," *African American Review* 36, no. 1 (Spring 2002): 121-35; Gates, *The Trials of Phillis Wheatley*, 27.

13. "Wesleyan Missionary Society," in *Missionary Register for 1819*, 5; Seeley, *Memoir*, 219.

14. Kilham, *Memoir*, 227; Peterson, *Province of Freedom*, 201.

15. Sibthorpe, *History of Sierra Leone*, 32-33; Joe A. D. Alie, *A New History of Sierra Leone* (Oxford: Macmillan, 1990), 69; Peterson, *Province of Freedom*, 54-56, 108; "Register of Disposal of Captured Negroes," CO 267/38, TNA UK.

16. Anon., "Fair of Free Town," *Royal Gazette and Sierra Leone Advertiser*, 3 and 11 April 1819; "An Enigma," *Royal Gazette and Sierra Leone Advertiser*, 8 January 1819; "Fashionable Memoranda," *Royal Gazette and Sierra Leone Advertiser*, 26 February 1820; *Sixteenth Report of the Directors of the African Institution*, 335.

17. Tamba journal, November–December 1820, William Tamba papers, CMS.

18. Ibid.

19. Charlesworth, *Africa's Mountain Valley*, 188.

20. Seeley, *Memoir*, 241–44; Tamba journal, November–December 1820, William Tamba papers, CMS; Charlesworth, *Africa's Mountain Valley*, 161.

21. Seeley, *Memoir*, 149, 159.

22. Lowther, *Odyssey*, 217–25.

23. Seeley, *Memoir*, 249; Bacon, *Abstract of a Journal*, 6–7.

24. Bacon, *Abstract of a Journal*, 7, 10; *Proceedings of the CMS*, 1821–1822, 80.

25. Bacon, *Abstract of a Journal*, 9.

26. Tamba journal, March–June 1821, William Tamba papers, CMS.

27. Mill wrote his name without the "s" in his earlier letter to Bostock, though Europeans generally wrote Mills.

28. Bacon, *Abstract of a Journal*, 9–14.

29. *Proceedings of the CMS*, 1820–1821, 60; Mouser, *American Colony*, 95–96; W. Singleton, "Account of a Visit," 61–62.

30. Robert Bostock Documents, Beinecke Library; Tamba journal, March–June 1821, William Tamba papers, CMS; Special Court of Oyer and Terminer, TS 11/826/2732; Bacon, *Abstract of a Journal*, 9; Charles Johnson, *Bitter Canaan: The Story of the Negro Republic* (Boston: Boston University African Studies Center, 1988), 37.

31. Tamba journal, March–June 1821, William Tamba papers, CMS.

32. Bacon, *Abstract of a Journal*, 9.

33. Letter from Reverend Johnson, *Religious Intelligencer*, vol. 6, no. 28 (8 December 1821), 437; Bacon, *Abstract of a Journal*, 15; Tamba Journal, March–June 1821, William Tamba papers, CMS.

34. Letter from Reverend Johnson, *Religious Intelligencer*, 437–40.

35. "United States Colonization Society," *Christian Observer* 22 (1821): 60–62; C. Johnson, *Bitter Canaan*, 40; *Proceedings of the Church Missionary Society for Africa and the East, Twenty-Second Year: 1822–1823* (London: L. B. Seeley, 1823), 59.

36. C. Johnson, *Bitter Canaan*, 44.

37. J. T. Campbell, *Middle Passages*, 53; C. Johnson, *Bitter Canaan*, 41–44.

38. Holsoe, "Study of Relations"; James B. Taylor, *Biography of Elder Lott Cary: Late Missionary to Africa* (Baltimore: Armstrong and Berry, 1837), 36.

Chapter 23. Van Diemen's Land

1. Lieutenant Charles Jeffreys, RN, *Van Diemen's Land: Geographical and Descriptive Delineations of the Island of Van Diemen's Land* (London: JM Richardson, 1820), 159; David

Burn, *A Picture of Van Diemen's Land* (Hobart, TAS: Cat and Fiddle Press, 1973), 5; "Jeffreys, Charles (1782-1826)," *Australian Dictionary of Biography*; George William Evans, *Geographical, Historical and Topographical Description of Van Diemen's Land* (London: John Souter, 1822), 63, unnumbered note; James Boyce, *Van Diemen's Land* (Collingwood, VIC: Black, 2010), 155.

2. Edward Curr, *An Account of the Colony of Van Diemen's Land* (London: George Cowie, 1824), 3; Jeffreys, *Van Diemen's Land*, 8; Michael Roe, "Darwin in Hobart," *Island* 28 (1986): 16-18; *Godwin's Emigrants Guide*, 1; Evans, *Geographical, Historical and Topographical Description*, 26; W. C. Wentworth, *A Statistical, Historical and Political Description of the Colony of New South Wales, and Its Dependent Settlements in Van Diemen's Land* (1819; repr., Cambridge: Cambridge University Press, 2012), 182.

3. James Ross, *The Settler in Van Diemen's Land* (1836; repr., Melbourne: Marsh Walsh, 1975), 45.

4. Ross, *Settler*, 3, 15, 4, 1; Leonie C. Mickleborough, *William Sorell in Van Diemen's Land* (Hobart, TAS: Blubber Head Press, 2004), 27; Sharon Morgan, *Land Settlement in Early Tasmania: Creating an Antipodean England* (Cambridge: Cambridge University Press, 2003), 49; James Fenton, *A History of Tasmania: From Its Discovery in 1642 to the Present Time* (Hobart, TAS: J. Walch and Sons, 1884; repr., New York: Cambridge University Press, 2011), 50; Margaret Dillon, "Convict Labour and Colonial Society in the Campbell Town Police District: 1820-1839" (PhD diss., University of Tasmania, April 2008), 11; Kirsty Reid, *Gender, Crime and Empire: Convicts, Settlers and the State in Early Colonial Australia* (Manchester: Manchester University Press, 2007), 60-73; Mickleborough, *William Sorell*, 5-9, 11, 100-101, 104; Alison Alexander, *Governors' Ladies: The Wives and Mistresses of Van Diemen's Land Governors* (Sandy Bay, TAS: Tasmanian Historical Research Association, 1987), 70-76, 78.

5. Morgan, *Land Settlement*, 13; Mickleborough, *William Sorell*, 23-24, 43, 45-46; Burn, *Picture of Van Diemen's Land*, 14.

6. Classified advertising, *Hobart Town Gazette*, 14 April 1821, 2.

7. On John McQueen's activities in the colony: Application for a Joint Auctioneer's Licence, 15 January 1821, reel 6051, 4/1748, 95-97, NSWSRA; Granted an Auctioneer's Licence, 8 March 1821, reel 6070, 4/1265, 56-57, NSWSRA; Tendering Rebuilt *Endeavour*, 11 August 1821, reel 6051 4/1749, 410-12, NSWSRA; Reply to tendering proposal, 21 July 1821, reel 6008, 4/3504, 159, NSWSRA; Kirsten McKenzie, *Scandal in the Colonies: Sydney and Cape Town, 1820-50* (Melbourne: Melbourne University Press, 2004), 83-84; New Partner at MacQueen and Atkinson, 8 July 1822, reel 6055; 4/1761, 10, NSWSRA; "Sydney," *Sydney Gazette and New South Wales Advertiser*, 27 December 1822, 2; "Ship News," *Sydney Gazette and New South Wales Advertiser*, 16 June 1821; Classified Advertising, *Sydney Gazette*, 2 January 1819, 4; "Hobart Town: Ship News," *Hobart Town Gazette and Southern Reporter*, 23 January 1819, 1; Classified Advertising, *Sydney Gazette*, 15 July 1824, 1; *Hobart Town Gazette*, 25 December 1825; *Sydney Gazette*, 18 September 1823; *Sydney Gazette*, 15 July 1824; *Hobart Town Gazette*, 25 December 1825.

8. Colonial Secretary's Office, 2648, reel Z1787, AO of Tasmania. His supporter

Robert Thorpe also implied in his own court case in Britain that Bostock's claim was unsuccessful. See Dr. Thorpe's Case, CO 267/88, TNA UK.

9. Ross, *Settler*, 4; Joan Goodrick, *Life in Old Van Diemen's Land* (Adelaide: Rigby, 1977), 130; *Hobart Town Gazette and VDL Advertiser*, 12 October 1822; Morgan, *Land Settlement*, 45–46; Mary Nicolls, ed., *The Diary of the Reverend Robert Knopwood, 1803–1838* (Launceston, TAS: Tasmanian Historical Research Association, 1977), 383, 391.

10. Boyce, *Van Diemen's Land*, 158–60.

11. Goodrick, *Old Van Diemen's Land*, 167; Babette Smith, *Australia's Birthstain: The Startling Legacy of the Convict Era* (Sydney: Allen and Unwin, 2007).

Chapter 24. Liberty in White and Black

1. Z. Lewis, *American Missionary Register*, vol. 2 (New York: J. & J. Harper, 1822), 236–38.

2. Bacon, *Abstract of a Journal*, 39; William Fox, *Brief History of the Wesleyan Missions on the Western Coast of Africa* (London: published for the author, 1851), 265–66; S. A. Walker, *Church of England Mission*, 11–13, 183–84; Tyng, *Memoir*, 173.

3. Seeley, *Memoir*, 343; Butt-Thompson, *Sierra Leone*, 238–39; *Proceedings of the CMS*, 1823–1824, 229.

4. S. A. Walker, *Church of England Mission*, 157; Charlesworth, *Africa's Mountain Valley*, 156.

5. S. A. Walker, *Church of England Mission*, 169.

6. Seeley, *Memoir*, 338, 356.

7. Noah to CMS, "Speech of 1824; Seeley, *Memoir*, 363; S. A. Walker, *Church of England Mission*, 175–76.

8. Seeley, *Memoir*, 289.

9. Tamba to CMS, 10 February 1824, William Tamba papers, CMS; *Proceedings of the CMS*, 1823–1824, 96.

10. Tamba to CMS, 28 March 1824 and 9 April 1824, William Tamba papers, CMS; Noah to CMS, 24 March 1824, David Noah Papers, CMS.

11. Thomas Sylvester Johnson, *The Story of a Mission: The Sierra Leone Church* (London: S.P.C.K., 1953), 36, S. A. Walker, *Church of England Mission*, 222–23.

12. Noah to CMS, 17 November 1824; Tamba to CMS, 30 December 1824, William Tamba papers, CMS; S. A. Walker, *Church of England Mission*, 211, 234; *Proceedings of the CMS*, 1823–1824, 96.

13. Tamba to CMS, 10 February 1824 and 13 March 1827 (date crossed through), William Tamba papers, CMS.

14. Anon., "At a Meeting of the Agricultural Society . . .," *Sierra Leone Advertiser and Royal Gazette*, 7 October 1820; Seymour Drescher, *The Mighty Experiment: Free Labor versus Slavery in British Emancipation* (Oxford: Oxford University Press, 2004), 96–98.

15. Noah to CMS, 6 May 1826, David Noah Papers, CMS; Noah to CMS, "Report at Kissey for Michaelmas 1825," Noah Papers, CMS; S. A. Walker, *Church of England*

Mission, 268; Tamba to CMS, May 1825, William Tamba papers, CMS; Tamba report Wellington/Kent of 27 September 1826, William Tamba papers, CMS; Noah to CMS, "Report at Regent, 1827," David Noah Papers, CMS.

16. Noah to CMS, 6 May 1826; Tamba to CMS, 19 December 1827, William Tamba papers, CMS.

17. Tamba to CMS, 27 March 1828, William Tamba papers, CMS.

18. Noah to CMS, report of Gloucester and Regent, 1829; Noah to CMS, "Journal of a Visit to Bassa."

19. Noah to CMS, "Journal of a Visit to Bassa."

20. Birrell, *Mariners, Merchants*, 70-76; Thelma Birrell to author, personal communication, 2010; Colonial Secretary's Index, 4/3504, reel 6008, p. 45, NSWSRA; Lucille V. Andel, *Clerk of the House: The Reminiscences of Hugh Munro Hall, 1818-1882* (self published, 1984), 74, 81-83.

21. Ian W. McLean, *Why Australia Prospered: The Shifting Sources of Economic Growth* (Princeton: Princeton University Press, 2012), 54, 58.

22. Bennett and Warner, *Country Houses*, 92-97; Andel, *Clerk of the House*, 74.

23. Advertising, *Sydney Gazette and New South Wales Advertiser*, 2 September 1826, 4; classified advertising, *Sydney Gazette and New South Wales Advertiser*, 4 April 1828, 4; *Historical Records of Australia*, series 1, vol. 14, 156-57, 560; Mathew Hindson Account Book, p. 65, 1827-30, A151, Mitchell Library; Paula Byrne, "Freedom in a Bonded Society: The Administrative Mind and the 'Lower Classes' in Colonial New South Wales," *Journal of Australian Studies* 53 (1997): 51-58.

24. Probate packets, John McQueen, date of death 19 March 1829, series 1-383, NSWSRA; Karskens, *Colony*, 168-69. McQueen's death certificate gives his age as forty, but as all other ages for him—from his days in Africa through his period as a convict— coincide, it would seem that it is this one that was wrong, adding one or two years onto his actual age. Family Notices, *Sydney Gazette and New South Wales Advertiser*, 21 March 1829, 3.

25. Tamba to CMS, n.d., received by them Midsummer 1826, William Tamba papers, CMS.

26. Fyfe, *History of Sierra Leone*, 174-75; Huzzey, *Freedom Burning*, 209.

27. Half a rod is roughly 8.25 feet; each acre is 160 square rods.

28. Fyfe, *History of Sierra Leone*, 162; Rankin, *White Man's Grave*, 2:115-18.

29. Thelma Birrell, personal communication, 2010. See F. M. L. Thompson, *English Landed Society in the Nineteenth Century* (London: Routledge and Kegan Paul, 1963), 28; Re Approval of grant of tenement in Hunter Street to Mr. Bostock, 4 March 1819, reel 6006, 4/3500, 7, NSWSRA; Memorial for a Grant of 400 acres and indulgences, 1 October 1821, Fiche 3209, 4/1863, 28, NSWSRA; Reply to memorial for land, 13 November 1821, reel 6008, 4/3504A, 7, NSWSRA; McLean, *Why Australia Prospered*, 70.

30. Drescher, *Mighty Experiment*, 98-99.

31. Sibthorpe, *History of Sierra Leone*, 152; S. A. Walker, *Church of England Mission*, 221, 300.

32. J. Sweet, *Recreating Africa*; Walter Hawthorne, *Planting Rice and Harvesting Slaves: Transformations along the Guinea-Bissau Coast, 1400–1900* (Portsmouth, NH: Heinemann, 2003); Gwendolyn Midlo Hall, *Slavery and African Ethnicities in the Americas: Restoring the Links* (Chapel Hill: University of North Carolina Press, 2005).

33. The name Summers is not known among Krio surnames today, suggesting that he did not return, or at least that he changed his name or did not have any sons.

34. See Seeley, *Memoir*, 200; Thomas Eyre Poole, *Life, Scenery and Customs in Sierra Leone and Gambia* (London: Richard Bentley, 1850), 1:56–58.

35. Based on the fact that he swears on the Holy Bible while giving his testimony in 1821 (where many others did not), and on the Reffell family's own family history. Robert Wellesley Cole, *Kossoh Town Boy* (Cambridge: Cambridge University Press, 1960), 129–30.

36. "The Black Natives," *Hobart Town Gazette*, 11 November 1826, 2; Burn, *Picture of Van Diemen's Land*, 24.

37. Nicholas Clements, *The Black War: Fear, Sex and Resistance in Tasmania* (Brisbane: University of Queensland Press, 2014), 125; James Bonwick, *Last of the Tasmanians, or, The Black War of Van Diemen's Land* (London: Sampson Low, Son and Marston, 1870), 143.

38. Goodrick, *Life in Old Van Diemen's Land*, 208, 184; Van Diemen's Land, *Geelong Advertiser and Squatters' Advocate*, 6 July 1847, 1; "Family Notices," *Launceston Examiner* (Tasmania), 16 June 1847, 6; "Family Notices," *Courier* (Hobart, TAS), 16 June 1847, 2.

39. S. A. Walker, *Church of England Mission*, 427–48.

Epilogue

1. Alice Bennett and Georgia Warner, *Country Houses of Tasmania: Behind the Closed Doors of Our Finest Private Colonial Estates* (Sydney: Allen and Unwin, 2009), 198–207; Sherwood, "Trade in Enslaved Africans," 24.

2. Bain Attwood, *Possession: Batman's Treaty and the Matter of History* (Melbourne: Miegunyah Press, 2009), 15–17; Richard Osborne, *The History of Warrnambool* (Prahan, VIC: Chronicle, 1887), 14–16, 41, 77, 131, 135, 189, 202–3, 213, 238.

3. Robert Clarke, *Sierra Leone: A Description of the Manners and Customs of Liberated Africans* (London: J. Ridgeway, 1843), 47–48.

4. Walter Rodney, *How Europe Underdeveloped Africa* (Nairobi: East African Educational, 1972), 141; Stephen Frenkel and John Western, "Pretext or Prophylaxis? Racial Segregation and Malarial Mosquitos in a British Tropical Colony: Sierra Leone," *Annals of the Association of American Geographers* 78, no. 2 (1988): 211–28. Bostock's children Eliza, Augustus, and James—his eighth-, ninth-, and eleventh-born Australian children—all lived into the twentieth century. See Birrell, *Mariners, Merchants*, 38.

5. Huzzey, *Freedom Burning*, 17; Rolf Boldrewood, *Old Melbourne Memories* (New York: Macmillan, 1896), 51, 65–69.

6. Tony Roberts, *Frontier Justice: A History of the Gulf Country to 1900* (St. Lucia: University of Queensland Press, 2005), 184; 211; Deborah Bird Rose, *Hidden Histories: Black*

Stories from Victoria River Downs, Humbert River and Wave Hill Stations (Canberra: Aboriginal Studies Press, 1991), 180, 260.

7. Roberts, *Frontier Justice*, 88; F. J. Gillen, *Gillen's Diary: The Camp Jottings of F. J. Gillen* (Adelaide: Libraries Board of South Australia, 1968), 3:485–87, 492; Alf Chambers, *Battlers of the Barkly: The Family Saga of Eva Downs* (Rockhampton: Central Queensland University Press, 1998), 55; Tony Austin, *I Can Picture the Old Home So Clearly: The Commonwealth and "Half-Caste" Youth in the Northern Territory, 1911–1939* (Canberra: Aboriginal Studies Press, 1993), 3–4; Tony Austin, *Never Trust a Government Man: Northern Territory Aboriginal Policy, 1911–1939* (Darwin: Northern Territory University Press, 1997), 19–20, 44–45; Anna Haebich, *Broken Circles: Fragmented Indigenous Families, 1800–2000* (Fremantle, WA: Fremantle Arts Centre Press, 2000), 288.

8. Austin, *Never Trust*, 17, 195–97; Haebich, *Broken Circles*, 195.

9. Haebich, *Broken Circles*, 155, 192–93, 343; Richard Broome, *Aboriginal Australians: Black Responses to White Dominance* (Sydney: Allen and Unwin, 1994), 120.

10. Beetaloo Station Pty. Ltd. v. Minister for Lands, Planning and Environment, Bruce Godilla, and Pompey Raymond Administrative Law, http://www.supreme court.nt.gov.au/archive/doc/sentencing_remarks/0/98/0/NS000520.htm.

11. Interview with Shauna Bostock-Smith, 2012.

12. Interviews with Raila Sanusi-Ball and Nafisatu Deen, Eastern Freetown, March 2009 and 2011; Christopher Fyfe, "Four Sierra Leone Recaptives," *Journal of African History* 11, no. 1 (1961): 75–85, 82; Jean H. Kopytoff, *Preface to Modern Nigeria: Sierra Leonians in Yoruba* (Madison: University of Wisconsin Press, 1966), 51; Wyse, *Krio*, 20–21; T. J. Barron, "James Stephen, the 'Black Race,' and British Colonial Administration, 1813–1847," *Journal of Imperial and Commonwealth History* 5 (1977): 131–50, 137; J. T. Campbell, *Middle Passages*, 81.

Bibliography

Archival Documents

United States of America

BAKER LIBRARY, BLOOMBERG CENTER, HARVARD BUSINESS SCHOOL
D'Wolf Papers.

BEINECKE RARE BOOK AND MANUSCRIPT LIBRARY, YALE UNIVERSITY
Robert Bostock Documents Concerning the Slave Trade, James Marshall and Marie-Louise Osborn Collection.

BRISTOL HISTORIC AND PRESERVATION SOCIETY, RHODE ISLAND
D'Wolf Papers.

HUNTINGTON LIBRARY, PASADENA, CALIFORNIA
Papers of Thomas Clarkson.

JOHN HAY LIBRARY, BROWN UNIVERSITY
Fales Family Papers.

NATIONAL ARCHIVES AND RECORDS ADMINISTRATION
Index to New England Naturalization Petitions, 1791–1906.

OTTO G. RICHTER LIBRARY, THE UNIVERSITY OF MIAMI
Edward Spalding Papers.

RICHARD J. DALY LIBRARY, THE UNIVERSITY OF CHICAGO AT ILLINOIS
E. H. Columbine Papers.

United Kingdom

LIVERPOOL RECORD OFFICE

Robert Bostock Letterbooks 387 MD 54-55.

Bickerton Papers, 942 BIC 1.

THE NATIONAL ARCHIVES, LONDON, ADMIRALTY

ADM 1/1674: Letters from Captains, Surnames C, 1820.

ADM 1/1813: Letters from Captains, Surnames F, 1816.

ADM 1/2535: Letters from Captains, Surnames S, 1813.

ADM 1/2536: Letters from Captains, Surnames S, 1813.

ADM 1/2537: Letters from Captains, Surnames S, 1813.

ADM 1/2538: Letters from Captains, Surnames S, 1814.

ADM 1/2539: Letters from Captains, Surnames S, 1814.

ADM 1/2540: Letters from Captains, Surnames S, 1814.

ADM 1/4226: Letters from Secretaries of State, July–September 1813.

ADM 7/605: Captain Denman's Trial, Slave Factories, Gallinas, 1840–1848.

ADM 7/606: Slave Trade Cases, Admiralty Miscellanea, 1850.

ADM 37/4430: Ships' Musters (Series 2), Ship *Thais*, 1 January 1812–30 June 1813.

ADM 37/4431: Ships' Musters (Series 2), Ship *Thais*, 1 July 1813–31 August 1814.

ADM 37/4462: Ships' Musters (Series 2), Ship *Albacore*, 1 August 1812–28 February 1814.

ADM 43/64: Navy Board: Head Money and Papers, Vouchers, 1813.

ADM 51/2180: Captains' Logs, *Bann*, 1812–1820.

ADM 51/2914: Captains' Logs, *Thais*, 1812–1816.

ADM 52/3462: Masters' Logs, *Thais*, 1813.

THE NATIONAL ARCHIVES, LONDON, BOARD OF TRADE

BT 98/62: Registry of Shipping and Seamen, Agreements and Crew lists, Series 1, Muster Rolls.

THE NATIONAL ARCHIVES, LONDON, COLONIAL OFFICE

CO 267/36: Sierra Leone Original Correspondence, Secretary of State, 5 January–23 March 1813.

CO 267/37: Sierra Leone Original Correspondence, Secretary of State, 24 March–27 December 1813.

CO 267/38: Sierra Leone Original Correspondence, Secretary of State, 1814.

CO 267/39: Sierra Leone Original Correspondence, Secretary of State, 1814.

CO 267/40: Sierra Leone Original Correspondence, Secretary of State, 1815.

CO 267/41: Sierra Leone Original Correspondence, Secretary of State, 1815.

CO 267/49: Sierra Leone Original Correspondence, Secretary of State, 1819.

CO 267/51: Sierra Leone Original Correspondence, Secretary of State, 1820.

CO 267/55: Sierra Leone Original Correspondence, Secretary of State, 1821.

CO 267/88: Sierra Leone Original Correspondence, Secretary of State, Dr. Thorpe's Case, 1815–1827.

THE NATIONAL ARCHIVES, LONDON, FOREIGN OFFICE

FO 72/182: Foreign Office, General Correspondence, Spain, 1 April 1815–31 April 1815.

THE NATIONAL ARCHIVES, LONDON, HIGH COURT OF THE ADMIRALTY

HCA 32/1308: Prize Court, Papers, War of 1812, nos. 1644–1651.

HCA 42/455/680: Appeals for Prizes, Papers, Napoleonic Wars, 1815, Captured Ship: *Juan.*

HCA 42/488/982: Appeals for Prizes, Papers, Napoleonic Wars, 1816, Captured Ship: *Nuestra Senora De los Dolores.*

HCA 42/488/983: Appeals for Prizes, Papers, Napoleonic Wars, Captured Ship: *Phoenix.*

HCA 49/97: Vice Admiralty Proceedings, Sierra Leone, 1808–1817.

HCA 49/101: Vice Admiralty Proceedings, Various, 1793–1831.

THE NATIONAL ARCHIVES, LONDON, HOME OFFICE

HO 17/1/1: Home Office, Criminal Petitions (Series 1), 1813.

THE NATIONAL ARCHIVES, LONDON, TREASURY SECRETARY

TS 11/823/2712: Papers, George Cook vs. Charles William Maxwell and others, Chancery and King's Bench, 1816–1820.

TS 11/826/2732: Papers, Robert Bostock vs. Edward Scobell, King's Bench, 1820.

TS 18/58: General Series Papers, Criminal Cases, Slave Factories at Gallinas, 1840.

TS 18/60: General Series Papers, Criminal Cases, Liberation of Slaves by HMS Alert at Gallinas, 1855.

THE NATIONAL ARCHIVES, LONDON, WAR OFFICE

WO 12/10344: African Corps, General Musters, 1813.

WO 12/10345: African Corps, General Musters, 1814.

UNIVERSITY OF BIRMINGHAM

William Tamba, 1820–1829, Original Papers—Missionaries: Church Missionary Society papers. Available on microfilm, Church Missionary Society (Wiltshire: Adam Matthews Publications), section IV, part 5, reel 94, CA 1 O203.

David Noah, 1824–1829, Original Papers—Missionaries: Church Missionary Society papers. Available on microfilm, Church Missionary Society Papers, Microfilm (Wiltshire: Adam Matthews Publications), section IV, part 5, reel 89, CA1 O165.

UNIVERSITY OF HULL

Thomas Perronet Thompson Papers, 1783–1869.

Australia

ARCHIVES OFFICE OF TASMANIA
Colonial Secretary's Office, 2648, reel Z1787.

MITCHELL LIBRARY,
STATE LIBRARY OF NEW SOUTH WALES
Joseph Arnold Journals, 1810–1815.
John Thomas Bigge: Appendix to Bigge's report of 1822, returns of Births, Deaths and Marriages.
Hassall family—Papers, 1793–2000.
Mathew Hindson Account Book, 1827–1830.
Captain John Piper Papers and Correspondence, 1790–1845.

NEW SOUTH WALES STATE RECORDS' AUTHORITY
Bostock and McQueen's pardon, 4/4472, pp. 9–11.
Information regarding allotment of convicts, reel 6004, 4/3494, p. 66.
Re land grant, fiche 3266, 4/438, p. 9.
Application for a Joint Auctioneer's Licence, 15 January 1821, reel 6051, 4/1748, pp. 95–97.
Granted an Auctioneer's Licence, 8 March 1821, reel 6070, 4/1265, pp. 56–57.
Tendering Rebuilt *Endeavour*, 11 August 1821, reel 6051 4/1749, pp. 410–12.
Reply to tendering proposal, 21 July 1821, reel 6008, 4/3504, p. 159.
New Partner at MacQueen and Atkinson, 8 July 1822, reel 6055; 4/1761, p. 10.
Colonial Secretary's Index, 4/3504, reel 6008, p. 45.
Probate packets, John McQueen, date of death 19 March 1829, series 1–383.
Re Approval of grant of tenement to Mr. Bostock, 4 March 1819, reel 6006, 4/3500 p. 7.
Memorial for a Grant of 400 acres and indulgences, 1 October 1821, fiche 3209, 4/1863, p. 28.
Reply to memorial for land, 13 November 1821, reel 6008, 4/3504A, p. 7.

Sierra Leone

SIERRA LEONE NATIONAL ARCHIVES
Liberated African Letterbooks.
Birth Certificates.

Cuba

ARCHIVO NACIONAL DE LA REPÚBLICA DE CUBA
Tribunal de Comercio, Legajo 161, Exp. 17.

Tribunal de Comercio, Legajo 30, Dossier 199, Apresamiento de la *Rosa*, 1816.
Junta de Fomento, Legajo 86, Exp. 3506.
Legajo 44, Number 3, Consulado 3572.

Newspapers

United States of America
African Repository and Colonial Journal (Washington), vol. 7, 1831–1832
American Missionary Register (New York), vol. 2, 1822
Boston Recorder, 1819
City Gazette and Commercial Daily Advertiser (Charleston), 1807
Religious Intelligencer (New Haven, CT), vol. 6, 28 December 1821
Religious Reporter (Middlebury, VT), September 1820
Washington Theological Repertory, vol. 1, 1819

United Kingdom
Asiatic Journal and Monthly Miscellany (London), vol. 2, 1816
Bath Chronicle and Weekly Gazette, 1812
Cheltenham Chronicle, 1811
Chester Chronicle, 1811
Christian Observer (London) vol. 22, 1822
*Church Missionary Paper: For the Use of Weekly and Monthly Contributors to the Church Edinburgh
    Review, or the Critical Journal*, vol. 21, February–July 1813
Evangelical Magazine and Missionary Chronicle (London), vol. 26, 1818
Gore's Liverpool Directory, 1790
Liverpool Mercury, 1813
Missionary Society (London), vol. 18, Midsummer 1820
Observer (London), 2001
Times (London), 1808–1815, 1840, 1980

Sierra Leone
African Herald (Freetown, Sierra Leone), 1809
Royal Gazette and Sierra Leone Advertiser, 1817–27
Sierra Leone Gazette, 1808

Australia
Courier (Hobart), 1847
Geelong Advertiser and Squatters' Advocate, 1847
Hobart Town Gazette and Southern Reporter, 1818–1825
Launceston Examiner, 1847
Sydney Gazette and New South Wales Advertiser, 1815–1929
Sydney Herald, 1834

Printed Publications (1900 and Before)

African Institution. *Eighth Report of the Directors of the African Institution, Read at the Annual General Meeting on the 23rd of March, 1813.* London: J. Hatchard, 1814.

————. *Eleventh Report of the Directors of the African Institution, Read at the Annual General Meeting on the 26th of March, 1817.* London: J. Hatchard, 1817.

————. *Fifth Report of the Directors of the African Institution, Read at the Annual General Meeting on the 27th of March, 1811.* London: J. Hatchard, 1811.

————. [First] *Report of the Committee of the African Institution, Read to the Annual General Meeting on the 15th of July, 1807.* London: J. Hatchard, 1811.

————. *Fourth Report of the Directors of the African Institution, Read at the Annual General Meeting on the 28th of March, 1810.* London: J. Hatchard, 1814.

————. *Ninth Report of the Directors of the African Institution, Read at the Annual General Meeting on the 12th of April, 1815.* London: J. Hatchard, 1815.

————. *Second Report of the Committee of the African Institution, Read at the Annual General Meeting on the 25th of March, 1808.* London: J. Hatchard, 1812.

————. *Sixteenth Report of the Directors of the African Institution, Read at the Annual General Meeting on the 10th of May, 1822.* London: J. Hatchard, 1822.

————. *Sixth Report of the African Institution, Read at the Annual General Meeting on the 25th of March, 1812.* London: J. Hatchard, 1812.

————. *Special Report of the Directors of the African Institution, Read at the Annual General Meeting on the 12th of April, 1815.* London: J. Hatchard, 1815.

————. *Tenth Report of the Directors of the African Institution, Read at the Annual General Meeting on the 27th of March, 1816.* London: J. Hatchard, 1816.

————. *Third Report of the Directors of the African Institution, Read at the Annual General Meeting on the 25th of March, 1809.* London: J. Hatchard, 1814.

————. *Twelfth Report of the Directors of the African Institution, Read at the Annual General Meeting on the 9th of April, 1818.* London: J. Hatchard, 1818.

American State Papers, Legislative and Executive of the Congress of the United States, 1818–1826: Foreign Affairs. Vol. 5. Washington, DC: Gales and Seaton, 1826.

Anderson, Benjamin. *Journey to Musardu.* New York: S. W. Green, 1870.

Anon. *An Account of All Sums of Money Paid or Claimed under the Acts Passed for the Abolition of the Slave Trade, or under Any Orders in Council, as Bounties for Slaves or Natives of Africa, Condemned in Any Court of Vice Admiralty Navy Office, 28th June 1817.* London: printed for the House of Commons, 1817.

————. "American Colonization Society: Purchase of Land for a Colony at St. John's River." *Quarterly Christian Spectator* 3, no. 7 (1821): 649–53.

————. "A Brief Sketch of the State of Sierra Leone, in 1814, from the National Intelligencer." In *The Christian Herald*, edited by John Edwards Caldwell, 2:341–43. New York: John E. Caldwell, 1816.

————. *Extracts from the Report of the Commissioners Appointed for Investigating the State of the Settlements and Governments on the Coast of Africa.* London: Printed for the House of Commons, 1812.

————. "Hints for Improving the Colony of Sierra Leone." *The Philanthropist, or Repository for Hints and Suggestions Calculated to Promote the Comfort and Happiness of Man*, 2:41–56. London: Longman, 1812.

————. "Sierra Leone." *The Friend: A Religious and Literary Journal*, 3:301. Philadelphia: John Richardson, 1830.

————. *The Trials of the Slave Traders: Samuel Samo, Joseph Peters and William Tufft*. London: Sherwood, Neeley and Jones, 1813.

————. [Godwin]. *Godwin's Emigrants Guide to Van Diemen's Land, More Properly Called Tasmania*. London: Sherwood, Jones, 1823.

Ashmun, Jehudi. *A Memoir of the Exertions and Sufferings of the American Colonists Connected with the Occupation of Cape Montserado: Embracing the Particular History of the Colony of Liberia from December 1821 to 1823*. Washington, DC: Way and Gideon, 1826.

Bacon, Ephraim. *Abstract of a Journal Kept by E. Bacon, Assistant Agent of the United States, to Africa*. Philadelphia: Clark and Raser, 1822.

Boldrewood, Rolf. *Old Melbourne Memories*. New York: Macmillan, 1896.

Bonwick, James. *Last of the Tasmanians, or The Black War of Van Diemen's Land*. London: Sampson Low, Son and Marston, 1870.

Boyle, James. *A Practical Medico-Historical Account of the Western Coast of Africa*. London: S. Highley, 1831.

Brayley, Edward Wedlake, and John Britton. *The Beauties of England and Wales*. Vol. 4. London: Vernor, Hood, Longman, 1805.

Brooke, Richard. *Liverpool as It Was during the Last Quarter of the Eighteenth Century: 1775–1800*. Liverpool: J. Mawdsley and Son, 1853.

Burke, John. *A Genealogical and Heraldic Dictionary of the Landed Gentry of Great Britain and Ireland*. Vol. 2. London: Henry Coulburn, 1847.

Buxton, Thomas Fowell. *African Slave Trade and Its Remedy*. London: John Murray, 1811.

Caswell, Henry. *Martyr of the Rio Pongas*. London: Rivingtons, 1857.

Chamier, Frederick. *The Life of a Sailor by a Captain in the Navy*. New York: J & J. Harper, 1833.

Charlesworth, Maria Louisa. *Africa's Mountain Valley; or, The Church in Regent's Town, West Africa*. London: Seeley, Jackson and Halliday, 1856.

Church, Mary. *Sierra Leone; or, The Liberated Africans, in a Series of Letters from a Young Lady to Her Sister in 1833 and 34*. London: Longman, 1835.

Church Missionary Society. *Proceedings of the Church Missionary Society for Africa and the East, Seventeenth Year: 1816–1817*. London: L. B. Seeley, 1817.

————. *Proceedings of the Church Missionary Society for Africa and the East, Eighteenth Year: 1817–1818*. London: L. B. Seeley, 1818.

————. *Proceedings of the Church Missionary Society for Africa and the East, Nineteenth Year: 1818–1819*. London: L. B. Seeley, 1819.

————. *Proceedings of the Church Missionary Society for Africa and the East, Twentieth Year: 1819–1820*. London: L. B. Seeley, 1820.

————. *Proceedings of the Church Missionary Society for Africa and the East, Twenty-First Year: 1820–1821*. London: L. B. Seeley, 1821.

————. *Proceedings of the Church Missionary Society for Africa and the East, Twenty-Second Year: 1821–1822*. London: L. B. Seeley, 1822.

————. *Proceedings of the Church Missionary Society for Africa and the East, Twenty-Third Year: 1822–1823*. London: L. B. Seeley, 1823.

————. *Proceedings of the Church Missionary Society for Africa and the East, Twenty-Fourth Year: 1823–1824*. London: L. B. Seeley, 1824.

Clarke, Robert. *Sierra Leone: A Description of the Manners and Customs of Liberated Africans*. London: J. Ridgeway, 1843.

Clarkson, Thomas. *The History of the Rise, Progress and Accomplishments of the Abolition of the African Slave Trade*. London: John W. Parker, 1839.

Coke, Thomas. *An Interesting Narrative of a Mission Sent to Sierra Leone, in Africa, by the Methodists, in 1811*. London: printed for the author, 1812.

Collier, G. R., Sir Charles Macarthy, et al. *West African Sketches*. London: L. B. Seeley and Son, 1829.

Curr, Edward. *An Account of the Colony of Van Diemen's Land*. London: George Cowie, 1824.

Dodson, John. *A Report of the Case of the Louis, Forest, Master: Appealed from the Vice Admiralty Court at Sierra Leone*. London: John Butterworth, 1817.

Drake, Richard. *Revelations of a Slave Smuggler*. New York: R. M. DeWitt, 1860.

Du Bois, W. E. B. *The Suppression of the African Slave Trade to the United States of America, 1638–1870*. New York: Longmans, Green, 1896.

Edwards, Bryan. *The History, Civil and Commercial, of the West Indies*. Vol. 4. London: G. & W. B. Whittaker et al., 1819.

Ellis, A. B. *History of the First West India Regiment*. London: Chapman and Hall, 1885.

Equiano, Olaudah. *The Interesting Life of Olaudah Equiano, or Gustavus Vassa, the African*. London: printed for the author, 1794.

Evans, George William. *Geographical, Historical and Topographical Description of Van Diemen's Land*. London: John Souter, 1822.

Falconbridge, Anna-Maria. *Two Voyages to Sierra Leone during the Years 1791-2-3*. London: printed for the author, 1794.

Fenton, James. *A History of Tasmania: From Its Discovery in 1642 to the Present Time*. Hobart, TAS: J. Walch and Sons, 1884; repr., New York: Cambridge University Press, 2011.

Fisher, George. *The Instructor, or American Young Man's Best Companion Containing Spelling, Reading, Writing, and Arithmetick*. Worcester: Isaiah Thomas, 1786.

Fox, William. *Brief History of the Wesleyan Missions on the Western Coast of Africa*. London: published for the author, 1851.

Garnon, William. "Memoir of the Late Rev. William Garnon, First Chaplain of the Colony of Sierra Leone." In *Missionary Register*, 237–42, 285–95. London: L. B. Seeley, 1819.

Griffiths, T. R. "On the Races Inhabiting Sierra Leone." *Journal of the Anthropological Institute of Great Britain and Ireland* 16 (1887).

House of Commons. *Journals of the House of Commons, from November the 4th 1813, in the 54th*

Reign of King George the Third, to November the 1st 1814. Vol. 69. London: H.M. Stationery Office, 1813.

——. *Journals of the House of Commons, from November the 8th 1814, in the 55th Reign of King George the Third, to January the 17th 1816*. Vol. 70. London: H.M. Stationery Office, 1816.

Jameson, Robert Francis. *Letters from the Havana: During the Year 1820*. London: John Miller, 1821.

Jeffreys, Lieutenant Charles, RN. *Van Diemen's Land: Geographical and Descriptive Delineations of the Island of Van Diemen's Land*. London: JM Richardson, 1820.

Kilham, Hannah. *Memoir of the Late Hannah Kilham, Chiefly Compiled from Her Journal*. London: Darton and Harvey, 1837.

Laing, Alexander Gordon. *Travels in the Timannee, Kooranko, and Soolima Countries in Western Africa*. London: John Murray. 1825.

Leonard, Peter. *Records of a Voyage to the Western Coast of Africa in His Majesty's Ship Dryad; During the Years 1830, 1831, and 1832*. Edinburgh: A. Shortrede, 1833.

Macaulay, Kenneth. *The Colony of Sierra Leone Vindicated from the Misrepresentations of Mr. McQueen of Glasgow*. London: Hatchard and Son, 1827.

Marryatt, Joseph. *Thoughts on the Abolition of the Slave Trade, and the Civilization of Africa*. London: JM Richardson and J. Ridgway, 1816.

Marshall, John. *Royal Naval Biography; or, Memoirs of the Services of All the Flag Officers, Super-annuated Rear-Admirals, Retired-Captains, Post-Captains, and Commanders*. London: Longman, Hurst, Rees, Orme, Brown and Green, 1824.

Mayer, Brantz. *Captain Canot; or, Twenty Years of an African Slaver*. New York: Appleton, 1854.

Melville, Mrs. E. H. *A Residence at Sierra Leone*. 1849; repr., London: Frank Cass, 1968.

Missionary Register for 1816, Containing the Principal Transaction of the Various Institutions for the Promulgation of the Gospel, vol. 4. London: L. B. Seeley, 1816.

Missionary Register for 1817, Containing the Principal Transaction of the Various Institutions for the Promulgation of the Gospel, vol. 5. London: L. B. Seeley, 1817.

Missionary Register for 1819, Containing the Principal Transaction of the Various Institutions for the Promulgation of the Gospel, vol. 7. London: L. B. Seeley, 1819.

Missionary Register for 1820, Containing the Principal Transaction of the Various Institutions for the Promulgation of the Gospel, vol. 8. London: L. B. Seeley, 1820.

Missionary Register for 1824, Containing the Principal Transaction of the Various Institutions for the Promulgation of the Gospel, vol. 12. London: L. B. Seeley, 1824.

Mockler-Ferryman, Augustus Ferryman. *British West Africa: Its Rise and Progress*. London: Swan Sonnenschein, 1900.

Munro, Wilfred H. *The History of Bristol, R.I.* Providence: J. A. and R. A. Reid, 1880.

Napier Hewett, Captain J. F. *European Settlements on the West Coast of Africa, with Remarks on the Slave-Trade and the Supply of Cotton*. 1862; repr., New York: Negro Universities Press, 1969.

Newton, John. *The Select Works of the Rev. John Newton*. Edinburgh: Peter Brown and Thomas Nelson, 1831.

Nyländer, Gustavus Reinhold. *Grammar and Vocabulary of the Bullom*. London: Church Missionary Society, 1814.

Oliver, Vere Langford. *The History of the Island of Antigua*. Vol. 1. Antigua: Mitchell and Hughes, 1894.

Osborne, Richard. *The History of Warrnambool*. Prahan, VIC: Chronicle, 1887.

Park, Mungo. *Travels in the Interior of Africa*. Edinburgh: Adam and Charles Black, 1858.

Pierson, Arthur T. *Seven Years in Sierra Leone: The Story of the Work of William A.B. Johnson, Missionary of the Church Missionary Society, from 1816 to 1823 in Regent's Town, Sierra Leone*. London: James Nisbet and Co., 1897.

Poole, Thomas Eyre. *Life, Scenery and Customs in Sierra Leone and Gambia*. London: Richard Bentley, 1850.

Rankin, F. Harrison. "A Visit to Sierra Leone, in 1834." *Carey's Library of Choice Literature*, no. 41, part 2 (2 July 1836): 276–349. Philadelphia: L. E. Carey & A. Hart.

———. *White Man's Grave: A Visit to Sierra Leone in 1834*. London: Richard Bentley, 1836.

Reid, Thomas. *Two Voyages to New South Wales and Van Diemen's Land*. London: Longman, Hurst, Rees, Orme and Brown, 1822.

Ricketts, H. J. *Narrative of the Ashantee War: With a View of the Present State of the Colony of Sierra Leone*. London: W. Simpkin and R. Marshall, 1833.

Robertson, G. A. *Notes on Africa: Particularly Those Parts Which Are Situated between Cape Verd and the River Congo*. London: Sherwood, Neely and Jones, 1819.

Ross, James. *The Settler in Van Diemen's Land*. Hobart, 1836; repr., Melbourne: Marsh Walsh Publishing, 1975.

Seeley, Robert Benton. *A Memoir of the Reverend W. A. B. Johnson*. New York: Robert Carter and Brothers, 1853.

Singleton, William. "An Account of a Visit to the Gambia and Sierra Leone." In Anon., *Report of the Committee Managing a Fund Raised by Some Friends for the Purpose of Promoting African Institution*. London: Harvey, Darton, 1822.

Slight, Henry, and Julian Slight. *Chronicles of Portsmouth*. London: Lupton Relfe, 1828.

Smith, William. *A New Voyage to Guinea, Describing the Customs, Manners, Soil, Climate, Habits, Buildings. . . .* London: John Nourse, 1745.

Spilsbury, Francis B. *Account of a Voyage to the Western Coast of Africa*. London: Richard Phillips, 1807.

Taylor, James B. *Biography of Elder Lott Cary: Late Missionary to Africa*. Baltimore: Armstrong and Berry, 1837.

Thorpe, Robert. *A Letter to William Wilberforce, ESQ, MP, Vice President of the African Institution. . . .* London: Law and Gilbert, 1815.

———. *A Reply "Point by Point" to the Special Report of the Directors of the African Institution*. London: F. C. and J. Rivington, 1815.

Trollope, Anthony. *The West Indies and the Spanish Main*. London: Chapman and Hall, 1860.

Tyng, Stephen H. *A Memoir of the Rev. W. A. B. Johnson, Missionary of the Church Missionary Society, in Regent's Town, Sierra Leone*. New York: R. Carter, 1853; repr. Memphis: General Books, 2010.

Uring, Nathaniel. *A History of the Voyages and Travels of Captain Nathaniel Uring.* 1726; repr. London: C. Cassell, 1928.

Vernice, Jeremiah. *Jeremiah Vernice of the Island of Saint Thomas, Merchant, Claimant of the Cargo as the Property of Juan Bailey, of the Island of Parto Rico, Merchant.* London: S. Brooke, 1814.

Wadström, C. B. *An Essay on Colonization.* Vol. 2. London: printed for the author, 1795.

Walker, Samuel Abraham. *The Church of England Mission in Sierra Leone.* London: Seeley, Burnside and Seeley, 1847.

———. *Missions in Western Africa, among the Soosoos, Bulloms &c.* Dublin: William Curry, 1845.

Wentworth, W. C. *A Statistical, Historical and Political Description of the Colony of New South Wales, and Its Dependent Settlements in Van Diemen's Land.* London: G. & W. B. Whittaker, 1819; repr. Cambridge: Cambridge University Press, 2012.

Wilberforce, Daniel Flinkinger. *Sherbro and the Sherbros; or, A Native African's Account of His Country and People.* 1886; repr., Charleston, SC: BiblioBazaar, 2010.

Williams, Gomer. *History of the Liverpool Privateers and Letters of Marque.* London: Heinemann, 1897; repr. Cambridge: Cambridge University Press, 2010.

Winterbottom, Thomas. *An Account of the Native Africans in the Neighbourhood of Sierra Leone.* London: John Hatchard, 1803.

Printed Publications (post-1900)

Afzelius, Adam. *Sierra Leone Journal, 1795–6.* Edited by Alexander Peter Kup. Uppsala: Almqvist und Wiksell, 1967.

Ajayi, J. F. Ade, and B. O. Oloruntimehin. "West Africa in the Anti-slave Trade Era." In *The Cambridge History of Africa*, edited by John D. Fage, 5:200–201. Cambridge: Cambridge University Press, 1976.

Alexander, Alison. *Governors' Ladies: The Wives and Mistresses of Van Diemen's Land Governors.* Sandy Bay, TAS: Tasmanian Historical Research Association, 1987.

Alie, Joe A. D. *A New History of Sierra Leone.* Oxford: Macmillan, 1990.

Allen, William E. "Liberia and the Atlantic World: Convergence and Effects." *History in Africa* 37, no. 1 (2010): 7–49.

Andel, Lucille V. *Clerk of the House: The Reminiscences of Hugh Munro Hall, 1818–1882.* Self-published, 1984.

Atkinson, Alan. "The Moral Basis of Marriage." *Push from the Bush* 2 (1998): 104–15.

Attwood, Bain. *Possession: Batman's Treaty and the Matter of History.* Melbourne: Miegunyah Press, 2009.

Austin, Gareth, Joerg Baten, and Bas Van Leeuwen. "The Biological Standard of Living in Early Nineteenth-Century West Africa: New Anthropometric Evidence for Northern Ghana and Burkina Faso." *Economic History Review* (26 September 2011): 1–23.

Austin, Tony. *I Can Picture the Old Home So Clearly: The Commonwealth and "Half-Caste" Youth in the Northern Territory, 1911–1939.* Canberra: Aboriginal Studies Press, 1993.

———. *Never Trust a Government Man: Northern Territory Aboriginal Policy, 1911–1939.* Darwin, NT: Northern Territory University Press, 1997.

Balkun, Mary McAleer. "Phillis Wheatley's Construction of Otherness and the Rhetoric of Performed Ideology." *African American Review* 36, no. 1 (Spring 2002): 121–35.

Banton, Michael. *West African City: A Study of Tribal Life in Freetown.* Oxford: Oxford University Press, 1970.

Baptist, Edward E. *The Half Has Never Been Told: Slavery and the Making of American Capitalism.* New York: Basic Books, 2014.

Barcia, Manuel. *The Great Slave Revolt of 1825: Cuba and the Fight for Freedom in Matanzas.* Baton Rouge: Louisiana State University Press, 2012.

———. "Sugar, Slavery and Bourgeoisie: The Emergence of the Cuban Sugar Industry." In *Sugarlandia Revisited: Sugar and Colonialism in Asia and the Americas, 1800–1940,* edited by Ulbe Bosma, Juan Giusti-Cordero, and G. Roger Knight. New York: Berghahn Books, 2010.

Barron, T. J. "James Stephen, the 'Black Race,' and British Colonial Administration, 1813–1847." *Journal of Imperial and Commonwealth History* 5, no. 2 (1977): 131–50.

Barry, Boubacar. *Senegambia and the Atlantic Slave Trade.* Cambridge: Cambridge University Press, 1998.

Bayly, C. A. *The Birth of the Modern World, 1780–1914.* Oxford: Blackwell, 2003.

Beckert, Sven. *Empire of Cotton: A Global History.* New York: Knopf, 2014.

Beckles, Hilary McD. "Emancipation by Law or War? Wilberforce and the 1816 Barbados Slave Rebellion." In *Abolition and Its Aftermath: The Historical Context, 1790–1916,* edited by David Richardson, 81–82. Abingdon, UK: Frank Cass, 1985.

———. "The Slave-Drivers' War: Bussa and the 1816 Barbados Slave Rebellion." *Boletín de Estudios Latinoamericanos y del Caribe* 39 (December 1985): 85–110.

Beltran, G. Aguirre. "The Rivers of Guinea." *Journal of Negro History* 31, no. 3 (1946): 290–316.

Bennett, Alice, and Georgia Warner. *Country Houses of Tasmania: Behind the Closed Doors of Our Finest Private Colonial Estates.* Sydney: Allen and Unwin, 2009.

Bennett, Norman Robert, and George E. Brooks, eds. *New England Merchants in Africa: A History through Documents, 1802–1965.* Boston: Boston University Press, 1965.

Bergad, Laird W., Fe Iglesias García, and María del Carmen Barcia. *The Cuban Slave Market, 1790–1880.* Cambridge: Cambridge University Press, 1995.

Birrell, Thelma. *Mariners, Merchants — Then Pioneers.* Self-published, 1993.

Bledsoe, Caroline. "Political Uses of Sande Ideology." *American Ethnologist* 11, no. 3 (August 1984): 455–72.

Blight, David W. "If You Don't Tell It Like It Was, It Can Never Be As It Ought to Be." In *Slavery and Public History: The Tough Stuff of American Memory,* edited by James Oliver Horton and Lois E. Horton. Chapel Hill: University of North Carolina Press, 2008.

Bolster, W. Jeffrey. *Black Jacks: African American Seamen in the Age of Sail.* Cambridge, MA: Harvard University Press, 1997.

Boone, Sylvia Ardyn. *Radiance from the Waters: Ideas of Feminine Beauty in Mende Art.* New Haven, CT: Yale University Press, 1986.

Boyce, James, *Van Diemen's Land*. Collingwood, VIC: Black, 2010.

Braidwood, Stephen J. *Black Poor and White Philanthropists: London's Blacks and the Foundation of the Sierra Leone Settlement, 1786–1791*. Liverpool: Liverpool University Press, 1994.

Broadbent, James. "Macquarie's Domain." In *The Age of Macquarie*, edited by James Broadbent and Joy Hughes. Melbourne: Melbourne University Press, 1992.

Brooks, George E. *Eurafricans in Western Africa: Commerce, Social Status, Gender, and Religious Observance from the Sixteenth to the Eighteenth Century*. Athens: Ohio University Press, 2003.

Brooks, George S., Jr. "A View of Sierra Leone ca. 1815." *Sierra Leone Studies* 4, nos. 13–14 (1960): 24–31.

Broome, Richard. *Aboriginal Australians: Black Responses to White Dominance*. Sydney: Allen and Unwin, 1994.

Burn, David. *A Picture of Van Diemen's Land*. Hobart, TAS: Cat and Fiddle Press, 1973.

Butt-Thompson, F. W. *West African Secret Societies*. London: H. F. Witherby, 1929.

Byrd, Alexander X. *Captives and Voyagers: Black Migrants across the Eighteenth-Century British Atlantic World*. Baton Rouge: Louisiana State University Press, 2010.

Byrne, Paula. "Freedom in a Bonded Society: The Administrative Mind and the 'Lower Classes' in Colonial New South Wale." *Journal of Australian Studies* 21, no. 53 (1997): 51–58.

Campbell, James T. *Middle Passages: African American Journeys to Africa*. New York: Penguin, 2007.

Campbell, Mavis C. *Back to Africa: George Ross and the Maroons*. Trenton, NJ: Africa World Press, 1993.

Carney, Judith A. *Black Rice: The African Origins of Rice Cultivation in the Americas*. Cambridge, MA: Harvard University Press, 2001.

Caulker-Burnett, Imodale. *The Caulkers of Sierra Leone*. Bloomington, IN: Xlibris, 2010.

Chambers, Alf. *Battlers of the Barkly: The Family Saga of Eva Downs*. Rockhampton, QLD: Central Queensland University Press, 1998.

Chartrand, René. *British Forces in the West Indies, 1793–1815*. London: Osprey, 1996.

Checkland, S. G. "Economic Attitudes in Liverpool." *Economic History Review* 5, no. 1 (1952): 58–75.

Childs, G. Tucker. *A Grammar of Kisi: A South Atlantic Language*. Berlin: Mouton de Gruyter, 1995.

Childs, Matt D. *1812 Aponte Rebellion in Cuba and the Struggle against Atlantic Slavery*. Chapel Hill: University of North Carolina Press, 2006.

Christopher, Emma. *A Merciless Place: The Fate of Britain's Convicts after the American Revolution*. New York: Oxford University Press, 2011.

———. *Slave Ship Sailors and Their Captive Cargoes, 1730–1807*. New York: Cambridge University Press, 2006.

———. "'The Slave Trade Is Merciful Compared to [This]': Slave Traders, Convict Transportation, and the Abolitionists." In *Many Middle Passages: Forced Migration and the Making of the Modern World*, edited by Emma Christopher, Cassandra Pybus, and Marcus Rediker. Berkeley: University of California Press, 2007.

———. "'Ten Thousand Times Worse than the Convicts': Rebellious Sailors, Convict Transportation and the Struggle for Freedom." *Journal of Australian Colonial History* 5 (2004): 30–46.

———, dir. *They Are We*. New York: Icarus Films, 2014.

Clements, Nicholas. *The Black War: Fear, Sex and Resistance in Tasmania*. Brisbane: University of Queensland Press, 2014.

Cole, Robert Wellesley. *Kossoh Town Boy*. Cambridge: Cambridge University Press, 1960.

Coleman, Deirdre, ed. *Maiden Voyages and Infant Colonies: Two Women's Travel Narratives of the 1790s*. London: Leicester University Press, 1999.

———. *Romantic Colonization and British Anti-Slavery*. Cambridge: Cambridge University Press, 2005.

Colley, Linda. *Britons: Forging the Nation, 1707–1837*. New Haven, CT: Yale University Press, 1992.

Cooper, Helene. *The House at Sugar Beach: In Search of a Lost African Childhood*. New York: Simon and Schuster, 2008.

Corker, Sylvester, and Samuel Massaquoi. *Lofa Count in Historical Perspective*. N.p. [1972?].

Costello, Ray. *Black Salt: Seafarers of African Descent on British Ships*. Liverpool: Liverpool University Press, 2012.

Coughtry, Jay. *The Notorious Triangle: Rhode Island and the African Slave Trade, 1700–1807*. Philadelphia: Temple University Press, 1981.

Craton, Michael. *Testing the Chains: Resistance to Slavery in the British West Indies*. Ithaca: Cornell University Press, 1983.

Creel, Margaret Washington. *A Peculiar People: Slave Religion and Community-Culture among the Gullahs*. New York: New York University Press, 1989.

Crooks, J. J. *A History of the Colony of Sierra Leone, Western Africa*. London: Browne and Nolan, 1903; repr., London: Frank Cass, 1972.

Dalby, David. "Banta and Mabanta." *Sierra Leone Language Review* 2 (1963): 23–25.

Davidoff, Leonore, and Catherine Hall. *Family Fortunes: Men and Women of the English Middle Class, 1780–1850*. Abingdon, Oxon: Routledge, 2002.

Davis, David Brion. *The Problem of Slavery in the Age of Emancipation*. New York: Knopf, 2014.

Day, Linda. "Afro-British Integration on the Sherbro Coast, 1665–1795." *Africana Research Bulletin* 12, no. 3 (1982).

De La Rue, Sidney. *Land of the Pepper Bird: Liberia*. New York: Putnam, 1930.

Dennis, Benjamin G. *The Gbandes: A People of the Liberian Hinterland*. Chicago: Nelson-Hall, 1972.

Dennis, Benjamin G., and Anita K. Dennis. *Slaves to Racism: An Unbroken Chain from America to Liberia*. New York: Algora, 2008.

DeWolf, Thomas Norman. *Inheriting the Trade*. Boston: Beacon Press, 2008.

Diouf, Sylviane. "Devils or Sorcerers, Muslims or Studs: Manding in the Americas." In *Trans-Atlantic Dimensions of Ethnicity in the African Diaspora*, edited by Paul E. Lovejoy and David V. Trotman. London: Continuum, 2003.

Dominguez da Silva, Daniel B. "The Atlantic Slave Trade to Maranhão, 1680–1846: Volume, Roots and Organization." *Slavery and Abolition* 29, no. 4 (2008): 477–501.

Donnan, Elizabeth. *Documents Illustrative of the Slave Trade to America*. Vol. 4. Washington, DC: Carnegie Institution, 1930–35.

Dorjahn, V. R. "Initiation of Temne *Poro* Officials." *Man* 61 (February 1961): 36–40.

Dow, George Francis. *Slave Ships and Slaving*. Mineola, NY: Dover, 2002.

Drescher, Seymour. *Capitalism and Antislavery: British Mobilization in a Comparative Perspective*. Oxford: Oxford University Press 1987.

———. *Econocide: British Slavery in the Era of Abolition*. Pittsburgh: University of Pittsburgh Press, 1977.

———. *The Mighty Experiment: Free Labor versus Slavery in British Emancipation*. Oxford: Oxford University Press, 2004.

Drewal, Henry John. "Mami Wata: Arts for Water Spirits in Africa and Its Diasporas." *African Arts* 41, no. 2 (Summer 2008): 60–83.

Duncan, Nester H. *Family Life in Lofa County, Liberia: Kissi, Gbandi, Loma, Mandingo, Kpelle.* N.p. [1970?].

Dunn, Elwood D., Amos J. Beyan, and Carl Patrick Burrowes. *Historical Dictionary of Liberia*. Lanham, MD: Scarecrow Press, 1995.

Dunn, Michael. "Early Australia: Wage Labour or Slave Society." In *Essays in the Political Economy of Australian Capitalism*, edited by E. L. Wheelwright and Ken Buckley. Vol. 1. Sydney: Australia and New Zealand Book Company, 1975.

Dyde, Brian. *The Empty Sleeve: The Story of the West India Regiments of the British Army*. St. Johns, Antigua: Hansib, 1997.

Earthy, E. Dora. "The Impact of Mohammedanism on Paganism in the Liberian Hinterland." *Numen* 2, no. 3 (1955): 206–16.

Elliott, Jane. "Was There a Convict Dandy? Convict Consumer Interests in Sydney, 1788–1815." *Australian Historical Studies* 26, no. 104 (1995): 373–92.

Ellis, M. H. *Lachlan Macquarie: His Life, Adventures and Times*. Sydney: HarperCollins, 2010.

Eltis, David. "Welfare Trends among the Yoruba in the Early Nineteenth Century: The Anthropometric Evidence." *Journal of Economic History* 50, no. 3 (September 1990): 521–40.

Eltis, David, Philip Morgan, and David Richardson. "Agency and Diaspora in Atlantic History: Reassessing the African Contribution to Rice Cultivation in the Americas." *American Historical Review* 112, no. 5 (December 2007): 1329–58.

Everill, Bronwen. *Abolition and Empire in Sierra Leone and Liberia*. London: Palgrave Macmillan, 2012.

Farrow, Anne, Joel Lang, and Jenifer Frank. *Complicity: How the North Promoted, Prolonged and Profited from Slavery*. New York: Ballantine Books, 2005.

Flannery, Tim, ed. *The Birth of Sydney*. Melbourne: Text, 1999.

Franco, Juan Luciano. *Comercio Clandestino de Esclavos*. Havana: Editorial de Ciencias Sociales, 1985.

Frenkel, Stephen, and John Western. "Pretext or Prophylaxis? Racial Segregation and Malarial Mosquitos in a British Tropical Colony: Sierra Leone." *Annals of the Association of American Geographers* 78, no. 2 (1988): 211–28.

Fulton, Richard M. "The Political Structures and Functions of the Poro in Kpelle Society." *American Anthropology* 74, no. 5 (1972): 1218–33.

Fyfe, Christopher. "The Foundation of Freetown." In *Freetown: A Symposium*, edited by Christopher Fyfe and Eldred Jones. Freetown: Sierra Leone University Press, 1968.

———. "Four Sierra Leone Recaptives." *Journal of African History* 11, no. 1 (1961): 75–85.

———. *A History of Sierra Leone*. Oxford: Clarendon Press, 1962.

———. "A View of Freetown, Sierra Leone." *Sierra Leone Studies* 1 (1953): 26–27.

Gates, Henry Louis, Jr. *Faces of America: How Twelve Extraordinary People Discovered Their Pasts*. New York: New York University Press, 2010.

———. *The Trials of Phillis Wheatley: America's First Black Poet and Her Encounters with the Founding Fathers*. New York: Basic Civitas, 2003.

Gillen, F. J. *Gillen's Diary: The Camp Jottings of F. J. Gillen on the Spencer and Gillen Expedition across Australia, 1901–2*. Vol. 3. Adelaide: Libraries Board of South Australia, 1968.

Gomez, Michael A. *Exchanging Our Country Marks: The Transformation of African Identities in the Colonial and Antebellum South*. Chapel Hill: University of North Carolina Press, 1998.

Goodrick, Joan. *Life in Old Van Diemen's Land*. Adelaide: Rigby, 1977.

Gould, Eliga H. *Among the Powers of the Earth: The American Revolution and the Making of a New World Empire*. Cambridge, MA: Harvard University Press, 2012.

———. "The Wars of 1812." *Journal of the Early American Republic* 34, no. 1 (Spring 2014): 109–14.

Grace, John J. "Slavery and Emancipation among the Mende in Sierra Leone, 1896–1928." In *Slavery in Africa: Historical and Anthropological Perspectives*, edited by Suzanne Miers and Igor Kopytoff. Madison: University of Wisconsin Press, 1977.

Green, David R., and Alastair Owens. "Gentlewomanly Capitalism? Spinsters, Widows, and Wealth Holding in England and Wales, c. 1800–1860." *Economic History Review* 56, no. 3 (August 2003): 510–63.

Haebich, Anna. *Broken Circles: Fragmented Indigenous Families, 1800–2000*. Fremantle, WA: Fremantle Arts Centre Press, 2000.

Hague, William. *William Wilberforce: The Life of the Great Anti-Slave Trade Campaigner*. San Diego: Harcourt, 2008.

Hainsworth, D. R. *The Sydney Traders: Simeon Lord and His Contemporaries, 1788–1821*. Melbourne: Cassell, 1972.

Hair, P. E. H. "An Account of the Liberian Hinterland c. 1780." *Sierra Leone Studies* 16 (1962): 218–26.

———. "Africanisms: The Freetown Contribution." *Modern African Studies Review* 5, no. 4 (1967): 521–39.

Hall, Catherine. *Civilising Subjects: Metropole and Colony in the English Imagination, 1830–1867*. Chicago: University of Chicago Press, 2002.

Hall, Gwendolyn Midlo. *Slavery and African Ethnicities in the Americas: Restoring the Links.* Chapel Hill: University of North Carolina Press, 2005.

Hancock, David. *Citizens of the World: London Merchants and the Integration of the British Atlantic Community, 1735–1785.* Cambridge: Cambridge University Press, 1995.

Harley, George W. "Notes on the Poro in Liberia." *Papers of the Peabody Museum.* Vol. 19. Cambridge, MA: Peabody Museum, 1941.

Harris, Sheldon H. "An American's Impressions of Sierra Leone." *Journal of Negro History* 47, no. 1 (January 1962): 35–41.

Haslam, Emily. "Redemption, Colonialism and International Criminal Law: The Nineteenth Century Slave-Trading Trials of Samuel Samo and Peters." In *Past Law, Present Histories,* edited by Diane Kirkby, 7–22. Canberra: ANU Press, 2012.

———. "Silences in International Criminal Legal Histories and the Construction of the Victim Subject of International Criminal Law." In *Critical Approaches to International Criminal Law: An Introduction,* edited by Christine Schwöbel, 181–95. London: Routledge, 2014.

Hawthorne, Walter. *Planting Rice and Harvesting Slaves: Transformations along the Guinea-Bissau Coast, 1400–1900.* Portsmouth, NH: Heinemann, 2003.

Helfman, Tara. "The Court of Vice-Admiralty at Sierra Leone and the Abolition of the West African Slave Trade." *Yale Law Journal* 115, no. 5 (March 2006): 1124–56.

Hetherington, Tim. *Long Story Bit by Bit: Liberia Retold.* New York: Umbrage Editions, 2009.

Heuman, Gad J., and James Walvin, eds. *The Slavery Reader.* London: Routledge, 2003.

Hirst, J. B. *Convict Society and Its Enemies.* Sydney: George Allen and Unwin, 1983.

———. "Or None of the Above: A Reply." *Historical Studies* 22, no. 89 (October 1987): 519–24.

Holsoe, Svend E. "The Condo Federation in Western Liberia." *Liberian Historical Review* 3 (August 1966): 1–28.

———. "Slavery and Economic Responses among the Vai." In *Slavery in Africa: Historical and Anthropological Perspectives,* edited by Suzanne Miers and Igor Kopytoff. Madison: University of Wisconsin Press, 1977.

———. "A Study of Relations between Settlers and Indigenous Peoples in Western Liberia, 1821–1847." *African Historical Studies* 4, no. 2 (1971): 331–62.

Horne, Gerald. *The Deepest South: The United States, Brazil and the African Slave Trade.* New York: New York University Press, 2007.

Howard, Allen M. "Nineteenth-Century Coastal Slave Trading and the British Abolition Campaign in Sierra Leone." *Slavery and Abolition* 27, no. 1 (April 2006): 23–49.

Howe, Mark A. DeWolfe. *Bristol, Rhode Island: A Town Biography.* Cambridge, MA: Harvard University Press, 1930.

Howe, George. *Mount Hope: A New England Chronicle.* New York: Viking Press, 1959.

Humphries, Jane. *Childhood and Child Labour in the British Industrial Revolution.* Cambridge: Cambridge University Press, 2010.

Huzzey, Richard. *Freedom Burning: Anti-Slavery and Empire in Victorian Britain.* Ithaca: Cornell University Press, 2012.

Hyde, Francis E., Bradbury B. Parkinson, and Sheila Marriner. "The Port of Liverpool and the Crisis of 1793." *Economica* 18 (November 1951): 363–78.

Innes, Gordon. "A Note on Mende and Kono Personal Names." *Sierra Leone Language Review* 5 (1966): 34–38.

Jackson, Michael D. *Life within Limits: Well-Being in a World of Want.* Durham, NC: Duke University Press, 2011.

———. *The Palm at the End of the Mind: Relatedness, Religiosity, and the Real.* Durham, NC: Duke University Press, 2009.

Jasanoff, Maya. *Liberty's Exiles: American Loyalists in the Revolutionary World.* New York: Knopf Doubleday, 2012.

Jedrej, M. C. "Structural Aspects of a West African Secret Society." *Ethnologische Zeitschrift* 1 (1982): 133–42.

Johnson, Charles. *Bitter Canaan: The Story of the Negro Republic.* Boston: Boston University African Studies Center, 1988.

Johnson, Thomas Sylvester. *The Story of a Mission: The Sierra Leone Church.* London: S.P.C.K., 1953.

Jones, Adam. *From Slaves to Palm Kernels: A History of the Galinhas Country, 1730–1890.* Wiesbaden: A. Schröder, 1983.

———. "White Roots: Written and Oral Testimony of the 'First' Mr Rogers." *History in Africa* 10 (1983): 151–62.

Kallon, Michael F. *Idols with Tears.* Bloomington, IN: AuthorHouse, 2005.

Kaplan, Herbert H. *Nathan Mayer Rothschild and the Creation of a Dynasty.* Stanford: Stanford University Press, 2006.

Karasch, Mary C. *Slave Life in Rio de Janeiro, 1808–1850.* Princeton: Princeton University Press, 1987.

Karskens, Grace. *The Colony: A History of Early Sydney.* Sydney: Allen and Unwin, 2009.

———. *The Rocks: Everyday Life in Early Sydney.* Melbourne: Melbourne University Press, 1998.

Kelly, Kenneth G., and Elhadj Ibrahima Fall. "Employing Archaeology to (Dis)entangle the Nineteenth-Century Illegal Slave Trade on the Rio Pongo, Guinea." *Atlantic Studies* 12, no. 3 (2015): 317–35.

Kercher, Bruce. "Perish or Prosper: The Law and Convict Transportation in the British Empire." *Law and History Review* 21, no. 3 (2003): 527–84.

Kettner, James H. "The Development of American Citizenship in the Revolutionary Era: The Idea of Volitional Allegiance." *American Journal of Legal History* 18, no. 208 (1974): 208–42.

———. "Subjects or Citizens? A Note on British Views Respecting the Legal Effects of American Independence." *Virginia Law Review* 62, no. 5 (1976): 945–76.

Kidd, Colin. "Ethnicity in the British Atlantic World, 1688–1830." In *A New Imperial History: Culture, Identity and Modernity in Britain and Empire, 1660–1840*, edited by Kathleen Wilson. Cambridge: Cambridge University Press, 2004.

Klein, Herbert S. *The Atlantic Slave Trade.* Cambridge: Cambridge University Press, 1999.

Klein, Herbert S., and Stanley L. Engerman. "Long-Term Trends in African Mortality in the Transatlantic Slave Trade." *Slavery and Abolition* 18, no. 1 (1997): 36–48.

Kopytoff, Jean H. *Preface to Modern Nigeria: Sierra Leonians in Yoruba.* Madison: University of Wisconsin Press, 1966.

Kup, A. P. *Sierra Leone: A Concise History.* Devon: David and Charles, 1975.

Lamp, Fredrick. "Ancient Wood Figures from Sierra Leone: Implications for Historical Reconstruction." *African Arts* 23, no. 2 (April 1990).

Landers, Jane. *Atlantic Creoles in the Age of Revolution.* Cambridge, MA: Harvard University Press, 2011.

Langley, E. Ralph. "The Kono People of Sierra Leone: Their Clans and Names." *Africa* 5, no. 1 (1932): 61–67.

Lawrance, Benjamin N. *Amistad's Orphans: An Atlantic Story of Children, Slavery, and Smuggling.* New Haven, CT: Yale University Press, 2014.

Linch, Kevin. *Britain and Wellington's Army: Recruitment, Society and Tradition, 1807–15.* London: Palgrave Macmillan, 2011.

Liston, Carol. "Colonial Society." In *The Age of Macquarie*, edited by James Broadbent and Joy Hughes, 30–31. Melbourne: Melbourne University Press, 1992.

Little, Kenneth. "The Function of Medicine in Mende Society." *Man* 48, no. 142 (1948): 127–30.

———. *The Mende of Sierra Leone: West African People in Transition.* Oxford: Routledge, 1951.

Lloyd, Christopher. *The Navy and Slave Trade: The Suppression of the African Slave Trade in the Nineteenth Century.* London: Longmans, 1940.

Lovejoy, Paul E. "The Impact of the Atlantic Slave Trade on Africa: A Review of the Literature." *Journal of African History* 30, no. 3 (1989): 365–94.

Lovejoy, Paul E., and David Richardson. "The Initial 'Crisis of Adaption': The Impact of British Abolition on the Atlantic Slave Trade in West Africa, 1808–1820." In *From Slave Trade to Legitimate Commerce: The Commercial Transition in Nineteenth Century West Africa*, edited by Robin Law. Cambridge: Cambridge University Press, 2002.

Lowther, Kevin G. *African American Odyssey of John Kizell.* Charleston: University of South Carolina Press, 2013.

Mackenzie-Grieve, Averil. *The Last Years of the English Slave Trade, 1750–1807.* London: Frank Cass, 1941, 1968.

Mantoux, Paul. *The Industrial Revolution in the Eighteenth Century: An Outline of the Beginnings of the Modern Factory System in England.* London: Routledge, 2006.

Maris-Wolf, Ted. "'Of Blood and Treasure': Recaptive Africans and the Politics of Slave Trade Suppression." *Journal of the Civil War Era* 4, no. 1(March 2014): 53–83.

Marques, Leonard. "Slave Trading in a New World: The Strategies of North American Slave Traders in the Age of Abolition." *Journal of the Early Republic* 32, no. 2 (Summer 2012): 233–60.

Mason, Matthew E. "Slavery Overshadowed: Congress Debates Prohibiting Atlantic Slave Trade to the United States, 1806–1807." *Journal of the Early Republic* 21, no. 1 (Spring 2000): 59–81.

Maxwell-Stewart, Hamish. *Closing Hell's Gates: The Death of a Convict Station*. Sydney: Allen and Unwin, 2008.

McKenzie, Kirsten. *Scandal in the Colonies: Sydney and Cape Town, 1820–1850*. Melbourne: Melbourne University Press, 2004.

McLean, Ian W. *Why Australia Prospered: The Shifting Sources of Economic Growth*. Princeton: Princeton University Press, 2012.

Mickleborough, Leonie C. *William Sorell in Van Diemen's Land*. Hobart, TAS: Blubber Head Press, 2004.

Migeod, F. W. H. "Some Observations on the Physical Characteristics of the Mende Nation." *Journal of the Royal Anthropological Society* 49 (1919): 265–70.

———. *A View of Sierra Leone*. London: Kegan Paul, 1926.

Miles, Tiya. *Ties That Bind: The Story of an Afro-Cherokee Family in Slavery and Freedom*. Berkeley: University of California Press, 2005.

Misevich, Philip R. "The Origins of Slaves Leaving the Upper Guinea Coast." In *Extending the Frontiers: Essays on the New Transatlantic Slave Trade Database*, edited by David Eltis and David Richardson. New Haven, CT: Yale University Press, 2008.

Moore, Robin. *Nationalizing Blackness: Afrocubanismo and Artistic Revolution in Havana*. Pittsburgh: University of Pittsburgh Press, 1997.

Moreno Fraginals, Manuel, *The Sugarmill: The Socioeconomic Complex of Sugar in Cuba, 1760–1860*. New York: Monthly Review Press, 1976, 2008.

Morgan, Kenneth. "James Rogers and the Bristol Slave Trade." *Historical Research* 76, no. 192 (May 2003): 189–216.

———. "Liverpool's Dominance in the British Slave Trade, 1740–1807." In *Liverpool and Transatlantic Slavery*, edited by David Richardson, Anthony Tibbles, and Suzanne Schwarz. Liverpool: Liverpool University Press, 2001.

———. *Slavery and the British Empire: From Africa to America*. Oxford: Oxford University Press, 2007.

Morgan, Sharon. *Land Settlement in Early Tasmania: Creating an Antipodean England*. Cambridge: Cambridge University Press, 2003.

Mouser, Bruce L. "African Academy—Clapham, 1799–1806." *History of Education* 33, no. 1 (January 2004): 87–103.

———. *American Colony on the Rio Pongo: The War of 1812, the Slave Trade, and the Proposed Settlement of African Americans, 1810–1830*. Trenton, NJ: Africa World Press, 2013.

———. "Îles de Los as Bulking Center in the Slave Trade, 1750–1800." *Revue Française d'Histoire d'Outre-Mer* 83, no. 313 (1996): 77–91.

———. "The Nunez Affair." *Académie Royale des Sciences to D'Outre Mer* (1973–74): 697–742.

———. "Trade, Coasters and Conflict in the Rio Pongo from 1790 to 1808." *Journal of African History* 14, no. 1 (1973): 45–63.

———. "The Trial of Samuel Samo and the Trading Syndicates of the Rio Pongo, 1797 to 1812." *International Journal of African Historical Studies* 46, no. 3 (2013): 423–41.

———. "Women Slavers of Guinea Conakry." In *Women and Slavers in Africa*, edited by Claire C. Robertson and Martin A. Klein. Portsmouth, NH: Heinemann, 1997.

Murphy, William P. "The Sublime Dance of Mende Politics: An African Aesthetic of Charismatic Power." *American Ethnologist* 25, no. 4 (November 1998): 563–82.

Murray, David R. *Odious Commerce: Britain, Spain and the Abolition of the Cuban Slave Trade.* New York: Cambridge University Press, 1980.

Neal, David. "Free Society, Penal Colony, Slave Society, Prison." *Historical Studies* 22, no. 89 (October 1987): 497–518.

Nemer, Julie F. "Phonological Stereotypes and Names in Temne." *Language in Society* 16 (1987): 341–52.

Newton, John. *Journal of a Slave Trader, 1750–1754.* Edited by Bernard Martin and Mark Spurrell. London: Epworth Press, 1962.

Niane, Djibril Tasmir. "Africa's Understanding of the Slave Trade: Oral Accounts." *Diogenes* 45, no. 75 (1997): 84–85.

———. "The War of the Mulattos (1860–1880): A Case of Resistance to the Slave Trade on the Rio Pongo." *Black Renaissance/Renaissance Noire* 3, no. 3 (Summer 2001): 116–32.

Nicolls, Mary, ed. *The Diary of the Reverend Robert Knopwood, 1803–1838.* Launceston, TAS: Tasmanian Historical Research Association, 1977.

Nunn, Nathan. "The Long-Term Effects of Africa's Slave Trades." *Quarterly Journal of Economics* 123, no. 1 (February 2008): 139–76.

Nunn, Nathan, and Leonard Wantchekon. "The Slave Trade and the Origins of Mistrust in Africa." National Bureau of Economic Research Working Paper Series, no. 14783, March 2009.

Obadele-Starks, Ernest. *Freebooters and Smugglers: The Foreign Slave Trade to the United States after 1808.* Fayetteville: University of Arkansas Press, 2007.

Owen, Nicholas. *Journal of a Slave-Dealer: A View of Some Remarkable Axcedents in the Life of Nics. Owen on the Coast of Africa and America from the Year 1746 to the Year 1757.* Edited by Eveline Christiana Martin. London: G. Routledge, 1930.

Parsons, Robert T. *Religion in an African Society.* Leiden: Brill, 1964.

Pérez, Louis A. *Cuba: Between Reform and Revolution.* New York: Oxford University Press, 2011.

Perry, Calbraith Bourn. *Charles D'Wolf of Guadaloupe, His Ancestors and Descendants.* New York: T. A. Wright, 1902.

Peterson, John. *Province of Freedom: A History of Sierra Leone, 1787–1870.* London: Faber, 1969.

Phillips, Ruth B. "Masking in Sande Mende Initiation Rituals." *Africa* 48, no. 3 (1978): 265–77.

Piersen, William D. "White Cannibals, Black Martyrs: Fear, Depression, and Religious Faith as Causes of Suicide among New Slaves." *Journal of Negro History* 62, no. 2 (April 1977): 147–59.

Piot, Charles. "Of Slaves and the Gift: Kabre Sale of Kin during the Era of the Slave Trade." *Journal of African History* 37, no. 1 (1996): 31–49.

Pope, David. "The Wealth and Social Aspirations of Liverpool's Slave Merchants of the Second Half of the Eighteenth Century." In *Liverpool and Transatlantic Slavery,* edited by David Richardson, Anthony Tibbles, and Suzanne Schwarz. Liverpool: Liverpool University Press, 2001.

Popkin, Jeremy D. "Race, Slavery, and the French and Haitian Revolutions." *Eighteenth-Century Studies* 37, no. 1 (Fall 2003): 113–22.

Porter, Arthur T. *Creoledom: A Study in Freetown Society.* Oxford: Oxford University Press, 1963.

Pybus, Cassandra. *Black Founders: The Unknown Story of Australia's First Black Settlers.* Sydney: University of New South Wales Press, 2006.

———. *Epic Journeys of Freedom: Runaway Slaves of the American Revolution and Their Global Quest for Liberty.* Boston: Beacon Press, 2006.

Rediker, Marcus. *The Amistad Rebellion: An Atlantic Odyssey of Slavery and Freedom.* New York: Penguin, 2013.

Reid, Kirsty. *Gender, Crime and Empire: Convicts, Settlers and the State in Early Colonial Australia.* Manchester: Manchester University Press, 2007.

Richmond, E. C. "Simeon Lord: A Merchant Prince of Botany Bay." *Journal and Proceedings of the Royal Australian Historical Society* 30, no. 3 (1944): 157–95.

Roberts, Tony. *Frontier Justice: A History of the Gulf Country to 1900.* St. Lucia, QLD: University of Queensland Press, 2005.

Rodney, Walter. *A History of the Upper Guinea Coast, 1545–1800.* New York: Monthly Review Press, 1970.

———. *How Europe Underdeveloped Africa.* Nairobi: East African Educational, 1972.

Roe, Michael. "Darwin in Hobart." *Island* 28 (1986): 16–18.

Rose, Deborah Bird. *Hidden Histories: Black Stories from Victoria River Downs, Humbert River and Wave Hill Stations.* Canberra: Aboriginal Studies Press, 1991.

Russell, Sharman Apt. *Hunger: An Unnatural History.* New York: Perseus, 2005.

Ryan, Maeve. "'A Most Promising Field for Future Usefulness': The Church Missionary Society and the Liberated Africans of Sierra Leone." In *A Global History of Anti-Slavery Politics in the Nineteenth Century,* edited by William Mulligan and Maurice Bric. New York: Palgrave Macmillan, 2013.

Scanlan, Padriac X. "The Colonial Rebirth of British Abolition: The Liberated African Villages of Sierra Leone, 1815–1824." *American Historical Review* 121, no. 4 (2016): 1085–113.

Schafer, Daniel L. "Family Ties That Bind: Anglo-African Slave Traders in Africa and Florida, John Fraser and His Descendants." *Slavery and Abolition* 20, no. 3 (1999): 1–21.

Schama, Simon. *Rough Crossings: Britain, the Slaves and the American Revolution.* London: BBC Books, 2005.

Schwab, George. *Tribes of the Liberian Hinterland.* Cambridge, MA: Peabody Museum, 1947.

Schwarz, Suzanne. "Reconstructing the Life Histories of Liberated Africans: Sierra Leone in the Early Nineteenth Century." *History in Africa* 39 (January 2012): 175–207.

Scott, Cleve McD. "Bussa's Rebellion, 1816." In *Encyclopedia of Slave Resistance and Rebellion,* edited by Junius P. Rodriguez, 1:90–91. Westport, CT: Greenwood Press, 2007.

Shaw, Rosalind. *Memories of the Slave Trade: Ritual and the Historical Imagination in Sierra Leone*. Chicago: University of Chicago Press, 2002.

Sheridan, Richard B. "The Guinea Surgeons on the Middle Passage: The Provision of Medical Services in the British Slave Trade." *International Journal of African Historical Studies* 14, no. 4 (1981): 601–25.

Sherwood, Marika. "The Trade in Enslaved Africans and Slavery after 1807." In *Colonialism, Slavery, Reparations and Trade: Remedying the Past*, edited by Fernne Brennan and John Packer. Oxford: Routledge, 2012.

Sibthorpe, A. B. C. *A History of Sierra Leone*. London: Cass, 1970.

Sidbury, James. *Becoming African in America: Race and Nation in the Early Black Atlantic*. New York: Oxford University Press, 2007.

Singleton, Theresa A. "Slavery and Spatial Dialectics on Cuban Coffee Plantations." *World Archaeology* 33, no. 1 (2001): 98–114.

Sirleaf, Ellen Johnson. *This Child Will Be Great: Memoir of a Remarkable Life by Africa's First Woman President*. New York: HarperCollins, 2009.

Smallwood, Stephanie E. *Saltwater Slavery: A Middle Passage from Africa to American Diaspora*. Cambridge, MA: Harvard University Press, 2007.

Smith, Babette. *Australia's Birthstain: The Startling Legacy of the Convict Era*. Sydney: Allen and Unwin, 2007.

Solleh, Kumba Kemusu. *The Damby Tradition of the Kono People of Sierra Leone, West Africa*. Bloomington, IN: AuthorHouse, 2011.

———. *Kono Gold or Koine Gold: Onomastics, the Human Naming Tradition*. Bloomington, IN: AuthorHouse, 2009.

Solow, Barbara L. "Capitalism and Slavery in the Exceedingly Long Run." *Journal of Interdisciplinary History* 17, no. 4 (Spring 1987): 711–37.

Sparks, Randy J. *Africans in the Old South: Mapping Exceptional Lives across the Atlantic World*. Cambridge, MA: Harvard University Press, 2016.

Spitzer, Leo. *The Creoles of Sierra Leone: Responses to Colonialism, 1870–1945*. Ile-Ife: University of Nigeria Press, 1972.

Stipriaan, Alex van. "Watramama/Mami Wata: Three Centuries of Creolization of a Water Spirit in West Africa, Suriname and Europe." *Matatu* 27/28 (2003): 323–37.

Stobart, Jon. "Culture versus Commerce: Societies and Spaces for Elites in Eighteenth-Century Liverpool." *Journal of Historical Geography* 28, no. 4 (October 2002): 471–85.

Strickrodt, Silke. "African Girls' Samplers from Mission Schools in Sierra Leone (1820s to 1840s)." *History in Africa* 37 (2010): 189–245.

Swaminathan, Srividhya. *Debating the Slave Trade: Rhetoric of British National Identity, 1759–1815*. Farnham, Surrey: Ashgate, 2009.

Sweet, James H. *Domingos Álvares, African Healing and the Intellectual History of the Atlantic World*. Chapel Hill: University of North Carolina Press, 2011.

———. *Recreating Africa: Culture, Kinship and Religion in the African-Portuguese World, 1441–1770*. Chapel Hill: University of North Carolina Press, 2003.

Taylor, Alan. *The Civil War of 1812: American Citizens, Irish Rebels and Indian Allies*. New York: Vintage Books, 2011.

Thomas, Hugh. *The Slave Trade: The Story of the Atlantic Slave Trade*. New York: Simon and Schuster, 1997.

————. *Cuba: A History*. London: Penguin Books, 2010.

Thompson, F. M. L. *English Landed Society in the Nineteenth Century*. London: Routledge and Kegan Paul, 1963.

Thornton, John. "Witches, Cannibals and Slave Traders in the Atlantic World." *William and Mary Quarterly* 60, no. 2 (April 2003): 273–94.

Thornton, Tamara Plakins. *Handwriting in America: A Cultural History*. New Haven, CT: Yale University Press, 1996.

Tonkin, Elizabeth. "Jealousy Names, Civilised Names: Anthroponomy of the Jlao Kru of Liberia." *Man* 15, no. 4 (December 1980): 653–64.

Trouillot, Michel-Rolph. *Silencing the Past: Power and the Production of History*. Boston: Beacon Press, 2015.

Tuerk, Helmut. *Reflections on the Contemporary Law of the Sea*. Leiden: Martinus Nijhoff, 2012.

Turner, Michael J. "The Limits of Abolition: Government, Saints and the 'Africa Question,' c. 1780–1820." *English Historical Review* 112, no. 446 (1997): 319–57.

Tyler-McGraw, Marie. *An African Republic: Black and White Virginians in the Making of Liberia*. Chapel Hill: University of North Carolina Press, 2007.

Ukpabi, S. C. "West Indian Troops and the Defence of British West Africa in the Nineteenth Century." *African Studies Review* 17, no. 1 (1974): 133–50.

Utting, F. A. J. *The Story of Sierra Leone*. London: Longmans and Green, 1931.

Wahrman, Dror. *The Making of the Modern Self: Identity and Culture in Eighteenth-Century England*. New Haven, CT: Yale University Press, 2004.

Walker, James W. St. G. *The Black Loyalists: The Search for a Promised Land in Nova Scotia and Sierra Leone, 1783–1870*. New York: Africana, 1976.

Watkins, Mark Hanna. "West African Bush School." *American Journal of Sociology* 48, no. 6 (May 1943): 666–75.

[Watson, Frederick, ed.] *Historical Records of Australia*. Series 1: Governors' Despatches to and from England. Vol. 8: July 1813–December 1815. Melbourne: Library Company of the Commonwealth Parliament, 1916.

Watson, W. N. Boog. "The Guinea Trade and Some of Its Surgeons." *Journal of the Royal College of Surgeons* 14 (1969): 203–14.

Wheeler, Roxann. *The Complexion of Race: Categories of Difference in Eighteenth-Century British Culture*. Philadelphia: University of Pennsylvania Press, 2000.

Whyte, Iain. *Zachary Macaulay, 1768–1838: The Steadfast Scot in the British Anti-Slavery Movement*. Liverpool: Liverpool University Press, 2011.

Williams, Eric. *Capitalism and Slavery*. Chapel Hill: University of North Carolina Press, 1944.

Williams, Greg H. *The French Assault on American Shipping, 1793–1813: A History and Comprehensive Record of Merchant Marine Losses*. Jefferson, NC: McFarland, 2009.

Wilson, Kathleen. *The Island Race: Englishness, Empire and Gender in the Eighteenth Century*. London: Routledge, 2003.

Winks, Robin W. *The Blacks in Canada: A History.* Montreal: McGill-Queens University Press, 1997.

Wood, Marcus. *The Horrible Gift of Western Freedom: Atlantic Slavery and the Representation of Emancipation.* Athens: University of Georgia Press, 2010.

Wylie, Kenneth C. "Fountainheads of the Niger: Researching a Multiethnic Regional History." In *Studies in the African Diaspora: A Memorial to James R. Hooker,* edited by John P. Henderson and Harry A. Reed. Dover, MA: Majority Press, 1989.

Wyse, Akintola. *The Krio: An Interpretive History.* Madison: University of Wisconsin Press, 1989.

Yambasu, Sahr John. *Between Africa and the West: A Story of Discovery.* Bloomington, IN: Trafford, 2013.

Unpublished Secondary Sources

Dillon, Margaret. "Convict Labour and Colonial Society in the Campbell Town Police District: 1820–1839." PhD dissertation, University of Tasmania, 2008.

Holsoe, Svend Einar. "The Cassava-Leaf People: An Ethnohistorical Study of the Vai People with a Particular Emphasis on the Tewo Chiefdom." PhD dissertation, Boston University, 1967.

Hyde, Judith, and Kevin Bales. "Physical and Mental Health Aspects of Rehabilitating Children Freed from Slavery." Free the Slaves, Washington, DC, final draft submitted to the U.S. Department of Labor, Bureau of International Labor Affairs, May 12, 2006.

Jones, Denise M. "The Business Organisation of the Liverpool Slave Trade in the Eighteenth Century: A Case Study of Robert Bostock." Master's thesis, University of Liverpool, 2006.

Leopold, Robert Selig. "Prescriptive Alliance and Ritual Collaboration in Loma Society." PhD dissertation, Indiana University, 1991.

Malin, Beverly. "The Illegal Slave Trade, as Practiced by the De Wolf Family of Bristol, Rhode Island, 1790–1825." Master's thesis, Brown University, December 1975.

Misevich, Philip. "On the Frontier of 'Freedom': Abolition and the Transformation of Atlantic Commerce in Southern Sierra Leone, 1790s to 1860." PhD dissertation, Emory University, 2009.

Mouser, Bruce L. "Trade and Politics in the Nunez and Pongo Rivers, 1790–1865." PhD dissertation, Indiana University, 1971.

Ngovo, Benjamin Samule. "The Bandi of North Western Liberia: A Study of Continuity and Change in Bandi Society to 1964." PhD dissertation, Western Michigan University, 2011.

Porter, Dale Herbert. "Defense of the British Slave Trade, 1784–1807." PhD dissertation, University of Oregon, 1987.

Index